Banging On!

Banging On!

Bob Henrit

BANKHOUSE

First published in the United Kingdom in 2013 by

Bank House Books

PO Box 3

New Romney

TN29 9WJ UK

www.bankhousebooks.com

British Library Cataloguing in Publication Data

A catalogue record for this book is available from the British Library

ISBN 9780957305830

Photo Credits:

Richard Dunkley
Tina Korhonen
John Price
James Cumpstey
Gary Merrin

Editor: Simon Fletcher
Layout & Design: Dave Randle
Typesetting and origination by Bank House Books

Contents

Banging On!

My mate Keith Moon urged me to never let the truth get in the way of a good story.

In *Banging On* I hope I've managed to tell the truth – *and* a good story.

That said, I hope I haven't angered anybody I wasn't intending to!

My heartfelt thanks to Google, who made researching this book considerably easier than the last one.

RJH, 2013

Chapter One: IN THE BEGINNING

Growing up in a staunchly Catholic family has its good points and its bad points. Unfortunately you don't get to appreciate the good points for an awfully long time.

On the one hand you've always got somewhere to go on a Sunday morning and on the other you've always got somewhere you've *got* to go on a Sunday morning!

I was born into the aforementioned staunchly Catholic family on 2 May 1944 at approximately three in the afternoon to Marcelle and Harry Polson Henrit. My mother came from an Irish family that had moved to the north-east of England, the men to work in the coal and lead mines and the women to work 'in service'. My father was born in Arbroath on 14 April 1912 (the day the *Titanic* sank). The family moved to St Andrews, where my globe-trotting grandfather was a golf pro. My mother was born in Lanchester, County Durham on 22 July 1914 and my sister and I had two maternal grandfathers, one who survived the 'war to end all wars' and one who didn't. Both were called John, and unfortunately John Ward didn't have time to marry my grandma before he was cut down in the mud of Flanders. John Carroll survived the war and came home shortly after to take care of both the girls, but my mother never got over the shame of illegitimacy and bore the stigma all her life.

My folks met in St Andrews where my mother went to work as a silver service waitress in the Grand Hotel (that impressive red stone building with white turrets alongside the clubhouse you see in photos of the eighteenth hole on the Old Course). My old man was a gas-fitter by day and moonlighted as a lamp-lighter by night. He didn't drive and normally he would carry a ladder with him balanced across the saddle and handlebars of his push-bike to light the gas lamps of St Andrews. But if he was meeting my mother he left his ladder behind and simply shinned up the lamp-posts, taking care not to mess up his front-pleated grey-flannel trousers or his two-tone shoes. Fortunately for me Harry and Marcelle didn't opt to go back to County Durham (thereby probably condemning me to a life down the mines like my uncles and many of the other men in the family) when they decided to better themselves and move away from the windy east coast of Scotland. Instead they opted for the bright lights of London.

My dad found a job in the Royal Small Arms factory in Enfield, and they set up home in Waltham Cross where my older sister Patricia and I grew up. (Patricia was born at the end of 1941 on the day the Japanese attacked Pearl Harbor, which precipitated the entry of America into the war.)

Waltham Cross was a dormitory town on the very outer edges of London, tucked just inside Hertfordshire: near enough to claim you lived in the smoke but far enough out not to have to breathe it in.

Not long before the war the newly married Henrits rented a brand new three-bedroomed semi-detached house, which they eventually bought when they decided they liked the area enough to take out a crippling twenty-five-year mortgage on the place. They paid what was then the considerable asking price of £850. (To put this into perspective my dad and most other guys working in the armaments industry were probably earning less than £2 a week.) My old man had flat feet and was disappointed not to be able to enlist in the Forces with his brothers. Instead he ran the gauntlet of bombs dropping on him at the gun factory down by the River Lea at Enfield Lock. (My mother worked at Murex, making welding rods.) We were in a cul-de-sac a couple of miles away, with the Barkers (Nora and Edgar) living on one side of us and eventually the Cookes (Sonny and Dorothy) on the other. At the top of the road lived the Clements, a family who won the football pools and scooped the main prize of £64,000 – which was a hell of a lot of money at the end of the fifties. Like my parents, most people lived in Berkley Avenue for the whole of their lives. Like us the residents were typical working-class families, when that was something to be proud of.

In those days the town of Waltham Cross was surrounded by wide-open spaces. Farms, parks, playing fields, lakes and lots of healthy countryside were bounded in the east by the River Lea and the west by the arterial road that went to Cambridge and beyond.

Eventually two council estates were built directly behind us to take people from the London boroughs of Edmonton and Tottenham. They were built on the site of lakes that had resulted from Second World War bomb craters: older kids said that we would catch polio and die if we fell in.

As I said, the Royal Small Arms factory where my dad worked was a constant target for enemy bombers during the war, but the brush factory that stood opposite the church was said to be the only place in the town to suffer a direct hit from a German 'doodlebug'.

We trembled in the air-raid shelter in our garden as Hitler's V1 and V2 rockets droned overhead. My mother said her heart stopped beating as their engines cut out and they crashed to the ground, to explode on impact.

Our Lady of the Immaculate Conception and St Joseph's Church (with our Catholic junior school conveniently situated next to it) was just a half mile away from home. My mother was very active in the church and on its various social committees. We walked down an alleyway, left into the High Street, past the monument to Queen Eleanor (which gave the town its name), under the Four Swans arch, across the front of the post office and Barclays bank, the kindergarten, Handford's bike shop and Linscott's bakers, and there we were. There were a handful of pubs on the way to the church, in which we had no interest (even when we were of age), and a couple of cinemas. The Embassy and the Regent confronted each other across the High Street.

The 'Embo' was posher than the Regent, which was undeservedly called the 'Bug Hutch'. This perceived grandeur was possibly because it had a café on the first floor and us Henrit kids were dressed in our Sunday best and taken there for tea and cakes on what my mother would refer to as high-days and holidays. As we got older we took ourselves there for ice-cream with strawberry sauce, which was served in those tinny (and tiny) metal chalices, and watched the world go by along the High Street below, through the art deco windows.

When Patricia and I came home from school our house was characterised by the smells that defined the days of the week. Monday was always left-overs from the Sunday roast, more often than not rissoles of beef, pork or (my favourite) lamb. (In those days chicken and turkey were luxury meats we didn't see until Christmas.) Friday was a day of abstinence for us Catholics, so we had fish, or sometimes omelettes. Mid-week was boiled beef and carrots, or corned-beef pie, and every once in a while my mother rang the changes with corned-beef hash! At the beginning of the week all these evocative smells were mixed with those of the gas-boiler in the kitchen, which worked in tandem with the mangle standing outside the back door.

A decade later, when I became a musician, my mother invented the all day breakfast, which meant whatever time I got up from the gig the night before a cooked breakfast was waiting. And absolutely anybody who came to pick me up was presented with, at the very least, a sausage sandwich.

When we were kids television was in its infancy, and since we didn't have one until 1960 Saturday Morning Pictures was very much a part of our lives. We went to the Embassy as often as our pocket-money would allow, to keep up with serials featuring cowboys and Indians, spacemen, and Laurel and Hardy, as well as newsreels, cartoons and the like. I used to go with Harry and Donella, two of the kids next door who were part of a recently arrived Anglo-Indian family called the Webbs: their sisters were Jackie and Joan, their parents Rodger and Dorothy. They were lodging in one room in the Cookes' house alongside their cousins (nicknamed Happy and Chuckles), while they got themselves together and found a proper place to live. My 'auntie' Rita Bird was a local councillor and a friend of my mother's from St Joseph's Church who was able to pull strings to help the Webbs to get a council house. More of these people later

In the afternoon on a Saturday I walked, or rode my little blue bike with rod-pull brakes illegally but safely on the pavement, to Cheshunt public library and picked up an adventure book of one kind or another. (I say safely, but even now I remember the pain of braking too hard and going over the handlebars on one of these trips, and almost biting my tongue off!)

Most of what I read and re-read in those days would be deemed politically incorrect today, but in the fifties adventure stories of Biggles, the Swiss Family Robinson, Richard Hannay, the Scarlet Pimpernel, the Three Musketeers et al were not frowned upon and were very much part of my Saturday evening diet. I'd finish the book by the following Wednesday or Thursday and change it the next weekend. Fortunately this love of reading has stayed with me all my life, and has enabled me to wile away the thousands of hours I've spent travelling and cooling my heels in hundreds of identical hotel rooms.

As a young kid I was into the usual innocent things: stamp and birds' egg collecting, and even fishing – or rather chasing stickleback in shallow streams,

(I'm laughing with fear as I write this.) I remember Bernie's mother running out and telling the rest of the neighbours not to worry: it was only the boys playing with gunpowder!

St Ig's was something of a baptism of fire, and it was a struggle being a very small fish in a very big pond. Before this I'd been up there with the leaders, and invariably managed to come top, or in second place, in my class at primary school. For a start we were educated by Jesuits, and they ruled by fear. When I became a teenager (which wasn't particularly significant in those days) I was the unexpected recipient of the school's Third Line Progress Prize (a leather-bound Latin missal), but even that didn't change my jaundiced view of my education. The further I get away from my schooldays the more I feel that perhaps they weren't that bad. Time is a great healer, and I find myself thinking that I must have deserved everything that happened to me, which is, I guess, a typically Catholic way of dealing with the situation. Perversely, it may well have been the college's harsh punishment that pushed me to seek public adulation in a pop group immediately I left school. Fame was not revered at the college, and even though Edmund Purdom, Alfred Hitchcock, Clem Cattini, George Martin, Bruce Forsyth, Bernard Butler, Paul McKenna and the London IRA's Reginald Dunne were old boys, they weren't acknowledged for years.

Corporal punishment was the way of life at Jesuit colleges, and pretty much the only consequence of transgressing any of the written and unwritten laws. If you misbehaved in the street, arrived late, didn't hand your homework in on time, or worse still didn't wear your school cap all the way home on the bus as you passed all the girls' schools, you would be ordered to receive a certain amount of ferulas. These were very painful blows on the bare hand by a slipper-shaped piece of whalebone covered in leather, called the ferula. There was a time when I was led to believe I was the most punished kid St Ig's had ever had. Even then it seems I was looking for fame at whatever price.

There were two set times at which we received these punishments: around lunchtime and at the end of the school day. A line of unfortunates gathered outside the ferula room to receive their just deserts. There was a rota of teachers to administer the ferula, and as I recall the list was published each day so you had the opportunity to visit a teacher who actually liked you (or more accurately didn't hate you), and therefore might be more lenient with you. This didn't always work, as sometimes the less sadistic teacher wasn't in that day or was otherwise engaged. In that case he would invariably be replaced with one of the Maloney brothers, who as far as I remember didn't like anyone and positively enjoyed their extra-curricular activities. These tough guys invariably came round during the last lesson on a Friday to administer punishment to those stupid enough to have neglected to get it during the allotted seven-day period. This meant you would be given double the number of ferulas originally ordered. Invariably I received eight. It wasn't just the pain of the whacks which hurt, it was the anguish of sitting in class hearing the increasingly loud noises of punishment approaching down the corridor, and knowing from the ferocity and frequency of the blows which teacher was 'giving' that day. If the strokes followed one another quickly the pain was less than if the ferula master paused between each hit to give it the chance to take effect. Amazingly nobody ever screamed, cried, struggled or ran away. Instead we allowed ourselves to be led like lambs to the slaughter. Immediately afterwards we filed into the church for Benediction, to give thanks to God for being punished – or just once in a while for not being punished.

I'm intrigued to discover fifty years later (through the power of the internet) that ferula was originally the stalk of the giant fennel, used for punishing schoolboys and also a natural form of Lebanese Viagra (*ferula hormonis*). If only we'd known!

Several of my schoolmates were destined for the priesthood and teaching, thereby continuing to propagate the whole ethic of corporal punishment. It really was the most unlikely ones who went on to take the cloth. God certainly does work in mysterious ways.

Because of my paper round I was frequently late for school, and often ran to catch the 649 trolleybus, which was on its way up to Holborn via Stamford Hill, with newsprint all over my hands. Delivering papers wasn't a job for people who liked comfort or a lie-in, but since I was saving up for a drum kit it had to be done. Towards the end of my time at St Ignatius I was more and more involved with the group (more of which later!), so my schoolwork suffered. I'd frequently do my homework on the way to school. Writing on a lurching trolleybus was never easy, and my shaky handwriting frequently got me into trouble. Trouble with the Jesuits began with a capital T.

I always said that if I ever had sons I wouldn't send them to my alma mater, so when the vexed issue of schools for my sons came up as they rocketed towards secondary education my wife (a maths teacher) asked the new lay head of St Ignatius why we should send them there if their father hated his time at the school so much. The head did his best, but he couldn't persuade us to force them to follow my faltering footsteps.

Having been burdened with the stigma and guilt of Catholicism, James and Jos escaped the Jesuit education their father had endured, but still had to put up with supporting Spurs when all their pals supported the far more successful Arsenal.

Bernie B. had slightly older brothers, Garnet and John, who'd both gone to St Ignatius – which was probably why he didn't. They had a couple of things we Henrits hadn't acquired: a radiogram and a television. We cowered behind the settee to enjoy John Wyndham's *The Triffids*. Even in black and white on a 7 inch screen the sight of giant maize-like plants moving so threateningly was frightening.

It was to the Bensons' house that we went to listen to 78rpm records, including Bill Haley's arguably life-changing 'Rock Around the Clock'. It would be easy to say that this was the record that turned me on to music and drumming but it wasn't: it was actually Presley's 'That's Alright Mama' in 1954, followed a year or two later by 'Peggy Sue', that whetted my appetite. One day around this time I went to mess around at Bernie's house, and he said we were going to have a skiffle group: I was going to be the washboard player. He produced his mother's washboard from behind his back and I immediately got the green 310 bus down to the haberdashery department at Pearson's in Enfield to buy thimbles for all of my fingers and thumbs. You attached the thimbles, scraped them across the corrugated metal surface and made a racket that, to soon-to-be-adolescent ears, sounded vaguely reminiscent of steam trains clattering by.

Benson Père was a carpenter, handy with his hands, and he built his three sons a guitar – of sorts. As I recall it was a huge acoustic guitar with a large sound hole, but since it didn't have any frets it was probably completely useless as a musical instrument. But it made the right sort of sound.

Eddie Read was another pal. His parents owned a house next to the Bensons as well as the local newspaper shop, and since he actually owned a proper acoustic guitar he was invited to join our skiffle group, which was already named The Roulettes (more of this name later). Jim Wilkinson was the same age as us, and went to Cheshunt Grammar with Bernie. We invited him to join The Roulettes to play tea-chest bass. To be honest I'm not sure how many gigs Jim played at, but I do have him down as our bassist, something which I hope is not a result of false memory syndrome.

Skiffle was very much a do-it-yourself form of music which borrowed heavily, or should I say completely, from the folk/blues artists of America. Anyhow, just about everybody who ultimately made it in popular music at the beginning of the sixties got their start in a fifties skiffle group. We played the music of mostly long-dead guys who at that time we'd never even heard of, like Big Bill Broonzy, Leadbelly, Woody Guthrie, Blind Lemon Jefferson et al. Skiffle was single-handedly popularised by a Scotsman named Lonnie Donegan who, as was the fashion of that time, inevitably became known as 'the King of Skiffle'. Lonnie's real name was Tony, and he changed it in homage to an early and deceased blues musician called Lonnie Johnson.

The King of Skiffle was a proper musician who played banjo and guitar with Chris Barber's traditional jazz band, and we slavishly copied his music. His first hit was 'Rock Island Line', a song which we enthusiastically crucified before moving on to murder many of his (and other people's) subsequent hits including 'Putting on the Style', 'Worried Man Blues', 'Pick a Bale o' Cotton', 'Freight Train' and 'Cumberland Gap'.

There were estimated to be 50,000 skiffle groups all over the country during the mid-fifties, including The Quarrymen in Liverpool who went on to become firstly the Silver Beetles and eventually The Beatles. To be frank, all the other 49,999 skiffle groups will have been absolutely certain they sounded pretty good, like us – but I don't believe that more than a handful did. I know we Roulettes didn't, because we actually recorded ourselves in Eddie's house on a state-of-the-art Grundig tape recorder, which was the size of a large suitcase (with a magic eye to show if you were over-recording yourselves – which we ignored).

We played everywhere and anywhere for 5 shillings, which, as the old joke goes, was all we could afford at the time. Boom, boom . . .

I'm not sure I could have been described as sartorially elegant at this, or any other, stage of my life, although I certainly made the effort to be up to date. Aside from my school uniform (which doubled up for Sunday best), the sum total of my wardrobe was the odd (make that very odd) cardigan or jumper knitted by my mother, teamed with grey flannel trousers. So I bought myself a lurex shirt which was dark red with narrow black metallic stripes (surprise, surprise, it itched like crazy), and a pair of black cavalry twill trousers worn with my scuffed school brogues. With my Brylcreemed hair brushed into a side parting I was happening! I was so carried away with this illusion of style that I began to customise my school uniform, which at St Ignatius College was a complete no no. Instead of my well-darned grey woollen socks, I took to wearing white socks with my shiny-bottomed grey Dacron trousers. On the very first day I strutted my stuff I was summoned to visit the headmaster. I was berated in his office, which smelled of tobacco, while his equally smelly old dog looked on. The reviled Chang described me as 'half a Teddy Boy' which appeared to be worse than being a whole one. So I was caught in the act and found guilty by one man and his dog, and made to atone for my delusions of elegance with an order to collect four ferulas for my trouble. In retrospect I wondered whether the punishment for being a *complete* Teddy Boy would have earned me a lesser sentence. After all the head had already told me I was guilty of the more grievous crime of being an incomplete one. I couldn't have turned up dressed as a Teddy Boy because, to be honest, I only had the white socks. (My side-parted short-back-and-sides hair wouldn't have gone into a DA at the back however many tubs of my dad's Brylcreem I put on it.)

Actually I wouldn't acquire the rest of the uniform necessary to be a Ted until I joined The Kinks nearly forty years later. Young Russell Ballard (who was about to enter my life for ever) certainly did have the garb, however. He was just over a year younger than me and had the drape jacket, drainpipe trousers and brothel-creeper (aka beetle-crusher) suede shoes. When he was about ten years old even his parents described him as a little Teddy Boy. But I digress.

The next logical step for any washboard player with aspirations (delusions?) of percussion grandeur was the acquisition of a drum kit, as they were called in those days. My Scottish upbringing meant I didn't rush out and buy one, but borrowed one from a guy called Graham Boustred who was in the 3rd Waltham Cross (St Joseph's) scouts with me and Bernie. Once I realised I could adapt what I'd played on the washboard to the drums, it was time to make an investment. (Especially since Graham, my patrol leader pal from The Kestrels, wanted his drums back.) I thought his mahogany-finished Birmingham-built drums were nothing special at the time, but something like fifty years later I spotted an identical set at a vintage drum show and discovered they were highly collectable Windsors – and therefore worth a great deal.

As ever, my long suffering parents were nothing if not supportive. I kicked in the few shillings I'd earned each week from my paper round at Carr's newsagents, and they provided the rest. We went up to town to buy some drums.

Aside from Berry's in nearby Edmonton where they had one Egmont guitar, a Gigster snare drum with an attached cymbal and a Reslo microphone in the window (which we went up on the trolleybus to ogle every now and again), all the major music shops were in the West End of London. Pre-Wolfenden Soho was completely different in the fifties, and all the lamp posts were occupied by heavily made-up women looking for love. The music shops were mostly in two streets then: my first drumset came from Lew Davis's shop in Charing Cross Road and my second (a couple of years later) from Ivor Arbiter's dad's shop, Paramount, on Shaftesbury Avenue. It wasn't a pure drum shop because they didn't exist in those pre-'beat boom' days, but it was unique in that it had full-length mirrors so would-be Elvis Presleys could see what they looked like wearing the latest cheap and cheerful Spanish guitars – even though they had no idea how to play them. These were smuggled in by Ivor's 'jazzer' mates from a distributor in Holland.

Initially we bought a very, very basic drumset for me for £5 or so – which comprised a bass drum, snare drum, hi-hat and ride cymbal. The bass drum didn't match the snare drum and wasn't even from the same maker, but for the moment it did what I wanted. I still couldn't play 'Peggy Sue' properly, but if I threw the snares off I had a tom-tom of sorts. I really wanted to go to drum lessons but couldn't find anyone to teach me rock 'n' roll. There were any number of teachers in my area to teach me how to play dance band drums, but strict tempo wasn't for me. Like a great many others I just got on with it, made lots of mistakes and taught myself.

My mother, who was an accomplished dressmaker (and a schoolteacher who taught several of my girlfriends to sew), made some drum bags for me from pvc – probably bought from Phil Wainman's dad's stall in Holborn's Leather Lane. (Phil was a drummer who went on to own a recording studio and produce The Sweet, Mud, Bay City Rollers and The Boomtown Rats.) I used an old hatbox for the snare and the duffle-bag I put my smelly sports kit in for the rest of the bits and pieces. I could get on a trolleybus with the help of Bernie B., and put all my drums in the luggage bay. I was on my way!

Alongside music I was also into cycling, not seriously enough to join a club like Eddie Read, but enough to whiz around the country on my Sun Vitesse racing bike with not one but three derailleur gears, drop handle-bars with several rolls of grip-tape round them and GB brakes. I even had leather cycling shoes to fit into my Christophe toe-clips, although I never went as far as getting the cleats attached to my shoes. That was a step too far (if you'll pardon the pun). Sunday afternoon was spent touring the bike shops of North London with Jim Wilkinson and Eddie Read and ogling the minutiae/nuts and bolts of cycling which Bonners, Hetchins, Kamp Sports and countless others had in their windows. The Lord's Day Observance Society was active in those days so nothing, but nothing, was open on a Sunday. If you ran out of milk you were in trouble.

Hetchins in Seven Sisters Road was a mile or so from St Ig's, down Stamford Hill and my favourite shop because they sold unique bikes with hand-built frames with 'curly' back and chain stays: I couldn't get enough of looking at them. All these expensive bikes had gears made by an Italian firm called Campagnolo (which a half century later, when my wife and I went to see *Aïda* in Verona, I discovered also made pepper mills!). Mavic and Cinelli rims, Bianchi frames in Celeste blue, Reynolds 531 tubing, Mafac quick release flanged hubs, GB brakes, Maes bends and Chater Lea lugs were all on what seemed to be permanent display behind those dusty crowded windows.

Fausto Coppi, Rik van Looy, Bobby Simpson and many more exotic guys like them were eulogised in *Cycling*, in those days a weekly newspaper that I bought as and when I could afford it (but mostly read in the paper shop as I was getting my delivery together).

We cyclists used to steal Wall's or Lyon's oil-cloth ice-cream banners from outside sweetshops to wrap our wet weather capes in, so they fitted neatly and professionally under our Brooks saddles. Aside from plums and apples, which we scrumped from peoples' gardens, this was probably the first (possibly the last) thing I ever stole, and I've been consumed with Catholic guilt ever since.

On Sundays we got on our bikes after I'd delivered my newspapers and been to early mass, to pedal our way to easily accessible places like Southend (40 miles each way) and be back in time for tea. Unfortunately this meant missing my mother's Sunday dinner, which was served at about three o'clock, immediately after our favourite wireless programmes: *Family Favourites*, the *Billy Cotton Band Show*, *Round the Horne*, *Educating Archie*, *Life with the Lyons*, et al. Invariably the food would be left in the oven for me, and while the crispy remainders put me off gravy for life, they gave me a liking for overdone meat, stuffing, potatoes, sprouts, peas, cauliflowers and the like.

As we progressed with our music we began to listen to real rock 'n' roll, a great deal of which Eddie Read's cousin, Kenny Carr and Jim Wilkinson's brother Roger had in their record collections. Stuff like Link Wray's 'The Rumble' and 'Get a Job' by The Silhouettes, 'Come Go with Me' by the Del Vikings, Jackie Wilson's 'Reet Petite' and 'Little Bitty Pretty One' by Thurston Harris and the Sharps.

By this time, though, the baby boomers of Great Britain were discovering Radio Luxembourg. Because the BBC didn't play anything other than what they referred to as 'light' music on the Light Programme, this was our only real source of musical education, and can best be described as a trumpet – the fat end being the whole of America and its music and the thin end being the voracious, soon-to-be-teenagers of this sceptred isle.

So I listened to the likes of Elvis Presley, Buddy Holly, Little Richard, Larry Williams, Ricky Nelson, Jerry Lee Lewis, Chuck Berry, Bo Diddley, and Johnny Otis bursting through my home-assembled Delco crystal set and wearing my bakelite headphones, under the bedclothes in my freezing cold bedroom. The problem with Luxembourg was that listening to it wasn't so easy. As with wartime transmissions like 'Jairmany calling, Jairmany calling', the sound came (and went) in waves. But that wasn't at all important to us: it was part of its charm. All we cared about was hearing the latest music. There was another station that we could listen to. It was called AFN, and was set up during the war as a home-comfort for American Forces (and a propaganda medium against their latest enemy). A chap called Willis Conover played real jazz music with a smattering of fifties rhythm and blues. I don't remember him playing any rock 'n' roll.

Unlike our American counterparts, we embraced everything we heard without any concern as to its genre. It was all rock 'n' roll to us, and we were blissfully unaware that it might well be country and western, rhythm and blues or something that I later discovered was called race music.

Once I started playing with US guys towards the end of the sixties I discovered that contemporary young musicians in the States were completely uninterested in the stuff we listened to and played. Songs popularised by the likes of Pat Boone, Rosemary Clooney, Dean Martin or even Doris Day were dismissed because they weren't supposed to like them. And it appears they weren't always exposed to some of the music we heard. West coast music may not have been played on the east coast and vice versa. When we first arrived in America in 1970 I was astonished to discover that Conway Twitty, whose song 'It's Only Make Believe' was one of my favourites, was a country artist. I was even more surprised to discover that his portly and rapidly ageing group was called the Twitty Birds!

Eventually, when I was coming up to fourteen, I was head-hunted for another group (a band was something that specialised in strict tempo dance music in those days), and this was the beginning of a life-long friendship with Russell Ballard. He and his older brother Roy played together with a singer called Norman Jago in Rick Nicol and the Rebels, and I joined them in my first real rock 'n' roll band: Bill Brown played electric bass for the first time, Roy played piano, Russell played lead guitar and a chap called Lennie Gypps played rhythm guitar. The come-on for me was the use of a wonderful four-piece blue marine-pearl Carlton drumset that belonged to Les Ballard, who had been a local dance band-leader and was Roy and Russell's wonderfully supportive dad. No more 'Bitsa' set covered in white marine-pearl

Fablon from Woolworth's to make it look-like-it-was-meant-to-go-together-with-everything-coming-from-the-same-manufacturer: I was playing a genuine 'Made in England' drumset and I loved it. The new group was named Norman Eddy and the Imperials (Eddy after the guitarist Duane Eddy and the Imperials after our local dance hall in Waltham Cross).

I don't think I ever saw Russell's dad play drums, but I do recall him sitting with a biscuit tin full of all his smoking stuff on his lap and banging on it in time to music on the television or record player.

Eddie Read had given up the idea of a career in music, and when Bernie joined me on bass in the Imperials he threw himself into the world of club cycling. He bought a new racing frame from Freddie Grubb, bolted all the proper lightweight gear onto it and was ready to race. The local lads went out training once or twice a week and Eddie joined them. There were two training routes of around 25 miles, which went out from North London, one to Hertford and back, the other via Potters Bar to Hatfield and back. You waited on the road for the lads to ride by in a big long line, whereupon you jumped on to the back and pedalled like mad to keep up. Eddie was on the Hatfield loop at a place called Bell Bar when a car travelling south overtook another car and wiped him out. Eddie got up and said he was fine, but they decided to take him to our local hospital just in case. Unfortunately he'd broken a rib, which had punctured a lung. He died on the way to hospital. Eddie was the first of my contemporaries to die, and because of this I don't think we really took the whole thing in. We certainly didn't know anything about grieving and closure in those days.

Norman Eddy and the Imperials needed a place to rehearse, and since Roy and Russell Ballard played football for Cheshunt Boys Club and they had lots of space at their clubhouse next to the Arterial Road, we all joined for a couple of shillings a year and eventually became part of the fabric. Several other beat groups already rehearsed there including the Parker Royal 5 (who became The Hunters) and The Bluejacks. I never actually played football for the Boys Club, but we always stayed behind after rehearsals and played five-a-side in the hall.

As far as sporting activities were concerned I wasn't a bad runner and (according to me) reasonably coordinated, so I played cricket and football for St Joseph's followed by cricket and rugby for St Igs. I was once most surprised to be chosen to represent the college at 880 yards in the North London Schools championship. I borrowed some 'spikes' from my sister's boyfriend, Johnny Rogers, and ran on cinders for the first (and last) time at the Henry Barras Stadium in Edmonton. I came a creditable fourth, just out of the medals.

My brother-in-law-to-be sat behind me for four years at St Ig's, and we both played wing-forward for the school rugby team: Roger Cookson was on the blind side of the scrum and I was open side because I was faster than him and had further to run. I enjoyed playing rugby and cricket, but once I really got into playing music taking part in sport didn't mean that much any more – especially if it was an away game on a Saturday and interfered with getting to the gig.

The Boys Club was a brilliant place to be, and everybody was so supportive of what all the bands were up to, especially Stafford Young – who had been Russell's teacher at nearby Kings Road School. Stafford, whom I still called Mr Young up until his death in 2008, was originally from Northern Ireland, and had helped George Best with his football as he was growing up. Danny Blanchflower was also from Belfast, and part of our club. Since he was also Spurs captain, had already lifted the FA cup and would soon go on to achieve the double, he was very well liked.

Russell B. was on Spurs' books as a junior, but had a very serious accident when out playing in the woods near Temple Bar in 1958, being hit in the eye with a stone. Over the next couple of years he was in and out of London's Moorfields eye hospital and in and out of The Imperials, while the surgeons unsuccessfully tried to save it.

In 1959 The Imperials were entered in the National Association of Boys Clubs nationwide talent competition, and we won our way through to the finals at the Royal Festival Hall. We didn't win that year, but were highly commended. The next year we nailed it, albeit with a slightly different line-up. Our singer Norman Jago had left and been replaced by Buster Meikle, who'd been in the Parker Royal 5 until they changed their name to The Hunters, and found a dynamic new singer called Dave Sampson to back. When we acquired Buster we'd also taken on the Parker Royal 5's stage jackets, which fitted us where they touched. They were American-style red tuxedos with black 'shawl' lapels, purchased a few years before from Cecil Gee in Shaftesbury Avenue.

Lennie Gypps, aka Bruce Chips (after Bruce Welch, The Shadows' rhythm guitarist), had recently left The Imperials, eventually to enter the service of the Lord. He had his own highly un-evangelical words to Connie Francis's 'Lipstick on your Collar': 'Lipstick on your chopper told a tale on you . . .'

Bernie had replaced Bill Brown, and by this time I had saved up enough money to invest in a floor tom to add to Les Ballard's kit, so we could play 'Apache' by The Shadows properly, as well as 'Peggy Sue', 'New Orleans' and 'Running Bear'. One Saturday Roy drove me on his Lambretta scooter to Old Ford Road in London's East End to pick up a matching blue marine-pearl Carlton drum from Ted Warren's drum shop (as advertised in the *Melody Maker* classified pages). We tied it to the back of the scooter and I proudly over-used it that night at a gig in a dodgy pub in Enfield Highway – somewhat inappropriately called the Top House.

Poor old Russell was back in hospital again, so we needed a replacement lead guitarist to stand in for him. We found a chap called Billy Kuy, who at the time was playing with a very good local band called The Stormers. Billy knew more jokes than anyone, and he still owes me a pound he borrowed from me at a gig in 1960. He went on to be in The Outlaws, which was a band that backed Mike Berry and contained both Bobby Graham and Chas Hodges (of Chas and Dave fame). Anyhow, the newly named Buster Meikle and the Daybreakers duly fought their way through the heats, and we found our way into the grand finals, which we won, beating a real classical guitarist into second place. We received our trophy from Mr 'Give Me the Moonlight' himself, Frankie Vaughan, who was the patron of the Association of Boys Clubs. This was meant to be our entry into the big time, and in some ways it was. One Sunday soon after our victory we found our way up the newly built M1 to a TV studio in Birmingham to appear on a religious programme called *Sunday Break* with Cliff Richard. This may well have been his first opportunity to talk about his faith on national television.

Cliff Richard was the stage name of the Harry Webb who grew up next door to me and whom I'd gone to Saturday morning pictures with. He eventually went to Cheshunt Secondary Modern School with my sister – after she transferred there from the Holy Family Convent. Cliff was also a member of the Boys' Club, and at the beginning of the sixties when he was really making it big he came back to do a couple of charity shows: I suppose you could say The Daybreakers supported him. One was at his old school and the other at the Regal Cinema, Edmonton – an old theatre where I recently learned Marie Lloyd ended her career. I once stood outside with my ear on the door listening to a very muffled Jerry Lee Lewis!

The gig at the secondary school was interesting because we met Cliff's backing group, The Drifters, for the very first time. They hadn't yet been forced to change their name to The Shadows by the American vocal group of the same name. With Ben E. King as lead singer, they'd already had hits with Mort Shuman's 'Save the Last Dance for Me' and 'There Goes my Baby'. We all got dressed in the same classroom and were able to see their instruments up close for the first time. Hank Marvin's Antoria guitar was sitting in its open case on a school desk, and Russell tells me Jim Wilkinson, having gazed at it in awe, couldn't resist reaching down and gently strumming it. Hank heard this and growled, 'Leave it alone, son, it cost a lot of money!' This was probably only a couple of years before Russ wrote an instrumental originally called 'Atlantis' for The Shadows, which they recorded and renamed 'The Lost City'.

I met Tony Meehan for the first time at that concert, and he and I remained firm friends and admirers of each others' work until Tony's sad death in November 2005. Tony went on to be head of A&R at Decca, and malicious rumour has it that he was present at the infamous meeting where Dick Rowe turned down the Beatles. More about Tony later.

Cliff was playing a week in variety at Finsbury Park Empire and Tony was ill (mumps, measles?) and Mrs Webb told my mother they were looking for a replacement. They weren't going to ask me because I was still at school. So Laurie Jay got the gig at the Finsbury Park Empire with Cliff and I didn't. Oh well!

The Hunters were also on the bill at that secondary school show, and I thought I was about to be related to John Rogers, their bass player. He was courting my sister and they planned to get married.

I was coming up to sixteen, and GCEs were looming. All this music lark was taking my focus away from formal learning, although in the end I managed to scrape half a dozen passes, together with good results in English and maths, the subjects that I liked most.

One of the main reasons for my not focusing sufficiently on school work is that another group had secured my services, even though I was still gigging with The Daybreakers. I'd be picked up from school in a Ford Zephyr (with a bench seat in the front and a column shift) and whizzed off to many a late night show. Freddie King and the Bluejacks came from just round the corner from Cliff's family's council house in Bury Green, Cheshunt, and although they weren't as good as us they had an agent who got them a lot of well-paid gigs on American bases around the home counties. Fred Wilkinson was their guiding light and rhythm guitarist, John 'Nobby' Dalton was the bass player (he was destined to join The Kinks when Pete Quaife finally called it a day), the lead guitarist was Norman Mitham and the singer Joey Pallett. We travelled miles to US airbases and army camps to play in pitch-black bars to mostly drunken servicemen and their even more intoxicated women. (Frequently we'd be playing to just a few guys when suddenly the place would fill up, when what the Americans irreverently called 'the pig bus' arrived from the local towns.)

14

Nobby and I were both coming up to fifteen, and certainly not old enough to be in these places, so Fred lied about our ages. It was interesting: if we played for the families of American servicemen in the afternoon Fred would tell them we were only twelve, thereby getting more attention for us, and more drinks, food and take-away liquor for Fred and the older guys in the band.

These gigs were like an introduction to America for us, and Fred used to put on his best American accent as we pulled up at the gates: 'Band for the NCOs' Club.' I doubt any of us will ever forget the taste of the first hamburger (washed down with Pepsi-Cola) that we ate in the commissary at Bentwaters USAF base sometime in 1960. Fred Wilkinson was the salt of the earth, and had actually fought in the Korean War until the tank he was driving was blown up by the Communists. He woke up on a hospital ship, and all he could see was a blurred vision in white which he took to be an angel! He was like an older brother to us, and tour-managed for us through The Roulettes and Argent. He richly deserves a very special place in my musical upbringing.

We Daybreakers were getting quite a reputation as capable musicians, and we eventually found ourselves in demand to do our own show and also back some of pop Svengali Larry Parnes's stable of singers. This allowed the promoters to get a decent backing band for absolutely no extra money. These guys weren't particularly difficult to back because aside from their 'hit' (if they'd had one) they all sang the same songs: 'Great Balls of Fire', 'I Got a Woman', 'My Babe', 'Johnny B. Goode' and so on. This was fine as long as you didn't have too many of them on the bill at the same time. I remember one gig at Bognor Regis where there were three artists arguing with other because they all had much the same repertoire. In the end they all sang the same songs. Anyway, we backed the likes of Johnny Gentle, Michael Cox, Tommy Bruce, Nelson Keene and on one unmemorable occasion, at St Albans Corn Exchange, Ricky 'Tell Laura I Love Her' Valance. One of the only guys we never backed was Larry Page, who was billed as 'The Teenage Rage'. He went on to produce The Troggs and managed The Kinks – not once but twice.

Even though we were making some money we were still naïve, and frequently got cheated. (Ripped off would not be in a musician's vocabularies for another decade.) We once played at an unpaid audition at Barnet Drill Hall, organised by an ex-wrestler called Ron King who persuaded us, Neil Christian and the Crusaders (with Jimmy Page), Screaming Lord Sutch (with Ritchie Blackmore?) and several other bands to come along. Every band played for forty-five minutes, while Ron King counted all the half-crown coins he'd taken from the punters he'd sold tickets to.

Another thing you had to audition for was a programme on the Light Programme on Saturday morning. Imaginatively called *Saturday Club*, it was hosted by Brian Matthew. You had to go to their massive ex-skating rink studio complex in Maida Vale find the right studio among the dozens there, make a live recording and wait for a few days while Brian M. and the BBC hierarchy deliberated about your immediate future.

Of course what we really wanted to do more than anything was make records, and we jumped at the opportunity to record at the Acos factory in Waltham Cross. Acos was a company that made electrostatic loudspeakers, with a recording studio to demonstrate their sounds to interested parties. We backed a singer called Johnny

Carson, who was Cliff Richard's cousin, on a song called 'Dream On'. Aside from the Grundig, round at Eddie Read's parents' house, this was probably the first time we recorded. We also backed a guy called Roly Daniels on a record called 'Yo-Yo Boy', but I'm struggling to remember why, when and where.

Gigs were plentiful at this time for everybody, and even the smallest London suburb had several church halls as well as youth clubs, dance halls and cinemas where there was live music most weekends. We played at two or three local cinemas on Sundays during the break between films, and had to fit our instruments into the 3 or 4 feet available in front of the silver screen. No mean feat for a drummer, and like Roy Ballard I frequently had to play sideways. We played enthusiastically for nothing at both the Granada and the Regal in Edmonton, which was where all the package tours of the day went, but by far the worst of these gigs was in Ware at the Astoria cinema, where we had to take the Ballard family's upright piano. We manhandled it downstairs from their living room over the shop, and onto their open-backed lorry.

One winter's Sunday evening we played at Brady Boys Club, which was a Jewish club in a tough part of London's East End. We witnessed a fight while we played: rival gangs stood on each side of the hall, then suddenly ran at each other. Nobody told us what to do, so we kept playing as the fighting came closer and closer to the stage. Eventually, discretion being the better part of valour, we ground to a halt and fled to the relative safety of the dressing room.

Helen Shapiro was at the club on another night when we were playing there, and she asked us to back her. Among other songs we played 'Walking Back to Happiness' and 'Don't Treat Me like a Child', which were just beginning to be very successful for her. We obviously acquitted ourselves well, because she recommended us to her A&R man Norrie Paramour, who was looking after the recording careers of Cliff and the Shadows and Adam Faith at EMI. So we turned up early one Sunday evening at his mansion in The Bishops Avenue, Hampstead, and played a couple of songs for him. I'm sure this was the first time Roy played a Steinway piano.

Norrie liked what he heard in his front room, and arranged a recording session for us at Abbey Road. We played 'Yo-Yo Boy' again, and once we'd recorded another song called 'You Tell the Sweetest Lies I've Ever Heard' he came over to me. He said something along the lines of 'Well done', and then something I've never forgotten: 'You swing'. I had no idea at nearly sixteen what he meant, but hoped it was good! He immediately offered us a recording contract, but Buster Meikle decided he didn't want to be a pop star and that was the end of that. For the moment.

I played on a *real* record around this time. It was 'The Storm' by The Hunters, our club-mates from Cheshunt Boys Club, at Fontana Studios in Marble Arch. I arrived for my first real recording session with my complete drumset only to be told by the A&R man, Jack Baverstock that they didn't (and couldn't) record bass drums there. I was nonplussed, and told him that my whole 'rock-a-shake' rhythm would only work if the bass drum and snare played together. He made me play the rhythm and agreed the bass drum was very much part of it, and so we recorded it with a bass drum. He told me it was the first time they'd successfully recorded one.

The Hunters were an exceedingly accomplished instrumental group, who had already made an LP, comprising Brian Parker, John Rogers, Henry Stracey and their drummer Norman Sheffield. He once showed me how to play the drums, but at the time I was more interested in his wonderful Ajax drum kit than in how he played it.

He was considerably older than me and went on to found Trident Recording Studios. My mother took an immediate dislike to him. The Hunters wanted me to play on that particular record while Norman played timps. This was mid-1961, at which time they were a 'pro' outfit who worked on package tours, backing not only Dave Samson but also visiting US artists like Jimmy Jones and Bobby Rydell.

The Boys Club connection carried on with these guys, and when Cliff was on his first tour of America and it was too complicated (or expensive) to bring The Shadows back to play on the hugely popular and prestigious *Sunday Night at The London Palladium* TV show with him, he asked The Hunters to step in. Tony Meehan is on record as saying that during this arduous US bus tour if he wasn't playing the drums he was asleep.

To get the wherewithal to contribute to the price of my first 'bitsa' kit, I got a job one Easter holiday with my sister at nearby Oylers Farm, pulling spring onions. I think I got a shilling a day, and the worst thing about it was not that your hands stank of spring onions, but that those onions invariably grew right next to small and exceedingly virulent stinging nettles. I didn't let the grass grow under my feet, and actually had three jobs at one stage. One of them was working for Palmer's greengrocers as a delivery boy, also helping in the shop filling bins with vegetables and cooking beetroot.

I was also a newspaper delivery boy for Carr's newsagents. We loaded up our delivery bikes with all the papers ourselves, and were expected to remember our rounds and the papers that each house had ordered. Even more than half a century later I can still remember my paper round very clearly. It began by me dragging myself out of bed when my Westclox alarm clock sounded at exactly 5.30am, followed by a quick sprint on my racing bike to the paper shop to pack the exact number of unsorted papers and load them onto the carrier at the front of what used to be called a tradesman's bike. Some shops sorted the papers for their paper boys and pencilled the address on the top but not Carr's – we had to remember who had what. *Daily Sketch* to 1 Abbey Road, *Daily Herald* to number 5, *Daily Express* to number 7 with *Woman's Realm* on a Wednesday, and so on. The round went from the shop and a couple of miles down to the River Lea and back again, all before breakfast, followed by a mad rush via the trolleybus to school in Stamford Hill.

After breakfast on a Sunday morning I also had the much more difficult job of persuading people on the Waltham Newtown Estate to cough up the money they owed for the papers I'd delivered during the week. Often they'd cheerfully ask me to leave it till next week or more frequently hide behind the net curtains and not answer the door.

During the long summer holidays of my childhood, when it never rained and was so hot that the tar on the road bubbled, I had a bash at standing next to the London-bound trolleybus stop hawking evening papers. This necessitated a lot of shouting, which ultimately caused my voice to break.

I learned about what was going on in the world first thing in the morning from reading the headlines as I folded the papers to put them through letter boxes, and this was the way I discovered (like Don McLean) that Buddy Holly had died in a plane crash in Iowa in February 1959. This was something I mentioned to McLean when I was part of his And Friends backing group twenty-two years later. It was the one and only time I mentioned 'American Pie' and its enigmatic meaning. Don didn't dismiss me out of hand but looked at me in an interested way. Unfortunately he didn't follow it up by spilling the beans about the Father, Son and Holy Ghost.

But February made me shiver
With every paper I'd deliver.
Bad news on the doorstep;
I couldn't take one more step.

I can't remember if I cried
When I read about his widowed bride,
But something touched me deep inside
The day the music died.

Like all popular musicians, whether they admit it or not, I got into music to meet the opposite sex. There were two local girls who we as a group really fancied: Beverley Smith and Sue Nelson both looked just like Brigitte Bardot as far as we testosterone-burdened kids were concerned. We went so far as to serenade Beverley outside her parents' maisonette in Holmesdale Close – Bernie and Eddie with their guitars and me with Bernie's mother's washboard. She lived in a cul-de-sac, and the sound of my washboard overpowering the guitars echoed round the houses on three sides. I remember that neither her parents nor the rest of Holmesdale Close were music-lovers, because we were forced to flee the scene before they called the police.

In those days a magazine called *Spick and Span* taught us what the female form looked like, although Bob Cornish, one of our pals whose brother went on to direct *Top of the Pops*, showed Russell and me something stronger that his brother Mel, as an artist, had every aesthetic right to have in his bedroom. It wasn't even under his bed. Decades later we featured in *After Dark*, a gay magazine in America, which showed us topless and was cropped so we actually looked as if we were naked. In those days we'd do anything to sell records.

Carole Hayden was my first real girlfriend. I met her at a gig near where she lived in Enfield Wash. She was blonde and pretty, and got on well with my mother. I suppose we were sixteen at the time, and as soon as my aspirations of becoming a professional musician became a reality, a few months later, the romance fizzled out.

I can only assume I'd made some money from my nocturnal activities because I bought myself an almost new Trixon Luxus drumset. I acquired it from Paramount Music, Ivor Arbiter's dad's shop. It was solid black with tasteful gold speckles, and I was inordinately proud of it. Once equipped with Ajax cymbals, the best I could afford at the time, I was ready for a career in music.

Paternal Grandparents

*Maternal Granddad, Grandma
& my Ma*

My rather dapper Old Man

Old Bob, young Bobby & Harry Henrit: St Andrews 1949

Harry & Marcelle Henrit

My Mother's thirties finery

Berkley Avenue Coronation 1953 with Cliff's family's house on right

St Ignatius Under 13 XV

9 years old with sticky-out hair

Silver Service at Grand Hotel, St. Andrews – my mother stage right

Grandma Carroll

Marcelle at Bexhill-on-sea

*Outside St.
Joseph's church*

with Patricia - ticket to ride

Extended Henrit family outside Forgan's golf shop in St. Andrews

No place like home, Waltham Cross

More Waltham Cross

Twin Towers of St Ig's

Spotty teenage with Bernie

The happiest days of your life? The 5th form

Sun Vitesse & that itchy Lurex shirt

My first proper set, circa 1959

THE REGAL · EDMONTON

CLUB WEEK, 1960

GRAND CHARITY
CONCERT

WITH

CLIFF RICHARD

AND THE

SHADOWS

Block by courtesy of "New Musical Express".

Sponsored by Cheshunt Boys' Club

ALSO TALENT CONTEST FINAL

o n

Sunday, 30th October, 1960, 7 p.m.

Proceeds in aid of
New Headquarters
and Equipment Fund

LUCKY
PROGRAMME № 628 1/-

THANKS

WE, the Members and Management Committee of Cheshunt Boys' Club offer our SINCERE THANKS to all who have helped towards making our 1960 Club Week and Concert a happy and successful one.

Cheshunt Boy's Club concert programme 1960

"GOD SAVE THE QUEEN"

1. TRAD. versus ROCK
   MEMPHIS CITY JAZZ BAND
   JIMMY VIRGO AND THE BLUE JACKS

2. **THE ETCETERAS**
   North London's Top Vocal Group

3. **BUSTER MEIKLE**
   AND THE DAYBREAKERS
   MODERN RHYTHM
   Winners of Frankie Vaughan Award Trophy

4. **JUST JAKE**
   Miming His Own Business

5. **NEIL CHRISTIAN**
   AND THE CRUSADERS
   Britain's Brightest New Show-business Personality

6. **TALENT CONTEST FINAL**
   i CHERYL KENNEDY of ENFIELD.—Vocalist
   ii JOHN ALMOND of ENFIELD.—Saxophone Solo
   iii JUNE CARR of UPSHIRE.—Vocalist
   iv THE CRESTAS of HODDESDON.—Rhythm Group
   Introduced by Danny Blanchflower

7. FONTANA RECORDING STARS
   THE LANA SISTERS
   Swinging in Harmony

:: *INTERVAL* ::

AT THE ORGAN—PERCY VICKERY

8. **JAN ROHDE**
   Scandinavian TV. and Recording Star

9. KRAZY KOMEDIANS
   OLIVER AND TWIST
   A Dickens of an Act

10. **YOUR COMPÈRE ENTERTAINS**

11. TV. RHYTHM IN RELIGION AND
    FONTANA RECORDING ARTISTE
    JOHNNY CARSON
    AND THE CARSONAIRES

12. **"THE MUSIC TREE"**—
    AUDIENCE COMPETITION

13. FILM, RADIO, TV. AND RECORDING STAR
    # CLIFF RICHARD
    ## AND THE SHADOWS
    Currently Appearing at The London Palladium

14. PRESENTATIONS

15. FINALE—THE BOYS AND GIRLS SAY "GOODNIGHT"

COMPÈRE: ERIC FRITH   STAGE MANAGER: PETER BUSH
PRODUCERS: JAY NORRIS AND JOE CLARK
ORGANISTS: PERCY VICKERY AND CHRIS NICKOLDS

Cliff Richard & The Daybreakers

Daybreakers

Norman Eddy & the Imperials

Chapter Two: THE BIG TIME

My first brother-in-law-to-be Johnny Rogers met my sister at Cheshunt Secondary Modern School at the same time that Harry Webb was there. John was an excellent bass player who played first in the Parker Royal 5 and then The Hunters, and eventually wrote songs and produced records with Tony Meehan. I was told that when Tony left The Shadows that Jet Harris would follow him shortly afterwards, and this would leave two spaces to be filled. Brian Bennett was set to be Meehan's replacement but the battle for the bass chair was between John Rogers and Brian Locking, who had the advantage of having played with Brian Bennett twice before, with Vince Taylor's Playboys and the Krew Kats. Somehow it was arranged that whoever didn't get The Shadows' gig would join Adam Faith's backing group called The Roulettes. In the event The Shadows went with the devil they knew: 'Liquorice' Locking became a Shadow and John Rogers became a Roulette.

Maybe this wasn't so good for him but it worked out brilliantly for me, because within a month or two John, having taken over the leadership, decided they needed a new drummer and rowed me in. I was actually suffering from measles (or was it scarlet fever?) when the call came in for me to join Adam Faith's band, who were doing a week in variety at the Hippodrome in Bristol. I discussed it with my parents and we all agreed it was a great opportunity. My dad was especially pleased because he'd followed the big bands all his life and was surprisingly knowledgeable on the subject. He knew about drummers of his era like Jock Cummings, Joe Daniels, George Fierstone, Ronnie Verral and Jack Parnell. God willing, I'd soon be rubbing shoulders with them.

It should perhaps be noted that the Roulettes weren't a collection of spotty-faced musicians who'd grown up in the same area: we were a collection of acne-sufferers from different neighbourhoods. Russ Ballard and I had been in groups together since the late fifties but he didn't join 'Tel's Team' until a year or so after me. No, the Roulettes had been specifically formed as Adam Faith's backing group to replace John Barry's Seven.

I was just seventeen and didn't have a driving licence, so John drove me in the group's Ford Thames van down the dual-carriageway of the A4 to Bristol. I proudly set up my black with gold speckles Trixon Luxus drums and met the others in the band: Peter Thorpe the guitarist and Alan Jones the sax player. We rehearsed the show, including all Adam's hits, and I waited behind the drums for the great man to arrive. He turned up at about four o'clock for what in that legitimate part of mainstream showbusiness was known as band call. I was surprised as he strode across the stage to shake my hand: he was so short that his head almost seemed too big for his body. I know it's really unkind to say this, but he reminded me of the Mekon, an alien character who whizzed around on a small flying disc in 'Dan Dare, pilot of the future' on the front page of the *Eagle*, a comic I used to read on my paper round.

So we topped and tailed the intros and endings of all the songs we'd be playing in his forty-five-minute set ('When Johnny comes Marching Home Again', 'Hallelujah I Love Her So', 'I Got a Woman', 'What Do You Want', 'Do You Know What it's Like to be Lonesome' and so on), before we went to drop our bags at the theatrical digs we were staying in for the week. When we got back I put on the obligatory Max Factor pancake make-up (which was orange and arguably made you look less washed out under the stage lights) and some one else's made-to-measure 'Tonik' suit with a neat slit along the crease on the right leg where the original drummer's bass drum beater had ripped cleanly through. At least I didn't need to worry about it happening again.

I neglected to say I was also instructed in playing what was called tab music. When 'the turn' walked off, the band always played an uncomplicated up-tempo tune as the tabs (curtains) came across to end the show.

That was that: no audition, I was in. My passport could say I was a professional musician. I'd made it but, like everybody else who joined The Roulettes, I was on two weeks' probation.

I survived the first week and moved on to the next show, which was in Sunderland at the Empire. Unusually the whole variety show (including the pit orchestra) moved from one Moss Empire to another for ten weeks. Eventually I was told how much I'd be earning, and was astonished to discover that I would get £35 a week for backing Terry and extra for anything I did in the studio, on TV or radio. (In May 1962 most professional people would be earning £5 a week, except for Adam Faith who got £3,000.) This was a full-time job, and there certainly wasn't going to be a free moment for several years.

This was a traditional variety show, with Adam topping the bill and thereby closing the proceedings, with the next act on the totem pole closing the first half (depicted in slightly smaller capital letters on the poster). We had a vocal group called The Kestrels on the bill and a speciality act called Rondart and Jean: Ron blew darts out of his mouth at his wife Jean, who had a balloon or a cigarette nervously clamped between her teeth. There was also a fine comedian and trumpet player called Don Arrol, as well as Des Lane, the penny whistle man who danced a jig as he played.

Don used to ask us to help him during his act, which closed the first half. We had to hide in the audience and heckle him. At the end he'd announce that he'd like to finish with a beautiful tune called 'Cherry Pink and Apple Blossom White' (a well-known instrumental which had been a hit for Eddie Calvert). As he stood ready to start and lifted the trumpet to his lips we were to shout out 'Flight of the Bumblebee'. He'd ignore us and again lift his trumpet, whereupon we shouted out our request again. In the end he gave in: 'OK, then, but don't be surprised if it sounds like "Cherry Pink and Apple Blossom White"!' He'd then launch into an enthusiastic version of Rimsky Korsakov's 'Flight of the Bumblebee', which would bring the house down. It could be apocryphal, but up in Scotland I was told he was heckled during his act and asked by a drunk to play 'Melancholy Baby'. When he said he didn't know it the heckler shouted back, 'Well, show us your cock!'

I've always loved the story about a famous Scottish comedian called Chic Murray, who during the good old days of variety would take a taxi to the station at the end of the week. As he left he always stuffed something into the cabbie's pocket, saying, 'Have a drink on me.' Once Chic had gone the guy would put his fingers into his top pocket and pull out a teabag. Chic had a rather jaundiced eye, which produced the following memorable line: 'What use is happiness? It can't buy you money.'

The Kestrels contained three guys who within a year or two would leave their mark on the music industry: Roger Cook, Roger Greenaway and Tony Burrows. The two Rogers became David and Jonathan and wrote hits like 'You've Got Your Troubles' for The Fortunes and 'Melting Pot' for Blue Mink. Tony Burrows owns the distinction of appearing on a single episode of *Top of the Pops* in three hit bands: Edison Lighthouse, White Plains and Brotherhood of Man. He was also in the Flower Pot Men with Jon Lord and Nicky Simper, both of whom went on to found Deep Purple.

In those days we were expected to be all-round-entertainers, so Adam Faith worked out a little skit for me. Halfway through the set he announced that he had a new drummer who had only been with him for a week: he was French and spoke no English. His name was 'Robear Honro': would they like to hear him say something in French? Of course his adoring audience said they did, so he called me down to the front and asked me to say something in French. I was reticent at first, feigning shyness, but 'Tel' insisted. Eventually I would say 'Moe duh lawn' in my best French accent. Tel would give me a cod look and ask me to say it again, so I would. He'd then ask what it meant, whereupon I'd say 'Cut the grass' in a very English accent and run back to the drum rostrum ready for the next song.

We travelled around from gig to gig in a Ford Thames van and I got to know the other guys, Peter Thorpe and Alan Jones. Thorpey was a cheerfully uncomplex character who'd been the leader until John Rogers turned up, and his group had been the first to back Adam after the John Barry Seven left. He outlasted the rest of his group and played the show really well. He'd come from the same musical background as John and me, and seemed to have the depth of experience and repertoire we had. I never really got to know Alan Jones, because he didn't last for too long after I turned up. He was a slightly older 'proper' musician who'd played in dance bands and had the unfortunate nickname of Honk. This wasn't a term of endearment. When he got nervous, which was any time he played a solo, he over-blew his sax and produced an annoying honking sound. Of course the more he tried to stop this happening the worse it got. So eventually he went his own way back to Mecca.

As I said, the first variety tour went on for ten weeks, and we headed for a different city after the second show every Saturday. The week in the new theatre began with a band call, although this wasn't strictly necessary for us because the same

US acts found themselves supporting the likes of The Beatles, Stones or The Kinks.

The first package tour I did with Adam Faith was with Gene Vincent and Eden Kane, who were both backed by a group called The Echoes. I was new to it, and was surprised to find myself virtually alone in a dressing room one night with the guy who'd greatly influenced the music I liked with records like 'Bebop a Lula', 'Baby Blue', 'Lavender Blue', 'Lotta Lovin'', 'Say Mama', 'Git It' and 'Over the Rainbow' – most of which we'd played in The Imperials or The Daybreakers. We were sitting at a round table. Gene was in pain from the leg he'd injured in a motorbike accident in Virginia, and was swigging constantly from a square bottle of what I think was Jack Daniels. He was holding a Second World War Luger pistol he'd picked up in Hamburg, having just come to Britain after working in the Star-Club. I was told some forty-five years later that he shot up the club with that same pistol. We had no way of knowing whether it was loaded, how many painkillers he'd taken or how drunk he was, so when he pointed it at each of us in turn we took it seriously. Eventually he put the pistol down on the table and started spinning it around in front of him. I made my excuses and left. Gene was the epitome of an American rock 'n' roller, albeit now dressed in leather at the insistence of Jack Good, who found his image far too polite for a wild man. He possessed the same sort of perceived dangerousness that Adam Faith had – but I suspect Gene Vincent was sinister and tortured for real.

Another memorable package tour we did comprised Adam Faith, the Barron Knights, The Undertakers, a singer from Manchester called Lorraine Grey and of course us. We also had a compère named Dave Reid who linked all the acts. We criss -crossed the country in the usual convoluted way, but this time with a very zany bunch of performers. The Barron Knights were professionally zany but confined it to their act, whereas The Undertakers caused mayhem onstage and off. One night they armed themselves with pea-shooters, and as little Lorraine was singing her heart out with Cilla Black's 'Anyone Who Had a Heart' they let fly with their pea-shooters against my drums, which were set up at the back of the stage. The sound of dried peas on cymbals wasn't deafening, and had it been in time it would have been quite musical, but the sound of them dropping on toms, snare and bass drum was most off -putting for poor Lorraine.

The Undertakers were from Liverpool and they followed the same career path beaten by The Beatles, in other words clubs in Germany and playing a great many sets a night, but it had paid off and they'd just been successful in the charts with an American song called 'Just a Little Bit'. For many years Jackie Lomax, Chris Huston, Brian Jones, Geoff Nugent (aka The Rat) and Buggsy Pemberton were my favourite Liverpool band, and years afterwards when they'd given up all the craziness (and we hadn't) we'd bump into them on the west coast of America. On the tour we stopped at the newly built Blue Boar motorway café on the M1 for a cup of tea. Jonesy got his saxophone and he, Chris and Buggsy got on the long distance buses parked there, busking and collecting money in the top hats they wore on stage that had become their trademark. Jackie had a great voice and went on to be signed to The Beatles' Apple label, Buggsy emigrated to the mountains of California to become a carpenter and Chris Huston became a successful record producer having swept up and slept on the floor of studios in New York. The first thing he was involved with was 'Groovin'' for the Young Rascals, and without their knowledge (or permission) he added the distinctive congas that gave the record great flavour and, for my money, gave the Rascals a hit.

The Barron Knights had also had hit records with their mickey-takes of songs that had already been successful for other artists, like The Beatles and The Stones. They sequenced these together for 'Call up the Groups', in which Dave Clark's 'Bits and Pieces' became Boots and Britches – about being in the Army. They were merciless in their parodies, but didn't always get away with murder. Andrew Lloyd-Webber refused to give them permission to change some of his most famous and serious lyrics to 'Don't Cry for my Vacuum Cleaner'! Peanut, Duke d'Mond, Butch, Dave Ballinger and Barron were great guys, and we had a lot of fun together during the long hours we spent together on the coach.

As usual I was doing a drum solo each night during our set, and on the final night of the tour as I was bashing away the Barron Knights came on to remove bits of the drumset one piece at a time. Eventually I was left standing there with drum sticks and playing on the microphone stand! It was a brilliant piece of theatre, and no doubt if we'd been in summer season or panto we'd have kept it in every night.

When I began with Adam Faith music TV was just beginning to get going, and Jack Good (the godfather of music TV) was responsible for most of it. He was the Svengali who persuaded Cliff Richard to release 'Move It' as a single, and was a pal of Adam's. He sent Adam a lot of records from America by vocal groups we'd never heard of: The Marvelettes, The Contours, The Miracles and James Brown. As far as TV programmes were concerned we only had *6.5 Special* with Cliff, Adam, Marty Wilde and Joe Brown; and *Cool for Cats* with Kent Walton, who moonlighted by commentating on the wrestling (a sport that he insisted to us was absolutely genuine!). Ground-breaking programmes like *Thank Your Lucky Stars*, *Ready Steady Go*, *Boy Meets Girls*, *Wham!*, *Shindig* and *Top of the Pops* (which I honed my miming skills on) were just around the corner.

I was just eighteen, and had got my very first passport in June to go on holiday to Majorca with Michael Wood ('Mood') and Jim Wilkinson. They went, and were badly burned in the sun they weren't accustomed to, but I never got there. I was destined to go somewhat further afield for my maiden voyage – to Australia and New Zealand. My first trip out of the country and I was going halfway around the world!

We flew to Sydney via Bombay (or was it Calcutta or Delhi?) and I'll never forget getting off the Qantas plane in India in the early hours of what would have been an autumn morning in the UK. I was wearing an unsuitable grey flannel suit and walking down the stairs from the plane and stepping onto the tarmac was like walking into an oven. We stayed in uncomfortable transit – with fans in the ceiling moving the hot air around – for a couple of hours while they refuelled the Boeing 707, before heading off to Sydney via Perth. We crossed the line from the northern to the southern hemisphere, which was a big deal then, and they gave you a certificate to prove you'd achieved it. It wasn't quite like being on an ocean liner and someone dressing up as Poseidon with a trident, but it's something nice to tell my grandchildren – if I ever get any (see back page).

Flying in those days was completely different from today. The crew had to work out where they were using a sextant through a dome in the roof. The navigator stood on a stool in the aisle for ages while he looked at the stars through a bubble in the top of the fuselage.

We were in Australia when the indigenous population justifiably hated the Poms. If someone was needed to fill an official post they sent to the UK for a replacement, completely bypassing the native Australians. I recall doing a TV show for what I think was ABC TV, and all the technicians were from Britain. We weren't really meant to be in Australia because we were supposed to be touring New Zealand, but we took the chance to see such sights as we could. I distinctly remember the Sydney Harbour Bridge, because our hotel was just below it. We set off for Auckland, and arrived in a very rainy, very cold, rather old-fashioned city which somehow seemed reminiscent of a cowboy town in America, as portrayed in westerns we'd seen. The whole of New Zealand seemed like Ireland to us: green, wet and just as difficult to get around. We stayed in an old-fashioned hotel called the Coburg, and for the first time in my life I enjoyed the steak I saw on the breakfast menu. We weren't just playing with Adam Faith; we also backed Johnny Leyton, who brought along his own pianist. His name was Charles Blackwell, and believe it or not he'd just made an orchestral album of well-known skiffle tunes (it must be seriously collectible). John Leyton went on to be in *The Great Escape* and *Von Ryan's Express*, but these were his pop star years. He'd had hits with 'Johnny Remember Me' and 'Wild Wind', and since these tunes had the soprano voices of female opera singers on them, which John 'echoed', he and his Australian-born manager and record producer Robert Stigwood needed to audition classical singers at every city we went to. It made me chuckle to hear this going on because, to be frank, Johnny wasn't always the most tuneful of singers.

Robert Stigwood (known to his artists as 'Stiggy') was destined to become one of the greatest movers and shakers in the music business. A year or three later he was directly involved with, among others, The Beatles, Mick Jagger, Rod Stewart, David Bowie, Eric Clapton and the Bee Gees.

Johnny performed before Adam, and we went on in front of him with Charlie playing B. Bumble and the Stingers' 'Nut Rocker'. It was a proper backing gig, and we actually had real music to read: this was set up on the usual unstable and difficult to erect music stands. So John went through all of his hits, and at the end he threw in his version of Elvis's 'Such a Night', which was unintentionally hilarious. During the solo he grabbed the lapels of his suit jacket and pulled it off his shoulders so it fitted like a woman's stole. Then he did a sort of Chuck Berry duck-walk on tiptoes along an imaginary line from stage right to stage left. Now he did this without warning us: we weren't sure if he was sending himself up and whether we were supposed to laugh. When he did the same thing the next night we realised he was serious. Unfortunately we struggled not to burst out laughing. Eventually we realised that if we put our music stands high enough we could cover our faces, and we could cry tears of laughter while John did his shtick.

From Auckland we set off to Hamilton, Napier, Palmerston North and Wellington before taking off for the South Island. There we played gigs in Nelson, Christchurch and Dunedin. We were flying to the gig at Dunedin Town Hall when dense fog, in what was almost their summer, meant we couldn't land there. We flew on to Invercargill, which really is like a Wild West town. It took us four hours to drive back to Dunedin, which incidentally looks more like a Scottish city than most in Scotland. It's named after Dundee and Edinburgh.

It was September 1962, and we were in New Zealand at the time of the Cuban missile crisis. This was when Nikita Kruschev built installations for surface-to-air missiles in Cuba that were capable of bringing down American U2 spy-planes. John F. Kennedy reacted by sending battleships to blockade Cuba. Nobody knew what the outcome would be, but in the Antipodes we all figured we were as far away from the trouble as we could possibly be. Détente prevailed, and the superpowers backed down – so we were able to set off home. On the way we had been booked into a gig at the Town Hall in Hong Kong, and we flew there by way of Manila. We struggled through a thunderstorm with forked lightning all around us, which for someone on only his third or fourth flight, was absolutely terrifying.

The first (and last) Antipodean tour was over, and we headed back to the UK for lots more gigs, a package tour and eventually a pantomime in Bournemouth. We were busy!

Within a week or two of joining the Roulettes (and forty years before Richard and Judy's book club) I was chatting over beans on toast with Tel, and we got round to talking about books. I said I loved to read and that the idea of doing an English literature degree one day appealed to me. He took me under his wing, and I was astonished when he gave me a comprehensive list of books that he considered to be essential reading. This included some of the obvious modern classics by the likes of Steinbeck, Hemingway, Joyce, Scott Fitzgerald, George Orwell, Kafka, Evelyn Waugh, Günter Grass, Jaroslav Hašek, Victor Hugo, Harper Lee and Aldous Huxley, but also science fiction by Pohl and Kornbluth, Arthur C. Clarke, and dozens of others. It was an expensive list, but fortunately his fan club had a couple of lovely girls in it who worked for Penguin Books at Hounslow. They sent me two or three paperbacks each week, and eventually I had them all. They kept me going for a long time. Later I heard about a book called *University of One*, the story of a glamorous film star named Gloria Graham who was taken under the wing of a famous writer and given a reading list, which mirrored exactly what Tel had done for me. I'll always be grateful.

We also did TV shows, like *The Billy Cotton Band Show*, which gave me what was for many years my biggest musical thrill. We played an earlier Adam Faith hit called 'Lonesome', and Billy's orchestra came in behind us halfway through. No kidding, it was like being lifted up and pushed along.

As I said, these were the days when musicians were expected to be all-round entertainers, and nobody escaped. Evie Taylor was Adam's formidable manager; she also looked after Johnny Worth and John Barry as well as Jackie Dennis. The three words on his publicity handbill, diminutive, kilted and Scottish, pretty much sum him up, except that I'd say Evie managed to fashion a silk purse out of a sow's ear when one considers the lyrics of his first (and only) hit record: 'Lah-Dee-Dah, Oh boy, let's go, Cha, cha, cha . . .' I make no apologies for spelling, having never seen these prosaic lyrics in print – even the all-knowing Google can't help me!

Towards the end of 1962 John Rogers came to my parents' house with a white label record he wanted to play me by a new band called The Beatles, who had finally got into EMI's studios to record a single. On the family's Philips radiogram 'Love Me Do' was to my mind far more raw and energetic than the more sophisticated 'arranged' stuff we were hearing, like 'Good Luck Charm', 'I Remember You', 'The Young Ones', 'I Can't Stop Loving You' and even a couple of instrumentals, 'Telstar' and 'Wonderful Land', which were getting radio play and dominating the charts at the time. To state the bleeding obvious, 'Please Please Me' came along a couple of months later, and The Beatles and the rest of the Merseysound were off and running.

We were all booked with Adam into pantomime at the Bournemouth Pavilion for Christmas 1962. The cast for Emile Littler's latest production of *Aladdin* consisted of Tommy Fields (Gracie's brother), who played Widow Twankey, and Sid Plummer, a xylophone player who played Abanazar (boo, hiss). We rented a couple of freezing cold holiday flats in Canford Cliffs next to Sandbanks – forty years before the area became the most expensive real estate in the world. The programme didn't bill us as The Roulettes, we were the Adam Faith Musicians, but whoever we were we acted as Chinese policemen and emperor's guards and of course backed Adam at his wedding to the Princess Balroulbadour to close the show. We wore coolie hats, or ridiculous turbans, tunics and these short gold Wellington boots with curled up toes. These were difficult to play the bass drum and hi-hat with because the toes fouled the pedals. The very last part of the show was where we all took our bows, got into a long line across the stage and with gay abandon danced the latest craze: the Madison:

1. Step left forward.
2. Place right beside left (no weight) and clap.
3. Step back on right.
4. Move left foot back and across the right.
5. Move left foot to the left.
6. Move left foot back and across the right.

We got to drive home to London every Saturday after the show, but that particular year this was a great deal easier said than done. The winter of 1962 was hell, with fog and snow to be negotiated. We usually got home so late that I often spent the Sunday sleeping, only getting up in time for my mother's delicious roast dinner. On the Monday we'd get up early and retrace our steps through the snow for seven more performances. The company manager was Don Auty, who always wore evening dress (or at least a dinner jacket) at the side of the stage while policing the show. He made sure that nothing untoward went on, and during the panto had little to do. However, by the time he policed us again at the summer season at Bridlington in 1963 and again in Margate in 1964 the dynamic within the band had changed completely. For a start we were doing our own spot on the show as The Roulettes, we were making our own records and we had not one but two new members.

Henry Stracey was a great guy and a wonderfully musical rhythm guitarist, but I don't think he'd mind me saying he wasn't all-round-entertainer material, and with summer season only a few months away Tel was looking for someone who was. I don't believe he knew what he was looking for, but when Russell Ballard came along for a blow with us he knew he'd found him. Russell had primarily played lead guitar with me in The Daybreakers – but he also moonlighted on piano. Tel loved Russ's image, with the dark glasses he wore constantly because of his eye problems, and hired him immediately to play piano. Because he was so good on guitar he graduated to lead guitar, while Thorpey played rhythm mostly, with a bit of dual lead. As a band we were nearly there.

We were often employed to do gigs for Her Majesty's Forces through the auspices of ENSA, and one of these took us to Lüneburg Heath. We were contracted to play for the troops, and they put us up in what had once been Hitler's hunting lodge. We were there for several days, and as usual one of the top brass was assigned to look after us. His first name (or possibly his surname) was Cameron, and I have no idea what his rank was. Possibly he was a major. Anyway, we had lots of time to kill and when he asked what we'd like to do we decided we'd like to drive tanks. This from guys who couldn't even drive a car! So they kitted us out with overalls and berets with two badges on them, like General Montgomery's during the war. We drove two Churchill (or were they Challenger?) tanks, and burned the clutches out on them in no time at all. It was fun while it lasted. Cameron was a nice guy, but in common with his military brethren all over the world wasn't worldly enough to talk for long to a bunch of spotty teenagers who weren't under his command. In the end he stood 'at ease' with his hands behind his back, and enquired how they were treating us and if the food was all right.

We'd heard about the Hamburg clubs and the Liverpool bands there, and since we weren't a million miles from Hamburg we decided to go to see who was playing in the Star-Club on the Reeperbahn. I'm pretty sure we saw The Fourmost, Swinging Blue Jeans, Howie Casey and the Seniors and The Undertakers in an evening among the sex and violence of the Grosse Freiheit.

The most terrible sound I've ever heard woke me at about 5am on Monday morning 5 May 1963. It was my sister screaming. She was standing by the phone in the hall of my parents' house at 19 Berkley Avenue, and had just received the news from the police in Grantham that her fiancé Johnny Rogers had been killed in a road accident. The Roulettes' grey van had crashed head on, and the road manager was seriously hurt too. This guy, Chris, was such a terrible driver that we never went anywhere with him if it wasn't really necessary. For weeks in variety we all went on the train. I'd seen John in the hallway at my place at about ten on the Sunday night, and said I'd see him at the station in the morning. He said he was going in the van, and when I asked why he said he wanted to save money for the wedding. I said it was dangerous, because Chris was such an awful driver, but John insisted. We had a Commer J4 minibus with bench seats running east to west, and the gear was packed behind the seat that John was sleeping on, with amplifiers on the bottom, the drums alongside and guitars on top. If the opportunity presented itself he was capable of sleeping all the way to the Sunderland Empire. But the van collided with something, and the topmost guitar in its case shot forward and landed on John. That one guitar in its hard case broke one of his ribs, which punctured a lung, and that was that. I believe he would have survived had the guitar case hit him anywhere else.

Russell and I stood on our local station in Theobalds Grove on our way into King's Cross to catch the mainline to the north-east in complete shock; we didn't know how to deal with it. I know I got to Sunderland expecting it was all a ghastly mistake and that John would be there. He wasn't, of course, and we had to sort out our broken gear (I had cymbals bent inside out, and my wonderful Trixon snare drum, which had once belonged to Brian Bennett from The Shadows and been used on 'Dance On', was virtually a write-off.) The next thing we needed to do was get ourselves together for the show that night. I can't remember how we got through the show without a bass player, but assume that Russell took over, and I know that eventually we began to audition guys from near and far. Our first choice was Chas Hodges, who had just been offered the gig with his all-time hero Jerry Lee Lewis, so the timing was wrong for him. A lot of bassists who wanted to remain anonymous if they didn't get the job came up from London, but in the meantime we were using a local guy who was pretty good. This could be false memory syndrome on my part, but I think John Paul Jones who was playing with Tony Meehan at the time came to audition. (If I'm wrong this was said 'without prejudice', so please don't sue me.)

Eventually this local chap turned up from Hartlepool. He had a Teddy Boy haircut with a DA (when we were all sporting overgrown 'college boys', which came down over our collars), drainpipe trousers and was wearing the longest winkle-picker shoes (grey mock-crocodile Denson Pointers) I'd ever seen. He played bass well and sang well, but what really got the management interested were his claims to be a dancer (which was true), a trumpet player (which wasn't) and a ventriloquist, which was something never put to the test. You'd never expect to find that in a rock group anyway. John Rogan was hired in the second week of May 1963. What endeared him to us most was his ridiculous sense of humour. He was immediately named 'Mod' (because he was such a rocker), and the Geordie chap who'd helped us out for a week left in high dudgeon – disgusted at the way he'd been 'tret'! We were now a proper rock group.

Because we were contracted to play in Sunderland for a week we weren't allowed to go to Johnny's funeral, and the indomitable Tilly, his mother, never forgave Adam Faith or Evie for it. Of course John would have understood perfectly, but his family didn't.

Unbeknownst to me, this week in variety was a warm-up for the summer season coming up in Bridlington, and the cast would be with us for thirteen weeks starting in June. In the meantime, though, we had other stuff to do.

We had a few gigs for the Army, one of which was in Kuala Lumpur, and another at what I believe was called the Happy Valley Stadium in Singapore. All of this was long before they turned KL or Singapore into modern cities, and that double -barrelled KL tower would have been a figment of somebody's nightmare. I can't remember anything about it other than somebody being stabbed through the open window of the car we were travelling in! Eventually we found our way on various antiquated Fokker aircraft to Singapore and the Goodwood Park Hotel. We stood in the bar alongside William Holden and Capucine who were filming *The 7th Dawn*, and watched this agile-looking guy with a completely bald head swimming length after length in the outdoor pool. This swimmer was none other than Noel Coward, who lived semi-permanently in a bungalow in the grounds. He invited Terry and the rest of us in for tea, and regaled us with his best show-biz stories about the great and good of stage, screen and radio. Unfortunately we were all so jaded from the travelling and the oppressive climate that at least two of us fell asleep where we sat on the floor.

I had lunch once overlooking the lake in Montreux with Graham Payn, the great man's biographer and companion, and he laughed uproariously as I told him my story. In retaliation for falling asleep at his feet, Noel Coward described us Roulettes in one of his books as 'hideously skinny and horrendously loud'! We played the gig in Singapore, and Noel sat in the front row in a white suit. From the look on his face and his agitated reaction he seemed to like what he saw – even if it was skinny and loud!

When we were in the dressing room we found a beetle that was hand-sized, so big we didn't dare pick it up. Eventually, though, we tried to flush it down the loo. This animal/insect wasn't having any of that, and did its utmost to escape. The best we could do was put the lid down and run.

Before the days of unisex and long-haired guys going to ladies' hairdressers we Roulettes went to an old-fashioned barber in Acton. Eddie Jones was an old friend of Adam's, and we battled our way round the traffic-bound North Circular Road to his place every month or so to have our hair trimmed. Eddie was outrageously gay at a time when the word referred to the demeanour of girls dancing around maypoles. Unsympathetic people would probably have called him a pansy. Homosexuality was neither cool nor within the law in those days. He always had a fund of great risqué jokes, one of which has stayed with me for nearly fifty years. A gay couple take a room above a pub for a party with all their friends, and are having a whale of a time dancing around and camping it up. It's a really old pub and the upstairs floors aren't at all safe. One of the guys falls through the floor, crashes on to the bar and the beer pump penetrates him in the obvious place. The poor guy's screaming as all his friends rush down to help him. They assess the situation and decide to grab him under the arms and lift him gently off the pump. They lift him most of the way off, whereupon the victim whispers, 'Now down!'

After our inauspicious dalliance with Noel Coward we came home, and during 1964 were well into our normal round of recording sessions, TV stuff and live shows. I got a phone call from an unknown American who was making a record with a fairly new band and asked if I would come and play drums at IBC Studios the coming Friday morning. I said that as I was playing a week in variety at the Wimbledon Theatre with Adam Faith I could easily fit it in. Now, one of my problems is that I'm too honest, and I've spent my whole life working in an area where honesty is invariably *not* the best policy. So I told Adam what was going on, and was surprised when he told me I couldn't do it because I might be late for the show. I couldn't dissuade him, and since he was paying me a retainer to guard against these eventualities that was that. So I phoned the unknown American back (he turned out to be Shel Talmy) and told him I couldn't make it. The Kinks booked Bobby Graham to play drums on 'You Really Got Me', so I missed out. In 1984, when I finally joined them, Dave Davies said that if I'd made that session I would probably have hated him twenty years earlier. Surely not!

Another record I nearly made was 'Whiter Shade of Pale'. How this happened is a long and convoluted (but possibly interesting) story. Adam Faith and The Roulettes were doing a charity gig with The Hollies and various other artists, including Tony Rivers and The Castaways in the Concorde Theatre (or was it the Waverley), where South London meets Essex, and a young girl called Sandra Goodrich was singing 'Everybody Loves a Lover' in Tony's band's dressing room. Russell and I heard her and were very impressed, so we took her to Tel to see what he thought. Tel liked her and brought Evie Taylor in to look her over and allegedly she wasn't impressed. (This is my version, but to be frank everybody involved seems to have a slightly different take on the subject. But no matter.)

Sandy was working at the Ford factory in Dagenham, and began to call me on her way to work in the morning – which was unfortunate for me since she started work at 7am. Eventually, even though romance couldn't blossom between us at that time of the morning, her career did blossom, and both Evie and Terry took her on for management. They changed her name to Sandie Shaw and took away her shoes! Chris Andrews wrote songs for her, and within a very short time she was off and running on the treadmill of radio and TV shows, and of course package tours. Eventually she won the Eurovision Song Contest with 'Puppet on a String'. To do most of these shows she needed a band, and some pals of ours who we'd toured with were rowed in to back her. The Paramounts were Southend's finest, and unique in the sort of music they played. They did authentic versions of R&B hits and Diz, their bass player, was the most wonderful gospel pianist. We toured with them and Sandie in 1965 with the Barron Knights, Patrick Kerr (the dancer from *Ready Steady Go!*) and a comedian called Freddie Earle, who shot himself in the hand with a starting pistol while doing a James Bond skit. There are no prizes for knowing that Gary Brooker and Robin Trower of The Paramounts were in the original Procol Harum, and I got a call sometime in 1967 from a lyricist named Keith Reid to ask me to play on the session that gave rise to their massive hit record. I had something else on and couldn't do it, so missed out on appearing on the most played record of the last forty years. The guys ultimately brought in a much more jazzy player in Bill Eyden (who was Georgie Fame's drummer).

Three years before this Adam Faith and The Roulettes began a series on Radio Luxembourg sponsored by Ever-Ready Batteries. It lasted for approximately half an hour a week on a Sunday, and we recorded several episodes in one hit at their studios at 38 Hertford Street, behind the newly built Hilton Hotel. We had to come up with an instrumental each week: tunes like 'Walk Don't Run', 'Summer Place' and even 'Exodus'. For Tel's songs we trawled through all the stuff we'd played in previous groups: 'I Got a Woman', 'Hallelujah I Love Her So', 'You Must Have Been a Beautiful Baby', 'Multiplication' and so on. Time was of the essence during these hurried sessions, and gave rise to a vehicle and a phrase much employed throughout my playing career – the Radio Luxembourg Ending. We'd watch each other intently and stop as quickly and as elegantly as possible at the end of a song, without the added complication of having to learn an ending. (This is up there with another vehicle known as the American fade-out. The Americans had no trouble with fading a song out during a single bar if they didn't have a proper ending, while we were more generous in the UK – taking up to four bars to disappear.) The show always finished with Tel's song 'The Time Has Come', with slightly different words: 'The time has come for me to say goodbye again'.

I remember Stirling Moss lived in Mayfair at the back of the studios, and we bumped into him (although fortunately not literally) every now and again on our way to the nearest restaurant, Tiddy Dolls Eating House.

I was booked for sessions at these Radio Luxembourg's studios for a Lionel Bart musical, which I think was *Quasimodo* but may well have been something else. I remember it was a reading session: I was nervous and found it exceedingly tough to get it right. Fortunately Ross McManus, Elvis Costello's dad, was singing on these sessions and helped me immensely.

One of our variety weeks was in Liverpool at the Empire, and in its review the *Liverpool Echo* mentioned the sounds of The Roulettes rattling around the old theatre like bullets. I'm sure they did, and it's difficult to envisage what we sounded like on stage in 1963. We always used the theatre's PA for vocals, but to make sure his voice was crystal clear Adam took his own Shure microphone with him. It's laughable in these days of sonic sophistication and sound reinforcement to think that anyone would think a half-decent mic on its own could make any difference at all. Anyway, Bert Harris, Tel's roadie, reverently carried the sacred microphone everywhere and presented it to the stage manager to plug into the great metal cabinet of an amplifier, invariably on stage left. This was in turn connected to a couple of column speakers frequently fixed to the walls in front of the proscenium arch.

While I was in Liverpool that week I went into the drum department downstairs in Hessey's and asked the guy behind the counter what music was happening in Liverpool, and who was making it. He immediately mentioned a group called The Beatles who were doing well in Hamburg. I commented that this was a weird name, and that was that.

A few weeks later I was back in the West End getting measured for a bespoke pair of boots at Annello and Davide's and sitting next to these four guys with northern accents. There were half a dozen chairs in a line in the middle of the shop with wall to ceiling shoe boxes on three sides. The window onto Charing Cross Road was full of ballet shoes, character shoes and various different versions of elastic-gusseted Chelsea boots. My Scouser friends were sitting together next to me, and the farthest two appeared to be arguing loudly. I was getting leather boots, but they were interested in suede boots, up until that precise moment simply called ski boots. I chatted to the guy nearest to me and asked if they were a group. He replied they were, and I asked in the usual way what they were called. The guy hung his head, and in the sheepish way you do when telling people who've never heard of you, said, 'We're called the Beatles.'

'Oh, I've heard of you,' I replied. 'I was in Hessey's music shop a couple of weeks ago, and they told me about you.'

Paul McCartney smiled and replied, 'I thought you were French!'

We learned long after the event that, with The Beatles making it in America for Epstein during the beat boom, the impresario Lew Grade was looking for a beat group to promote as an alternative in the biggest market in the world. He came to Evie with The Roulettes in mind. She said no, that we were with Adam, and Sir Lew looked elsewhere – ending up with the Dave Clark 5. We suspect that by this time, after the success of 'The First Time', the act was what it said on the record: Adam Faith *and* The Roulettes rather than Adam Faith *with* The Roulettes – and for safety's sake, to guarantee her investment, she was determined to keep it that way.

The next time we bumped into the Fab Four they were wearing their 'Beatle boots' and things were really happening for them. We were all taking tea together in the Carlton Hotel on the seafront in Great Yarmouth just before going to our respective gigs. They were appearing at the ABC cinema and we were on the Wellington pier. Anyway, we started chatting, and after our crit in the *Liverpool Echo* about bullets spraying off the walls got to talking about volume, and they said they played the same volume everywhere. I remember that several girls came into the room looking for autographs, and in a roomful of beat boom musicians all sporting college boy haircuts, shiny Tonik (by Dormeuil) suits, and Anello and Davide boots weren't sure who was a Beatle and who wasn't – except for John Lennon, because of his glasses. Lennon helped them. Pointing to Mod and Thorpey, he said 'There's Paul and Ringo.' The guys signed as instructed, so somewhere out there are a handful of completely spurious Beatles autographs. That said most groups were capable of forging the signatures of missing members when necessary. I know there are quite a few Adam Faith signatures that weren't written by him!

We'd moved on to a new tailor called Dougie Millings, in Soho's Great Pulteney Street.

He made us these cutaway Tonik suits with black collars, which were a copy of some worn by the Everly Brothers (or was it The Crickets?) on a 1960 album cover. The Beatles asked where we got them, and the rest is history. Dougie had a fitting room below the shop, and he let us rehearse there – which was very convenient as it was right in the West End. Dougie's son Gordon helped his old man out in the shop, and these days he goes around the world talking at seminars about The Beatles.

Terry admired Lonnie Donegan, and they got on really well as they had the same disaparagingly wry sense of humour. Every now and then we were on the same show. Lonnie had a Martin acoustic guitar, when they were like gold dust in the UK, and Tel wanted it. It was unique in that it had a built-in microphone when nobody was doing that commercially. Eventually the 'King of Skiffle' gave in, and sold the D45 to the 'Prince of Pop'.

Tel had been in a skiffle group with Wally Whytton, called the Worried Men, and we were playing a skiffle medley in the act. We ploughed through various songs, and at the end of 'Putting on the Style' he threw this very rare guitar from the front of the stage to the back, and I leapt up to catch it over my head. I'm sure it looked spectacular, but its success depended on two things: Terry throwing it far enough and straight enough and me getting to it. I was leaping around the rostrum like Bert Trautmann (Manchester City's goalie), but as you'd expect sometimes I was beaten by the flight of the guitar. This wasn't so bad if we had curtains behind, because the guitar would get caught up in the drapes and slip gently to the floor, where the excess material would cushion its fall, but if we weren't in a theatre there was nothing to stop it flying on until something hard put a stop to its flight. That rare, double celebrity-owned guitar was often unavailable because it was being repaired.

Sometime in 1964 we played at a Tupperware convention in Rome, and Tel went out a couple of days early. When we arrived we were besieged by paparazzi at the airport, and they took hundreds of photos of us doing sixties-style zany poses and generally jumping up and down like loonies. Tel had come to meet us and looked on in amazement. The show was the next day, and as usual we Roulettes did a few songs before Terry came on. Afterwards we heard people talking: 'Adam Faith was good, but The Beatles didn't play enough on their own!' I don't know quite what (or who) Tupperware were expecting, but this might have been a serious case of misrepresentation. Even as we walked around Rome people came up to us singing Beatles' songs. We stayed in a very grand Grand Hotel, and for the first time saw those shoulder-shaped wooden coat hangers with sticks below the crossbar, so you could lift your suits up to hang them high in the air in a double-decker wardrobe. We were much taken with these, and decided to borrow some to take home for our stage suits. We packed them in our suitbags, but we weren't careful enough. Having carried them downstairs ourselves, we allowed the porter to take them to the taxi for us. He tried to bend the suitbags over his arm and couldn't. We were rumbled, and all the suitbags were searched on the marble floor of the foyer in full view of the great and good who were staying in the hotel. Fortunately we let The Beatles take the blame.

Towards the very end of our career The Roulettes were somehow selected to play in Montreux at the Golden Rose Artists Festival with Julie Rogers, Esther and Abi Ofarim, and a load of artistes we'd never heard of. This was in 1967 when Zapata Mexican moustaches were very much in fashion. We wanted to be up to date but didn't have time to grow them, so we went out and bought some. After the show we sat at a table with these American record company people, and after a few hours the moustaches (or perhaps the glue holding them on) became very irritating. Eventually we went to the loo, took them off and came back as if nothing had happened. I'm not sure the Americans noticed or were they too polite to comment?

Buster & the Daybreakers at Cheshunt Boy's Club'

Moody & magnificent

Roulettes mark 1

Roulettes uncomfortably warm black & white jackets

Roulettes: signed, sealed & delivered

With incriminating suitbags

With Chris Andrews at EMI, 'It's alright

Lonnie with Tel's Martin

Roulettes Mk 2

Roulettes in Manchester Square

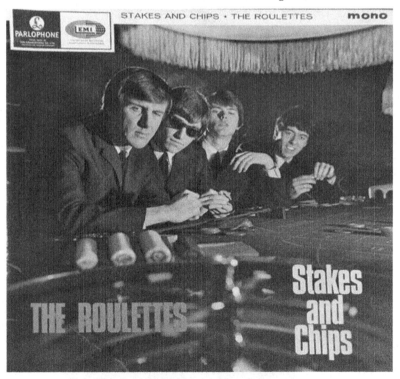

Stakes and Chips

THE
HUNTERS

The Hunters

Roulettes Mk 1

Tel and Russell's Sunbeam Rapier

Buster Meikle and the Daybreakers, Derby Locarno

Fred selling deckchairs: note the essential lipstick on the minibus

Risqué Rouletttes

Beauty Queen, Margate

Chapter Three: A TABLE NEAR THE BAND

Even though we'd started out as a backing group, by this time we Roulettes were as tight knit a unit as any band that had grown up together, and we were happily making records without Adam. Like him we were signed to Parlophone, which meant we recorded at EMI's studios – conveniently situated alongside the world's most famous zebra crossing in Abbey Road, St John's Wood.

The way we made records went something like this: John Burgess, our A&R manager, would phone Evie Taylor to tell her it was time for a new Roulettes record, and the session was booked for a couple of weeks' time. Only then would he ask if we had any material. In the early days we'd say no, and John would say something like 'OK, I'll find something.' He'd send along an acetate demo by someone like Neil Sedaka, and we'd learn the song and then find our way to the studio on the designated day for a 9.30 start. I don't believe there was ever any procrastination from us, or interference from John, and that's pretty much the way it went until Chris Andrews came along. With Chris's input there were always more than enough songs available to record. (All this was just before Russell B. got into writing his own great songs, although he and I had collaborated on the 'flip' side of our version of Marvin Gaye's 'Stubborn Kind of Fellow' in 1964, called 'Mebody'.) We eventually recorded one of Tommy Moeller and Brian Parker's songs, 'Long Cigarette'. The lyrics were still unfinished when we got to the studio to put the track down, so I finished them off and wrote the last chorus:

> Baby looks fine, boy,
> I wish she were mine, boy,
> I'm glad baby's come,
> Knew she wouldn't forget,
> She's worth waiting for,
> I should never have bet,
> Some other sucker she's met,
> Smoking a long cigarette

We'd arrive at EMI, set up the gear by 9.30, record the all-important A-side and then the less-important B-side, all by one o'clock – including an obligatory tea break. Then we'd all go to the canteen for lunch and the recording engineers in their white lab coats, with slide rules in the top pockets, would get on with the balancing of our work (turning three tracks into one track so that a mono single could be cut).

Technically EMI was more state of the art than any other studio, although that meant three-track tape machines and a battleship-grey mixing desk, which we likened to a Lancaster bomber because of its faders, which were like the throttles found in the planes' cockpits. Alongside John Burgess in the studio we had engineers like Geoff Emerick (who eventually engineered *Sgt Pepper*, *Abbey Road*, *Revolver* and the *White Album* for The Beatles); Peter Bown of Pink Floyd fame, who also engineered 'All Together Now' and 'Hold Your Head Up' for Argent; or Malcolm Addy, who engineered Britain's first real home-grown rock 'n' roll hit record: 'Move It' for Cliff Richard. He worked on all Cliff's other records until 1966, whereupon he graduated to Bell Sound Studios in New York and recorded the likes of Ella Fitzgerald and Duke Ellington.

These Roulettes sessions went on for three years, producing eight singles and one LP, and it wasn't until we finally left Tel that we were told sessions at EMI went from nine o'clock until one o'clock. We'd been wasting half an hour of valuable recording time for years! This 9.30 arrival got us to the studios too late for a place in the small car park, so (before meters arrived) we were forced to park round the corner, near the tube station in St John's Wood. Despite all this, our album *Stakes and Chips* has the distinction of being one of the exceedingly rare albums of all time and, providing it has the biographical insert, is worth 500 times more than the few quid it cost in 1965.

That same year we did a summer season at Margate, with roughly the same cast as the year before, but with the addition of Tel's comedian pal Dave Reid – who always ended his act with 'I have to go now, the lights are fading my suit.' We had a soprano named Liz Laurie, unkindly called Moonface, and an orchestra leader called Bert Waller, who'd played piano with Jack Hylton. This time the dancers were billed as The Lovelies.

Things had moved on a bit by summer 1964, and we were billed just under Adam. By 1964 we'd made a couple of records as The Roulettes and were taken much more seriously by the management. We had our own stuff to do, including a drum solo from me called 'Quite a Party', where I got to stretch out – although within certain rhythmical parameters, because Tina Scott (the show's soubrette) danced to it.

Proper billing didn't mean we behaved ourselves, though. We used to judge the heats of the Miss Margate competition, and as red-blooded nineteen-year-olds this was a great way to meet these attractive locals, and several short-term 'friendships' were formed.

Since a summer season always lasted for thirteen weeks, obviously we needed to find something to fill our time and stop us going stir crazy. In Bridlington the year before we'd taken up golf for a while and all went to a few lessons. Having a grandfather who was once a professional at St Andrews, I was bitterly disappointed to discover that golf wasn't in my genes. Having discovered it needed to be worked on, and having heard stories of professional musicians who got so hooked on golf that they'd rather chase a small white ball around the countryside than make music, I lost interest. Even though my granddad, my old man and all my uncles were naturals, I wasn't. (It was even more galling to discover that both of my sons could play from a very early age!) Of course I then became disparaging about the sport and, like Mark Twain, looked upon it as a good walk spoiled. As an aside, we were at our North London tennis club during the German exchange weekend with Wuppertal Tennis Club one summer when my wife asked one of the older German players if he played golf. 'No, my dear,' he replied. 'I'm still sexually active.'

I had learned to drive in a Ford Anglia during the summer season at Bridlington in 1963, but the very first car I owned was an Austin Mini. It's interesting to note that in 1951 there were 2.25 million cars on our roads and by 1964, when we were still with Adam Faith in Margate, there were 8 million. Anyway, I was one of those 8 million because when I came back to North London I bought myself a red Mini (5783 MD) and had it souped up by one of Fred's acquaintances. I was now liberated, and could drive myself anywhere I wanted to go. (The downside was that I could drive my friends anywhere they wanted to go too!) The Mini wasn't the greatest car for a drummer because the bass drum had to go on the front seat, which made selecting first gear impossible. You had to get used to starting off in second, which could be a problem on a hill. The floor tom sat on the back seat with the traps case. The ridiculously small boot had only enough room for the snare drum and the smallest tom. Cymbals went behind the driver's seat. It wasn't ideal, but better than the VW Beetle we once had, which had an engine in the boot and enough room for a very thin cymbal case under the 'bonnet'.

We needed to keep ourselves entertained during the show, because playing nine performances a week for all that time could drive a bunch of teenage guys crazy. So we began to mess around with the show, not maliciously or drastically, but just enough to make us and some of the others smile. We were dressed as cowboys with neckerchiefs to sing 'Cats and goats and geese better scurry', or Hooray Henrys in blazers and boaters to sing 'Joshua, Joshua, nicer than lemon squash you are', and to cope with this humiliation we often blacked out our teeth and frequently made the already rickety scenery rock. Donald Auty, in his dinner jacket, would knock on the door, shake his head sadly and say, 'Now, boys'.

Inexplicably we opened the show, and as the orchestra struck up and the curtains opened we marched two from each side of the stage to the centre, then turned sideways, facing back the way we came, put our hands out like Al Jolson and belted out:

> Why, don't, you, make it tonight, make it a holiday;
> Make it tonight, make it a jolly day,
> Your castles won't come tumbling down
> If you start out now and paint up the town.
> Just make it tonight forget tomorrow, it's just another day,
> Things will turn out right if you make it tonight.

It wasn't exactly Rodgers and Hammerstein but the audience loved it, except for one time when I tricked Russell into marching earlier. We had four bars to wait before starting our march, and I always told Russell when to go by saying 'And' – which was what dance people said when they were going to begin a routine on the very next beat. To see if he was concentrating I said 'And' after two bars, and Russell, who obviously had infinite and misplaced trust in me, marched on two bars early. The rest of us arrived centre stage in fits of laughter, and again we were greeted with Mr Auty's 'Now, boys' speech as soon as we got off the stage. This time he reported us to Tel, who did his best to keep a straight face while he ticked us off and told us how unprofessional we were being. I took this badly because as a boy I'd been kicked out of my sister's tap-dancing lessons, run by the redoubtable Madame Yandy, for being useless – but now it appeared I was capable of marching on the spot and singing at the same time. I felt this was progress and meant I was *really* professional! I was so good I was chosen to waltz the soprano to the front of the stage for her to sing 'It's a Grand Night for Music'. To be honest this wasn't to do with my terpsichorean prowess but more because I ended up closest to her after we'd taken part in another piece of rhythmical moving around the stage with the dancing girls.

We had proper dancing to do with 'Les Girls' too: lifting them onto our shoulders, having first put our feet into third position, grasping them around the waist and keeping our backs straight, then bending our legs sideways in a plié before hoisting them aloft onto our shoulders, where they would balance precariously. All this was years before Billy Elliott, but as I said we were meant to be all-round entertainers, and we did our best.

We even took part in the sketches with Tom Mennard and Bobby Dennis where we had to nod vigorously in response to questions like 'Filled in your forms? Passed your test? Well, sit over there then.' I can't remember what the purpose of this was, but I'm sure it made people laugh.

During that Margate season we were staying in Broadstairs, where we had a bungalow that was always overflowing with friends. It was 4 or 5 miles from the theatre, and as the weeks wore on we left our summer home later and later and had to drive faster and faster to The Pavilion, with just about time to squeeze into our Tonik suits with under-the-collar bow ties and rush to the sides of the stage before the orchestra struck up with our entrance music.

Unfortunately theatres in those days insisted we wore 'slap'. This was pink (make that orange) pancake make-up from Max Factor, which you put on with a damp sponge and which, as far as I recall obliterated the contours of your face and made your eyes sink into your head. But 'rules is rules' and this was showbiz, so we religiously put the nasty stuff on for each and every gig – providing it wasn't a Sunday. (The Lord's Day Observance Society decreed you couldn't 'don the motley' on the Sabbath.) It took a while to get this stuff on, and if we were late we invariably did it badly (if at all), and again we'd have the 'Now, boys' comment. Sometimes there weren't four Roulettes in the theatre by curtain up, so three (or sometimes two) of us had to march on to the strains of 'Make it Tonight'. Thanks to Tina Scott we eventually discovered Max Factor Sun Goddess, having messed around with Pancake Number 8 for too long. Pancake had a little round applicator made from crumbly sponge which you moistened slightly (with water if you had it, spit if you hadn't), before rubbing it over the top of the make-up then smearing it on. Sun Goddess was a vastly superior powder which was far quicker to apply, didn't ruin your shirt collar and, if you were secure in your sexuality, you might just get away with wearing in the street between shows.

One prank took quite a few weeks to come to fruition. We were vaguely dressed as cowboys for an Oklahoma piece and were issued with saws with which to pretend to cut through a piece of 4x2 while singing 'Spring, Spring, Spring'. We made a forward movement with the saw on each word and brought it back on the 'and', so really the piece of wood should have easily lasted for thirteen weeks. It would have done had we not come into the theatre early to do some surreptitious sawing. Eventually Mod sawed completely through his bit, which meant the wood broke in two and sprang up in the air, taking our saws with it. The result was yet another 'Now, boys' conversation with the company manager – and of course a new plank of wood.

Long-standing showbiz tradition said that if a 'turn' was doing a show in the town he had licence to 'pass in' to any other shows they had on, including cinemas. We were doing a week in variety at the Palace Theatre in Manchester in 1965 when the film of *The Sound of Music* was released and we decided to go to see it one afternoon. Fred Wilkinson didn't quite understand the concept of a musical, and when Julie Andrews sang the reprise of 'Climb Every Mountain' at the end of the film he was heard to say, 'Gor blimey, there she goes singing again.' It was the very same week that we were sitting in the dressing room late one afternoon when we heard Harry Secombe rehearsing a song from *Pickwick* (a show he was trying out before taking it to London). He was singing Leslie Bricusse's 'If I Ruled the World' with the rest of the cast, a capella, and it sounded so wonderful we all sat on the stairs to listen with the hairs standing up on the back of our necks. The next time I heard this song was in a lift going up to Lionel Blair's flat in Notting Hall when his pal Ray Martine parodied 'If I ruled the world, you'd all be poof for a start!'

Fred Wilkinson had been in the army in the fifties, and found himself posted to Korea during that particular struggle between the forces of good and evil. If he woke us up in the morning his greeting would invariably be in the voice of a sergeant-major: 'Hands off cocks, hands on socks.' He drove us and looked after the gear for years, therefore having access to the float provided by the management, which allowed us to fill up the van with petrol for something like 10 shillings. This was the time of Green Shield stamps, where every gallon of juice supplied several sheets of these: they could eventually be traded for various luxury goods. These stamps were deemed to be the crew's exclusive property, and were known as 'roadies' perks'. If the band decreed they weren't allowed to keep them they'd simply cut off their noses to spite our faces and go to a petrol station that didn't provide them. Now Fred would happily drive past non-Green Shield stamp garages in the Commer van with the fuel level dangerously low while searching for one that would elicit, in the fullness of time, the wherewithall to get presents for his wife and three children. Mostly the gods smiled on him, until one morning when we were heading home on the A10 just as the dawn came up like thunder, funnily enough at Thundridge, a village about a dozen miles from where we lived. We conked out just as Fred managed to coax the van into a garage that not only didn't give stamps but was closed. Our hero was undeterred, and having found an empty bean can walked purposefully towards the two-stroke pump. Two-stroke was used for motorbike engines. Because oil had to be mixed with the petrol it needed to be pumped by hand. A do-it-yourself lever stuck out from the side, so Fred did it himself. To stop ton-up bikers from pilfering, the nozzle was padlocked into the pump. Undeterred, Fred pumped away until the mixture overflowed down the outside of the pump and sometimes into his strategically placed tin can. Far more of it went onto the ground than into the can, but eventually he had a whole canful, which he poured into our tank. Many canfuls later, with an alarmingly large puddle forming at his feet, Fred decided we had enough to get home. He clambered back into the driver's seat reeking of two-stroke, and we set off down the A10 in a cloud of smoke caused by the oil in the petrol, combined with whatever had originally been in the can Fred had found.

Dear old Fred died of cancer in the mid-eighties, and we really won't see his like again. I'll give you another small anecdote about him. When some tea-leaf made off with my bag of Zildjian cymbals as he was loading the van after a gig in Sunderland, Fred watched him do it but didn't chase him until he'd put his Lotus mechanic's overalls over his best Tonik suit. Fred came back with the cymbals a few minutes later, with bloody knuckles and a satisfied smile on his face.

'The Weekend Starts Here' was the slogan for a television show that had a huge impact on youngsters at this time. *Ready, Steady, Go!* began in 1963 and was unique in that it had a live dancing audience (even though groups mimed to their records initially). It started in Kingsway Studios in Holborn and was transmitted on the commercial television network. Eventually it was transferred to another studio away from the central London congestion in Wembley, just a stone's throw from the Empire pool and the famous stadium. It was presented by Keith Fordyce, assisted by an attractive young girl called Cathy McGowan, who had long dark hair cut into a fringe. She auditioned for the programme when the director, Elkan Allan, invited applications from 'normal' girls for the position of presenter. By the time the programme got going she certainly wasn't normal or ordinary, but she was attractively ingenuous and eventually acquired the title 'Queen of the Mods'. We were pretty friendly for a while and exchanged late night phone calls while sitting on the stairs in the draughty hallways of our respective parents' homes.

There were dancers on the programme to show the kids how it should be done. One of these guys was Patrick Kerr, who was also a singer who'd toured with us, along with his wife Theresa Confrey and a chap called Paul Gadd, also known as Paul Raven in those days. He ultimately became famous, then infamous, as Gary Glitter. That said, he once sold me a brilliant military overcoat which I wore for years.

We were on the show a dozen times with the likes of Dusty Springfield and Petula Clark, although never with Dave Clark who somehow features in all the videos! Could this be because he bought the rights to all the programmes?

Top of the Pops came along in 1964, and very shortly afterwards *Ready, Steady Go!* decided to change their format drastically and insist that acts played live. We Roulettes were on the first *Ready Steady Goes Live* in April 1965. The producers had brought in another female presenter, this time a blonde called Gay Singleton. I hope she won't be insulted, but Gay was an Essex girl before they were invented, and fancied Russell. On this programme I played with The Kinks almost twenty years before I joined them. As well as The Kinks there were other great acts on that day: The Manfreds, Dionne Warwick, Cliff Bennett, Zoot Money, The Yardbirds and The Artwoods, as well as Tom Jones who, for some reason, was allowed to mime. For the finale we all joined in playing an R&B classic we sort of knew by Don Gardner and Dee Dee Ford called 'I Need Your Loving'. I remember The Beatles joined in too, although I can't find a reference to them being on the programme.

Another milestone is that my future wife and I were in the same room together at this gig. We didn't meet. She was with her then fiancé Derek Griffiths, who played in Ronnie Wood's brother's band, The Artwoods.

The Roulettes had just appeared on *Ready, Steady Go!*, and since it was still not eight o'clock we decided to go to one of the nearest clubs for a drink on the way home. The Chez Don in Dalston was bordering on being in a rough area, just round the corner from my old school, so I often bumped into one or two of my contemporaries from St Ig's there when we went there every now and again on a Friday to meet the opposite sex. Of course Russell was with me that night, because we lived near each other, along with my friend Mood, Ian Clark and various others who'd been at the show. The next part is confusing, but suffice it to say that everybody there had seen us on TV that night. Depending on their sex they were either highly impressed or distinctly (make that violently) unimpressed. Russell began chatting to someone who was impressed, but she happened to belong to someone who definitely wasn't. In retrospect it wasn't a good idea to go somewhere where they weren't used to personalities, and to chat up someone's woman was asking for trouble. Trouble was exactly what we found. On leaving the club to walk back to the cars we suddenly realised about twenty guys had followed us outside. We walked on, and all of a sudden were the centre of a fight that was nothing to do with mods and rockers. A guy from my old school threw the first punch at me, and before long blows were raining in from all sides. In that situation all you can really do is stay on your feet and hit out as much as you can to stop them hitting you. Sometime later we were bruised and bloodied and once the adrenalin wore off it began to hurt – a lot. Woodsy Aka Mood was lying on the ground in pain, and there was no sign of Russell. It turned out Mood had a hole in his jacket where someone had stabbed him in the back with a sharpened hacksaw blade – which had broken off inside. He desperately needed an ambulance to take him to hospital. There was no sign of Russell while we waited, and I was concerned that he might be lying in an alleyway in the same condition as Woodsy. We didn't want to tell Russell's parents there'd been a fight and we couldn't find their son: first things first, we needed to get Woodsy to hospital. Luckily we learned that the blade had missed his vital organs by a millimetre or two, and he wasn't in any danger. The next problem was Russell. My antique dealer pal Ian Clarke and I searched everywhere for him, and as it approached midnight we decided to give up, drive to his house and tell his folks we didn't know where he was. As it happened, Russell had had the good sense to escape the violence by jumping on a passing trolleybus as it slowly cruised by. In an hour or so he'd got home and gone to bed.

The next day we were on a popular TV show in Birmingham called *Thank Your Lucky Stars*, and my face and eyes showed very obvious signs of what had happened the night before.

So far I've only been in jail once in my life, and that wasn't at Her Majesty's pleasure. It was decided to take a version of *Ready, Steady Go!* into Wormwood Scrubs. It was us with Adam, Patrick, Theresa with a team of attractive dancers, and the lovely Muriel Young. Fred Wilkinson drove us through the dauntingly massive studded wooden doors, and as they slammed behind us we knew we were in jail – and it wasn't a reassuring feeling. But Fred knew what to do. He'd stocked up on cigarettes and his pockets were loaded, so the inmates loved him. They showed us

41

the stage and introduced us to the stage manager, ex-Sergeant-Major Emmett Dunn. We knew him from the Sunday papers because he had strangled his German mistress's soldier husband at a barracks in Wales, and hanged him by his neck in a stairwell to make it look like suicide. He led the party that discovered the body, and would have got away with it had the Military Police not been suspicious when he inadvisedly married the dead soldier's wife too shortly afterwards. He was tried and found guilty in Germany, but since the Federal Republic had no death penalty and he couldn't be hanged in the UK, he was sentenced to life imprisonment and began it in Wormwood Scrubs. There was another infamous celebrity in the audience who possibly wasn't so interested in Theresa and her highly attractive friends: William John Christopher Vassall had been caught in a homosexual 'honey trap' set up by the KGB, so he was probably more appreciative of us long-haired musicians in tight trousers. He was just beginning his eighteen years of porridge for spying on us for the Russians.

I'd like to say I enjoyed my time inside, but that wouldn't be entirely true: we all breathed a sigh of relief when we were eventually released a few hours later. It was a lesson to me about what prison is all about, and I feel that any young person who looks as if they're going off the rails should spend a day inside to show them what the future might hold.

Bobby Elliott played drums with The Hollies, and I first bumped into him in Rhyl on a summer Sunday concert in 1963. He was playing with Shane Fenton and the Fentones, who were slightly lower down on the bill. We'd arrived from Bridlington without stage clothes and had been forced to borrow some matador jackets from the theatre. Fred went out to buy cavalry twill trousers to go with them. We got on pretty famously, and bumped into each other at TV shows like *Thank Your Lucky Stars* and *Ready Steady Go!*, and even at the Blue Boar on the M1 where the world of rock 'n' roll fetched up for beans on two toast on the way home from gigs. (On any given night you'd find the heroes of the age there. One night we were there with The Beatles, The Stones and Unit 4+2. We were just leaving when Manfred Mann turned up, with Jack Bruce and Tom McGuinness facing backwards out of the back window of their estate car.) Some time in 1965, as there hadn't been any real drum singles since Sandy Nelson's 'Let There be Drums', we decided to have a bash at making a record together. The tune in question was 'Drum and Coke' and the flipside was 'Why Won't They Let Us Drummers Sing'. We recorded at IBC Studios, and once the record was finished we took it to EMI to release. Unfortunately The Roulettes and The Hollies had two different A&R men: mine was John Burgess and Bobby's was Ron Richards. Even though I'd written both tunes Ron Richards felt I was using Bobby, and refused to let him have anything to do with it. It's a shame really because it was actually pretty good. That said, Fred Barker and Ollie Beak, a glove puppet dog and an owl on *The Five O'Clock Club*, a children's TV show with Auntie Mu (the lovely Muriel Young) and Wally Whyton (who'd been in the Worried Men with Adam Faith) wanted to record my B-side with new words: 'Why won't they let us fellers sing?' I'm not sure if it came out.

> Why won't they let us drummers sing, it seems to me it
> really is a waste,
> Why won't they let us drummers sing, could it be they've
> really got no taste

It isn't fair to keep us always stuck right up the back,
Singing softly to ourselves with voices that they lack,
If they would only listen they would say we're all right Jack,
So why won't they let us drummers sing?

Bobbie remains a good friend. He called me when Argent began to be successful, and asked if we'd got the management right. If he was reading the signs correctly, it looked as if it was going to be important to be handled by the right people, especially since America was going to be crucial to our careers.

While he was in The Roulettes Thorpey had a problem with his Gretsch Country Gentleman guitar, which needed to be sent away for attention. Having taken it into Ivor Arbiter's Sound City, he asked whether they had anything he could borrow. Bob Adams was a lovely guy who, according to Ivor, was even worse at paperwork than me, which was slightly unfair. Frequently at both Drum and Sound City the 'loan book' went missing, because that way nobody would be implicated as to the whereabouts of lots of gear that had left the shop and nobody could trace. Anyway, Bob Adams said that the only other available Gretsch in the shop belonged to George Harrison. It had had something done to it and they were waiting for someone from The Beatles to come in and pick it up. He was sure George wouldn't mind if Thorpey borrowed it. So he took what was at the time the most famous Gretsch in the world, and since he was never asked for it back it sat under his bed with several beige Vox amplifiers for years. One day, long after the Roulettes and even Argent had called it a day, Adam Faith was looking for a semi-acoustic guitar and Thorpey remembered the Gretsch. Tel took it away, and that was that. Fast forward to a get-together with all of us just before Nobby Dalton's charity gig in the nineties, when the subject of the immense worth of celebrity-owned guitars (like the one Hendrix gave to Mitch Mitchell, which had sold at Sotheby's for several hundred thousand dollars) came up. When George's guitar was mentioned as being possibly number two on the most-sought-after-instruments-ever category, Tel went even whiter than usual when he realised he had no idea where it was! So somewhere out there is a Gretsch Country Gentleman that once belonged to the lead guitarist in the most famous band ever – and nobody knows it!

As I write this it occurs to me that Tel's own Martin Dreadnought, which he'd coveted for years before finally spiriting it away from Lonnie Donegan, was probably worth a lot of money on the celebrity-owned circuit too. But he thought he'd loaned that to a chap called Mick Rogers, who was first in his band after us in the mid-sixties and later with Manfred Mann's Earth Band.

We all loved Tel, but he had his idiosyncrasies. If we went for breakfast on our travels, Tel would always pay while we were in the restaurant then demand the money once we were on our way. 'Right, who had the extra beans?' If we were in a hotel restaurant being served by an older, invariably star-struck waitress, he would deliberately mumble, 'Tickle your arse with a feather, my love?' The poor lady wouldn't understand what he'd said, and would ask him to repeat it, whereupon Tel would say, 'Particularly nasty weather my love!'

My twenty-first birthday was on 2 May 1965, and for some strange reason we were booked for a few days into the Ideal Home Exhibition, for once not taking place in its traditional home in Earls Court but in a large exhibition hall in Leeds. We were playing in a pretty small theatre inside the main hall several times a day, and the audience, which was almost on top of us, was composed of punters of a certain age who were there firstly to buy labour-saving gadgets and secondly (maybe thirdly) for the music. These light-music-loving, foot-tapping, on-beat-clapping couples frequently complained that the music was too loud, and Tel would feign anger and ask us to turn it down. The other guys simply turned a volume knob on their amplifiers but it wasn't that easy for me. Fortunately my little Gretsch drumset had extra-large knobs on each damper, and I'd go to the front of the drums and pretend to turn them. The audience was always very happy with the results, and felt that they'd contributed something to the show. Terry became friendly with several of the stall-holders, and one of them gave him a circular, neon-tubed bathroom light with an infra-red centre, which lit and warmed the bathroom at the same time. I'm not sure how successful this 'must have' accessory proved to be at the show, but Tel passed his on to me as a birthday present!

My folks gave me the traditional coming-of-age present: a gold wristwatch which was wafer thin. It was so beautiful that I always took it off when I was drumming, but this was its downfall, and unfortunately it was stolen from our dressing room at Fillmore East in New York, along with one of Russell's guitars, almost exactly five years later.

Terry's road manager had been a coach driver and I believe had once been a professional wrestler. Along with our Fred, he was the salt of the earth. He delighted in going up to the ladies in greasy spoons and ordering 'egg and chips for Adam'. He'd driven package tour buses for a company called Timpson's, who in the sixties provided transport for just about all the groups and solo artists who were held captive for up to a month on often preposterous tours going around Britain. London to Newcastle, followed by Newcastle to Birmingham, then Birmingham to Sunderland was the sort of thing we put up with. It was said that agents worked out itineraries by throwing darts at a map – but in those days I was too young and excited to mind.

We had a new record out, and Evie Taylor booked us onto *The Mike and Bernie Winters Show*, which was prime-time Saturday evening TV. We were plugging 'Bad Time', which was a Chris Andrews song that was getting a lot of radio play, especially on the pirate stations. We did the run-through with Evie in the control room, and afterwards she came out to tell us we were too static and needed to move about more. She showed us what she wanted us to do and we were flabbergasted to see she wanted us to do the same cross-over box step that the Shadows were famous for. We protested, and she replied that if we didn't do it she would 'wash her fucking hands of us'. We didn't and she did! I don't believe we ever heard directly from her again.

I'm not sure whether Evie liked me or not, but I have every reason to suspect she didn't. After each show she'd go up to 'the turn' and growl, 'The drummer's too fucking loud.'

Evie was a brilliant manager from a showbiz family (Sid Field was her dad). She used to be on the boards with her own act, which climaxed in her lifting her long skirts up to expose a cymbal fastened to the inside of each knee, which she vigorously banged together. She was married to a Jewish guy called Maurice Press who epitomised the ideal of a Yiddish manager. I learnt a great many Yiddish words from him (some of which even surprised Ivor Arbiter, whom I was yet to meet in anything other than a retail capacity). 'Morrie' often came on tour with us, possibly to get away from Evie, and made us laugh all over the world with his dry humour and his rapidly fading man-of-the-world attitude.

We'd been doing clubs and cabaret in our own right as The Roulettes for quite some time, and often found ourselves battling up motorways with Fred behind the wheel of our grey Morris J4 mini-bus to do one or sometimes two gigs a night at dance halls in the Midlands, like the Torch in Tunstall, the Ritz in Kings Heath and the Plaza in Old Hill. The last two were owned by an ex-teacher called Ma Regan, who managed a Midlands band called The Redcaps who, for that reason, seemed to support us whenever we played there. Further north we'd double at the Princess and Domino in Manchester, where you changed in the extremely smelly gents' loo while the punters relieved themselves around you. Rock 'n' roll!

We worked up an act for The Roulettes that was designed to show off our 'all round entertainer' side. We did all the usual rock 'n' roll tunes, but interspersed them with what we fondly believed was what the more discerning punters, enjoying their chicken in the basket, might be interested in. We had a skiffle medley where I ill-advisedly had a washboard hanging round my neck on catapult elastic; Russell and Thorpey with 'two guitars in perfect harmony played 'Summer Place'; Russell played 'Chaconne' on Spanish guitar; there was some tap dancing from Mod (to 'Me and My Shadow'); a drum solo from me; and the *pièce de résistance*: a foreign folk song! We learned it phonetically from the Esther and Abi Ofarim album with 'Cinderella Rockafeller' on it, and it went something like this: *'Doy pa ullitzay, mitzay, mitzah, mitzyo, zah–ah–ah, mitzay, litze, moy mil in qui itzyo...'* If anybody recognises this and can tell me what language it is, other than Gibberish, please get back to me.

How could we possibly get paid off with an act like this? I have selective memory syndrome on this, and optimistically think we survived the week. The others seem to remember we took an early bath.

We'd just finished a Roulettes' solo gig in Birmingham when Fred Wilkinson dropped a bombshell. He had thought we were going home that night so he hadn't booked a hotel. We sent him packing to find one, but at 11.30 at night – even in the centre of the 'second city' – there was nothing doing. We sat glumly in the van for a while contemplating sleeping in it before someone had the bright idea of going to a police station. It was a rock 'n' roll version of an urban myth that the police would always let you sleep in the cells! That may have been the case once, but this particular night in 1964 the cells in Snow Hill were packed full of bad guys. So we sat in the waiting room on hard chairs entertaining ourselves by watching the miscreants being brought in before being interviewed and charged (or is it the other way round?). Eventually we couldn't take the hard chairs any more and left the rozzers to their own devices as the sun came up.

We had a girlfriend from the Black Country called Carole Williams, who I suspect was secretly in love with all of us. As a schoolgirl she faithfully turned up at our gigs, TV shows and even 'live' recording sessions with Adam up and down the country. By 1966 she had a job at a music agency called Astra in Wolverhampton, which was run by a bunch of guys – one of whom (Maurice Jones) was destined to be Argent's agent a few years later. It was Carole who persuaded her agency, partly owned by a drummer named Tony Perry, to get us these gigs. Every Friday she called all the groups that Astra acted for: The Montanas, Finders Keepers, Listen, The

Vendors (who became first the N'Betweens, then Ambrose Slade and finally Slade) and others, to remind them to come in to pick up their money. The young singer in Listen wasn't very good at getting up, and she always had to call him several times to get him to come for his £15. He turned up late one Friday and could tell Carole wasn't too happy. She told him it was because her pals The Roulettes were playing at the 7 Club in Shrewsbury and she had no way of getting there. The singer, who was soon to join the Band of Joy, said he'd take her in his car, a black Ford Popular. Off they went, and they eventually turned up at the gig. She introduced us to this guy called Robert, and we weren't sure about him – so Russell, Fred and I took him outside to advise him there'd be big trouble if he didn't take care of Caz. We offered her a lift back with us but she said she'd be fine with him. On their way back to Wolverhampton he admitted to her that he hadn't taken a driving test yet. Forty years later she told us Robert's surname – it was Plant!

All good things come to an end, and in early 1966 we parted company professionally with Terry Nelhams. We kept our name, and were soon booked as backing musicians for several artists on a TV show called *A Tale of Two Rivers*. The programme was directed by our old pal Mike Mansfield and its *raison d'être* was the rivers Seine and Thames. Unit 4+2 were also on, but we backed several people including Mark Wynter and a French chanteur named Richard Anthony. The lovely Petula Clark was on too, although I don't believe we backed her. The idea was that Les Anglais sang songs about London and Les Francais sang about Paris. Mark Wynter had a go at 'London by Night', and in my humble opinion made a pretty good fist of it until we got to the ascending part of 'some people say they love London by day'!

Richard Anthony had made a fortune taking songs that had been hugely successful in Britain and America and writing his own French words to them, thereby getting half of the writing royalties. 'Concrete and Clay' was one of these tunes, and when we played it on Two Rivers he was hugely impressed, and asked us if we'd like to work with him all over Europe that summer. Since we no longer had Tel to fall back on we decided to throw our lot in with Monsieur Anthony. This was easier said than done. The intransigent and fiercely nationalistic French Musicians' Union couldn't understand why he wasn't using a French orchestra. However, Richard's manager, a fishy chap called Poisson, began the negotiations and eventually persuaded the Union des Musiciens Francais to allow us to work. They gave in, as long as we had a French *chef d'orchestre*. Marcel Hendrix duly turned up to rehearse with us. He was an accordionist! There we were, a hard-rocking little four-piece band with an accordionist conducting us from the back. Fortunately he also played keyboards well and turned out to be a jolly nice garçon, whom I actually wrote some songs with. I've got a great unpublished Christmas song I wrote on the nudist beach with him at St Tropez if anybody's interested:

> While the snow falls thick on the roof-tops
> And the earth is hushed and still,
> You can hear the sound of his sleigh-bells,
> Ringing clear through the air so chill . . .

In the beginning it was difficult to find a nice phrase to describe Claude and Alain, the two French equipment/management guys who travelled with us. They had both been Paras, and worse still had fought in the Algerian war against the *pieds-noirs*. It was very clear they didn't agree with the decision of the union to allow us into la belle France in the first place. These guys made life as difficult as they could for us, and deliberately set off at breakneck speed so we couldn't follow them. Fortunately we had the indomitable Fred Wilkinson with us, who could not only drive fast (having worked for world champion F1 driver Jim Clark), but could find his way anywhere – even with poor directions. The crew thought they'd escaped from us one day on the way to Luçay-le-Mâle. We came racing round a corner in our Renault 16 to find the big Citroen ID shooting brake lying on its roof in a ditch, with all the drums, guitars, amplifiers and gear spilling out of the back door. The equipment guy was in the act of throwing his lucky charm troll into the bushes just as we arrived on the scene. We loaded as much gear as we could into the back of our car and sped off to the gig, leaving Alain to sort himself out.

As it happens, we saw terrible accidents just about every day we drove through France, sadly often involving Britons near the Channel ports who were unused to driving on the 'wrong' side of the road. Fortunately we didn't have to drive too often, because Richard had his own aeroplane: a twin-engined Piper Aztec with the letters NDK on the wing, its call-sign being November-Delta-Kilo. There was just enough room for me, Thorpey, Russell and Mod to be crammed in the back with Richard and the pilot in the front. Richard was always the co-pilot, but didn't have a flying licence: this didn't matter so long as the guy with the licence was there, but when for some reason he stopped coming and Richard still flew we became a little concerned. Not that we knew anything about flying, other than it was a necessary evil: luckily Monsieur Anthony seemed to be able to do it. But this little detail meant that he needed to contribute to various flying charities wherever he landed – or be grounded.

I only remember one dodgy moment in the plane when we were flying into St Tropez, where Richard lived when he wasn't in Paris or in his penthouse suite above the Hilton in Park Lane. This guy had money! In the sixties San Trop's airstrip was just a long, narrow field with a wind sock and trees on each side – with no room for error. Unfortunately Richard made an error, and the wind took us towards the trees at something like 100mph. Somehow he managed to wrestle the plane away from the trees, I suspect more by luck than judgement. This was the closest I had come to aviation death, although mathematically the more you fly the more chance you have of something going wrong. We had to jettison fuel once when, having taken off from Beirut on our way back from Singapore, the pilot felt something was wrong and decided to abort the mission. Once they open the taps the juice leaks out, but it takes an awfully long time to get rid of enough aviation fuel to get you back to the UK from the Middle East. I hope it's not another incidence of false memory syndrome, but I'm pretty sure Eric Morecambe and Ernie Wise were on that plane. I recall we were forced to abort a landing at Gatwick in the Aztec because we were only half a mile down range of something 'heavy' that was landing in front of us. Its turbulence would have flipped us over, and as the song goes, they'd have been scraping us off the runway like a lump of strawberry jam'.

At the time when contemporaries like Charles Aznavour were singing poignant songs like 'She', Richard was singing songs with 'Ya Ya Twist', 'Tchin, Tchin' and 'Yé, Yé' in the titles. You couldn't knock it, though: he was hugely successful. One show-stopper was 'Le Deserteur', a song set in an indeterminate time about a conscripted soldier who refused to go to war and kill people. It was written in 1954 by an engineer named Boris Vian, and since my French was good enough to understand it, it really struck a chord with me:

> Monsieur le Président,
> je vous fais une lettre,
> que vous lirez peut-être, si vous avez le temps.
>
> Je viens de recevoir
> mes papiers militaires
> pour partir à la guerre
> avant mercredi soir.
> Monsieur le Président,
> je ne veux pas le faire,
> je ne suis pas sur terre
> pour tuer de pauvres gens.

Through the auspices of my new best friend, the internet, I discover there's a brilliant English version by a chap called James Prescott from 1983. He hasn't just made a direct translation but a highly skilful adaptation addressed to the King of England.

The tour with Richard was designed to journey around the casinos of France, Belgium Italy and Spain, although, as is the way with these things, not in a particularly logical manner. (Show-biz agents in France were no exception as far as convoluted itineraries were concerned.) We ultimately criss-crossed Europe numerous times, but Cassis, which is just outside Marseilles, was our very first gig in a very glamorous casino. Halfway through the show Monsieur le Chanteur turned round to say, 'You guys are fabulous'. He was prone to mood-swings because of the slimming pills he was taking, which also made him sweat profusely, so he didn't always think we were fabulous. We didn't only play in glamorous casinos in exotic places like Juan les Pins, Antibes and Monaco; we also played at country fairs in the middle of nowhere, where couples danced on special wooden floors which had been laid on the grass.

Richard had signals for us, which consisted of waving his hands behind his back (like a doubles tennis player at the net) so the audience couldn't see them. Unfortunately he never told us what they meant, so we never did know whether he wanted it faster, slower, louder or softer. I do know that, unlike any other singer I ever backed, he actually liked drum fills. I rather think from his hand signals he'd have let me do one every other bar if I'd wanted!

I mentioned earlier that when the turn walked off at the end of a show the band had to play what was called tab music as the curtains came across. Richard Anthony was no different: we played something which wasn't a real tune, just a single 2/4 riff that didn't modulate. It wasn't until we got to America and appeared on Johnny Carson's *Tonight* that we discovered Paul Anka had become a multi-millionaire from his 'Toot Sweet', the tab music that Doc Severinsen's Orchestra played at the beginning and end of each section before the adverts came on, every night for decades. Talk about a licence to print money! Give me strength.

We had a great time in France and learned a lot about the country, its food, its people and its culture. We had to learn some of the language to be able to exist there. You couldn't be in the back-of-beyond places we went to without various key phrases like '*je cherches une chamber pour ce soir*', or '*moi je prends le steack haché*', '*autre bière*', '*l'addition, s'il vous plaît*', '*j'aime pas les anchois*', and the ever useful '*mon postillion a été frappe par la foudre*'. It was also useful to be able to say '*Je suis un rockstar. Je joue avec Richard Anthony.*' The biggest problem with this is that once you initiate a dialogue the foreign person you're talking to immediately assumes you can understand every single word of his language.

We were coming up from Marseilles, for once on a scheduled flight, having left very early to get home in time for Sunday lunch when fog at Heathrow meant we couldn't land there. Air France kindly dropped us off at Charles de Gaulle and we had to get a train and a ferry home in the same carriage as Jimmy Edwards. Like the Duke of Wellington and his Prussian friends, we eventually got to Waterloo – although not until well after midnight.

Another interesting aviation incident occurred with Richard. We were flying north from the South of France towards Paris one cloudless day when all of a sudden this huge glistening Super-Fortress which was on exactly the same heading flew overhead and headed off rapidly into the distance. Now I know there's supposed to be 1,000 feet between planes on the same course, but I don't believe there was – and knowing Monsieur Anthony, who was flying at the time, I have my doubts he knew it was there until it overhauled us. That said, it was a breathtakingly beautiful sight.

As I went to foreign countries I managed to collect enough words in German or Spanish to find my way to the gig, hotel or restaurant: *Haben sie eine zimmer frei? Direknung bitte. Tienes una habitación? La cuenta por favor.* Strangely it was never necessary to learn any words of Dutch, even though in my next musical existence with Argent we seemed to go to Holland every weekend. The Dutch didn't seem to want us to speak their language, and after at least forty years of going there I still don't know the words for Yes and No. However, I've stopped in remote petrol stations for directions and had long, lucid conversations in perfect English about London football clubs with the ordinary Dutch guy behind the counter!

If I had a favourite place in France in those days it would be Salon, down in the south, which was a place to which Napoleon retreated when he wanted to rechargé his batteries. Richard had a friend with a pizzeria there who made the most delicious pizza (outside Ralph's in New York) and fabulous chips with garlic. Nowadays my favourite French town is Collioure down near the Spanish border, where I've spent several New Years' Eves and with which I have a real affinity. Maybe in a previous life . . .

So we travelled around Europe with Richard having fun and generally misbehaving ourselves, while living the lives of the rich and famous.

I could probably write a whole chapter on flying incidents, but I'll just share a couple more with you. After 'Hold Your Head Up' had worked its magic for us in America, we were heading south on a plane when the stewardess came and asked if we were a band. Since we all had extremely long hair and were dressed in off-duty rockstar clothes this was something of a redundant question, but one we were asked daily. Jim had a stock answer: that we were a midget basketball team. Anyway when we told the Southern belle that we were indeed a band she went to the cockpit to tell the captain.

Soon she came back to ask us if we'd like a drink with him. Of course we said we'd be delighted. The next thing we knew we were instructed to fasten our seatbelts, which seemed strange since we were flying through distinctly unturbulent weather. The captain strolled down from the cockpit as the flight attendant delivered our drinks, and he started his pitch. He owned a residential recording studio outside Atlanta with state-of-the-art equipment and would do us a fantastic deal if we were interested. As he filled us in on the technicalities of the desk, outboard gear and twenty-four-track tape-machines the plane droned on. Eventually, clutching his business card we assured him we would give the matter a great deal of thought and he went back to get on with flying the plane. Now I'm convinced that there was no-one flying it during the sales pitch, and we certainly didn't see anybody else in charge, other than the pilot and the stewardess!

We were dragging ourselves through the endless corridors of La Guardia airport midway through the second Argent US tour on the way to catch a connection, and just within sight of our gate we spotted an extra large pram parked at the side. In this pram was what was obviously a very small person pretending to be a baby. As we passed the baby jumped out and run away. We all kept on walking, without reacting at all to what had just happened, and sat down at our gate. We had just been filmed for an episode of *Candid Camera*, and the next thing we knew we were besieged by a film crew and the US presenter, whose name was Alan Funt. They gave us all a disclaimer to sign and were very unhappy when we admitted we were in the American Federation of Musicians, because it would cost money if they used us. We watched dispassionately while they set up the shot again, and waited for the next suckers to arrive. They showed us how we should have reacted had we been Americans instead of jaded English rockers. They shrieked and screamed as the vertically challenged guy escaped from the pram, and generally got into the ridiculous spirit of the thing. I suppose our footage may have turned up on a bloopers programme about how not to do it, but if it did, in common with just about every other TV programme we've done in America, we haven't been paid for it yet!

We'd finished a long tour in Miami and were more than ready to go home, but fog in London stopped us taking off. We waited for five days at British Airways' expense and I'm sure nobody at home believed us. They all thought we'd gone for a well-earned rest. To be frank, if we were desperate for a holiday Miami would not have been our first choice. The place was populated by old-aged pensioners who wandered round among the fading grandeur in crocodiles so they didn't get lost. This was in the early seventies before Miami became cool, and it was the place 'snowbirds' went, to unintentionally shorten their lives: it was a fatal shock to their systems to replace the frozen north of America that they were used to with relentless heat and sun.

Speaking of heat and sun, I was sitting by the pool browning my God-like body at a hotel in Phoenix, Arizona, talking with a guy who was the support band's pilot. It was so hot by the time we'd run the few yards from the water back to our poolside rooms that we were dry. Anyhow, this young and (as it turned out) tragically hip pilot told us all about his job, which was piloting Chase, 'triple-high C' trumpeter Bill Chase's band, from show to show in what I think was an old Dakota. To keep himself entertained he liked to operate a 'Super-Trouper' spotlight at the shows, and to get himself into the mood to rock he liked to have several beers and maybe a few 'toots'. I asked whether he should be relaxing when the show was on, ready for the forthcoming flight, but he said there was no need: he could handle it. Not long after this the Dakota crashed, killing Bill Chase and the rest of his rhythm section, aside from the bass player,.

Just say no!

Fast forward twelve years to The Kinks flying into Philadelphia for the start of yet another US tour. We were sitting up-front in a BA Airbus and were descending into Walt Whitman airport after an uneventful and reasonably sober flight. I was looking out of the window at the Walt Whitman bridge when all of a sudden the captain pulled the stick back and the plane started clawing its way into the air again. I was still looking out of the window when this twin-engined plane skidded right underneath us at right angles to our flight path. Eventually we went round again and landed safely. As we left the plane I asked the purser if that counted as a near-miss. She pretended not to know what I was talking about, so I asked why we'd had to gain height quickly and abort the landing. She said it was because the captain thought he should try again. It seems no airline ever wants to admit to a near-miss in case they lay themselves open to being sued.

All my generation's musical knowledge came through the medium of Radio Luxembourg, and from those heady days in the fifties listening on my crystal set under the bedclothes in my unheated bedroom I never suspected I'd find myself visiting the Grand Duchy, let alone kneel on the floor and be interviewed by one of the DJs. I think I'm correct in saying we were gigging at Le Grand Palais with Richard, and somehow managed to get ourselves interviewed by the 'Royal Ruler' himself, Tony Prince. He hadn't been there long, having arrived from Radio Caroline immediately after Harold Wilson's government had passed the Marine Broadcasting Offences Act, which had instantly put paid to pirate radio. But offshore radio was great while it lasted, and certainly didn't do the various groups I'd been in any harm as far as radio plays were concerned.

It was never a bad idea to be friendly with the radio DJs: simply by playing your record they could guarantee a hit. This of course was long before the days of playlists, and the DJs could play what ever they liked – so long as it didn't have any 'F words' in the lyrics. We're not talking payola here but simply being friendly with guys like David Jacobs, Jimmy Savile, Tony Blackburn, Bob Harris, Annie Nightingale, Stuart Henry, Alan Freeman, Ed Stewart, Tony Windsor, John Peel, Kid Jensen, Keith Scuse and Kathy McGowan (who wasn't a DJ in the real sense). John Peel was deadly serious about independent music, so he wasn't quite so easy to hang out with, and I was amazed to see him playing mandolin on Rod Stewart's 'Maggie May' on *Top of the Pops*. I particularly liked Kenny Everett and we once spent the night together, although 'all in the best possible taste' and several years before he realised his true sexuality. We were coming back from somewhere (up north?), and it seemed convenient for him to stay at my parents' house in Waltham Cross rather than travelling on to London. He was in the bedroom not long vacated by my sister, and I was in the icy box-room over the alleyway that I'd been in for most of my life.

I particularly liked Kenny Everett and we once spent the night together, although 'all in the best possible taste' and several years before he realised his true sexuality. We were coming back from somewhere (up north?), and it seemed convenient for him to stay at my parents' house in Waltham Cross rather than travelling on to London. He was in the bedroom not long vacated by my sister, and I was in the icy box-room over the alleyway that I'd been in for most of my life.

Russell reminded me long after the very final corrections for Banging On! should have been done and dusted that I actually wrote a radio jingle for Kenny at that time. It went very much like this:

> K - E, Double N- Y, E-V-E-R-E- Double T
> and ended with Kenny Everett, Don't Forget!

Unfortunately I had completely forgotten it until Russell reminded me.

Moving a few years ahead here, when Argent were starting the big push into Moving a few years ahead here, when Argent were starting the big push into America we found ourselves on the Allison Steele late night radio show on WNEW in New York. She was billed as 'The Night Bird', and arriving at the studio in the early hours of the morning we were unsure about what to expect. We knew we needed to be on this particular programme because she played progressive rock like us, and in the days of extemporisation, when the tracks could be over twenty minutes long, she played them in their entirety. Reading about her forty years after the event, I discover that initially she wasn't into progressive rock and wasn't even a DJ but because she was 'promoted' to the graveyard shift it suited her to play long tracks by the likes of: Yes, Genesis, King Crimson, Iron Butterfly, Gentle Giant, Van der Graaf Generator and of course Argent.

We sat outside the studio listening to her smoky, seductive Julie London-type voice until we were called into her lair. The studio was dark, except for a single light on Allison who looked like she sounded – voluptuous and sexy. I'd like to say she was dressed provocatively and the room was full of smoke from her cigarette, but that could be another incidence of 'false memory syndrome'. She died in the mid-nineties. I've searched the web for a picture of her and came up with only one, which suggests how alluring she was to a twenty-something British rocker.

1966 was of course the time of our greatest footballing achievement, and we watched the final of the world cup in Majorca in the Hotel del Mar, surrounded by Germans. We were playing at the Tago Mago in Palma, and for some reason we were sitting at a table in the hotel with the captain of an American aircraft carrier that was visiting the Ballearics on a goodwill mission. I asked him what made the job interesting in peacetime and he replied, 'If you're a fireman you have to go to a fire from time to time'!

We recorded with Richard at Abbey Road, where he recorded the Stones' 'Baby You're Out of Time'. As usual he'd written his own words to cop 50 per cent of the writing royalties. As I recall, The Stones' lyrics were quite poignant, being about somebody who was born in the wrong era. Richard's had nothing to do with that: 'Baby, Baby, Baby, je penses a toi . Ne me commences pas!'

I saw him on a TV programme a year or two ago when I was in Paris on drum business, and he had evidently lost the battle with his weight and with the authorities. He looked the image of Demis Roussos (including the beard and kaftan), and in the recent past had been sent to jail for tax evasion. He had boasted that he could claim everything he spent on tax, including the tyres on his plane. It would appear he was wrong.

Having returned to the UK, I was booked to play on a record for an all-girl group ostensibly from Canada called the She Trinity, who were being produced by Micky Most at Rak Studios near Hyde Park. I played drums, Thorpey guitar and John Paul Jones, who was Micky's MD at the time, played bass. I'd met John Paul when he played bass with Tony Meehan's group, and this particular session was a couple of years before he helped found Led Zeppelin. The song in question was 'I Fought the Law' (which I think they changed to 'He Fought the Law'). This was every drummer's favourite song, because of the half-note triplets played over the end of the first line of the second verse: 'Robbing people with a six-gun'. I know Jon Hiseman's wife Barbara Thompson was in the band but don't recall seeing her at the studios.

Many, many years later I played with Sonny Curtis from The Crickets who'd written 'I Fought the Law', and he told me an interesting story about it. Just after the Bobby Fuller Four had had a hit with it, he was between tours and returned to Lubbock, Texas, the home of Buddy Holly. He went to visit his local garage and the owner asked him what he was doing. Sonny replied that he was a songwriter. The mechanic thought for a moment, then asked if he could write down the words for 'Home on the Range' for his brother! Sonny Curtis was not only great to play with; he was a proper songwriter who'd written quite a few of my favourite songs: 'Love You More Than I Can Say', 'Rock Around with Ollie Vee', 'Love is All Around' and my favourite 'Walk Right Back'. I actually got to play the proper version of this with him, with a second verse which begins: 'Those eyes of mine which gave you loving glances once before . . .' The Everly Brothers had been in such a hurry to record it that they hadn't had time to wait for Sonny to write a second verse, and simply repeated the first. We also played the repeat turnaround at the end of the song which Waylon Jennings, who should have been on the plane with Buddy Holly, the Big Bopper and Richie Valens, used on his version.

I was never a jazz player, because too many drummers in progressive rock fancied themselves as jazz players without having the necessary looseness the music demanded. At the time few drummers other than Aynsley Dunbar managed to cross over. Of course the nuts and bolts were just the same, but rock drumming had an inherent straightness that jazz certainly didn't need. It also had off-beat, which again jazz didn't need until perhaps the last rousing 'shout' chorus (if at all). However, I had some celebrated jazz-playing friends who played at a pub in Finchley called the Tally Ho, where Johnny Richardson let me sit in alongside a bass-playing trumpet player called Jerry Salisbury. Johnny had been the manager of Drum City with my pal Gerry Evans, and always gave me a shuffle or two to play, which was easy for a rocker to handle. The Cromwellian, Klooks Kleek and The Bag o' Nails were other places where there was the possibility of a 'blow' if you knew the band. I remember Keith Moon sat in at The Cromwellian if he could, and I know he got up with Mike Cotton's band when Jim Rodford was playing there. The band was playing something like 'My Girl', but in his inimitable way Moonie was playing 'My Generation'! I loved to sit in with Mike because of course they had a horn section, and I indulged myself playing all the accents with them on songs like 'Papa's Got a Brand New Bag' and 'Barefootin'. They were a really hard-working band – and they offered me a job in 1966. I turned it down because I was going off to France with Richard Anthony.

I mentioned Unit 4+2 earlier. They were a bunch of guys from the boys' club, who started out as a vocal group like the Four Freshmen and were very good at those very American close harmonies. They were really more of a folk group, but like most musicians of my acquaintance in the area they got the chance to make records. Brian Parker was with them, and so was Buster Meikle. Sometime around Christmas 1964 I came back from a tour, and along with Russell B. was asked to play on the group's third record. The session was to be at a small studio called Nova Sound in Marble Arch, just behind Oxford Street. The song was 'Concrete and Clay', and Brian had written it with Tommy Moeller, who was their lead singer. He had envisaged it to be more like a Drifters' song with a much cooler beat, but we played it in a much rockier way, still with a cross-stick off-beat on 4 in the verse and on 2 and 4 in the chorus. I don't think he was too happy with it (at least not until it sold its first million and became number 1 around the world).

I always bought an American magazine called *Downbeat* if I could find it in Dobell's record shop near Leicester Square, mostly for the adverts which often said evocatively 'prices slightly higher west of the Rockies'. How cool was that? Around this time they reproduced the music for a new musical style called bossa -nova, which had originated in Brazil. It had been around in Latin America since 1958 but was popularised by Antonio Carlos Jobim and Joao Gilberto, and was evidently doing well in cool jazz circles in America. I hadn't really been into it before, but having studied the drum part in *Downbeat* out of curiosity and worked out how the bass drum went against the Cuban 'clave' cross-stick rhythm and the eighth notes on the hi-hat, I slowly began to play it. Anyhow, even though the song was much faster I decided I'd try to play this bossa beat in the solo, and it worked. Everybody liked it and Russell played a great and award-winning acoustic guitar solo against it. Having recorded the song, I felt the track would benefit from a cowbell playing the bass drum part, which was a single beat on 1 and a double on &3 known as a baion. This was over-dubbed by the engineer, Leo Pollini, (who had been Tommy Steele's drummer) on to a three-track machine, and while I was at it, having discovered a little bell in the studio, I decided to overdub it on the offbeat with the cowbell on the 1 and &3 over my two bar count in. And that was that. We finished the session, submitted our invoice for five pounds fifteen shillings and sixpence and got on with being in The Roulettes. The only difference between this and the various other records I played on at the time for other artistes was that it became a rip-roaring success around the world. Thanks to this, John Barker (Unit 4+2's manager and self-styled 'producer') decided to keep the same team of musicians together, and Russell and I played on the next dozen or so singles, from 'Hark' to Bob Dylan's 'Ain't Going Nowhere'.

The first of these were easy sessions along the lines of the hit, but when the band became more ambitious to recapture the millions of sales achieved by 'Concrete' they decided to put us together with an orchestra. This was recorded at Decca Studios in West Hampstead, and gave me the fright of my life. It is an act of suicide in the music industry to claim you can read music if you can't, and I've always been conscious of not over-stating my claim in that direction. I don't profess to read 'fly shit', but given time, peace and quiet I can work out what's required of me; however, it's always nice to have a part to look at to use as a road map. Having been booked for this session, I asked for a top line and was told I wouldn't need it because it was 'only rock 'n' roll' and I'd easily get it. The song was called 'You've never been in love like this before' and unfortunately it wasn't 'only rock 'n' roll' at all – it was complicated. (As I speak to more and more of my contemporaries, pals like Clem Cattini, Bobby Graham and Brian Bennett, the more I realise I wasn't alone in this experience, and we all wanted the earth to open and swallow us up.) Fortunately the percussionist was Johnny Deans (who'd played in the pit on the very first weeks in variety I'd done): he put me straight and nodded where the accents came and so on. Of course when you're playing with hugely experienced orchestral musicians, capable of sight-reading anything, who are watching you struggle with sardonic smiles on their faces, panic sets in – and it just gets worse and worse.

Clem Cattini put it into perspective for me recently. The fixers and producers like Charlie Katz were booking us young rockers by name because they wanted us for what we could bring to the party. The orchestral guys were being booked as *a* violinist, *an* oboist, *a* harpist or *a* tuba player. Anyone available would get the gig. It was good to know this some forty years later, but at the time I just wanted to faint so I could escape in an ambulance. Clem also assured me that lots of the other players were bricking it, and nobody noticed. A great trombone player of my acquaintance, when faced with complicated 'dots' for Gene Pitney that he had no chance of sight-reading, took his trombone with him, climbed out of the window of the toilet at the Fishmongers Arms in Wood Green and went home.

I realise I'm going out of sequence, but here's another story while we're on the vexed subject of reading music. Chris White from the Zombies was producing a record for Diana Dors, who had been one of the unattainably glamorous women I'd grown up ogling in magazines like *Tit Bits*, *Film Fun* and the like. I was engaged to play drums for her, and we all met at Roundhouse Studios in Chalk Farm one Sunday morning. Diana Dors, née Fluck, flounced in in a starry haze accompanied by her MD. The first tune we put down was one of Chris's compositions, so no problem at all – we were rocking. If the session went past midday we'd have been eligible for double session money, so we were keeping a hopeful eye on the clock. With fifteen minutes to go it looked like there was no B-side and we were beginning to relax. Suddenly the MD burst in apologetically with the charts for the next track. The pages looked black, as if a spider had crawled all over them, and to make things worse there were lots of crossings out. It was a nightmare, a Las Vegas show-type jazz part that had been written for a big band – and we were a small rock group. I'm told there's an obvious difference. We tried to busk it, but being a Vegas arrangement it was fast and 'interesting': all the verses had different accents. We were in trouble but we struggled manfully. It's another record that may or may not have seen the light of day.

The business of having a hit record was too important to be left to the record-buying public. Pluggers worked away at the job, taking DJs, programme directors, journalists and TV producers to lunch, as well as buying drinks in the BBC bar after *Top of the Pops*. At one time the record companies simply said which records they'd sold most of, and the one that had sold most was top of what was then called the Hit Parade. Obviously this relied on honesty, and it's also fair to say that this wasn't abundant in the music biz. After all, it was always possible a secretary's fingers might slip and add a couple of noughts to the sales figures she was typing. By 1966 they had changed how the sales figures were collected, and introduced the top secret 'chartshop list', where a number of shops up and down the country sent their sales figures in every Wednesday. There were loopholes, and it was possible to take the thing into your own hands by clandestinely getting hold of the chartshop list – and getting someone to visit as many of the shops named as possible to buy records. These record shops reported their sales and orders to the BPI, and the numbers were used to make up the top fifty bestselling records in the UK that week. It was designed to be an exact science, and it probably was as far as the big retailers like HMV were concerned, but to make it regionally fair they blanketed the country. Once you got into Devon and Cornwall or Lancashire and Yorkshire (say), the list relied on someone having the enthusiasm to accurately report what was going on, while getting on with the real business of selling Max Bygraves or Val Doonican records to mums and dads – or painting their nails! It was the numbers of orders that made the whole thing manipulable, because they would show up as sales. So all you needed to do was get someone to go into the shop in question and order a record, and if you got it right you'd end up just inside the Top 50, which would allow your manager to get you on TV in a 'bubbling under' spot.

For some stupid reason, probably a financial one, we decided to visit the record shops ourselves. We set off in Thorpey's car (a powder blue Ford Zephyr or possibly a Vauxhall Velox, with a matching metal dashboard) and whizzed off to visit as many shops as we could in as short a time as possible. We arrived at the town with the relevant chart shop (say Bacup) and parked the Zephyr around the corner. One of us would go in and ask for 'I Can't Stop' by The Roulettes. The person behind the counter would (of course) say they didn't have it, but they could order it if we paid up front. We'd pay over a few shillings, leave the shop and that was that. The second Roulette went in half an hour later and went through the same rigmarole, followed at thirty minute intervals by the third and the fourth. All this nefarious activity took an hour and a half, which meant that with travelling we could only hit three or four shops in a day – which wasn't enough. So we came to the conclusion that if two of us went in together we'd do it in a third of the time. We tried this, and to all intents and purposes it worked – although the second pair certainly alerted the shop assistant that something weird was going on. Eventually we cut down the time between each pair, and then decided, fuck it, we'd all go in together. So there we were, four Roulettes asking for one each of 'I Can't Stop', although, hang on, I could do with a couple! Eventually we were rumbled when one of the more observant shop assistants recognised Russell's dark glasses and asked for his autograph.

As it happens, the time on the road was well spent. 'I Can't Stop' (our ninth record) went into the charts at number 49. You needed around 50,000 sales to get just inside the top 50 in the mid-sixties and I understand that those sales would make you number 1 in the twenty-first century.

As I said, John Barker managed Unit 4+2, and he looked after us once we'd left Adam and Evie. He had offices at Lionel Bart's HQ in Shaftesbury Avenue, conveniently next to Velotti's café. This was where Apollo Music, which published 'Concrete and Clay', was run from. They had a little songwriting studio with a Ray Charles-era wooden Wurlitzer electric piano, where the likes of the Alex Harvey Band, Steve Darbishire and the Yum Yum Band, Status Quo, Pete Dello, Ray Kane and the other Honeybus guys used to work their magic. As it happens, I never made records with Alex Harvey or the Quo, but I did with all the others. Ray Kane produced an album for Nicol Williamson, a Shakespearean actor who was the most accomplished pub pianist I ever heard. He flowed tunes from one to another with ease. He wasn't actually playing on the album, but sang songs in a recitative Rex Harrison-like way, although more like Richard Harris did with Jim Webb's 'McArthur Park'. Having trawled the internet I can't find any evidence the album was ever released. As I said the original, pre-exclusively twelve-bar blues 'Pictures of Matchstick Men' Status Quo were also part of the Apollo music gang, and we spent many a happy hour talking nonsense together in the demo room there.

We saw Lionel every now and again. As a comedian he made a very good songwriter! He made a terrible mess of the world-famous joke about the masturbating astronaut at the office Christmas party in about 1966. Leslie Paul was Lionel's accompanist and the MD of Apollo, who very cleverly translated the melodies his boss hummed into such classic pieces of music as 'Fings Ain't Wot They Used T'Be', 'Where is Love', 'Consider Yourself', 'Reviewing the Situation', 'Food Glorious Food' and my favourite, 'As Long As He Needs Me', resurrected by the Barron Knights as 'As Long As He Drinks Tea'.

Les also interpreted the straight pop songs like 'Living Doll', which Lionel had written for my one-time next-door neighbour Cliff Richard, and 'Easy Going Me', as sung by my first boss Adam Faith.

We hadn't been back long from that interesting year in France with Richard Anthony when Russell B. and I threw our lot in with Unit 4+2, whose records we'd played on while working with Adam Faith. Prog rock with Argent was another year away.

We stopped being the Roulettes at the end of 1966, but there's a group purporting to be us still playing gigs as I write. They can't be accurately described as a tribute band, since they appropriated our history of playing with Adam, although they didn't go as far as to lay claim to our names. My niece Emma was so incensed by their impersonation of us that she phoned to ask how much they would charge for a wedding. Having lulled the 'Roulette' she was talking to into a false sense of security, she innocently asked if Russ Ballard would be doing the gig if she booked them. No, was the response, he's in LA now – so we don't see too much of him! We decided to let sleeping dogs get on with their lying – the only verb to describe what the bogus Roulettes were up to.

Hold the presses . . . I've just spotted a New York indie girl band called

CHECK UP ON
THE UNDERTAKERS!

Brian Jones (alias Boots) on saxophone. Aged 23, dark-haired and got his nick-name from the high-heel cowboy boots he always wears for a show. Joined the group two years ago after attending secondary school and a technical college where he was training to be an electrical engineer. Once ran his own group—The Rebels. Keen on blues singers, especially Ray Charles.

Chris Huston on guitar. Aged 20 and the only fair-haired member of the group. One of the original Undertakers, he played with two groups before. Started playing the guitar as a hobby four years ago. Worked as a commercial artist before becoming a professional musician. Keen on blues—with a special fancy for Cliff Bennett and the Rebel Rousers.

Geoff Nugent on guitar. Aged 20. One of the original Undertakers and the group's most experienced musician. Started in show business at the age of nine when he sang in a Workers Playtime concert. Later played many solo-spots in concerts and played with Bob Evans and the Five Shillings and The Topspots before becoming an Undertaker.

Jackie Lomax on guitar. Aged 19. Bought a guitar and taught himself to play and joined The Undertakers 18 months ago. Former grammar school pupil, he gave up wanting to be an artist to try his luck as an entertainer. Keen on Ray Charles.

Warren Pemberton on drums. Aged 18, nick-named "Bugs". Attended Art School before becoming a professional 18 months ago. Before that, he had played with a local group alongside Jackie Lomax. Spent all his savings on his £300 set of drums.

LORRAINE GRAY

Encouraged by her success in a holiday camp talent contest last summer, Lorraine Gray pleaded with a Rochdale club owner for a chance to sing with his resident group and, despite a marked lack of enthusiasm from this gentleman, Lorraine persisted until he allowed her to do a couple of numbers for the sake of peace and quiet.

From that moment, Lorraine's life exploded into a frenzy of activity: she was introduced to one of the north's leading agencies, recording tests were fixed, clothes were bought and intensive rehearsals started with a group formed specially to accompany her.

Her professional debut at the Oasis Club, Manchester, was witnessed by a critical audience of teenagers and her new-found agents and this pert sixteen year old soon dispelled any doubts that may have lingered with her astonishingly mature voice and style delivered with the assurance of an artiste we beyond her years.

Her first record release on the Fontana label—"Your Little Toy"—confirmed opinion that Lorraine was capable of making tremendous impact in 1964. Her second disc is due for release at the end of May.

THE BARRON KNIGHTS

ONE of North London's most successful groups, The Barron Knights, features all six members, vocally, as soloists, plus duets, trios, and songs involving 4 and 5 singers. They concentrate mainly on versatility with humour.

Recently, they completed a highly successful summer season at Great Yarmouth with Billy Fury and Joe Brown, and on 22nd December they are strongly featured on the Beatles Christmas Show, at Liverpool "Empire" 23rd December, Bradford "Gaumont" 22nd and Finsbury Park "Astoria" 24th December to 11th January.

Record-wise, their next issue on Columbia is likely to be "Give Me More" (3rd January, 1964) and they have already cut their L.P. which is pending release.

They have broadcast on "Let's Go" (B.B.C.) and have appeared twice on "Teenage Special" on Grampian T.V. Soon they will be featured on "Saturday Club".

The group comprises of "Barron" Antony (rhythm guitar, bass, drums, harmonica), Don Ringaell (bass, ballad singer), P'nul Langford (lead guitar, comic), Duke D'Mond (feature singer), "Butch" Baker (lead guitar, comic), "Sharkey" (drums).

THE SWINGING BLUE JEANS

SWINGING BLUE JEANS' NEXT SINGLE "YOU'RE NO GOOD" (H.M.V. Pop 1304) RELEASED 29th MAY. DRAMATIC CHANGE OF STYLE ON THIS BEAT BALLAD.

"HIPPY HIPPY SHAKE" REACHES MILLION MARK IN WORLD SALES.

THE SWINGING BLUE JEANS' first big date was a talent contest at Liverpool's Empire Theatre some four years ago. The S.B.J. won the contest, and found a new member—guitarist Ralph Ellis. Ralph, who lead the group that were runners-up, joined Ray Ellis (guitar), Les Braid (bass-guitar) and Norman Kuhlke (drums), to complete a personnel that has remained unchanged. The group built up a big following in the North of England, and became the first beat group to have a resident spot at the CAVERN. The four boys turned professional in September, 1961, and enjoyed a successful season at THE STAR CLUB, HAMBURG—Germany's famous beat centre. THE SWINGING BLUE JEANS returned to England, took up resident spots at Liverpool's Mardi Gras and Downbeat clubs, and began broadcasting regularly—long before the tag "Merseybeat" was invented.

Early in 1964, THE SWINGING BLUE JEANS gained top pop honours when they reached the No. 1 spot in the "Disc" Hit Parade with their version of "Hippy Hippy Shake". "Hippy" gained the S.B.J. the first silver disc awarded in 1964. The record's high chart-placings in twelve countries gave the four boys an international reputation.

Was it something I said, Tel?

Rehearsing 'Aladdin and his Wonderful Lamp'

Adam Faith and the Shadows

Panto, Bournemouth 1962

LICENSED RESTAURANT
ADAM FAITH
"ALADDIN"

Adam and his brother Dennis

roulettesroulettesroulettesroulettesroulettesroulette
sroulettesroulettesroulettesroulettesroulettesroulett
esroulettesroulettesroulettesroulettesroulettesroule
Musicians are discerning people—their favourites of today are usually everyone's favourites of tomorrow. Naturally enough, good musicians (and bad) choose only to admire great musicians. One group admired by nearly all British musicians is the 'Roulettes'.

Roulettes album insert

roulettesroulettesroulettesroulettesroulettesroulette
sroulettesroulettesroulettesroulettesroulettesroulett
esroulettesroulettesroulettesroulettesroulettesroule

MOD ROGAN

PETER THORP

BOB HENRIT

RUSSELL BALLARD

Sole Direction   JOHN L. BARKER ASSOCIATES LTD.

Personal Manager   **ANNE C. NIVEN,** JOHN L. BARKER ASSOCIATES LTD. 164 Shaftesbury Avenue, London, W.C.2 COVent 0572

Agency   ERIC EASTON LTD., 1 Little Argyll St., London, W.1 REGent 4536

Publicity   ROD BUCKLE... PROD... 164 Shaftesbury Avenue, London, W.C.2 TEMple 9686

Roulettes insert with Thorp inexplicably spelt correctly

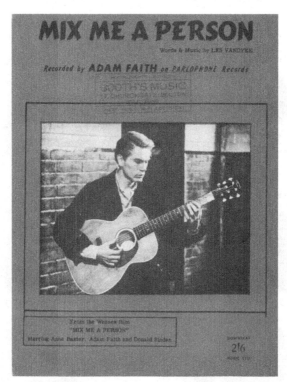

Tel with that famous Martin guitar

EMI Studios after recording 'Faith Alive'

Chapter Four: HOLD MY HEAD UP

After I'd left St Ignatius at sixteen, and during my year learning all there was to know about the opposite sex before it was too late at Cheshunt Grammar School, I became friendly with a chap called Nic Kinsey and his infinitely more highly attractive sister Rose. Their dad Ray was a documentary cameraman and sound recordist who'd been all over the world making films, and regaled us with stories of flying transatlantic on Stratocruisers, buying 2 dollars-worth of food in New York and generally experiencing what the world had to offer. He'd been in the RAF, and even though he didn't have a handlebar moustache it wasn't difficult to imagine where one had been. He was without a doubt the first 'man of the world' I'd ever met, and a somewhat exotic figure. He had the best radiogram-type sound system I'd ever seen and Russell, Bernie and I spent lots of time round at their house listening to records sounding their very best, rather than the way they did on our mono Dansette player. It was here we marvelled at the spread sound of 'living' stereo for the first time.

Nic was destined to do something big in the technical side of sound production and recording, and had a lot of boffin friends who turned out to be useful to me as time passed. So Nic earned himself a state scholarship and went off to Manchester University to read electronics, and our paths crossed for a bit of harmless fun whenever we played the clubs and theatres of Lancashire's capital, backing Adam, or on our own as The Roulettes. Somehow or other we often managed to stay with him in the tower block that was his hall of residence. It was conveniently placed near Mr Smith's club, which was where it all happened in Manchester in 1964 and 1965.

While Nic was away having a good time and studying really hard, at least for the last couple of weeks of every college year, Ray bought shares in a small recording studio installed in a church in Barnet, North London, which specialised in producing evangelical programmes for use throughout the world. Once Nic graduated and become part of the company we started to make decidedly non-religious music at Livingston, demos and experimental stuff to see what sounds we could get if we worked hard at it. Nic was interested in turning the studio into a commercial venture, so I don't believe we paid for any studio time. We listened to a great deal of Tamla-Motown music and worked out how to get those evocative sounds. Russell wrote a great song, which we recorded there with a view to it being a single, complete with a Motown-type recorder part (played by Nic). Even though it was a saga of lost and unrequited love, I suppose it's become something of a mantra for me: 'Help me to help myself . . .' Unfortunately it doesn't always work!

We spent a lot of time messing about in the old Livingston studio while Nic learned how to record, with us as willing guinea pigs. (It's fair to say we also spent a certain amount of time in the Railway Arms and slightly less in the nearby Golden Tandoori restaurant over Chicken Chilli Masala talking nonsense about life and the universe. John Verity was working on sessions for the first album of a heavy metal band called Saxon, and managed to eat Indian food (Bangalore phal actually) every night for over a month. Mind you, he was from Bradford so he was used to it.

Sainsburys decided to build yet another supermarket in New Barnet right next door to Livingston studios, so there went the neighbourhood. Nic, Mike Smee, Ray and the other guys decided to move to another church in Wood Green which was up and running. We'd done a lot of excellent stuff in the old place, including Russ's *Barnet Dogs* album, and the beginnings of the second Charlie album, which continued at the new studio. The new Livingston didn't have either of the old Neve desks from Barnet, but a super-duper, state of the art SSL mixing desk (which cost as much as a four-bedroomed detached house) in one studio and an upmarket Amec console in the other.

It's fair to say Nic's lifestyle of long hours in the studio seeing very little daylight, rubbish food and (it's fair to say), an awful lot of drinking in the Duke of Edinburgh finally took its toll, and he succumbed to a heart attack in the middle of 1994. It sounds like a Bernard Manning joke but he died in the pub, and the staff were so used to him falling asleep with his head on the bar that they didn't realise there was anything wrong with him until they were unable to wake him at closing time. I wasn't there, but I'm told Nic had a cheque in his pocket at the time for a six figure sum, which he hadn't quite got round to depositing in the bank. He was just fifty, and the world not only lost one of its most enthusiastic, belligerent and exasperating characters but also one of its most enquiring minds. Any conversation initiated with Nic invariably culminated in a response from him in his Bradford accent beginning 'No, but why?' It's curious, this accent thing, because I'd first met him at school in the leafy suburbs of Cheshunt, Hertfordshire, in 1960, and even then for some reason he had a broad Yorkshire accent – although I knew for sure he'd spent all his formative years in North London.

I described Nic as belligerent, and that's the adjective which sums him up best. I'll illustrate this with an anecdote. The studio had relocated from Barnet, and the guys were desperate for business, when an enquiry from the mighty EMI came in for emergency studio time. They were swamped with artists who needed to record and were jammed up at Abbey Road. They decided to do a trial session, and a very, very young and inexperienced band turned up with an equally young but highly attractive girl singer accompanied by the head of EMI's production staff. John Verity was a shareholder by this time and was engineering the session. Aside from a 'meet and greet' at the beginning, once the proceedings were under way Nic was warned to keep well away from the control room. According to John, the session started badly mainly because the young guys were nervous and, being unused to the studio, were struggling. John persevered, and by lunchtime he had managed to make them sound reasonably good. He'd almost disproved the old recording studio adage that you can't polish a turd – until the pubs closed at three-ish and Nic came back, that is. Forgetting he shouldn't be anywhere near the control room he wandered by the open door and was invited in by the chap from EMI to hear the great track. Completely unsolicited, he declared it to be 'fucking crap!' Twenty albums a year went elsewhere at that precise moment.

Anyway, this ever-enquiring single mind led to several inventions. One was the Inpulse One drum machine in 1985, which, having its own touch-sensitive pads on board and the ability to load in additional drum sounds, was years ahead of the opposition. I worked on encapsulating the sounds with him. Nic had another idea that certainly would have been hugely successful had he not died. This was the so-called Magic Mixer. As opposed to all the other upmarket mixing desks, which physically duplicated a highly expensive single bus and faders for as many mic and line inputs as the desk possessed, Nic's consisted of just a single bus with touch faders: the equalisation, panning and various other important bits of information about sound parameters were held in a computer, and you only needed the single controller bus to assign it. This was unique in that it used a computer over twenty years ago at a time when they weren't in any real evidence in recording studios.

Nic's single-mindedness didn't extend to clearing up any mess in the studio, or the living area he built for himself above it. As his dad once said, 'If Nick moved into a pig-sty pigs would move out!'

In 1971 my wife-to-be decided it was time for me to ask her to marry me. It didn't seem like an overly long courtship to me. We had met in 1967 in a studio in Marble Arch on what I think was the session for Bob Dylan's double-negative song: 'Ain't Going Nowhere'. Ricki was there with her old schoolfriend Wendy, who was soon to be married to Lem Lubin: he had been the guitarist in Unit 4+2 since the beginning. Manfred Mann was recording us, and we'd put down what they used to call a self-penned B-side called 'So You Want To Be a Blues Player'. It was tongue in cheek, but came at a time when lots of otherwise innocuous pop groups were re-inventing themselves as blues bands. (In those days it didn't really matter what was on the flipside of a record, but if you wanted half the publishing you simply had to write the thing yourself.) When we made records with Jonathan King he asked us to play any old riff and take it through a few chord changes for a few bars, and in the fullness of time it turned up on the other side of a 45rpm record with his name on it as writer.

The lovely Ricki's real name was Ann and her surname was Hedderick – which explains her nickname. After university in Birmingham she came to London, first to become a music and PE teacher and second to marry Adam Faith. You couldn't make it up!

Anyway, Ricki and I began courting after having 'accidentally' bumped into each other at a nightclub called Hatchetts. But there were complications: according to her friends I wasn't the marrying kind, and besides (as I've mentioned) she was engaged to a guitarist friend of mine named Derek Griffiths. Derek was better accepted by Ricki's family because before becoming a musician he'd been an accountant. He also had another big advantage over me, as far as her family was concerned: he wasn't a

Catholic. So while to my mind it hadn't been too difficult to persuade Ricki to fall in love with me (she once unwisely told me I was her knight on a white charger), it was a monumental task to persuade her dad to follow suit – especially as around this time I was getting ready for progressive rock, and my hair was halfway down my back – with green streaks!

Against all the odds we started courting, and I spent a lot of time in the flat she shared near the Edgware Road with Wendy and a couple of other girls. If I was there for supper I contributed half a crown to the kitty. The flat was in Nutford Place on the fringes of London's West End, near Hyde Park, so we were well situated for entertainment. Hatchetts was the club of the moment, which we went to a lot. I recall seeing Ike and Tina Turner there, and while their show was great they used what remains the strangest PA I've ever seen: a battered pair of the metal Tannoy speakers you normally saw at sports stadiums. After we'd been clubbing, to the theatre or to the cinema I'd see how quickly I could drive my red Mini Cooper back to my parents' in Waltham Cross. Each night I'd try to shave seconds off my best time of twenty-two minutes as I sped the 16 miles through the suburbs of North London. If we'd had an argument I could get home much more quickly than if we'd parted amicably!

When Ricki and I met I was still in Unit 4+2, and we were working hard at 'getting the band together, man'. We were so intent on doing this that we unwittingly signed up for a couple of weeks at the Storeyville club in Cologne. Like The Beatles before us, some nights we played nine forty-five minute sets (or, worse, till the last drunken punter left). But they were human, and once or twice they let us off and we only had to play eight times. Like most bands, Unit 4+2 had a repertoire large enough to fill three forty-five minute spots, so if we had to play nine times we simply played the sets three times each. This was tough for me because it meant I had to play three drum solos a night, but I looked on this as a challenge and coped with it pretty well. I spoke to Cozy Powell about playing for this length of time and, like me, he felt this was a great apprenticeship: if you couldn't handle it then music wasn't the right career for you. Certainly that training made it possible for me to enjoy some of the fourteen-hour sessions we did with The Kinks seventeen eventful years later. It actually didn't matter how many times you repeated a song in the Storeyville because the punters weren't there for the music, they were there for love. The bar was full of girls who, for a small fee, would help them find it. 'Women of negotiable affection' is an apt description I once heard in Alaska!

Even though I was enthusiastic about playing those long hours I was getting tired, and it was beginning to show. I always maintain that what I was doing in those days was like working down the mines, only harder. I believe it was one of the brothers who ran the hotel who noticed my plight, and told me that people who wanted to keep awake in Germany (students, lorry drivers, musicians and so on) took a legal stimulant called AN1, also known as psychotonikum: you bought it in the *Apotheke*. Well, it worked, and for a while we were all much more enthusiastic about the seventh, eighth and ninth spots of the night. But just like aspirin, if you took it for long enough it lost its potency and you had to take more: the usual drug spiral. Anyhow, we survived the drugs and the food and returned to the UK a new band.

This was early 1968. We carried on doing university gigs and were booked to do another extended residency, this time at the Carousel in Copenhagen, just round the corner from the Tivoli Gardens. We were playing for a long time again, so when fatigue set in we went looking for a Danish version of AN1. The chemist provided us with caffeine tablets. I can't say they gave us more energy but they certainly kept us awake – mainly because they give you a splitting headache, which you can't possibly sleep through.

Unit 4+2 were an interesting band. They'd play 'knuckles' in the van on the way to the gig until their hands were bruised and bloodied, so by the time they got on stage they'd have difficulty playing their instruments! We'd be driving along with Welsh or Scottish mountains towering over us, and someone would say, 'I could get to the top of that mountain in fifteen minutes.'

'No you couldn't.'

'Yes I could.'

'Prove it!'

And we'd stop the van, so they could attempt to climb a mountain that a mountaineer would take a whole day to scale.

We were pretty well received at colleges and clubs up and down the country and we managed to keep going, but we came to a point where one of us was drinking too much, which was adversely affecting his pitching. We were signed to an agency owned by Chris Barber and his sister Audrey to get us gigs, and they put an Australian called Johnny Toogood in charge of us. Johnny, after private consultations with the rest of us, decided to confront the perpetrator, and in a general appraisal of our performance after a gig at the London College of Printing said he could tell us what would improve our act in three words: 'Stop drinking.' We counted the words on two fingers, and couldn't stop laughing. The opportunity to make wayward members of the band more sober was missed.

Unit 4+2 lurched on. Somehow I heard that Spencer Davis was looking for a drummer and a bass player for a tour of American universities. Lem and I went along for a blow with Spencer and Ray Fenwick and got the gig. Obviously I knew the guys in the original Spencer Davis Group (Spencer, Pete York and the Winwood brothers) from various TV shows we'd appeared on together, and for a while Spencer lived not too far from me in Potters Bar. I was really looking forward to playing 'Gimme Some Loving', 'Somebody Help Me', 'I'm a Man' and the various other songs the band were famous for, including one that would eventually become Johnny Vee's tour de force: 'Stay With Me Baby'.

It would have been my first trip to the States but unfortunately, for reasons never explained to me, the tour was cancelled.

The worst thing that happened to us in 1967 may well have been the best as well, because we talk about it every time we Unit 4+2 guys get together. To set the scene, we had a one-night stand in Inverness, but our Ford Transit was kaput so we borrowed The Yardbirds' gear wagon. No bloody seats, no bloody heater, no bloody radio, no bloody good – but it got us safely the 573 miles or so from London to the gig in the Royal Inverness Hotel. We had a roadie, and instructed him to fill up the van with petrol before the drive home. (That's showbiz: drive 573 miles, play a gig and travel 573 miles back in one day!) We finished the gig, waited a couple of freezing hours for the singer to come back with the roadie from a party, told him exactly what we thought of him and got on our way. It began to snow just as we ran out of petrol in the skiing resort of Aviemore. Under intense interrogation the soon to be ex-roadie admitted he hadn't filled up. There was nothing to do, having sworn vigorously and imaginatively at him, but curl up on the amplifiers and try to sleep. It was snowing hard outside and there was permafrost on the ceiling. As you can imagine, not only did sleep not come easily, it didn't come at all. During this miserable night the lead vocalist began to laugh hysterically. When we asked him what was so funny he told us that in years to come we'd all be laughing about this. But there's more . . . Come the dawn we filled up with petrol and set off southwards. On the A1 just inside England we got a puncture in the nearside back wheel, and upon checking we discovered that while The Yardbirds had thoughtfully provided a spare wheel, there wasn't a jack. We dispatched the roadie to get help. Settling down to wait, after a while we decided we should try to help ourselves. We unloaded the gear from the back of the van into the pouring rain, and four of us held the back of the van up so the other two could change the wheel. It worked, and we soon sped off to find the roadie. We came to the unworthy predecessor of a motorway services, a restaurant called Gingham Kitchen, and there was the roadie having what a few years later the Americans would describe as brunch. He hadn't been able to get help, so figured the next best thing to do was get something to eat. He began work with Led Zeppelin as soon as he got out of the van back in London. Forty years later we can just about laugh about all this.

There were a great many things that happened to Unit 4+2, many of which beggar belief. One of these concerns rolling off the ferry from Newcastle to Göteborg in our relatively new long-wheelbase Ford Transit van, recently kitted out with two aircraft seats behind the driver and three more behind those. This was the height of luxury in the mid-sixties, and you were supposed to be able to recline your seat and go off to sleep. (In reality you couldn't, because all the gear was crammed in behind the back three seats.) Anyway, as we set off through the snow for a series of gigs somewhere in the frozen parts of Scandinavia the windscreen was hit by something hard, and broke. In those days a cracked windscreen crazed like a spider's web, except for a small piece in front of the driver that stayed clear so you could limp to a garage. Fred struggled manfully to drive while looking through the clear 12 square inches in front of him but eventually gave up the dangerous struggle and smashed the windscreen out from the inside. Fred had this massive full length sheepskin-lined Swedish Army greatcoat which he climbed into, and he drove with the collar up like a Battle of Britain pilot. We popstars cowered behind the two front aircraft seats in our flimsy leather jackets, covered in snow, until we got to the gig what seemed like many frozen hours later. We didn't pass any garages to enquire about a replacement windscreen the whole journey.

I described the van as being relatively new, but it didn't stay that way for long. One of our number (the one who'd been the singer in The Daybreakers) was so disgusting with his disposal of rubbish (old newspapers, magazines, drink containers, fish and chip wrappers, and worse) that the bus soon filled up with his detritus. We decided to take things into our own hands. We pulled up outside his house in Goffs Oak (just up the road from where the village's other accomplished musician, Posh Spice, would be born roughly seven years later). When he closed the front door on his way to bed, just as the sun came up, we emptied the contents of the van into his front garden and drove off. He never mentioned it and neither did we.

I've been heard to say that being in a band is exactly like being in a marriage: you have to work hard to keep it going. You turn a blind eye to the other person's idiosyncrasies in the interests of harmony. Unit 4+2 certainly didn't do this, and if someone absent-mindedly picked their nose, broke wind, burped, played pocket billiards or stank of garlic it would be brought to their attention – immediately and frequently.

Colour TV was launched in 1967, and I played on the first non-black and white music show. It was on BBC2 and imaginatively entitled *Colour me Pop*. In an effort to make the most of the new medium I wore an orange jacket, brown shirt, lime-green tank top, blue trousers and red shoes (at least I didn't wear flowers in my hair). I had forged a relationship with a couple of guys who owned a stall in Kensington market known professionally as Cockell & Johnson, and negotiated a deal whereby if I put their logo on my bass drum and used it on *Colour Me Pop* they would guarantee me free clothes for life. They went out of business not long after the show was aired. This proves another showbiz adage: there's no such thing as a free lunch!

I was playing a small black round badge Gretsch kit at this time, although through the sixties I also owned a couple of black Trixons, a silver glitter Ludwig set, a black Rogers, an equally black Slingerland and an ASBA set stored in France. (The three black American sets had originally been covered in those groovy and these days highly collectible three-dimensional moiré finishes, but I soon stripped them off and followed the boring trend of basic black.) My relationships with Ivor Arbiter, Gerry Evans and my 'Dolly Mixtures' Hayman drums were about a year away.

Many years after Unit 4+2 broke up a Dutch TV company decided to make a film about 'Concrete and Clay', and lobbied us to see if we were available. Russell and I were busy so couldn't make the first filming at the Coach and Horses, a pub in Northaw, Hertfordshire, that the guys used to frequent and even played at in the mid -sixties. Lem wasn't invited, but the film went ahead anyway. The crew finally got round to filming me at a hotel in Kensington, and I was ready to talk about bossa-novas, cowbells and the 'nuts and bolts' of how the record was made. Their first question on camera had nothing to do with this and hit me straight between the eyes: 'Why did you sack Buster Meikle from the band?' I was flabbergasted, and even though I know Buster feels it was my fault (or Russell's, or Lem's), because he brings it up from time to time, the decision was taken by the management and the band had nothing to do with it.

Unfortunately the writing was on the wall for Unit 4+2 and Russell and I were tentatively making plans to do something else.

Besides playing sessions for producers who wanted an aggressive young player rather than an older ex-jazzer on their records, I was also signed with Unit 4+2 to Fontana Records. We recorded in the same studio in Marble Arch where I'd played my first real session with The Hunters in 1960. By 1967 things had changed: Fontana had multi-track machines and the studio got a good sound.

I know media propaganda says that if you can remember the sixties you weren't there, and everybody was out of it all the time and making love and tons of money. The reality was that apart from the fortunate few the greater majority struggled along earning a few quid a week, and investing what they could into music. Nowadays it's laughable that then a brand-new Ludwig 400 snare only cost 50 quid or so, whle a loaf of bread was 6*d* – which makes the drum serious dosh.

I have never smoked, so I managed to survive the sixties, seventies and eighties without getting into substance trouble, something for which my brain and my lungs are grateful. Musos who did turn on were always planning to get started on their big project, but inevitably never did.

Towards the end of 1968 Russell and I had just finished playing a Unit 4+2 gig somewhere in Essex when we spotted Rod Argent and Chris White from The Zombies in the rapidly emptying hall. We knew they were getting a band together, and stood with them as they outlined their plans for world domination. The Zombies had just had (or were about to have) a monster hit with 'Time of the Season' in the US and the album it was taken from, *Odessey and Oracle* (mis-spelled by Chris White's artist pal Terry Quirke who painted the cover) was eventually successful too, and voted one of the best 500 albums of all time. But with all that going for them, they didn't want to be The Zombies any more. They wanted to try something new, and Russell and I were deemed to be the guys for the job. We were wanted for the project along with Rod's bass-playing cousin, who I knew from Mike Cotton's band. They had songs already, and we all gathered around at Chris's flat in Woodside Park in North London to listen to them. I remember getting in my car really buzzing and more elated than I'd ever been before. The material was great, Chris, Rod and Jim were great, what more could we want? The songs we heard that day were mature, with memorable tunes and great lyrics – 'Mr Galileo' was my favourite. I don't believe the song ever made it onto a record.

We didn't have any names at the time, and rather than call the band the New Zombies, I suggested it would make a lot of sense to call the entity Argent, in a somewhat sublime piece of trading-off. Jim Wilkinson, our tea chest bass-playing friend, had graduated from the Royal College of Art with an MA, and devised the futuristic logo and script for Argent the band and *Argent* the first album .

Before we did any Argent tracks we put down some stuff with Colin Blunstone, which came out as The Zombies. 'Imagine the Swan' was the A-side and 'Conversation off Floral Street' was the flip side.

> Well I have a picture in colour of you
> And it's there in my room to remind me of you
> So it was with surprise that I saw you today
> And I did not recognise you, girl, what more can I say?
>
> For the colours are gone
> You've become kind of gray
> And you're not like the swan
> That I knew yesterday...

Colin B. was pivotal at this stage of our career, because he had a manager named Mel Collins who also looked after the careers of (among others) Alan Bown, Mike Hurst (who I discovered recently was the real owner of Mel's office) and John Verity. Mel seemed to be an extremely well-connected chap, and he wanted us for his stable of artists. So with management taken care of by Mel's Active Management, production with Chris White and Rod's Nexus records and distribution through Epic and CBS, we set about making our own records.

Having routined the songs at Jim's local Pioneer Youth Club in St Albans, we went first to Olympic Studios in Barnes to put down a couple of tracks before moving to Sound Techniques Studio in Chelsea to record the remainder of the first album. The reason for this change of venue was that Jerry Boys who was engineering us was moving to the Chelsea studio, and we followed him. Even though EMI had a great reputation at the time, it never had an eight-track recording machine; Sound Techniques did, so we went for the multi-track option. (This isn't quite true: EMI did have an eight track but were still evaluating it, and it didn't have a clock to tell you where you were if you were overdubbing.) The guys at Abbey Road were making do with four-track machines, and in The Beatles' case were joining two together, with all the synchronisation problems that ensued.

Time was not on our side at Sound Techniques, because as soon as we finished the studio was closing to be refurbished. I haven't got that quite right: we had to be finished on the day they closed. This meant that the very first Argent album finished with a forty-eight hour session on 10 July 1969, the day Apollo 9 landed on the moon. We were not by any means an un-aggressive band and we played hard in the studio, but as good as the album was it wasn't as hard-hitting as I felt it was meant to be. The songs were great, as were the performances, but it came over as *soft* rock. One track called 'Liar', which was written by Russell and was our first single, wasn't a hit for us, but was gallingly successfully covered by Three Dog Night in the States. With more dynamics, it was a big success. (They also pinched one of Leo Sayer's songs and took it to the top of the charts in America but you don't know about my involvement with him yet.)

Having finished the recording and planned a release date, the next thing to do was to launch the band. There were a great many tried and tested places this could have been accomplished, but we somehow chose an art gallery that had never been used for music before. The lack of interest from the music trade in the ICA in The Mall was with good reason: it was completely concrete inside and didn't give the greatest sound you'd ever heard. It wasn't the worst either, but if you're going to expose a new band to the media for the very first time you really want great sound rather than OK. To be fair, the ICA looked great, as you expect a modern art gallery to, but the ultra-live acoustics made it tough for an aggressive band with lots of subtleties to get a good hearing. That said, almost forty years after our first (and last) appearance there, bands are still appearing at the ICA. Maybe they've had the acoustics mended, like the Albert Hall did?

The ICA wasn't the only prestigious London gig with difficult acoustics. To be honest, all of them were a problem to a loud rock 'n' roll band. The Festival Hall was the worst for a drummer: having been built in the fifties exclusively for orchestral music, it already possessed a very live sound. The Albert Hall had been built 100 years earlier and suffered from the same high frequency bias, until they decided to hang high-end-defeating acoustic flying saucers from the ceiling, which sort of cured the problem. But the winner of the Henrit prize for the worst-concert-hall-for-drummers-in-London goes to the Barbican. The acoustics there were (and probably still are) uncontrollable. The slightest tap on a snare drum produced a thunderous noise. (This was because acoustic engineers had deliberately installed this 'enhancement' from the beginning.) I played there shortly after it was built with a pal of mine called Mike Berry, who had a great voice. I'd known him since the very early sixties when he was in The Outlaws and had recorded an album called *Drift Away* with him. He'd had a chequered career, first as a singer, then as an actor, and made several hit records including 'Tribute to Buddy Holly' with Joe Meek, and an Edwardian love song written in 1915 called 'The Sunshine of Your Smile', which was produced and beautifully orchestrated by Chas Hodges:

> Give me the right to love you all the while,
> My world forever, the sunshine of your smile.

My favourite, though, was another Edwardian-type love song that I'm guessing Chas's mum used to play on the old joanna: 'What'll I Do'. It was written by Irving Berlin and, like 'Sunshine', had also been recorded by Frank Sinatra. It was known to us as 'the waddle song' for obvious reasons.

> What'll I do when I'm wondering who's kissing you, what'll I do?
> What'll I do with just a photograph to tell my troubles to?
> When I'm alone, with only dreams of you that won't come true, what'll I do?

In the early eighties I was touring with Mike and the usual reprobates: Dave Wintour, Johnny V. and an excellent keyboard player named Colin Stewart, who I lost touch with but hope went on to greatness. We arrived at the Barbican for the soundcheck, and from the first tap on the snare I was struggling. The place wasn't engineered for anything other than classical music. I couldn't control the volume of the drums: even with copious amounts of gaffer tape and loo roll on everything it was still too loud. The blonde and red-coated back-of-house manager came over to assist. 'You're knocking seven kinds of shit out of those drums,' she informed me helpfully.

I was desperately trying to produce a soft but still convincing sound, and was incensed by her remark. I replied as wittily as I could through clenched teeth. 'Madam, I assure you I'm capable of knocking seven kinds of shit out of these drums, but at the moment I'm trying to play as quietly as possible.'

I met one of the aforementioned highly paid sound engineers a couple of decades after I struggled to play at the Barbican. He was an opera singer who surprisingly doubled on drums, and we met when I sold him a Flats drum kit. While chatting about the unusualness of an opera singer playing drums he also admitted to being an acoustics engineer. I asked which concert halls he'd worked on and he mentioned the infamous Barbican. I sternly advised him against taking that particular set (or any other) for a gig there!

While I'm touching on the subject of dodgy-sounding gigs, Carnegie Hall was another concert hall whose acoustics were too good for rock 'n'roll. Remember the old joke about the old girl in New York who asks the cabbie how you get to Carnegie Hall. 'Lady, you gotta practice' is not quite correct. You have to practise playing *quietly* to get there! There's another marble-interiored building in Washington quaintly called the Daughters of the American Revolution, which is also unplayable as far as I'm concerned.

Mike Berry and I always got on pretty well, probably because we possessed the same stupid sense of humour. Some time after that tour which took in the problematic Barbican we discussed writing among other things a treatment for a children's TV programme. This was a project that Richard Stone, Mike's showbiz agent, had turned us onto. Mike was also an actor by this time, first in a kids' programme called *Worzel Gummidge* and later in *Are You Being Served?*, a popular sitcom set in a department store. Richard Stone put us together with a proper scriptwriter whose name escapes me, but I do know we met up at her cosy *pied-à-terre*, which used to belong to Errol Flynn, over Leicester Square tube station. I couldn't get any sensation of the great man's presence while we were there, although we did manage to put together a programme called *Outings*, which starred a red double-decker London bus that took a bunch of kids around the country, gently educating them by taking them to interesting places. Of course there was going to be music in it, and we wrote the theme together over the phone:

> *We're all going on an outing,*
> *We're staying out all day,*
> *Fun and laughter on our outing,*
> *Maybe we'll be down your way.*
>
> *We're going to find out*
> *What the world is all about,*
> *Maybe sing a song or two,*
> *We'll have some fun*
> *'Cos it's only just begun,*
> *So come on enjoy the view . . .*

How could we fail?

Funnily enough, while we were on that Mike Berry tour and coming back to town from a gig in Brighton Mike decided to look up a horror novelist friend of his. We went to this forbidding mansion and met James Herbert, who had actually been at school with me although we'd never met. I'd read several of his books including The Rats and Shrine, which delved into our mutual Catholic heritage. He's another celeb who doesn't figure on the school's website as a notable old Ignatian, even though he's written twenty-seven novels so far and sold millions and millions of books, three of which have been turned into Hollywood films, one by John Carpenter! (Clem Cattini, who's drummed as a session man on more great records than anyone I know and and 'Shaking all Over' arguably the first ever British rock 'n' roll record by Johnny Kidd and the Pirates, also goes unsung at the college.)

After Argent's ICA launch we decided we needed to do some concentrated playing before we headed to America, so we got our Wolverhampton agent Morris Jones to book us into the PN club on the Leopold Strasse in Munich for a couple of weeks. It was the same sort of thing we'd done with Unit 4+2, although we weren't envisaging having to play nine spots a night. Not without an argument, that is!

We had some interesting times on the way to Munich, a journey you couldn't do in one hit without overnighting somewhere. We always stopped in Frankfurt. Everything went well on the journey to the ferry, but after disembarking at Calais (or was it Ostend?) it was a different story. We had bought a powder-blue Ford Galaxie 500 convertible from our publisher Les Jones, which was so ostentatious it was immediately christened the Yobmobile, and we also had the largest van for the gear that you could get without a special licence: a Commer 'walkthrough'. We drove away from the port for a mile or two with Fred Wilkinson behind the wheel of the Yobmobile in convoy, until the big van came to a standstill. Our backline guy Brian Spencer, who used to be a window cleaner and had been at school with Russell, got out and walked back to the car looking concerned. We asked what was wrong, and he said he couldn't drive on the wrong side of the road. We were astonished, but it turned out he'd never done it before, so Jim and I jumped into the van to ferry it the 700 miles to Munich and Brian went to sleep in the back of the Yobmobile while we endeavoured to keep up with Fred. The Commer had one of those big steering wheels set horizontally, and like in those old black and white films the steering needed to be corrected constantly, which was fine on the straight, speed-limitless autobahns of Germany – but eventually we found ourselves at a chicane where the road was under repair and three lanes abruptly merged. Fred flicked the steering on the big American Ford and continued on course while I, with Jim by my side, wrestled with the wheel to make it first turn left then very, very shortly afterwards turn right. We careered along without hitting anything, and were soon back on course for Bavaria.

We did a certain amount of eating on the autoroute, but in those days if you didn't like underdone white sausages with German mustard you were out of luck. So by the time we arrived in Munich we were so hungry that we decided to blow all our *per diems* on a single meal in an upmarket restaurant called the Leopold. We sat down and looked at the menu, and most of us carnivores asked for steak or hamburger. Jim took a little longer to make up his mind, and decided on Omelette Surprise with chips. Brian (aka 'Nudger' because of his habit of digging you in the ribs with his elbow) decided he'd have what Jim had ordered. In the back of my mind I knew something about Omelette Surprise, but couldn't quite remember what it was. The steaks, hamburgers and beer arrived and a couple of plates of chips were placed in front of Jim and Nudger. We tucked in and the omelette eaters waited patiently. When they asked the waitress for their omelette she instructed them to eat their rapidly coagulating chips first. Unwisely they decided to wait. Eventually, once we'd all finished, she brought the Omelette Surprise. It was Baked Alaska: ice cream with sugary meringue around it very carefully and quickly cooked in the oven so the ice cream didn't melt. Served with sparklers. We shouldn't have laughed, but since we were in Germany Schadenfreude set in.

We were being put up by Pieter Neumann, the guy who owned the PN Club, at the apartment he also owned opposite – above a restaurant and a shop that sold the same Rosenthal crockery I was about to inherit as a wedding present the following year. All the PN bands stayed in this apartment, affectionately known as the Doom Pad, and it showed. It was terrible when we moved in – and it certainly wasn't any better when we moved out. Anyhow, we dropped our gear and headed out to see who was on at the club that night. The sign outside said 'Heute, Daddy'. I'm pretty sure Daddy was a working name for Supertramp, who, like us, were getting it together before heading off to America.

Besides not being able to drive in Europe, we discovered that Brian Spencer was unable to drink there either. We came out of the club that night to find him sitting in the kerb violently engaged in a Technicolor yawn. Oh, the miseries of free drink! So we carried him back to the Doom Pad and crashed out.

We were violently roused into wakefulness at 6.30am by a terrible, destructive noise – the sound of breaking glass. It was caused by a mobile machine that crushed beer bottles. Rather than take them away and reduce them to bite-sized chunks suitable for recycling, in 1969 they preferred to get the job done on the spot – and it only took about half an hour each morning. Fortunately the machine didn't fragmentise bottles from the bar immediately below our bunks on a Sunday, so we managed to get a lie-in. They were also digging up the whole length of the Leopold Strasse to put in the U-bahn for the tragic 1972 Olympics. This racket impacted on our sleeping patterns too.

Rod woke Nudger up one morning because he needed to discuss something to do with the gig.

'No one wakes me up when I'm asleep,' Nudger said angrily.

'When do they wake you up then?' said Rod.

We were on a budget and Jim, who'd been at the PN Club a couple of times before with Mike Cotton's band, suggested that the food in the Weinerwald below the Doom Pad wasn't too bad and was really cheap. Hackenmakengebratten was Jim's favourite and was indeed the cheapest thing on the menu. To be fair, it didn't taste at all bad, and it wasn't until we were told it was chicken guts that most of us stopped eating it.

Three really interesting, not to say far-reaching, things happened in Munich: we decided to visit Dachau, we went to the Rathaus Cinema to see *Easy Rider*, and we visited the Deutsche Museum.

Dachau was an awful place, which no one should take lightly. We walked around glumly. Of course we all knew what had happened there but weren't expecting what we saw. If you hadn't believed in the Holocaust before than you couldn't help believing it now. There was a real sense of foreboding about the place and for me it was a Road to Damascus experience. You couldn't fail to be touched as you walked through the gates with those hopeless words worked into the wrought iron: *Arbeit macht Frei*. We looked around the camp at the evil ovens and the huts that had once held human beings, and the railway lines that had brought millions to their deaths. It wasn't until we got back in the car on our way back to Munich that anybody said a word. The one thing we all commented on was that the camp was as silent as a grave: nothing grew there and no birds flew over it.

Easy Rider was a revelation to me too. I loved the sentiment and the music, but never having been to America I was shocked by the way the police dealt with the hippies in the film. Surely this was cinematic licence: it couldn't possibly be like that, could it? Not many months later I got the chance to put this to the test. We'd just played with John Mayall and Duster Bennett at Fillmore West, which was Bill Graham's gig at a theatre called Winterland in San Francisco, and were on our way south to LA to see The Kinks. We had a day off, and having heard they were on at the Palladium we decided to take a look. There are two ways to LA: the quick way via Route 1 and the slower, more scenic route alongside the Pacific via Big Sur on Route 101. As I recall we'd been to a party to celebrate our first gig on the West Coast the night before and everybody was jaded. Since for some reason I was less jaded than anybody else, it was decided I should drive and the consensus was we'd take the scenic route. This seemed crazy to me, because with 400 miles to drive the quickest way would surely be best.

Anyway, we set off and everybody went to sleep. So the only one capable of appreciating the scenery was involved in wrestling the car around countless bends at high speed, so couldn't possibly savour the view safely. Perhaps it's germane to mention what car we were travelling in: it was a Camaro, which went like shit off the proverbial shovel. Now I'd been in the US long enough to know what the speed limit was, but still couldn't understand why they were only allowed to drive at 55mph. The roads were great, and this car was capable of going twice that speed. So I persuaded it so to do! The mist was rolling in from the ocean as we barrelled along, eating up the miles. I was just beginning to think we'd be there in time when I spotted this red light in my wing mirror. At first I thought it was the rear light on a lorry, but looking down at the needle on the speedo, which showed the wrong side of 100, I figured that was unlikely. Eventually I realised it was a police car, and I was caught bang to rights. Over his loudhailer the highway patrolman asked me 'politely' to pull over. I stopped, and he invited me to 'step out of the car with my hands in full view'. Then he asked me to walk back to his car, where I sat in the front seat with a pump shotgun between my legs while he tried to work out the whys and wherefores of a numberless international driving licence. He asked me several questions, to which I responded in an accent which was a mixture of George Sanders and Cary Grant. I explained we were an English group, just arrived in America – maybe he'd heard of us – we used to be The Zombies but now we were called Argent. All this cut no ice, and neither did my informing him that we were in a hurry because we were going to see 'our chums' The Kinks who were performing in Los Angeles that very night. He asked me if I knew what the speed limit was in America, and I said I didn't realise there was one because in the films everybody seemed to drive much faster than we did in England. He assured me there was one, and it was 55mph. Did I know how fast I was going? I told him I was so intent on driving on the wrong side of the road that I wasn't really looking at the speedo. 'Well,' he said, 'I had to do 120 to catch you.' I wasn't sure whether to feel elated by this news, but at that precise moment all the doors on the Camaro opened and all the guys, who'd been asleep and had no knowledge of the bust, got out. The cop flipped out, produced his pistol and jumped into the crouch position behind the open driver's door – you know, the one you see in all the car-chase films. The rest of the Argents were highly shocked by this, and got back into the car as they were told.

My friendly cop said he'd do me a favour, and I thought I might be getting away with a ticking-off. But no: he meant that in the report he would say I was only doing 80mph. This would mean I could post bail (which means admitting the offence and paying the $120 fine), wouldn't have to come up before a judge the next morning and consequently wouldn't have to stay in jail overnight. Having recently seen *Easy Rider*, I was extremely relieved, and suddenly felt very vulnerable in my rock star's singlet, tight trousers and long hair. But the bad news was that to post bail we'd have to travel 25 miles back to Santa Maria, where he came from. I was formally arrested, and we chatted amicably about life and the universe as we headed off with the Camaro following until we arrived at the police station. Here the sort of uncompromising desk sergeant you see in films took my particulars (date of birth, mother's maiden name), fingerprinted me and because of the speed I'd been doing banned me from driving in California. As I left the desk $120 poorer he asked me if I was planning to stop anywhere on the way to Los Angeles, and when I said I wasn't his unsmiling response was 'Good!' And so Chris White drove me, Jim, Rod and Russell into Los Angeles for the first time in our lives, much later than expected.

We didn't see The Kinks, we didn't pass go, but fortunately I didn't go to jail. I don't know if I was banned for life as far as driving in California is concerned, but I'm certainly not going to put it to the test by asking the question almost forty years after the event.

The next time I made that trip was ten years later with my wife and the mother of my two children. I'll fill you in on the details when we get to that bit.

Ricki and I went out together for several years, and eventually decided it was time to get married. We set a date for early 1971, and the plans were well advanced until the slight elongation of Argent's second US tour with the likes of Jeff Beck and the Moody Blues got in the way. We had to postpone the wedding and the stag night organised by Lem Lubin for a while. The stag night was eventually held in the Golden Lion pub in Hoddesdon and carried on at Nic Kinsey's house round the corner, where we continued drinking and watched the traditional blue films. No one of a religious persuasion was compromised because this was the time when Standard 8 films had been superseded by Super 8 and the old projectors were completely incompatible – so much so that each frame burst into flames as it went through the gate of the projector, which kept us amused for almost two minutes. Nic had speakers set into the floor of his semi-detached house, and with the visual stimulation part of the evening gone we decided to carry on with the audio portion of the entertainment. Somebody must have been putting alcohol in my drink, because the next thing I remember was being woken up by Lem in a bus shelter a couple of miles away from Nic's place. He'd become worried, and even though he was what my kids describe as 'off his face' he'd sacrificed himself in those pre-breathalyser days to search for me on his Vespa GS scooter. Having found me, he realised he was too drunk to drive, so left it parked on the bus stop. We stumbled back to Hoddesdon together. Unfortunately, in his relief at finding the missing bridegroom-to-be, he forgot to switch the scooter's engine off, and it ran on through the night until the engine seized. It never worked again, and has been something of a bone of contention between us ever since!

I finally pledged my troth at my old church, St Joseph's in Waltham Cross. Tuesday 13 July 1971 was the beginning of life for me. (Prophetically Carole King was number 1 in the US with 'It's Too Late', but unfortunately for the music world Middle of the Road's 'Chirpy, Chirpy, Cheep, Cheep' was top of the pops here.) The night before we'd had a gig in the Midlands at Cannock Forum, and instead of going back to the flat opposite the King's Head on the green in Winchmore Hill where I'd been living 'over the broom' with Ricky for some time, I went to my parents' house in Waltham Cross. We weren't observing these proprieties for my strict Catholic parents (who by then were resigned to my immoral behaviour and only complained to each other about it) but for Ricki's dad, who was doing his best to put a brave face on the situation. He still hadn't fallen in love with me.

Lem from Unit 4+2 was by this time head of A&R for Rocket Records, and he had kindly agreed to act as best man. We turned up in a convertible Lotus Elite borrowed from my pal Woodsy (aka Mood), togged out in canvas suits (really) from Stirling-Cooper at the posh end of Wigmore Street. Mine was basic black with the amazingly close-fitting arms that clothes had in the early seventies, worn with some red patent leather shoes I bought in Munich. Lem's was much the same, but with white horizontal bands across the front which from a distance made him look like a skeleton. Ricki's lace dress came from Biba, and she looked absolutely stunning. She still has it just in case one of my rapidly ageing kids wants to get married one day. (That said, I can't imagine James or Jos looking right in it, mainly because they're too tall.) I haven't been able to look at myself in the wedding photos four decades after the event. My look is absolutely perfect for early seventies rock stars, but that doesn't mean I have to like it. Like just about everybody else at the event, my hair was long, dark and lustrous – except for the women. Their hair was long, *blonde* and lustrous.

The ceremony passed without a hitch, except for Ricki having to promise to let me bring up any children we might have in the Catholic faith, thus guaranteeing them somewhere to go on a Sunday.

Afterwards we journeyed out into rural Hertfordshire towards St Albans, to a country club owned by a seed merchant from Waltham Cross, where Ricki and I often went if I wasn't working. Fortunately the sun shone on the just and the unjust at the reception, so we were able to overflow onto the lawn to drink the champagne provided by Jon Waxman, who was head of A&R at CBS in New York. He eventually saw the error of his ways and left the artistic side of the 'shark-filled trench' that is the music business to go back to school to become a show-biz lawyer. (As Hunter S. Thompson once accurately wrote, 'The music business is a cruel and shallow money trench, a long plastic hallway where thieves and pimps run free and good men die like dogs. There's also a negative side.'

Ever since The Roulettes gave up the unequal fight, after our *bon temps en la belle France*, Johnny 'Mod' Rogan had fronted a trio strictly for functions like weddings and bar mitzvahs with Russell's brother Roy, so we didn't have to think too hard about who'd provide the music at our nuptials. It's a well-known fact among my friends and family that I live to dance, and to ensure that Ricki and I started off, the dancing Mod threatened to begin the proceedings with Simple Simon says, with his own unexpurgated words! As soon as the food was served and the speeches were over Ricki and I, along with Russell and Janet, rushed to the airport for our honeymoon in Marbella. To set the record straight, even though Russell and I were friendly it wasn't *that* kind of honeymoon. Russell and Janet came with us to the Costa del Sol but stayed in a different hotel – taking advantage of the fact that the Henrits were honeymooning (so Argent couldn't be rushing up and down the motorways of Europe for a week) to grab a much needed break. Russell was becoming dangerously fatigued by the non-stop touring and recording schedule, but we certainly didn't know it then. I suspect we all thought we shared the same degree of tiredness and that we'd be rejuvenated after a week off and some TLC. In Russell's case we were badly wrong.

Russell's mental health had been deteriorating steadily over the years, and by the time Argent was at its height he had become increasingly less able to cope with the stresses and strains of stardom. He sought professional medical help from Dr Drexler, who was the band's expatriate American Harley Street doctor, who referred him initially to a psychiatrist named Sutton (who immediately asked for an autograph for his son). Eventually, after being prescribed the wrong pills and, as Russell puts it, consultations with 'shrinks' up and down Harley Street, he found his way to another chap called Dennis Freedman, who helped.

The views that Russell had about musical direction were quietly at variance with Rod's, and weren't helping his mental equilibrium at all. In short, if Russell was rock 'n' roll, Rod was jazz. Of course we were playing progressive rock at the time, which was designed to allow us musicians to stretch out in the same way jazz players did, but nevertheless the market-place we were in was all about songs and hit records. Hadn't 'Hold Your Head Up' had the long and brilliant keyboard solo taken out by the record label so it would be more acceptable to popular radio stations? To be fair, the albums were selling well because of these extemporisations rather than in spite of them, and if I'm honest I enjoyed seeing how far I could push my technique just as much as Rod did. But the fact remains that the world, according to CBS/Epic, having already been given something they liked in their millions, would have preferred 'Hold Your Head Up Mk II' or even 'Son of Hold Your Head Up'. The biggest surprise of my career was the relatively slow progress through the Top 20 of our single 'God Gave Rock and Roll to You'. I really expected it to be number 1 everywhere, as did CBS/Epic, but it wasn't. In retrospect it would probably have benefited from the same drastic editing by the record company that 'Hold Your Head Up' had received.

But there I go again. I was supposed to be talking about Russell. As I see it, the whole thing came to a head during our American tour of 1972 when he was struggling to do even the ordinary things in life, like washing, eating, drinking and sleeping; never mind standing up being a scintillating rock god in front of thousands of people. It seems strange to me now to remember that all the professionals around us, managers, record company people, agents and even doctors, felt that the best therapy for him was to give him the 'normality' of being on the road. We were playing gigs for three days with the fourth day off, ostensibly to save the guys' voices, but in reality simply allowing us to travel further and wider. American tour itineraries issued at the beginning of the tour, and known to everybody as 'the book of lies', listed cities, gigs, hotels and flight information, and invariably stated 'day off, long drive'.) It's possibly germane to mention that the first Argent tour had lasted fifty-one days, and the fiftieth plane we boarded brought us home.

It must have been hell for Russell, and of course unless we were experiencing his demons too we'd have no idea what he was going through. I had roomed with him all my life (or at least since mid-1963 when he joined me in The Roulettes), and as he withdrew into himself I was powerless to stop him. Fortunately he wasn't always under the black cloud, and every now and then the old Russell would be there, but the cloud came down without any warning. I remember stumbling among the concrete canyons of New York supporting Russell, who was crying on my arm, and frankly the noise, bustle and general pushiness of the city could make even an untroubled person feel dizzy and off-axis. So what the hell was he doing there? I recently confided in Russell that when he was at his worst I really felt I was being dragged into the abyss too. Frequently we all lost our equilibrium when we took the lift up to Epic on the thirteenth floor of the CBS building. Our visits there invariably coincided with jet-lag, but that said the Big Apple could have an adverse effect on anyone.

We all loved New York and beginning a tour there in all the bands I've been there with was like plugging yourself into the electricity system before starting out. We never felt quite as ready for it if we started in California, Florida or the Mid-West.

The result of Russell's invisible illness was that he left the band, ostensibly to pursue a solo career, but in my opinion there was a more deep-seated reason. As he gradually got himself back to normality he saw that he needed to get away from the pressures of rock 'n' roll, and especially Argent. The daily grind of touring followed by writing songs for the next record (which the record company was pushing for), followed by the actual recording process itself, prised him away from Janet and his young family. On top of this was the pressure and responsibility of not just writing any old songs: they had to be hit songs and better than the last hit songs. You really were only as good as your last million seller! Things were completely different in those days when you toured incessantly to sell more records. Nowadays you sell records to enable you to tour. The business has turned full circle, and the money is in bums on seats. The rest of us had to sacrifice our families to the great god of rock 'n' roll too, but we all hoped we could make amends when we got back home with our pockets full of money. That said, I still haven't taken my daughter Lucy to Disneyland, and even at a little past thirty-five years old she brings the subject up a lot!

Speaking of the recording process . . . when we got our first 'Advance against royalties' from CBS some time in 1969, Nic Kinsey suggested that rather than spend our soon-to-be-hard-earned money in somebody else's studio, we should use the advance to equip our own – ensuring that by the time we got the second advance of (say) £75,000 we'd have it all to ourselves – and we could hire out the studio to other interested parties when we weren't in it. Needless to say we ignored him, and when Argent finally came to an end we'd invested probably a dozen of those advances and extra money borrowed from the record company, with nothing other than the records we'd produced to show for it.

I remember in 1973 we went round to Mel Collins's house for a swim in his pool, whereupon he gave us a royalties cheque each for £3,000 and said we'd never have to worry about money again. As Bruce Welch succinctly put it in his book, 'Rock and Roll, I gave you the best years of my life.'

I was doing a gig at the Opera House in Milan. The promoter told us there might be trouble because throughout Europe anarchist students felt that all concerts should be free. While their Italian counterparts were anxious to see us they weren't going to pay for the experience, whatever anybody said. Nothing untoward happened and nobody stormed the building, so we got on with the show. Halfway through, at the usual spot in the show when Jim's bladder needed to be emptied, I launched into my drum solo aka The Fakir, threw my sticks away, attacked the cymbals with my belt and got stuck into the sensitive passage where I played with my hands. I had to keep my head down and really aim accurately, so I didn't inadvertently bloody my knuckles on sharp drum bits and cymbals, and I wasn't paying attention to the audience. All of a sudden this quiet booing started, which soon became deafening. I was miffed, because aside from a full and recently opened beer can whacking me on the back of the head in Paris once, nobody had ever taken exception to my drum solo. I looked up, and there was a line of dozens of Milanese riot police standing in front of me in case the building was stormed, wearing helmets with visors down, flak jackets, heavy boots, night sticks and riot shields. If they'd hammered on their shields in time with what I was doing the audience would have thrown bodies. As it was, the police's menacing presence quickly caused them to lose interest, and the gig was effectively over. Still, it wasn't all bad. We were staying in a hotel in a narrow side street called Via London, outside which all the ladies of the night congregated until the early hours. Our hotel was not particularly salubrious but very entertaining, since the bar was absolutely packed with these professionally friendly, semi-naked and highly colourful ladies. Of course, as they used to say in the more salacious newspapers I delivered on a Sunday, we made our excuses and left.

Argent played with Jo Jo Gunn in Detroit when 'Run, Run, Run' was doing well in the charts, and Asylum Records threw a reception for them in a suite in their hotel – the Hilton. We all got very drunk. I noticed Jim had disappeared, and finally discovered him at reception arguing loudly about what a terrible hotel it was, because the lock on his door had been changed and he couldn't get in. Unfortunately we were staying at the Howard Johnson – down the street – and the concierge pointed that out to him as reasonably as he could. We walked Argent's belligerent bass player back to Ho-Jo's as a police car cruised innocently past. Still seething from his encounter with authority at the Hilton, Jim shouted the well-known Fabulous Furry Freak Brothers phrase at the cops: 'Off the pigs!' Needless to say they U-turned immediately to chase us, as we sprinted with Jim the last few hundred yards back to the safety of Ho-Jo's. It was only relative safety, because Detroit's finest didn't give up. They wanted Jim badly, and having sealed off the place they started searching the corridors as we breathlessly managed to get into our respective rooms. We were touring incessantly in those days and all had identical Samsonite suitcases in different colours that we never really unpacked: we simply opened the lids and took out whichever freebie T-shirt was cleanest. Jim was sharing with Don Broughton, who was running sound for us, and as we bundled him into his room before fleeing next door to our own he nonchalantly threw up into his suitcase before collapsing on his bed. The next morning his search for the source of that awful smell led him in the direction of his suitcase – which had closed because of the force of his Technicolor yawn. Having discovered all the tomatoes and carrots he didn't realise he'd eaten the day before, he promptly blamed Don!

John Verity supported us in the UK while promoting his first album. This was at a time when the three Leslie speaker cabinets for Rod's Hammond organ were frequently stashed in the support band's dressing room, and the noise rendered it uninhabitable while we were on stage. This didn't exactly endear Argent to him, but because this was definitely going to be Russell's last tour, JV eventually had a phone call from Mel Collins asking if he would be interested in joining us. He says it had nothing to do with the racket he'd endured, but he refused at first – claiming he preferred to work on his own stuff. Eventually he gave in and threw his lot in with us. It was felt by some that if JV was going to take care of the vocals we would need a guitarist too. I didn't agree, but nevertheless an advert was placed in *Melody Maker* and we held auditions for a guitarist, with applications from lots of luminaries: Andy Summers, a guy from the New Seekers who turned up in a Rolls Royce, Garth Watroy from East of Eden and Pete Thompson, the Australian singer from Manfred Mann's Earth Band and lots more.

In the end a very young guy, only by coincidence from St Albans, called John Grimaldi got the gig. He was without a doubt a virtuoso, playing cello, violin and guitar, and ostensibly a most interesting character. He was not only a descendant of the European circus family and related to the clown the Great Grimaldi, but he was also the true heir to the throne of Monaco: according to him, his line had been usurped by the Rainiers who were nothing but pretenders to the throne. Naturally, like everything else in this book, I write this 'without prejudice' – but this was certainly his story.

John G. came from a privileged background and had rebelled against authority long before he joined us. He either ran away from an upmarket public school called Haileybury in Hertfordshire or had been expelled from it – or both. His family wasn't happy with him at that time, and I don't suppose they liked him getting involved with a long-haired rock band like Argent either. He really was a long curly-haired version of Harry Enfield's 'Kevin the teenager', and petulant in the extreme. As I said he had a prodigious talent and was capable of playing absolutely anything Rod asked of him, but discipline was not a word he understood. Even rock authority figures like record company executives, promoters, managers, agents and pluggers were all treated with absolute disdain. He was also the only guitarist I met who hated Jimi Hendrix!

Poor John G. died of MS. I don't want to speak ill, but to be honest he played with us for three years and I'm having trouble remembering anything good he did. I distinctly remember him throwing his guitar down onto the wooden stage and walking off during a gig in America because he felt Rod was soloing for too long! He had a double-neck guitar with twelve and six strings like Jimmy Page, but invariably forgot to turn off one neck while playing the other – which certainly didn't make for the cleanest of sounds. We went to watch the Chambers Brothers in a club somewhere in America, and John really didn't get it. They were responsible for a song called 'Time Has Come Today' and a wonderful 12/8 version of 'People Get Ready', and I really liked them. At the end of the show one of the brothers said politely he'd like to thank the audience for coming. and John's loud response was: 'I'd like to thank the Chambers brothers for stopping!'

John Verity tells me that he went to see John G. on his deathbed, and he apologized for his terrible behaviour. Despite everything, he was a good artist, and was responsible for the covers for both the albums he played on: *Circus* and *Counterpoints*.

This Mark II period of Argent coincided with John Vee's 'fitting' days. He was an epileptic who knew when the fits were coming but was unable to do anything about it – especially if we were on the stage. Every now and again he'd have to be taken off the stage and we'd finish the number abruptly. Rod would sing another song while John sat in the dressing room in the recovery position. This was at a time when the perceived wisdom was that the most important thing was to stop the poor person having the fit from swallowing his tongue. I recall the suggestion that we put a shoe into his mouth, which created another problem – a broken jaw. He decided he wasn't going to take his medication for the rest of his life, so weaned himself off it. I'm not sure if I'm spilling the beans here but John knew when the fit was coming because he saw red bubbles in the corners of his vision. He discovered that if he took cocaine at this time the whole thing went away. He talked to medical people about this breakthrough, but believe it or not they dismissed his findings!

Tel and us singing in Studio 2 at EMI

Ideal Home exhibition, Leeds

Adam Faith.

**Tel's autograph—or
possibly Russell's**

Roulettes at NZ airport in 1962

Roulettes—wallies with brollies

Roulettes Mk1—kicking

Rondart and Jean

Three or perhaps four beauty queens at Margate

Russell outside EMI and my
first 'Beetle'

Richard Anthony before

Richard Anthony after

The Units

Cricket at Margate

Tommy Moeller and Russell Ballard: three words

Alec Issigonis Mini

Grandad Bob's swing: note cocked wrists and completely straight left arm

Fred Dailey and my grandad at the home of golf

Bob and Bobby

*Why won't they let
these fellers sing*

Chapter Five: DOWN THE MINES AGAIN

I mentioned the Deutsche Museum earlier, which is huge and celebrates everything German. It's a tremendously interesting place which had at that time, besides an Apollo capsule with re-entry burns all over it, a U-boat cut in two from stem to stern so you could see everything –. my favourite exhibit there. I was frightened yet fascinated by it in the same way I'm morbidly fascinated by crocodiles and snakes. I realise my claustrophobia wouldn't have allowed me to go down in it were I to have been unfortunate enough to have been born with a 'ze' at the end of my surname and conscripted into the German submarine service during the war. That said, I was most disappointed to discover they'd removed it when I went there while doing a short German tour with Russell B. in 2007. All was not lost because they'd replaced it with a desert-camouflaged Messerschmitt 109 of the Luftwaffe's Spanish Condor squadron. I've always had an affinity for the Spanish Civil War, so maybe I was there in a previous life – although I suspect if I was I'd have been one of those unfortunates Franco's Nationalistas and Hitler's Luftwaffe were bombing the life out of around Guernica.

In the afternoon on a Sunday at the PN club German bands came in to play, and we were all mystified by one called Amon Düül 2. They were a punk band in 1969 (several years before punk was invented) who sat on the floor and were either terribly good or terribly bad, I couldn't work out which. Rumour had it that the original band, Amon Düül (without any designative number), had all committed suicide. Curious!

At the time I was affecting a new sartorial style, which consisted of a navy blue school-type Burberry raincoat worn in all weathers, small Fair Isle jumpers from a very expensive shop called W. Bill on London's Bond Street, Levi 501s, and big hair. I had learned how to back-comb it having seen Oliver Tobias wearing this style when he was appearing in *Hair* in the West End. I went to see the show in 1968 at the Shaftesbury Theatre, but resisted the urge to get up on the stage. rip my clothes off and dance naked. However, I rather think that my wife-to-be, who went with dangerous friends, gave into the temptation.

There was a clothes boutique next to the club and I was ready for a new pair of Levis, so I went in wearing my mac. Because the young lady behind the counter didn't understand my 'Haben sie Funf Nul Ein, bitte?' I was forced to demonstrate to her what I was looking for by opening my raincoat up and showing her my jeans with a button fly. Unfortunately I'd not been too diligent last time I visited the loo and it was an *un-buttoned* button fly. She was very young and very shocked, and I was lucky I wasn't arrested for flashing!

Funnily enough we did a song from *Hair* in the Argent set. It was 'Aquarius', hardly a 'prog rock' tune – but we certainly turned it into something it wasn't. It was a tour-de-force. We went through all sorts of musical styles and time signatures before coming back to the tune ten minutes later (although it was in 6/8, which certainly wasn't the same meter as the original). As I recall Russell and I thrashed-out the idea for this while walking along a beach in St Tropez.

Active management had allowed us to have a rest, and we decided to take the Yobmobile to our old haunts in the South of France. We booked a villa for me, Ricki, Janet and Russell just outside Beaulieu. It had an airfield that we'd landed at a couple of years earlier when flying into the Nice and Cannes area. (This was one of the landing places where Richard Anthony had to donate to airport charities after landing without a licensed pilot.) We spotted this villa in the *Sunday Times*, where it was described as quiet, close to the beach and perfect for a relaxing holiday. It was indeed close to the beach, but much closer to the RN7 motorway to Nice, Cannes, Monte Carlo and the rest of the Cote d'Azur. To make matters worse, not only was the autoroute on one side but the high-speed TGV railway from Paris to Spain was on the other – and the noise was indescribable. We moved out 'tout de suite', lying to the owners that Russell was getting over a nervous breakdown and needed peace and quiet! One should never tempt fate. The owner gave us our money back, and we found our way further west to our old haunts in St Tropez. Our plan was to look-up Richard Anthony and perhaps stay with him, but he was out of town. Eventually we found a campsite at Cogolin, a few kilometres away from the hedonism and all-night traffic jams of 'San Trop' itself. We stayed in these giant upturned parasol-topped polystyrene cups for a restful few days, until the lovely Ricki went swimming in the Mediterranean with all our money hidden in her bikini! We had just enough money to get home, and I drove the Yobmobile all the way back in something like twelve hours, non-stop. Ah, those were the days!

We took this 'Aquarius' idea to its illogical conclusion on the stage for the first show in the PN, because while the club wasn't packed we could pretty much do as we liked. What we actually did was start our daily marathon nine show stint by playing the old John Lee Hooker song 'Dimples' as a shuffle. As minutes went by, with just a nod or a look I'd change the feel of the tune or the time signature or the tempo, and keep on changing it until it was time to take a break forty-five minutes later. This was great fun, and among other things it's where we got the idea for the rumba-type rhythm we used in 'Hold Your Head Up'. For the rest of the half-a-dozen spots we'd do our usual stuff like 'Stepping Stone', 'My Days Are Numbered', 'Natural Woman' (albeit with slightly different, more macho lyrics: 'I make you feel, I make you feel, I make you feel like a natural woman . . .' We also played various Zombies songs like 'She's Not There' and 'Time of the Season', as well as a few rock 'n' roll standards like 'What'd I Say' and 'Hi-Heel Sneakers'. In the last show of the night the indefatigable Fred Wilkinson used to get a chance to sing his own composition, which was a twelve bar blues shuffle, which consisted solely of these evocative lyrics: 'One, two, three, four, five, six, sev-en, eight, nine'.

There was a shoe shop on the other side of the road from the PN where I bought a pair of black and and a pair of red patent leather slip-on shoes. The red ones were destined for my bottom-drawer and I wore them for my wedding a year or so later.

At the very end of the roadworks, which had completely taken over the length of the Leopoldstrasse in preparation for the 1972 Olympics, was a very modern café called Le Drugstore, where unusually I found myself all alone to eat one afternoon. Normally we ate together before the show; maybe that day the others were obliviously tucking into chicken guts at The Weinerwald, while I knew the truth. I looked at the menu. Each meal had a number in front of it: all you had to do was order by number. I fancied something a bit different. Recognising that 'schweine' was probably gammon I ordered that with chips: 'Nummer drei, bitte.' I refuse to believe it was my accent, but instead of the gammon that I had my taste buds ready for, the Bavarian waitress brought me nummer zwei – tripe and spinach with a sloppy egg on top. As a musician, there's not a lot I haven't eaten of necessity, but to say I hate all three of these things would be a huge understatement – I detest them! But I didn't have sufficient words in German to say 'Please take this terrible food away' although I could say 'nein' and 'sheiss kuchen'. Anyway in the end I was so hungry I ate everything on the plate. I'd like to say I'm now more comfortable with eating tripe, but it certainly isn't true: it's still cow's stomach cooked in milk. I haven't eaten any since.

This language thing in Germany, although often problematic, was actually fun, and we'd often make-up the German equivalent of Franglais. Somehow in Munich we learned a new phrase: 'Die plattenspieler ist kaput'. One day we came into the club and there was no music playing. Norbert behind the bar told us why: 'Die plattenspieler ist kaput'. I believe Norbert 'batted for the other side'. He had his moments of reporting us to the owner, who could best be described as a despot, if we transgressed by playing a set that was a couple of minutes short. But sometimes he surprised us by giving us free drinks when we'd used up our meagre allowance of beer tokens. In some clubs these were coins engraved 'Gut fur eine bier', but at the PN they were small, easily mislaid, easily spent certificates.

I mentioned Herr Pieter Neumann was something of a despot, but he was more of a dictator. We realised this on the very first day when we were manhandling the gear down the narrow twisting stairs into the club. On the very walls on which we were bashing our precious knuckles, because of the PA cabinets, Hammond organ and Leslies, were murals of PN himself with his bristling moustache, holding the strings of rock group marionettes with Beatle haircuts, narrow ties and tight-fitting suits. He saw himself as a manipulator, and in his domain he certainly was. Still we didn't care, we were taking advantage of his facilities to hone our act and get it ready for the upcoming US tour.

A little later we played at the Zoom club in Frankfurt, which was a lot more rock 'n' roll than most clubs in Germany. Something had changed: people weren't there to buy sex (although they probably wouldn't turn it down if it was free); they were there for the music. This was great for us because we actually had an appreciative German audience, and we didn't have to play until the club owner said we could stop. We only played three, sometimes four spots a night. The Zoom didn't allow much room for the band, and by this time we had so much gear we filled up all but the most accommodating of club stages. I had two bass drums by this time and two floor toms, Rod had at least a Hammond organ, one or two mini-Moogs, a Hohner Pianette electric piano (left over from the Zombies) and a clavinet. (Fortunately he hadn't acquired a mellotron yet!) Even though Russell and Jim weren't using as many 4x12 cabinets for their amplifiers as they owned there still wasn't much room, and we stood very close to one another.

Funnily enough we played at the Cavern in Liverpool around then, and there was so little space for all our gear that we set up in a line with me at the back, Jim in front of me, then Rod with Russell in front of him. No wonder The Beatles held their guitars at such an acute angle, John, George and Paul couldn't have stood alongside each other inside one of those brick arches otherwise.

But I digress. A couple of nights into the Zoom Club residency we started the first show with 'Stepping Stone', and all of a sudden Russell was back in the drums alongside me holding the mic stand with one hand and his guitar with the other. At first I thought he was just doing what we called 'freaking out', in other words really getting into the act – even though it was only the first song. Eventually the penny dropped when I noticed a fierce blue light arcing around the whole of his body and the guitar, even around the tuners on his Fender. I realised he was in trouble and stood up to steady him, grabbing him with both hands. In some ways this was a big mistake, because it meant I took the electric shock across my heart too, but it meant I was sharing the voltage and he wasn't getting quite so much of it. I was dressed in my usual stage clothes: dungarees tucked into long leather boots with rubber soles from Miss Selfridge (please don't ask!), so I was isolated from the stage and able to kick out frantically with my feet. Eventually I bent the microphone stand, which wrenched the wires from the microphone and thankfully broke the circuit between it and the guitar. Everything went deathly quiet, and the next thing I remember was a bunch of paramedics arriving to work on Russell, swiftly followed by a squad of Grenzpolitzei to close the club while they investigated what went wrong. Russell went to hospital for a thorough check-out, and we all returned to continue the gig a couple of days later.

For many years the guys trusted their lives to some circuit-breakers that we bought from a company in Newcastle, and I remember us telling Alex Harvey's brother Les about them at a gig once in about 1972. Unfortunately he didn't have time to buy one since he was electrocuted at a gig at Swansea Top Rank ballroom while playing with Stone the Crows very shortly after. One day somebody decided to test the Argent ones, and guess what? They didn't work!

I have another electric-shock story. This happened to The Roulettes when we were doing a Sunday concert in Weston-Super-Mare (that has to be the most pretentious seaside place-name in Britain) at the Winter Gardens. Anyhow, the stage at the theatre was a semicircle, and the curtains ran around the circumference. We started the second half with our usual few minutes before Tel came on, and as the curtains opened Thorpey, Mod and Russell walked forward and nonchalantly held the mics and their guitars ready to sing. Then, spectacularly, Thorpey and Mod went straight up into the air in an arc like Flash Gordon rocket ships, before crashing down. They lay there completely immobile, and it was immediately evident something had gone terribly wrong. The curtains closed as Tel ran onto the stage. He knew exactly what to do – and kicked their feet vigorously and determinedly until they regained consciousness. He was a black belt in aikido and karate, having studied with Thorpey during our Bridlington season, and had been taught that kicking the soles of the feet was the antidote to electric shock. It worked, and thanks to Tel another rock 'n' roll tragedy was averted. Some time afterwards, when we were at last able to laugh about the incident, I was able to tell them I'd had a bird's-eye view of the proceedings, and that with Russell in the middle their trajectory had taken them in equal arcs out to stage left and stage right. It was fantastic, but hopefully never to be repeated!

I've had lots of untoward things happen onstage over the years, but one of the most potentially dangerous was when we were in New York with Argent. We were beginning the second tour just as 'Hold Your Head Up' was really beginning to happen. At the end of the very last encore we were all what we called 'building a shed' on the last chord, when Russell would make his guitar feedback and swing it round above his head. (He'd have his fingers in the holes that Jim Wilkinson had bored into the guitar more or less for that purpose.) When we'd made enough racket and were running out of steam he'd throw the still screaming guitar into the air while I carried on with my roll; then as he caught it I would shut the door. It looked great and we'd done it successfully many many times before. Unfortunately nobody saw fit to warn the house lighting guy about what was going on, and as the guitar sailed into the air the lights went out. Blackout. We all knew the heavy and solid Fender guitar was in the air, but didn't know where. Eventually Russell found it, or rather it found him. Like a circus performer he had his eyes looking up, and the guitar bashed him on the nose. *Variety*, the showbiz magazine, specialised in succinct headlines – and they reported it as: 'Ballard Bends Beak'.

I have a great many of these stories, so stop me when you're getting bored.

In the 1970s everybody had an intro tape to get the audience into the right mood before the show, and Argent's was Ravel's 'Bolero'. There'd be at least fifteen minutes of it before we were on. As soon as we got to the bit which I called the elephants trumpeting I knew we were close, although often as Ravel reached a crescendo we still wouldn't be ready. Invariably the first thing Rod would say to the audience was, 'Sorry to keep you waiting.' To avoid this anti-climax I always thought we should have started the music when we were ready – but we never did!

Anyhow we found ourselves at The Agora, a huge club in Columbus, Ohio, and even though we'd done the soundcheck Russell hadn't explored the stage. Once Ravel had done his thing one of the Super-Trouper spotlights would pick me up as I hit the gong and another would pick-up Russell as he played the four bar arpeggiated riff while walking forward, a bit like Bonnie Raitt. On the first beat of the fifth bar I'd whack the gong again and we'd be into the first section of an instrumental called 'The Coming of Kahoutek'. After two bars he found the step on the stage that he hadn't noticed before, and as he stumbled down it the guitar strap came off its button and the Fender 'kerranged' to the floor! It was yet another Spinal Tap moment, and all we could do was laugh and start again.

For those of you who don't know, Kahoutek was a huge anti-climax, much like the beginning of the show that night. It was a comet which was due to arrive in 1971 and supposed to be the biggest comet since Halley's, which had last appeared in 1910. But after all the hype, Kahoutek's trajectory made it nearly invisible. Unfortunately our album *Nexus*, which had 'The Coming of Kahoutek' as its first track, was already made by the time the comet failed to arrive.

Normally when something untoward happened, like a serious equipment malfunction, the only remedy to try to keep the audience happy was for me to do an impromptu drum solo. This was fine providing it didn't take too long to fix the problem. We were at the very beginning of the second US tour. Having learned our financial lessons from the first tour, we hadn't bought our own gear with us. We weren't used to what we had and were playing in the middle of an American football field at Varsity Stadium in Toronto. I remember the headliners didn't turn up but can't recall who they were (Ten Years After, Wishbone Ash, the Moody Blues?). If you ask Jim Rodford he'll tell you. We were promoted to closing the show and the first song went fine, but something major went wrong with the amps immediately afterwards. No problem: I launched into the aforementioned impromptu drum solo. The amps were fixed, and we played a few more songs before the organ packed up, so another drum solo was necessary. The only problem was that once the organ was fixed it was time for 'The Fakir' – which was my drum solo!

Incidentally, even though it was *de rigueur* at the time, the real reason we had a drum solo in Argent was because of Jim's weak bladder! He needed to go to the loo quite a lot, but his problems really began when we were in the Kinks together. Because we didn't have a drum solo to allow him to legitimately leave the stage, he needed the insurance of a bucket in the wings.

On the first Argent tour we played at a college in Dayton, Ohio, and as we were coming off the great B.B. King was going on. He put his arms around 'Lucille' to protect her as our paths crossed, beamed at me and said, 'Sounds good, man!' It was another special moment, and I'm really hoping BB doesn't say that to every body he plays with.

A few weeks later back in the UK we were playing with Uriah Heep at University College London (the building you see as a hospital in all those black and white films about doctors). There was quite a step from the dressing room to the stage down several darkened corridors and through several glass doors. This was long before glass doors had flying birds on them so you knew they were there, and Russell, in his anxiety to get to the stage, walked straight through one and split his nose. There was blood and glass everywhere, and we couldn't begin the gig until the bleeding had stopped.

We flew to America a great deal in those days, and like the Kinks and assorted other bands we always went with Air India, who gave us all sorts of concessions since we were deemed CIPs: Commercially Important Passengers. The only downside was their planes didn't always take off for New York on the day they were supposed to. This was a tour-manager's nightmare because it meant you didn't dare book a gig for the day after you landed. The Kinks' tour manager, Ken Jones, secured them an even better deal with Gulf Air, a Middle-Eastern carrier that gave them a deal on flying the equipment too.

The first time we went to New York we took off on time and we enjoyed ourselves immensely. In those days the in-flight entertainment was very different to nowadays. Even though the music was available at your seat via painful in-ear headphones, which you needed to pay a couple of dollars for, the film was shown on screens that unrolled from the ceiling in some planes or were on the bulkhead behind the galleys on others. This first transatlantic flight showed *Cabaret*, and since we had bulkhead seats we had to slip down as low as we could in them to watch it. This of course made Liza Minelli's face look much narrower than usual. I'm guessing we might have had a drink or two, but it was still light when we arrived so we could see the whole of the evocative New York skyline through the porthole. Fred turned to me shook my hand and said, 'We made it!' I knew I'd been waiting with bated breath all my life for this moment but I didn't realise old 'salt of the earth' Fred had too.

The first US tour in 1970 was a huge learning curve for us. We shipped everything across the Atlantic by air and took everything we used with us at a cost of £4,000 each way. We even took Rod's Hammond organ. It was a C3 especially built for European use, and therefore worked on a different Hertz rate (US was 60cps and UK was 50). So the Hammond needed a cycle-changer transformer the size of a substantial suitcase to make it go – but it was erratic and didn't always put out the right current. This made the tuning waver and could (and did) result in a very obvious pitch deviation from A440, sometimes in the middle of a song. Had this pitch change been constant and controllable it would have been really good for 'The Fakir', which was in quarter-tones anyway – sort of in the cracks between regular notes. It wasn't exactly 'desafinado' but 'close enough for jazz', and unfortunately it wobbled dangerously as and when it wanted to.

We'd sit on planes on this first tour hearing bumping below us as drums, guitars, amplifiers, organs and even cycle-changing transformers were thrown into the hold. At the end of the tour Dave Basely, our third equipment guy, left at home in the UK for economic reasons, asked whether he should bring a truck to pick up the remains of our gear or a skip! We hadn't heard about flight-cases, and by the time we had it was far too bloody late. Fifty planes in fifty-one days had put paid to any residual value the equipment might have. Fortunately we were heavily endorsed in those days, so most of the gear was easily and painlessly (make that cheaply) replaced.

After the first dizzying attempt I have never smoked, and neither had the other Argents, and at the time we first went to America this was a very good thing. It meant we weren't likely to take anything that was given to us when we had no idea where it came from, or what was in it. It's always been my view that this Russian-Roulette aspect should be enough to stop anybody doing drugs in the first instance. You know what it's supposed to be but there's certainly no guarantee that's what it is. Robbie Williams famously said something along the lines of, 'Often the only thing you have in common with the guy who's selling it to you in some dodgy bedsit at three in the morning is the drug itself.' This tour was around the time that Robbie Mackintosh, the Average White Band's drummer, died taking something he thought was something else. It was also when the keyboard player from Atomic Rooster flipped out after someone generously spiked his drink with an hallucinogen. I don't think Vincent Crane ever recovered. This drink spiking was something we had to guard against in those days, and we would never knowingly return to a beer we'd left earlier. We'd always open a new one.

Therefore it was a travesty of justice that the single 'Sweet Mary' (from our second album *Ring of Hands*), which was well on the way to being a sizeable hit, should have been stopped in its tracks by being banned on the radio for drug references. We all know now that 'Mary' was slang for marijuana in America at the time but nobody told us, especially not CBS. As bad luck would have it the Roulettes record 'Long cigarette' was also removed from playlists a decade earlier, when the BBC banned tobacco advertising.

I wasn't exactly naïve about drugs, but apart from the AN1 episode in Köln and the headache-inducing caffeine tablets I'd taken with Unit 4 I hadn't indulged. As non-smokers we didn't have the ability or mechanism to do it. And, having seen the whole audience lying flat on the floor at Fillmore West when we played there with John Mayall and Duster Bennet, this didn't exactly make us rush to join them in getting high. (We were already getting a vicarious hit from what the audience were indulging in whether we liked it or not.) That said, everybody we knew who turned on was always going to 'get it together, man' while they were high, but mostly never remembered what they had said when they were straight. That said, a lot of them never got straight again.

When we arrived in LA in May '71 we were invited to Eric Burdon's thirtieth birthday party. It was a glittering affair where there were more stars than you could shake a stick at, including Jimi Hendrix. Eric had just recorded with his new group War (the record being produced by none other than Chris Huston), and of course they played. I remember getting up for a jam with Mike Nesmith, whose song 'Flying down to Rio' remains one of my favourites: It's only a whimsical notion, to fly down to Rio tonight, I probably won't fly to Rio, but then again I just might . . .' I don't remember playing any Monkees songs that afternoon. I was chatting to Mitch Mitchell, Hendrix's drummer, and he had this big chap next to him trying to look as conspicuous as he could with a large bulge inside the jacket of his mohair suit. Noel Redding had one of these guys too, so I asked Mitch who they were and he told me they just appeared one day and said they were going to look after them from then on! Mitch, Jimi and Noel each had one of these chaps, who went everywhere with them.

Someone had provided a birthday cake, which was reputed to be full of hash (or was it grass?), and since we had a gig that night at the Hollywood Palladium we resisted the temptation to indulge – but we took some to eat later when we had a couple of days off. We put it in a drawer at the infamous Hyatt House on Sunset and forgot about it. By the time we ate it a few days later the cake was stale although the drugs inside weren't. We had it for breakfast with a nice cup of tea and headed-off for our first visit to Disneyland in Anaheim. It seemed to be an absolutely wonderful experience, but I think this may have been more to do with the potency of the 'compressed trichomes of the cannabis plant' than Walt Disney's vision of entertainment. I remember being much taken with the Pirates of the Caribbean ride, which surely wasn't really as colourful and exciting as I experienced it that stoned day.

Years later Walt's descendants set up another Disneyland outside Paris, which puts me in mind of a question that was asked at the time. It may well be a joke (or maybe not). What's the difference between Disneyland California and Disneyland Paris? In Paris Snow White doesn't shave under her arms!

While I'm doing confession I might as well admit that somebody (actually Lem Lubin's wife Wendy) once gave me a small piece of magic mushroom to eat while I was in Henrit's Drumstore in Wardour Street, and I walked through the West-End with what would best be described as the most intense and powerful sense of sexual well-being. It was a shame it didn't last until I got home!

Our first album was succinctly called *Argent*, and was mostly recorded at Sound Techniques in Chelsea. The second album was *Ring of Hands*, which we recorded at the EMI studios in St John's Wood. The next one was *All Together Now*, which had a cover with a photo of everybody associated with the band: managers, agents, publishers, press officers, roadies, co-ordinators and their various significant others.

Not long before the second US tour in 1971 something magical and far reaching happened to us. We played at the CBS world-wide convention, which just happened to take place in London. Please allow me to set the scene. Rather like the Olympics the mighty Columbia Broadcasting System picked a city every year to host their convention, which was always a no-expense spared event. Literally everybody who was anybody in the company, directors, A&R men, promotions men, label managers, personal assistants as well as a handful of the most important press and DJs from all over the world descended, and were wined and dined to excess. They had a whale of a time, but CBS wouldn't chuck their money around for nothing. It wasn't just a 'jolly'. As soon as the convention was over these people went back to their own countries and enthused about the things they'd done, but more importantly the new acts they'd seen. As good luck would have it they all loved London, because everybody wanted to come to the 'home' of the Beatles, the Queen, Winston Churchill, William Shakespeare, Charlie Chaplin, Henry VIII and the Beefeaters. And, as even more good fortune would have it, they all loved Argent. We performed along with a lot of other artists like Andy Williams at the Grosvenor Hotel in Park Lane to great acclaim, and the record company bigwigs assured us we would have a hit record.

Imagine the scene. A US 'plugger' goes into a radio station programme director's office with a jar of Harrod's whisky marmalade on the Monday morning after his long weekend in London. Having been given the jam, the PD would ask how the trip had been, and the plugger would tell him how great it was and how he'd seen this band called Argent who were destined to make it to number 1 with their great record called 'Hold Your Head Up'. The PD was the first one in the US to hear it. What did he think? Would he add it to the radio playlist. (The programme directors had absolute control over the playlist, and without their blessings we were sunk.) Of course this was going on on our behalf all over America at different radio stations, and lo it came to pass that we had a hit record, just as the mighty Clive Davis and Ron Alexenberg had said when we chatted together after the convention. It didn't make it to the top spot everywhere, because nationally it was kept out by a naff song called 'Brandy' by a New Jersey group called Looking Glass:

Looking Glass sank in that sea without trace a couple of records later, but a lifetime later their song was inexplicably covered by the Red Hot Chilli Peppers.

'Hold Your Head Up' was actually a reissue in the UK. It had been released a while before in all its progressive glory, when it lasted five or six minutes. This didn't make it the sort of record that would get played on ordinary AM radio, where records had to be under three minutes long. To be fair the long version got plays from some DJs, like Alan Freeman and Bob Harris, among others, but it wasn't enough to get it into the charts. Eventually CBS took the bull and the record by the horns and edited it down by themselves to three minutes, without the organ solo, and the rest is history. Rumour has it we got to number 1 in Australia too, twice, although I don't believe this feat was reflected in any royalties we received from down under. Don't get me started!

We didn't make the number 1 spot in the UK either ('Amazing Grace' played on bagpipes by the band of the Royal Scots Dragoon Guards kept us out), but the record was certainly number 1 in Cincinatti where we played with The Kinks on Nobby Daltons's twenty-eighth birthday. I don't think the Dangerous Brothers were too happy that the support band had the top spot and they didn't. We were watching their act from the side of the stage, and were moved away because they didn't like anybody watching from the wings. Life is strange, since within a very few years Jim would join them, followed eventually by yours truly.

The policing of the stage, a peculiar phenomenon (and alien to us), was something that they specialised in on the other side of the pond. Keeping the support band in their place was something all US bands and road crews were exceedingly well versed in. They ensured that even though you had lights and sound as prescribed in the contract, you never had all the lights or all the sound. The p.a. would be run at half strength, as would the lights. There were always technical problems with these things for the opening bands, which were miraculously cured by the time the headliners came on. This extended to the sound-check too, and if the main band hadn't intentionally finished theirs on time you might find yourself without one or having to do it with the audience in position – something of an anti-climax. The other things that were unfairly rationed were the amount of room on the stage available to the support band as well as the number of monitors, length of time on stage, number of dressing rooms, and number of complimentary tickets available, along with lots of other things designed to demoralise. If the support-band ran over their allotted time it wasn't unusual for them to have the power switched off in mid song.

On the tour before Russell left for some reason we agreed to do a few US dates with Queen as co-headliners. The flaw in this plan is that somebody on a co-headlining show has to go on last, thereby becoming the headliner! I'm sure the idea was that we would close the show on alternate nights, but have no recollection of that happening. My only recollection is of animosity and unhappiness. As always, Brian May was friendly, but the others certainly weren't. Everything that could go wrong with equipment during our show did. Lights at half-intensity, no-one to man the spotlights, sound only working on one side, insufficient space for our gear; I'm sure you get the picture. All of these faults were of course be fixed by the time Queen hit the stage with 'Killer Queen'! Passaic was the first gig in New Jersey, and we were all really dispirited after the gig. It doesn't matter how good you are if the audience can't see or hear you. To be honest the band may not have known about us being upstaged, but their management and road-crew certainly did.

We also agreed to tour with a very jazzy and progressive outfit called the Mahavishnu Orchestra, which was making huge waves among the progressive-rock audiences of America. They had such a fearsome reputation that nobody wanted to tour with them and be shown up musically. Argent, though, decided they could handle it, and though I say it as shouldn't we fared pretty well. Billy Cobham was their explosive drummer and the guitarist was an Englishman from Doncaster called John McLaughlin, whom I'd last seen in March 1964 wearing a Harris-tweed sports jacket with a packet of French cigarettes in the top pocket, a blue Oxford button-down shirt and a knitted tie. He was playing rhythm guitar with me and Russell in EMI's number 3 studios on an Adam Faith track called 'If He Tells You'. Now he was the world's most revered guitarist, wearing robes and leading the most progressive band on the planet. John was very spiritual and exuded good vibes, and even if he was behind me I could feel he was there. Spooky!

It was on this tour in Atlanta that something went wrong and Billy Cobham didn't make the gig, so Mahavishnu didn't go on. He was said to be asleep in his room, but I'm not sure. I know we went on twice that night to fill the gap. As it happens, Billy was a nice chap, but on this tour he was just getting into photography and always got to the front of the stage to take photos during my drum solo. He had one of those big cube-shaped Hasselblad cameras with a viewfinder in the top and a winder on the side, and even though I tried to blot him out, seeing him there was off-putting. Years later I told him how difficult it had been to play a solo with him standing in front of me every night. He said I had no need to worry because he was only being a photographer. I said that normally I had no trouble with showing off in front of photographers, but this one just happened to be the greatest drummer on the planet.

There are those who would unkindly say that I'm not a musician, I'm only a drummer (see www.drummersjokes.com), but my immediate family certainly are musicians. Ricki played piano and flute, Lucy played piano and a bit of drums, James played proper classical guitar, piano and drums, while Jos, unhindered by musical talent, became a drummer like his old man. He went through the Guildhall exams up to grade six, then taceted for good - or so we thought. Originally he wanted to play guitar, and his brother had taught him a few things before his first proper lesson at Enfield Grammar School. Like his sister, Jos is left-handed, which is excellent for tennis and cricket but not quite so good for playing guitar. We had to get a pal to change the nut on his acoustic guitar so it could be strung upside down. The teacher was singularly un-impressed with this and told him so. He also refused to teach him because he hadn't got a footstool! (If this attitude had prevailed in the '60s none of my pals would have ever made it into music.)

All the little Henrits had piano lessons, although in Jos's case the money wasn't exactly well-spent. He preferred to be out on the tennis court, the football field or the cricket pitch with his brother. Lucy was a real performer though and often did recitals with her piano teacher, Mrs Foster. I was too nervous to be in the concert hall when she was performing; I'd feel physically sick and have to leave.

I wasn't great at watching the boys play competitive tennis either. They were both very good juniors, although once they grew up Jos would have the edge over his brother – but even now I suspect James would kill himself to beat him. James learned his tennis etiquette from John McEnroe, and it became an expensive business keeping him in rackets. (He also used words on the court which frankly he wouldn't have heard a great deal at home. Not from me anyway, although possibly from his mother!) Eventually he found a sport which positively welcomed his aggression and bad language: he began to play water-polo at county level. So far the sibling rivalry between James and Jos hasn't been the same as with Ray and Dave, although if they'd been in a band together I suppose it could have exploded in the same way.

Some time after 'Hold Your Head Up' and around the release of 'God Gave Rock and Roll To You' my old boss came back into my life with a project he wanted me for. Adam Faith had met Dave Courtney, a songwriter who coincidentally had replaced me on drums in The Roulettes and was about to produce records with him. The recording sessions were to take place at Roger Daltrey's studio, a converted barn at his house in Sussex. Dave lived near Brighton and had discovered a harmonica player just down the road in Shoreham-by-Sea and was writing songs with him. The harmonica player's name was Gerry Sayer, soon to be changed to Leo by Adam's wife Jackie, who thought he looked like a lion with his mane of curly hair. Russell Ballard was going to play guitar with me on drums, our pal Dave Wintour on bass and Dave Courtney on piano. A chap called John Mills engineered Roger and Leo's albums. He claimed to have been trained at Tamla Motown! We never managed to verify it, though, and it seemed strange that a guy round the corner from me in Palmers Green could somehow find his way to Detroit and get hired by Berry Gordy. I suppose stranger things have happened in music.

Roger's studio was equipped with one of Moonie's old kits, a red Premier with two mounted toms, something I hadn't experienced before. In Argent I had a single mounted tom between my two bass drums and a couple of different sized floor toms. I reasoned that I wouldn't have two toms the same size, so why would I have two basses the same size? They were an 18in and a 22in, which I was able to put alongside one another with their heads in a straight line to create a new look – and, because their pedals were close together, make them not too stressful to play! I remember Mick Tucker from The Sweet copied me with this, with a pair of larger bass drums. This made me chuckle: they must have had a real impact on his wedding tackle! But I digress. Moonie's kit had a pair of identical sized small toms and, having tuned them to put out different tones, I really got into the concept.

I was living in Winchmore Hill at the time and London to Sussex every day wasn't the easiest of commutes, but we did it, and the results for Leo were excellent. We polished off the *Silverbird* album in double quick time between the barn in Sussex and The Beatles' Apple studios in Savile Row, whereupon Roger Daltrey (who'd been around for all the sessions and liked what he'd heard) decided he wanted an album too. Dave and Leo had a backlog of songs destined for the next album. These were channelled towards Roger, and we all got cracking on that. Strangely Roger's album, *Daltrey*, came out before Leo's. 'The Show Must Go On' got to number 2 in the UK charts in December 1973 and 'One Man Band' to number 6 in June 1974, while Roger had his first solo hit with 'Giving It All Away' in 1973.

The consensus of opinion was that Leo's first hit, 'I'm a One-Man Band' needed a banjo, and since nobody had one a battered example was removed from the wall of the saloon bar at the Kicking Donkey, Roger's local. It was put to very good use. This puts me in mind of a joke. What is the definition of perfect pitch? When the banjo you throw into the rubbish bin lands directly on top of the accordion!

I have an anecdote about One Man Band. Years after the hippies had left the west coast of India for good, Ricki and I went to Goa for a holiday and stayed in a hotel complex on the beach at Bambolim, where I over-indulged my love for Indian food for breakfast, lunch, tea and supper. After supper every evening performers came to the pool area to entertain us. Goa used to be a Portuguese protectorate, and its music is an attractive fusion of Indian with Latin. So this Goan chap arrived, set up his gear and launched into 'Everybody knows down Ladbroke Grove . . .' It was weird hearing 'One Man Band' being played in the sweltering heat while looking-out over the Arabian Sea, considering it was first recorded in a barn deep in the Sussex countryside. Mind you, not as astonishing as hearing an instrumental Muzak version of 'Hold Your Head Up' in a lift in an American skyscraper. If you made it onto a Muzak list you knew you'd really arrived! (Hold the presses. I understand the Ukelele Orchestra of Great Britain do a blinding version of 'God Gave Rock and Roll To You' in their show!)

Having completed these albums, the world woke-up to the songwriting/production team of Faith, Courtney and Sayer, and two more albums were made – one for Tel and another at Le Chateau d'Herouville in France (Elton John's Honky Chateau) for Dave Courtney. The studio had originally belonged to a volatile French composer called Michel Magné, although when we were there another chap called Laurent Thibault was responsible for it. Fleetwood Mac had been there, as well as many progressive bands like Pink Floyd, Jethro Tull, Uriah Heep and even the slightly less-than-progressive Grateful Dead (who had evidently done a live gig in the grounds). Strawberry Studios was what it was called, although I'm not sure it had anything to do with the Manchester studio of the same name.

Russell wasn't coming this time so John V, Jim Rodford and I all flew to Paris to get to the chateau, and having settled in and sorted ourselves out we went to bed early. I had a very comfortable chintzy room all to myself, looking out over a gravelled courtyard. It's pertinent to mention that the night before I'd been to the cinema with Ricki to see David Bowie in *The Man Who Fell to Earth*. I enjoyed the film, and thought David was excellent in it. About midnight I heard crunching on the gravel outside and looked out of my window to see David Bowie bathed in light looking up at my window! He'd arrived there with Iggy Pop and they were looking for a place to hang-out. The chateau was perfect, and the pair of them stayed for a few days. They made suggestions while we routined Dave Courtney's songs in the brick 'cave' that had been the original Chopin Studio. I understand that Bowie was working on *Pin Ups* while he was there with us with Iggy (now known to us as Jim), but I certainly didn't see (or hear) any evidence of it.

As a result of the idyllic surroundings it was a very interesting and relaxed album to make – maybe even too relaxed. The food was fantastic, as were the wine and the ambience after we'd finished for the day. We had Roger Daltrey's cousin with us (Graham Hughes) as official photographer of the proceedings, and he took some evocative pictures. We had to stop recording for a while at around four o'clock each day because clicks kept appearing on the tape. I deduced it was either Chopin's ghost or the French housewives switching on their electric cookers for 'le diner'. It was rumoured that Chopin's ghost inhabited the studio, and one of the rooms is permanently locked because of it. Anyway, the sound of live piano playing was frequently heard at the chateau, when the only piano in the village was at the studio. It was in the vicinity that Fryderyk had his liaison with George Sand.

I don't believe Dave Courtney's record came out at the time but you can certainly get it now: it's called *Midsummer Madness*. I remember Pete Henderson engineered it and Geoff Emerick mixed it. We had a great time.

Just before he left Argent Russell wrote a song called 'I Don't Believe in Miracles', which Colin Blunstone recorded at Abbey Road. I think he had it in mind for Argent, but in the event 'Blunders' got it, although Jim, Rod, Russell and I backed him on it in 1972. I remember I used my new, vintage 'fat' Ludwig and Ludwig snare drum on it, which I'd bought from an Englishman working at Lou Adler's Music Shop in New York on our first tour, for $40.

We always started an American tour by visiting the record company on 6th Avenue, aka Avenue of the Americas, in New York. By the time you got to Epic Records on the thirteenth floor of the CBS building at 51 West 52nd Street, at the corner of 52nd and Sixth Avenue, they'd be playing your record! The A&R department was like an Aladdin's cave, and we always left with boxes of albums which they kindly shipped home for us. I don't know if we were ever billed for this, but I know we ultimately picked up the tab for limos, lost vehicles, and various other things the record company went out of their way to remember.

Like Argent, many bands of the era made a big mistake in the way they contracted themselves to the record company. We all signed in America so we could have 100 per cent of the royalties in the biggest territory. (If you signed in the UK you received reduced royalties for the rest of the world.) The mistake, I'm told, was not signing directly to the record company. Chris and Rod had a production company called Nexus that produced our records and sold them to the Epic division of CBS. At the time this meant nothing when records were selling in their millions, but once we'd left Epic and they wanted their money back it made a *big* difference.

Because, like all record companies, CBS didn't stand still, it was inevitable that eventually we would become part of the furniture. When you leave a record company all the advances against royalties are totted up and set against sales, and only when there's a zero balance can you dream of making money. Unless, of course, you've signed to them indirectly through a production company, in which case you're screwed and as far as I can ascertain you'll never see any money at all! Mind you, hope springs eternal, and it's only around thirty-four years since we left. Still this hasn't stopped them packaging our life's work and putting it out willy-nilly.

As I said, CBS have behaved strangely to us since we left them in about 1975 and I still haven't received any statements from them, even though they're still releasing our stuff sporadically and (in my opinion) ineffectually. As it happens, just as I was doing the final cutting and pasting for this book, John Verity called me to say he'd just bought a box set on eBay of everything Argent had ever recorded for Epic. It was called *Original Album Classics* and had apparently been released in March without any recourse to anybody involved with playing on the records. I suppose, since they'd never seen fit to account to us over three and a half decades, they saw no reason to start dealing with us on details now. The worst thing was they wouldn't even send us a free box set to keep for posterity in lieu of royalties.

Things have moved on a great deal since the late '60s, and as I intimated there was always something inequable then about the way songwriting shares were apportioned, which frequently caused groups to break up acrimoniously. I certainly don't want to bang on about it, but it may be interesting to you to know the way bands worked was often like this. One guy would bring an idea to the rehearsal room (say a guitar phrase), then the rest of the band would work out something to play to complement it. In hours, days or weeks a song would be born. A recording would be made, and on the record label underneath the song's title would appear the name of the person who had dreamed up the original guitar phrase. Now it's blindingly obvious that the other players had a huge input too, but they wouldn't be recognised for their creative endeavours financially as far as the publishing was concerned. Of course, I hear you saying, they'd still get their record royalties – and I refer you to the paragraphs directly preceding this one! That said, frequently one of the group would bring a fully formed arrangement of a complete song to the rehearsal and tell everybody what to play. The huge difference, of course, is that publishing/writing royalties are nothing to do with the record company, so aren't frozen when a band leaves a record label.

I'm a great fan of Iain Banks, whom I've never met but would like to have a beer with in the unlikely event that he gets to read this. In a work of fiction called *Espedair Street* he came up with the perfect solution to the royalty issue. The book is about a Scottish band that makes records in the way I just described. After a certain amount of animosity, rather than allowing the rest of the band to seethe, the guy with his name under the song title decides to give them part of his publishing royalties in the form of an arrangement fee. I have no idea if Iain Banks was ever in a band, but he's certainly come up with a brilliant plan. By the way, Genesis always split the writing royalties equally, whoever came in with the guitar phrase.

Argent was coming to the end of a US tour, and we'd ended up once again in Miami. Lem Lubin was tour-managing and his father phoned him with a strange request. Lem's dad Paul was an entrepreneur who recognised the financial opportunities offered by American-style ice-cream parlours in Britain. He'd approached Baskin and Robbins to secure a franchise to sell their delicious products, and they had eventually refused him, preferring to let the Belgian distributor take care of the UK in his own time. This wasn't good enough for Lem's dad, so he asked us to bring back a sample of every one of B&R's thirty-one flavours. We went at it with a will, first buying a cooler to transport them in ice and a load of small plastic bags to take home one small sample of ice-cream – so it could be copied. Everything went well, apart from a certain amount of stomach-ache caused by eating the other 90 per cent of the ice-cream we couldn't bring ourselves to waste. Everything was packed and ready to be taken as hand luggage on the plane, when we got a call from Good Earth management about an emergency gig for lots of money in Toronto. Instead of flying home from Miami we had to go Toronto and do a gig first.

By the time we landed in Canada the ice in the cooler had melted. We decided dry ice would be colder so we set off to get some. Twenty pounds weight of dry ice was the least we could buy and our lump was wrapped in brown paper. We threw it in the back of the car and headed for the freeway. It was autumn, so we kept the windows up. Soon we realised we were hopelessly lost. We couldn't concentrate on the map and didn't really care; even though we had a gig that night we were happy to drive around aimlessly. Eventually we realised the carbon dioxide was seeping out of the parcel and clouding our judgement. Opening the window fixed that, but once we got back to the Four Seasons and chopped off enough pieces to fill our cooler we still had almost 20lb of dry ice to get rid of. We were going to put it on the balcony and leave it to evaporate, but thought it would be dangerous if the maid picked it up the next day while we were on the big silver bird heading for home. So we did the only thing we could: filled all our baths with water and dumped a few pieces in each. Finally we flushed the remainder away down several loos. Plumbing in hotels is joined vertically, so our toilet in room 2008 was directly above the one in 1908, which in turn was above 1808, and so on. Nothing happened for a while, until I found myself standing in a mist that was seeping out from under my bathroom door, rolling along the floor and out into the corridor. When I opened the door of the room I found the whole corridor was fogbound: it was coming from all the other Argent rooms. But there was worse to come: scary mist was coming out of all the loos below ours. We were swiftly banned from that particular Four Seasons, although I have stayed there since with the Kinks under an assumed name. Still, it was worth it, because once Lem's old man opened his Dayvilles shops we had ice cream for life, or at least as long as the business lasted. We had so many giant tubs of Rocky Road, Chocolate Chip and Maple Nut at home that we had to buy another freezer just for ice-cream. My kids say they can't remember it, but they certainly loved it at the time.

Eventually we got ourselves a new manager and carried on with what turned out to be the last US tour for Argent. This was the infamous Winnebago tour, which began in New York and finished up in Miami, unfortunately via the West Coast! This was the tour to end all tours and should have put us off for ever – but of course it didn't. Roger Myers, who was involved with Tony Visconti (who produced our final album at his house in Shepherds Bush), told him it was his intention to manage us – and his first task, having successfully negotiated a record deal, was to set up this American tour.

I should perhaps make it clear what a Winnebago is and what it's capable of doing. It's what the Americans call an RV, a Recreational Vehicle, a caravan with an engine built on a truck chassis and furnished like an inferior hotel room – including the shag pile rugs. The clue to the vehicle's capabilities is in the first word – recreational. The Winnebago Chieftain was built to convey a medium- sized family from one luxurious campsite to the next in clement weather, and it was at its best doing no more than 30 miles in a day. We were going to be travelling coast to coast and back again in winter, across mountains and plains, through fog, sleet, wind and snow, and averaging at least 250 miles a day (and/or night). We'd also be conveying the equivalent of a quite large and frequently bolshy family: Rod, Jim, John Grimaldi, John Verity, the tour manager known as the General, Les Lambert (who ensured all the electronics worked) and yours truly.

We were staying at the Mayflower hotel in New York, which was an old hotel we'd stayed in a lot. You had an apartment with a kitchen you could cook in –if you dared! The first time we were there (in 1970) was our introduction to the cockroaches of New York City, all of whom seemed to live in the Mayflower's kitchenettes. This fact alone ensured that only the terminally desperate ever cooked there. Anyway the guy with the Winnebago arrived and proudly took us out to see it parked directly on Central Park West. It was impressive, roomy and solid, with a big awning over the side door and a very large spare wheel securely bolted to the back. We looked inside at the galley and the combined shower and loo – dubiously marked 'no solid waste'.

We shot off first to Canada to play in an ice-rink in Montreal with Rainbow, who would eventually have a hit with a Russ Ballard song, the demo of which I'd played on: 'Since You've Been Gone'. As I recall we managed the first few gigs without any problems as far as the transport was concerned, but eventually the Winnebago began to show what it was made of – literally. I'm guessing we were in the wilds of Ohio and Jim was driving along a pretty narrow road, which all of a sudden became even narrower where it went over a fast flowing river. There was a bailey bridge over the river, and as bad luck would have it we entered at one end as a huge lorry loaded with tree trunks entered from the other. We all breathed in, but Jim was forced to squeeze over too far and the awning was neatly ripped off by the stanchions of the bridge and deposited into the raging river below. It could have been worse; we could have gone with it. We stopped as soon as we could to inspect the damage, and found gaping holes in the thin aluminium sidings through which you could see the polystyrene inside.

We criss-crossed the country in winter, and because I was just over hepatitis I was allowed to fly on the longer journeys (probably the only positive thing about that horrible debilitating illness, which left me weak and in despair). The tour went from East Coast to West Coast, then back to the South East and Florida: 10,000 miles would be a conservative estimate. We had a gig in Indianapolis, followed by another in Seattle, and I flew the 2,287 miles to wait for the others who were due there thirty-four non-stop hours later. I checked into the Edgewater Inn (made famous by Led Zeppelin), where you could pick up rods from reception and fish from your window, and waited, waited and waited. It was almost a week before the rest of the band and the crew had battled across the snowy Rockies at what was the worst possible time of the year. As if that wasn't enough, the Winnebago decided to play up. The guys lost a day while repairs were carried out, then left their hotel one evening with John V. at the controls. John had invested in a few packets of 'No-Doze' to keep him awake, and having ingested a handful of these truck driver's friends he promised to drive through the night until they wore off. Within a hundred yards the engine stopped and they ground to a halt, so they trudged back to the hotel to phone the mechanic, who couldn't do anything to help till the next day! John's eyes were open wider than usual all night. Anyway, after more breakdowns and detours around snowy impassable passes, they arrived, and we did the gig in Seattle with Steppenwolf.

I got on rather well with John Kay, who lost no time in telling me he *was* Steppenwolf, and I frequently sat with him discussing life and the universe. I promise you no drugs were involved, only alcohol. Even though he was a German, who'd relocated to Canada in the '50s, he didn't seem to know much about the book they'd taken their name from, or Hermann Hesse. I was surprised to discover John was legally blind, and even more shocked to hear him do his own off-stage announcement. 'Ladies and gentlemen, will you please welcome one of the true living legends of Rock and Roll: John Kay and Steppenwolf.' When I first heard it I thought he'd said one of the *two* living legends and wondered who the other one could be!

Eventually we loaded ourselves back into the smelly RV, which still had full black-water tanks, and made our way further south to the warmth of California and Bakersfield. It's about time for the other embarrassing drum rostrum story I promised.

The Bakersfield Auditorium was packed and we decided to keep back 'Hold Your Head Up' for the first encore. After we'd left the stage it took the audience some time to realise they hadn't heard our most successful song, and the shouted demands for an encore were so slow in coming that in the darkness the roadcrew assumed we had finished. The drum tech began to dismantle my big Pearl drum set as the shouting got louder, and we rushed back on for the encore. This was three or four years after 'Hold Your Head Up' had been a hit and we had played it literally hundreds of times since. It began in complete darkness with two spotlights on me standing up and rolling dramatically around the six toms before crashing all the cymbals and sitting down. After I'd established two measures of the rhythm the rest of the guys came in:

Bum, diddy-bum, diddy-bum, diddy-bum, pah
Bum, diddy-bum, diddy-bum, diddy-bum, pah

On the second 'pah' I sat down where the stool had been before we walked off: Andy Mackrill hadn't had time to put it back! Ten thousand people laughed uproariously. I don't know what hurt most, the embarrassment or the pain in my arse.

We continued to LA and parked our home on wheels outside the Hyatt House. Two interesting things happened, the first being that the huge spare wheel attached to the back disappeared. Not only had we remodelled the whole nearside, rendered the shower/loo room unusable, and almost completely rebuilt the engine, but we'd also lost the spare wheel. We weren't too concerned because the only trouble we'd avoided was a puncture, but we thought the owner might be a little miffed. In the event he was unconcerned, and swiftly arranged for us to pick up a replacement. We were initially taken aback by his lack of concern, and it wasn't until my fertile/devious mind started mulling over what had happened I came up with a hypothesis. We were innocent mules running a spare-wheel-full of Class A drugs from the East Coast of America to the West. (If that were the case, there's a distinct possibility we did the same thing from the West Coast to Miami!)

The second thing that happened was that the overworked roadcrew were anxious to score something to relax themselves on a rare day off, and in the Hyatt they bumped into a guy with a Zapata moustache who looked like he could help them. He wasn't wearing a T-shirt with 'Official Drug Dealer' on the front, but he might just as well have been. He was a black dude dressed like Superfly. From his slouch hat, through his tight-fitting velvet jacket, big-collared shirt, wide-bottomed loon pants and platform shoes, he looked the part. He took the guys upstairs to where the drugs were and, having passed over the necessary money, they waited round a corner as he went into his pal's room to score. They waited and waited and waited, until eventually they walked back around the corner to look for him and discovered a dead-end with a wide-open fire exit! The one thing this drug-dealer didn't have was drugs.

Eventually we found our way to Miami via Texas, Alabama, and, since it was a tour, many points in between. In the Holiday Inn in Birmingham, Alabama, we had a night off and the tour manager, who was a fully paid-up member of the Wine Club of Great Britain, decided he was going to treat himself to a great bottle of wine. Having called for the wine waiter, who he was taken aback to find was dressed exactly the same as the LA drug dealer who'd stiffed him, the General asked expectantly for the wine list: 'No list, man. We've got bottles of red or we've got bottles of white!'

We called the owner of the Winnebago as soon as we arrived in Miami to advise him he could pick up its remains whenever he liked. He turned up and we stood nervously outside the hotel as Vinnie inspected it for wear and tear. I doubt it would have managed the 1,200 miles up to New Jersey, but the guy was completely unconcerned. We were expecting a huge bill from the record company, but since we haven't seen it in thirty-three years I presume it got lost in the post along with our royalties.

After all this fun we came home to regroup and think what we would do next. In the event we (Jim, John V. and me) decided that since the best way to get a mansion in the country was to write songs that was what we would have to do. Chris and Rod, the songwriters involved with Argent, were so prolific (not to say financially successful) that I was always daunted by presenting my offerings to the band. As the old drummer's joke goes: What's the last thing a drummer says in a band? 'Hey, guys, why don't we try one of my songs?' There goes another rib! That said, when the *Circus* album was in pre-production I submitted a song called 'Prayer' for it: an imaginary hymn that a trapeze artist or tightrope walker might say before stepping out into the abyss: 'Oh dear God, please take care of me, it's not for myself but those who count on me, keep me safe, hold me in your hand, one slip could mean disaster, lying in the sand.' John V. did a great vocal and solo on it, but it didn't make it onto the album.

Now most bands cross-collateralised their income into keeping the band afloat, but no songwriter I heard of was ever crazy enough to do that. As I said, most of them quite rightly ploughed it into the mansion in the country. So we decided the way forward was to have ourselves a power-trio and write our own stuff. Out of the ashes of Argent would come Phoenix. Having just finished the infamous Winnebago tour we had a lot of adverse on-the-road experience to write about:

Ten thousand miles doesn't seem so far,
When you're travelling by plane and you're a shooting star,
But when times get tough you've got to change your plan,
You've got to pack up and get on the road . . .you rock and
roll band.
Winnebago, that's the way,
It's the only way to see the USA.

Argent had run its course when we started with Phoenix, so it was time to wield the new broom. Roger Meyers had moved on to the more lucrative activity of opening chains of hugely successful restaurants around the world, having realised that financially showbiz wasn't all it was cracked up to be! We wanted a new manager and immediately thought of Trident Records, which was ex-Hunters drummer Norman Sheffield's company which he ran with his brother Barry. They'd started out with a record shop around the corner from me in Waltham Cross and dabbled with recording there before going the whole hog and setting up a highly professional studio in St Anne's Court in Soho. But what interested us most was the fact that they also guided the careers of Queen. There were other guys involved, but all in all from where we were standing they'd done a wonderful job. They also had a film arm called Trillion, which had been responsible for arguably the world's first real pop video with 'Bohemian Rhapsody'.

We'd already started work on writing songs which we'd turned into demos at the studio in John V's home in Willesden. We took them with us to a meeting with the Trident guys, who liked them, and the contract was duly signed, sealed and delivered. We had a launch party to celebrate our liaison with Trident and I remember having a quiet chat with Brian May who asked me what the hell we were doing getting involved with Norman Sheffield. Queen had written a song about him called 'Death on Two Legs', which I guess conveyed the depth of their feelings. That said, even though he eventually completely blotted his copybook with me some time later, during our Phoenix years he was more than supportive.

The first album was recorded at Trident Studios, which, since it was owned by the company that managed us, was as good as being 'in house' so no money needed to be passed over. We had unlimited time to ourselves. which, even though we'd already routined the songs at John's place beside the railway in Cricklewood, gave us the opportunity to experiment.more than usual because nobody was watching the clock. Since we did a great deal of this in downtime, when the studio was empty, we probably didn't owe them too much money. And anyway CBS were footing the bill.

Trident had assigned one of their chaps to look after us, Dave Thomas, and eventually with input from all the various interested parties the album was finished. We were pleased, and in many ways we broke new ground as a power trio. Everybody had contributed to the writing and the garden looked rosy. The album was called *Phoenix* and the black cover featured a gold drawing of a rather benign-looking golden bird emerging from the ashes of a fire. Because it was so unthreatening it became known as the budgie. With the help of the record company we decided to get on the road, heading from London up north, with various stops, then retracing our steps. All this was before we really got back on the road for a proper big-venue tour with Aerosmith. I distinctly remember that when we played at JBs in Dudley we were told Robert Plant was in the audience, although we didn't see him. He may have been frightened after the dire warnings he'd been given when he drove Carol Williams to see The Roulettes! However, that's not the main reason I remember the JB's gig. John V. and I were rooming together at this time, and after a typically rock 'n' roll after-show drink or three I fell asleep instantly. Fortunately we weren't sharing a bed (although circumstance dictated that was something we'd done in the past), for reasons that will become apparent. I was awoken by a strange sensation: I could have sworn my feet were wet. I opened my eyes to find John weeing on the bottom of my bed. He said it wasn't malicious and he thought he was in the bathroom. Unfortunately for me we didn't have a bathroom: the nearest was down at the end of the corridor! I swiftly leapt into his bed and left the 'wet patch' to him.

That tour was the UK's introduction to Phoenix, so we obviously began with as much of the new album as we could get away with, swiftly followed by 'God Gave Rock and Roll to You', 'Hold Your Head Up' and the like. When we were playing in Sheffield we were just about to get to the Argent stuff when an exasperated voice from the audience shouted, 'Play summat we know!' Nobody ever wants to be educated at a gig, not even a Kinks one.

So we put the work in on the show to get match-fit before starting on the video to go along with the album. Bruce Gowers was Trillion's in-house director, who just happened to have been responsible for Queen's seminal 'Bohemian Rhapsody' video, and he was brought in to come up with a dynamite video. I still have it somewhere. It was filmed at Shepperton Studios and is extremely good, though I say it as I shouldn't. Others might cruelly say it has more to do with Spinal Tap, since as I recall I spent the whole time semi-naked in front of every drum and percussion instrument I owned. John V. is mostly in soft-focus, with a floaty top and a feather earring, henceforth known as the parrot. Jim struts around looking dark and menacing with a sinister moustache and beard, a lot like Johnny Depp in *Pirates of the Caribbean*.

One of the reasons we were touring with Aerosmith was because their management was Steve Leber and David Krebbs, who had masterminded Argent's career in the US at the beginning of the '70s. They helped us immensely. (Eventually these guys would look after everybody who was anybody, but in Argent's day the rest of the roster was along the lines of Aerosmith, the New York Dolls and Ted Nugent.) The other reason was that Aerosmith and Phoenix were both contracted to CBS.

The UK gigs were at the Liverpool Empire, Glasgow Apollo and Birmingham and Hammersmith Odeons. The vibes between us and Aerosmith were extremely good because we'd bumped up against them many times in our previous incarnation as Argent. However, they had a tour manager who still saw fit to wield the keep-the-support-band-down-so-they-don't-upstage-the-headliners sword, which we'd seen so much of when we first toured America. This guy made life really complicated for us as far as facilities were concerned, and although we put up with it for the UK leg things erupted when we reached Amsterdam on the European leg. I think I mentioned elsewhere that John and Jim had hidden reserves of anger which they kept concealed for as long as they could. We'd finished our show and everything had gone well, and we were having a beer on the side of the stage with David Krebbs, watching Aerosmith do their thing. John was sitting on top of a 5ft high wardrobe trunk when the aforementioned tour manager came up to him and demanded he got down. John refused, so the guy pulled him to the ground. This of course is a dangerous and stupid thing to do to a performer half-way through a tour. John got to his feet and set about the tour manager with the energy that had been pent up for the whole tour. Pausing for breath, John got him by the throat and uttered the immortal words: 'If you come near me again you'll be D, E, fucking D dead!' The tour manager might not have understood the spelling but he got the gist of the message - especially when David Krebbs appeared from the shadows and assured him John was right and he was wrong. Their tour manager lost so much face with his own road crew that he was sent home the very next day.

Somehow somebody made a pretty good bootleg of our show that night. It's called *Dykes and Dirty Water* and is, as far as I know, the only live evidence of the band.

The tour ended and CBS withdrew their support, and Dave Thomas went shopping for a new record company. He found Tony Stratton Smith's Charisma label, which was home to artists as diverse as Genesis and Monty Python's Flying Circus. *In Full View* was soon to be the result of that affiliation, but not before we went to America for a not particularly auspicious attempt at it. Jim had left the band by this time and his place in Phoenix 2 was taken by Ray Minhinnett, who was a guitarist. This wasn't the end of the world, because John V. was going to play bass and if we needed any other musicians we had carte-blanche to buy them in.

Norman Sheffield and Dave Thomas had worked hard to persuade the rest of the Trident company to give us the money to go to California to make this second album, which in hindsight turned out to be a huge and expensive mistake. We decided to record it on the West Coast and flew to LA to get the job done. I had recorded in America before but only a track for a Pepsi-Cola advert with Argent, never an album. We get off the plane, picked up an extremely battered estate-wagon from Rentawreck, followed by a phone from Bell Telephones, the bare minimum of food from Ralphs and a couple of six packs of beer before we proceeded to Oakwood Apartments on Barham Boulevard. Within an hour or two we had a couple of apartments and a complete LA lifestyle. Traditionally musicians staying in LA just long enough to make an album stay in Oakwood, as do scriptwriters who sit by the pool working on their tans armed with yellow legal-pads and printed synopses of how characters like Starsky and Hutch or Cagney and Lacey would behave in any given situation.

Those were the days when the right producer's name on album credits and the right sidemen positively guaranteed plays on FM radio. We worked in several studios with Stuart Alan Love, a producer with a track record. He was insisted on by the record company, was meant to be helping John V. but whom John eventually took over from. Kendun Recorders was a very upmarket studio in Burbank where we began, but when we ran out of time there we moved to Cherokee on Fairfax, which had no less than four Trident mixing desks. It was far more funky and I preferred it. Carmine Appice was making the 'Hot Legs' album (*Foot Loose and Fancy Free*) with Rod Stewart at the time, and had a whole studio to himself and his drums. Jeff 'Skunk' Baxter was also working there at the time, although probably not with the Doobies, and we helped him by marching on gravel for a track he was putting down. He said he owed us a session but so far he's never paid us back. All this was years before he became involved with missile defence systems and the US government.

It was an interesting time for us all, and we soon picked-up the way of life and could find our way around LA without any problem. However, some of the things took a great deal of getting used to. At lunchtime a very tall black guy on rollerskates would turn up with a wicker basket full of sandwiches, and he was most surprised when we bought some: they were simply there to cover the diverse cocktail of drugs in the bottom of the basket!

We needed a keyboard player for most of the tracks, and a guy called Ronnie Lee Cunningham turned up. He was brilliant. Another excellent musician we used was Snuffy Walden who'd played with Free, and turned up with the most brilliant demos of his songs, which in hindsight sounded like Toto. We used one of them called 'I Don't Mind'. Snuffy went on to write theme and incidental music for film and TV, and I often see his name on the credits for successful series like *My So-Called Life*, *The Wonder Years* and *The West Wing*, which he deservedly received an Emmy for.

Again we ran out of time and relocated to Crystal Studios on Santa Monica, which had been hugely successful in its day with the likes of Phil Spector but was now in decline and desperately needed a facelift. We'd put down one of Russell's songs called 'Just Another Day in the Life of a Fool' and decided a sax solo would be just the thing. Having cast around for a player with a suitable sound we came up with Jim Horn, who'd played with Duane Eddy. The negotiations began. He wanted a return ticket from San Francisco, what Americans call 'triple scale', and a couple of grams of extras!

I was outside the studio taking the air when he arrived in this great boat of a beaten-up vehicle, which surprised me since we'd allegedly flown him to LAX, and this certainly didn't look like a rental car. Two saxes were sitting innocently on the back seat: a tenor and an alto. I watched him deliberate before picking up the smallest one. The guy who had brought us 'Rebel Rouser', 'Good Vibrations', 'Going Up The Country', 'Tears of a Clown', 'Goat's Head Soup', 'Crazy Horses' and 'Strangers in the Night' hadn't even heard the track, but he knew which instrument would suit it best – the one that was easiest to carry! He walked into the studio and having listened to the track asked us where his part was. Eventually the penny dropped and we realised what he meant – he needed a notated sheet of music. John V. said there wasn't a part: we just wanted him to do his thing. Jim replied that this wasn't how it worked with him: 'I don't make things up, I need the music!' (It begs the question as to how he got on working with Brian Wilson and the rest of the Beach Boys, along with Canned Heat and Phil Spector.) As it happens, we knew we wanted a solo like Ralph Ravenscroft's famous one on 'Baker Street' (emulated eons later by Lisa Simpson). John sang it to him. He played it exactly how he was told, and went home. Triple scale, a couple of grams of marching powder, return ticket from San Francisco, and we had to tell him what to play. (Like a great deal else on that album, the sax part was replaced when we got back to London – although not by Ralph!)

Eventually we were finished and on our way home with an album-full of unmixed tracks.

We sat together on the plane, and Ray listened intently to the tracks on his Walkman. To get himself into the correct relaxed mood he was having a few drinks at the same time. Unfortunately he ran out of batteries at roughly the same time that the cabin crew ran out of patience and stopped serving him alcohol. Still, no matter, he had his duty-free supply to keep him going. Eventually two kind American girls on the other side of the aisle offered to lend him their ghettoblaster, but unfortunately his headphones didn't fit it. For a while he listened to it quietly, but eventually though he wanted it louder and, having turned up the volume, the whole plane was soon able to listen to the rough mixes of Phoenix's second album, soon to be called *In Full View*. I hadn't witnessed this before, but cabin crew have a straitjacket ready for belligerent customers. Around the time they were threatening to fit it the miscreant fell asleep. It's an awfully long way back from LA when someone next to you is misbehaving, and I prayed for sleep for myself that wouldn't come.

Lest I forget, I have a story about John V. on a long-distance flight. He's not the greatest of passengers and, having taken sleeping tablets, as soon as we sat down he was fast asleep. Unfortunately the plane developed a fault and was grounded, whereupon we had to leave the plane and take another flight. John was fast asleep and couldn't be woken, so they took him off in a wheelchair. He woke up at Heathrow hours later, thinking we'd arrived at our destination!

Unfortunately the results of our West Coast endeavours once we got them home were frankly disappointing, although we did get the opportunity to redo the work on them once we returned to Trident Studios with Ronnie Lee Cunningham who we flew in. *In Full View* came out in 1979.

The original Phoenix hadn't been going very long when the phone rang. It was Phil Collins to tell me Peter Gabriel was leaving the band, and even though he had no idea what was going to happen he wanted me to be part of Genesis. We'd known each other for years and he'd always been impressed by my playing through my Adam Faith days, when I flamboyantly showed off my playing style and stick-spinning skills on black and white TV on many a '60s Saturday evening. He'd also depped for me on an Argent album called *Counterpoints* when I had hepatitis, and I was told he was offered the gig if I died! Just before we decided to draw a discreet veil over Argent we were playing a gig in Guildford, and as we were on stage I looked into the wings and spotted Phil standing there. He wasn't there when we finished, and I wondered later whether that was my audition for Genesis.

We'd only just begun, and all the signs were that Phoenix had a good shot at success. We had solid management, CBS were back as our record company and we had the old management for the US who still looked after Aerosmith, who were just about to do another big-time tour of Europe with us in support. So we talked about it and, call me stupid if you like, I decided to stay put. My wife still calls me 'stupid if you like' over this (and other things I haven't done, like joining John Mayall or becoming a property developer), and if it weren't for the statute of limitations I'm sure she could use my alleged lack of ambition to join Genesis as grounds for divorce. It's funny, though: a wise man once said that opportunities always look bigger going than coming.

There's another story associated with me and the original Genesis guys. I was in New York and went to see Peter Gabriel at a club called the Bottom Line. He was brilliant, and

I was very impressed when his band moved seamlessly from instrument to instrument and back to where they started. We chatted at the gig, and one autumn afternoon in about 1980 I was in Drumstore when Peter wandered in and took me aside to ask what I was up to. I told him I was recording with Charlie, and he said it was a shame because he would like me to go on tour with him. This time I didn't say no, but something happened and ultimately we never got to work together, even though I'd bump into him from time to time at Real World studios.

Funnily enough, to continue the connection, I went on to make an album with Mike Rutherford at the Genesis studios at Fisher's Lane Farm near Guildford; John Verity produced it. The drum booth in the studio was very bright (all glass and stone), and I sounded a lot like Phil.

Phoenix Mark II emerged from the fire after Jim had absented himself to the Kinks in about 1977. At this time we had two guitarists in John V. and Ray Minhinnett, me on drums and no bass players. At the time it didn't matter because John played bass on the records, and fortunately, perhaps, the studio was as far as we got. If we'd ever had any live gigs we'd have been in trouble!

Around the time of Phoenix, Leber and Krebbs, our US management, got us to do a heavy album with a girl called Kathy September, whom I guess they had an interest in. Her manager was a chap called Doug Smith, who I believe was an associate of Lemmy – formerly one of Hawkwind's bass players. One day Lemmy called John V. to ask for my number because he needed a drummer. John thought quickly and said he believed I was out of the country. He saved me from myself, knowing it was unlikely I would turn Lemmy (or anyone else) down!

In the end Phoenix amalgamated with Charlie, and even though we were still managed by Trident and Dave Thomas here in the UK we needed representation in America, and Bud Prager certainly fitted the bill. He had guided Foreigner, Megadeth and eventually Bad Company to stardom. We met him in his suite in the Intercontinental at Hyde Park Corner, and after we'd signed with him he congratulated us and said, 'Say goodbye to your marriages!'

We'd made a pretty good record by this time, but even though we made a hilarious slapstick video, where we dressed as bakers and covered each other with pie for a song called 'It's Inevitable'; while the record got good plays in America and was according to Wikipedia the band's best-selling single, the album never took off enough for us to go there, and we never actually did a gig. There were two drummers in the new Charlie: me and Steve Gadd, who was in the original band, along with Terry Thomas, Terry Slessor, John Verity and John Anderson. Things didn't go too well for Charlie, and while we waited for something to happen I moonlighted with Don McLean for quite some time. When the shit hit the fan Dave Thomas disappeared, and we didn't see him till the Kinks played at the Coliseum in LA. Unfortunately there was a long post mortem after the gig that night, so I didn't really get a chance to ask what went on. Even though he's back in the UK now I still don't know why he left. To sum the whole thing up, Charlie weren't successful but I'm still married. I'll settle for that!

In 2008 Ken Bruce played the full length version of 'Hold Your Head Up' on his weekday morning Radio 2 programme. He got to the end of the very long fade-out and asked, 'Have they stopped yet?' I'm sorry to say we had.

Argent on Old Grey Whistle *Test with Whispering Bob*

Brand new early seventies
Pearl Kit in flight cases

Argent's first tour in the land of opportunity

Argent's rock management's company's 'other' business venture

After Dark magazine shot

Satisfyingly large Hayman set

The father of all cymbals—with Alvedis Zildjan in Boston

Argent: Brighton Rock

Compulsory lunch in Abbey Road cabnteen

With Ricki in Village Road

Jimmy relaxing

John Grimaldi

John Verity

Playboys at La Guardia: a very interesting article

Russell and Les Lambert

With Jim, getting it together in Munich, man

More with Ricki

*The lovely and
fragrant Ricki*

Chapter Six: IN BETWEEN

I was sitting with justifiable trepidation contemplating the removal of my wisdom teeth in my dentist's surgery in Finchley. Coincidentally I sat alongside an equally nervous chap called Ray Hammond, who'd been the first magazine editor who'd commissioned me to write anything when he was working at what was up until then the only real music magazine we had in the UK – *Beat Instrumental*. (Of course we had *NME*, *Disc*, *Melody Maker* and *Record Mirror*, but they were newspapers.) To be honest, *Beat* was really something of a fanzine, but at least it had pictures of instruments and the odd advert, mostly for British-built instruments along with pictures of the stars of the day. In the main these were taken by a lovely guy named Dezo Hoffmann, whose only fault was he made all the groups look the same!

Though I say it myself, I'd always been pretty good at composing essays on the trolleybus on the way to school, and the copy I'd written for *Beat* was about useful drumming concepts rather than 'favourite colour: *navy blue*, favourite drink: *Coca-Cola*,. Drummer: *Joe Morello*, favourite girls: *blondes*, which was what most of the popular music media had specialised in. I wrote about subjects like making yourself heard above banks of amplifiers (play rim-shots at all times), how to make your hands hard (wee on them?), along with the pros and cons of various drums and cymbals. Anyway, Ray Hammond told me he was moving to pastures new with a brand new title ultimately to be called *International Musician & Recording World*, and did I fancy writing for it. Up until the seventies there was no consumer magazine along the lines of the Which? report for instruments. The only way for us to see new stuff was to go round the various dealers in the West End of London, who in those days specialised in just two or three different makes. You had to see what they had for sale and either make your own decision on a product, or take the salesman's word for it. *IM&RW* changed all that.

In 1975 I began to review drumsets and cymbals of the era, an activity that I'm not too shy to be absolutely certain I invented. Richard Desmond owned the title, and having begun the magazine in Drury Lane near Covent Garden tube station, which was easy to get to, eventually moved it to Earl's Court when he became involved with a couple of adult magazines: *Penthouse* and *Forum*. Eventually he was one of the first guys to move into Docklands, when that massive Canadian development began in about 1978. I remember that before we had the luxury of e-mail I used to drive there with my copy, and everywhere for miles around was a muddy building site other than the Northern and Shell building – which stood tall, proud and alone alongside one of the ancient docks for what seemed like a very long time. I wrote for *IM&RW* from 1975 until they stopped publishing it in about 1992. I'm proud to say I was the only one who achieved that distinction, and I outlasted a great many editors – many of whom, like Tony Horkins and David Lawrenson, were eventually assimilated into the mainstream press.

In the very beginning all the Argent guys were writing for *IM&RW*: Rod, Jim, Johnny V. and me. Initially I wrote my stuff in longhand and someone turned it into proper typing suitable to be set, but as you can imagine I didn't get away with that for very long. In 1976 I bought myself an Olivetti typewriter from a second-hand shop. There was only one problem as far as magazines were concerned – it printed in *italics*. I argued that it was very attractive, but several editors disagreed violently with me and when the eighties began I bought myself one of the new-fangled, decidedly non-user-friendly computers. It came complete with a huge learning curve, which I'm still climbing. This was in the days of the minute green screen that killed your eyes and the huge floppy disk you saved stuff to. After I'd written a few chapters of my book about electronic drums I found myself at the optician's getting my eyes tested. Wearing glasses for reading coincided neatly with joining The Kinks.

Henrit's Drumstore had opened its doors to the drum world in the middle of 1977, and while criticising drum products in a magazine as a player is highly acceptable, and even OK as a retailer, if you're a distributor it's suspected you might have your own agenda. We had begun to sell bits and pieces I picked up around the world, like Camco drums, and since no one else had the stuff we were deemed to be distributors: no one trusted me to broadcast my unbiased thoughts on their products. Other companies threatened to withdraw their advertising unless I was replaced.

Since I had a lot of articles already written I came up with a solution – why not use a *nom de plume*? With my tongue lodged firmly in my cheek I suggested Henry Roberts, but never thought I'd get away with it until someone wrote a letter to the magazine saying they preferred Henry Roberts's writing to Robert Henrit's. I liked the name so much that I used it as my 'nom de room' when checking into hotels with The Kinks. This was to ward off so-called 'Spiny Normans' who phoned every hotel in the city asking for Henrit, Rodford or Gibbons while searching for The Kinks.

Drumstore came about when Phoenix's manager Norman Sheffield approached me about the idea of a drum shop in Wardour Street. Trident Studios, which he owned, was just round the corner in an alleyway called St Anne's Court, and he had a vacant lease on the basement and ground floor of 112 Wardour Street. The Who's management was above us and so, believe it or not, were the guys who looked after the Stones! The Ship, a pub much frequented by rock stars, was handily situated on the same side of the road as us and adjacent, just across the entrance to the NCP. If you walked through this car park you came out into Bateman Street, where I think I remember Derek Block, Don McLean's agent, had his office. The Marquee Club was just along Wardour Street to the left, and if you walked with difficulty across its invariably sticky floor and past the back bar you'd arrive in the recording studio.

When we started Drumstore we had a dream, or at least a desire, to turn it into the best shop in the world catering exclusively for drummers. I'd seen all of the contenders while rocking all over the world, so knew exactly what I needed to model it on: Drum City in Hollywood, Frank's in Chicago, Jack's in Boston and, my favourite by a long way, Frank Ippolito's Professional Percussion in New York City.

Within a very short time we had a shop fitted out with clean white emulsioned walls and brown carpets waiting for our first deliveries of drums. We got my pal Jim Wilkinson in to devise us a logo and he came up with a drum key with a fob hanging from it with my signature, and this became what I'm reliably informed was called our house sign. We had it made up into an almost three dimensional sign, which hung outside the shop like a pawnbroker's three balls. (It now hangs inside one of my outbuildings with various other signs that were suspended over the various stick and accessory counters. These outbuildings mostly contain flight-cases full of more drums than you could shake a stick at, cymbals, stands, pedals, percussion instruments, magazines, programmes, backstage passes, photos, catalogues and so on. In short, the detritus of a life misspent playing the drums, and famously known to my lovely wife as my 'crap'.)

I suppose it was a natural progression for me to become a drum shop owner, having played the instrument for twenty years, written about drums and drumming for *Melody Maker*, *International Musician* and *Beat Instrumental*, invented the odd accessory and presented drum clinics in the UK and Europe.

We looked in all the obvious places for staff for Henrit's Drumstore and plundered all the most successful London shops. This gave us a headstart, since we disabled them for quite a while by stealing their key staff. There was no doubt we were an attractive prospect for the guys we purloined, although for a while we ended up with more chiefs than Indians.

We planned a champagne opening attended by the great and good of the drumworld, and while we were standing round feeling rather pleased with ourselves, we received our first customer – and an awkward one at that. Our pal Baz Ward walked in with a Ludwig Super-Sensitive belonging to Blinky Davidson from The Nice, for whom he was working as a roadie. The snare drum needed mending, and since we had a workshop downstairs but no tools yet, this presented an insurmountable problem. We managed to persuade Baz to have a drink and leave the drum with us, and one of the guys brought the necessary tools in to effect the repair the very next day.

We were unique (and probably misguided) in having a bar for our esteemed clientele. This was situated downstairs, out of sight and close to the area where the drum hire was carried out. As I recall the public phone was also originally downstairs, giving drummers (and arguably some of the more racy members of staff) the opportunity to get gigs and (I was told many years later) order various commodities.

Like all drum shops, beside the professional members of staff we also had various 'resting' drummers, like the completely zany Steve Gadd (whom I eventually played with in a band managed by Norman Sheffield called Charlie) and Steve Rodford, who was Jim Rodford from Argent's son, who I think was playing with Princess Caroline of Monaco at the time.

We had a Saturday boy called Mike Dolbear, who was so desperate to make a career in drumming that his father insisted he learned the business from the ground up, starting in retail. The problem was that Mike lived in Brighton, which was approximately 65 miles from the Drumstore: he came up on the train every week with his dad, who left him at 10am and came back when we closed around 6 pm. I can't remember how much we paid Mike for the day, but I guarantee it didn't cover the price of two return tickets from Brighton, even if one of them was a child's fare! I must ask Dolbear senior next time I see him what he did for eight hours in Soho on a Saturday for all the years Mike was with us!

Keith Moon was an enthusiastic customer. He turned up at the most inconvenient times to put a stop to what was going on, just to make us laugh. He died in 1978, and when the dust died down I contacted Pete Townshend to see what they were doing about a drummer. Pete was an editor at Faber and Faber at the time, and I got a very nice letter back from him on their headed notepaper saying that unfortunately even though I was Keith's favourite drummer and they all liked my playing, they'd already signed Kenney Jones. Bum, poo, willie!

This is as good a time as any to tell a true story about Rod Argent's Keyboards, which was a sister shop inasmuch as it was part owned by Gerry Evans, who was one of my three partners in Drumstore. (The others were Norman Sheffield and John Vernon.) The shop was in Denmark Street, or Tin Pan Alley as it used to be known, and on the other side of the Charing Cross Road from us.

It was during the summertime when the manager was away on holiday that this guy came in and asked if the manager was around. The relief manager said no, and he wouldn't be back for a week. The guy was put out, and explained he had a carpet outside in the van that the shop had ordered, and he had to drop off that day. The relief chap said no problem, and told him to put it at the back of the shop. When the van driver had done this he asked for 800 quid, 'as agreed'. The relief manager said he couldn't give him a cheque because only the owners could sign it. The carpet man said a cheque was no good anyway: the deal was for cash, and if he didn't get it he'd have to take the carpet away and sell it elsewhere. The relief manager began to be concerned, thinking he'd be in deep trouble when the real manager came back if the carpet wasn't there. So he checked the till and discovered that as they'd had a pretty good day there was more than enough cash available. To quote Don McLean, everybody was happy for a while. Returning from his holiday, the real manager was astonished to discover a huge roll of carpet. His first question was why was it there and his second was who the hell had ordered it? The relief manager said 'You did', and explained. When it got to the part where he admitted to handing over £800 the manager hit the roof. The hapless shop assistant would have the money deducted from his wages if he couldn't find the villain who'd conned him and get the money back. The chap went out and, believe it or not, after quite some time he managed to find the van driver and confront him.

The van driver said he was just on his way back to the shop because he'd suddenly realised he'd made a mistake, and the carpet should have gone to another shop around the corner. He didn't have the cash any more, but would come round to Denmark Street, load it in his van and come back with the cash from the rightful owner. He disappeared with the carpet, and never came back!

Gerry had a great many stories along these lines. One of them concerns a Ludwig drumset disappearing from Drum City one Saturday afternoon. It had been a busy day and the shop had been packed, which made everybody happy until they started to lock up at closing time, when they discovered a brand-new four-piece Ludwig drumset had made its way out of the door.

I had a pal in a completely different life who told me some great music shop stories. We met at the tennis club and played together quite a bit at one time. I knew his dad had been in the music business, making amplifiers, and Derek worked for him as a young boy. His job initially was to go with his dad to London's West End music shops and pick up the amplifiers they'd agreed to mend. His old man chatted to the owners while Derek loaded the amps into the van. Sometimes he made 'a mistake' and began to load unbroken gear, and if this was was discovered he'd get a whack round the head from his old man and the gear would be returned. If nothing was spotted they'd be in a winning situation. But the resourceful family had a way of making sure they always won. Derek would put on his best Carnaby Street clothes and walk into a non-mainstream music shop like Blanks in Kilburn and talk about this great new group he was managing, which EMI/Decca/Pye/Phillips/CBS had just signed a deal with, and they had no instruments to go out on tour with. The guy behind the counter would get excited by this, and Derek would reel him in. They needed a couple of guitar amps, a bass amp, something for the keyboards and of course a sophisticated PA. The assistant would show him what they had and Derek would patiently listen. Once the sales pitch was over he'd say he'd heard really good things about 'XYZ amplifiers' (made by his dad): could they get them? The assistant didn't want to admit he didn't know much about the product and lose the sale, so he'd always say he could get it but it would have to be a special order, so he'd need to take a deposit. Derek would be happy to pass over a few quid, the shop would order all the goods and at the appropriate time the amplifier company would invoice them. Then Derek would disappear.

Another couple of good retail scams I know about concerned a very brazen guy who walked into an extremely busy Harrods at sale time with his own till, which he plugged-in in a corner and started to take money – cash only! Of course people at Harrods' sale are desperate to pay for what they want quickly in one department and move on to the next. I'm not sure how that guy was ever rumbled.

Two guys who were eventually caught, although not for a long time, carried out a great scam in another department store, in Oxford Street this time. They put on the white lab coats usually worn by guys working in John Lewis's dispatch and service departments, went to the electrical goods or white goods and picked up what they wanted, the bigger the better. Two guys in white coats carrying a television or a washing machine didn't look suspicious. They took the stuff downstairs and into their van, strategically parked at the back of the building, and drove off . . .

Henrit's Drumstore had a hire department, which was a core part of the business. One day the notorious Kray twins' older brother Charlie came in with a punk band he was 'managing' to hire some drums and percussion to make an album. The guys knew what they wanted, and when it came time to settle up for the stuff Doogie Bradford, the Scottish guy who ran the hire department, asked Charlie for a passport as security until the gear was returned. Charlie laughed. 'Do I look like the sort of person they'd give a passport to?' We all had to agree that he didn't. (If

Charlie had to leave the country his journey was more likely to start from an unknown airfield in the Home Counties in the dead of night rather than via immigration at Heathrow.) 'I tell you what, though, you can take this sovereign ring as security,' he said. And he handed over this massive piece of golden 'bling' with Queen Victoria's unsmiling profile in the middle. It would have been untrusting and possibly dangerous to have bitten into it to check its veracity, so it was put into the safe awaiting the return of our expensive gear. Well, you've probably guessed that the gear didn't come back, so the ring sat in the back of the safe for several years. Eventually when the shop closed I took it to a jeweller to get an opinion, and having examined it the guy went off to call the police! I explained the situation, and he said that he'd seen rings like this before, and they were meant to defraud. The body was made from lead, with a farthing set into it so you couldn't see the wren or the word farthing, only the monarch. The whole thing was then gold plated. I don't suppose Queen Victoria would have been any more amused than we were. I don't know what happened to it, but a quarter of a century after the event there was a sale at Sotheby's of Kray personal memorabilia. We might just have got our money back!

I have another pal at the Tennis Club who told me a story about a very different 'victimless crime'. At the height of their fame Queen were appearing at an open-air gig in a country home in Hertfordshire (possibly Knebworth). Someone he knew rather well, but absolutely certainly wasn't himself, had genuine tickets for the show. Arriving at the bank of turnstiles to go in and claim his own patch of mud, he was astonished to discover an unattended one. Seizing the moment, he took charge of it and, having worked out the complex mechanics of operating the machinery with his foot, was soon in business taking 'cash only' from punters anxious to get the best positions in front of Freddie Mercury and away from the mud. Nobody twigged, and he went home a great deal richer.

John V. and I had some time on our hands in about 1979 when Phoenix amalgamated with Charlie. We decided to have some fun, make a ridiculous record and see if we, make that Dave Thomas our manager, could sell it. We decided to record a cover version of the old Contours' classic 'Do You Love Me (Now That I Can Dance)', also stolen by Brian Poole and the Tremeloes and the Dave Clark Five quite a few years earlier. Johnny V. had a studio at his house, and to get a big sound we put the drums in one bedroom while all the other instruments played elsewhere. Russell B. played piano, and we put down a 'tongue in cheek' version with a backing track, which, as is often the way with throw-away tracks, sounded pretty damn good. Now the record has a recitative at the beginning which goes like this: 'You broke my heart 'cos I couldn't dance, you didn't even want me around, but now I'm back to let you know I can really shake it down . . .' This is before the two bar build into the chorus, and on The Contours' record a very black and soulful American voice recounts it. On our record it was decided I would say it in a really excruciating cockney (make that mockney) accent, which is making my toes curl even as I write: 'Yer broke me 'eart 'cuz I couldn't dance, you di'nt even wan' me aroun' . . .' I won't go on because my cheeks are burning, but I'm sure you get the picture. Russell wisely decided he didn't want to be part of it, but Dave Thomas punted the demo around under the name of The Juniors, and believe it or not we got a one record deal for it. That should really have been the end of it, but inexplicably we were getting plays on the radio. Now John Verity and I were really embarrassed, because we needed to support the record by doing TV shows. We engaged a stylist, and had some moody studio photos taken with us emoting, with just a hint of eye-shadow: it showed up in the *Radio Times* trailing a television programme. Possibly the Great British Public was spared our rendition of that great song because neither JV nor I can recall doing the programme. We may be suffering from selective amnesia because we're ashamed of ourselves!

In 1981, when I'd just returned from my mammoth stint with Don McLean, Johnny V. produced the Searchers at PRT and invited me along to play on the album. I was expecting it to be typical Searchers stuff with a ringing twelve string guitar, but it wasn't that at all. As it happened they didn't even possess a twelve string. All this was just before The Searchers split into two factions: The Searchers, with John McNally and Frank Allen, and Mike Pender's Searchers. Only one single, 'I Don't Want To Be The One' backed with 'Hollywood', was released, while the rest of the tracks surfaced as the Searchers' *40th Anniversary* collection in 2004.

I also made a record with a Scottish lassie called Clare Grogan, who was the singer with a band called Altered Images. I went into Livingston Studios with John Verity, put the tracks down and that was it. I didn't meet her then and I haven't met her since. It wasn't exactly rock 'n' roll, but that was the way some records were made.

Long before this Rod Argent and I very nearly had a record out that was commissioned by my friend Gerry Evans. He felt a compendium of disco hymns along the lines of Jive Bunny would be what everybody wanted in their stocking for Christmas. Rod played the organ, and my contribution was programming the Linn drum machine that I think we borrowed from Russell. The record had a 'four-on-the-floor' disco beat, and Rod segued seamlessly through 'Jerusalem', 'Land of Hope and Glory', 'Onward Christian Soldiers' and (as they say on all the compilations) many more. I know you'd like to think this is a figment of my imagination, but if you don't believe me ask Rod.

Argent's old agent Morris Jones sent me a message to tell me that AC/DC were looking for a new drummer because Phil Rudd had 'left'. He'd kindly put me forward for the gig. They were sending me a ticket to New York, and I was booked into the Parker Meridian hotel on W57th street (close to Carnegie Hall) for the whole weekend. We'd played with AC/DC several times before, but I only had a nodding acquaintance with the songs. I went out and got all the pertinent songs I figured they'd want to play and headed for the New World, spending the whole journey learning the likes of 'For Those About to Rock', 'Highway to Hell', 'Back in Black' et al. By the time I landed I could nail the stuff. There were a lot of famous drummers up for the gig, and by the time we got together I had the distinct impression the guys had had enough. The rehearsals were in Studio Instrument Rentals, and I remember it wasn't too long after Bon Scott had drunk himself to death and Brian Johnson had replaced him. Angus, Malcolm and the others seemed to be overdosing on tea, pots and pots of it! Talk about 'A Whole Lotta Rosie'. There were evidently quite a few famous drummers up for the gig although I only saw the back of one of them: I was told it was Denny Carmassi, who was playing with Heart at the time. In the event it never happened for me, but not to worry, it was 1983 – and though I didn't know it, Ray and Dave Davies were just around the corner.

During my years between Argent and The Kinks, when the UK's musical instrument industry was going to the wall, I contrived to get myself sent to China. I was writing for *IM&RW* every month, and because many of the drum companies whose products I was reviewing had upped sticks to Taiwan for economic reasons, I felt I should definitely go there and have a look around. Easier said than done, because in those days you needed a visa, and they were a bit suspicious about anybody entering their country openly stating he was there to look around the factories. They scrutinised my music industry magazines thoroughly for pornographic content before relieving me of quite a bit of cash to allow me to enter the country.

Anyway, the Pearl Drum Company coughed up for an airline ticket to show me round their factory in Taichung, and because I flew into Taipei I decided I might as well have a look at the other percussion factories there. KHS is a huge music company in Taipei responsible for brass, woodwind and fretted instruments as well as percussion, and since they also made bikes under the brand name Giant I was anxious to visit their factory. But it wasn't a factory as we know it at all: it was a massive complex behind high walls that included, as well as a large factory, living accommodation, cinemas, schools, swimming pools, tennis courts, a hospital and even a baseball diamond to keep the workers happy. I spent happy hours there witnessing them building various OEM drum lines for companies whose products I had already reviewed. I was interested in production numbers, but they were uncharacteristically cagey about these matters.

Other than Pearl I hadn't expected much from manufacturers in Taiwan, and I wasn't disappointed, but KHS were desperate to make waves with their drum products and worked hard at building them. There's not too much of my sort of drumming goes on in Taiwan, so when they took me out to lunch they picked my brains about their product. Their main drum line at that time was Linko, which wasn't by world standards anything to get too excited about, so when they told me they wanted to move further up market my ears pricked up. They told me they wanted to make drums from maple, and asked what I thought of the name Sabre. There's no such thing as a free lunch! I told them that all the world's most famous and successful twentieth-century drum companies had proudly carried their proprietor's names: Ludwig, Gretsch, Slingerland, Rogers and so on. I said that Sabre had none of these connotations. They nodded thoughtfully, and wisely decided to call the new drumset Mapex. Mapex has been highly successful, and I'm absolutely certain that the lunchtime over dim sum I saved the world's distributors from flogging a dead horse as they tried to sell a product unevocatively named after a curved, single-edged sword!

En route for Taichung and Pearl's refurbished factory, also behind high walls in what they called an Economic Processing Zone, I stopped off at another factory, which I refuse to name, where I saw drum manufacture at its very worst. The facility was inside a huge shed in the middle of a paddy field, and I watched them build a shell with dismay. The modern way of shell building is to take single 1mm plies of wood and coat them with glue, before carefully putting them one after another into a heated former shaped like a large saucepan. Once all the plies are neatly in place triangular segments, like laughing cow cheeses, are forced out under extreme pressure and left in position to fuse the thin pieces of wood together. Now because these thin sheets of wood have thick glue on them they don't always slide neatly into place to create a nice edge, where the head will sit once it's shaped and smoothed; therefore they have to be coerced into place. In Europe we persuade them into position with a rubber mallet. At this factory in the Taiwanese boondocks they did it with a ball pein hammer, which broke the edge and necessitated a repair as soon as it came out of the former. I was devastated. I'd expected the worst, but in the back of my mind I'd hoped things weren't going to be that bad. My lifelong love affair with drums looked like it was going to end right there in a soggy Chinese field. I wrote about all this on the way home on the plane, but in the end decided not to turn in the highly critical copy – since it served no real purpose. After all, everybody suspected cheap drums were made badly: they didn't need me to reinforce that particular view. It wouldn't have been good for the magazine either.

Fortunately there were good things to write about the new Pearl factory, which had started out producing cheap Maxwin drums for one US distributor and recently moved the vast majority of its production across the East China Sea from Japan.

Eventually I caught the bus from Taipei to Taichung, and since this was the Republic of China there were no signs on the buses in English saying where they were going. Fortunately I was prepared, and had memorised the symbols for Tai, meaning Taiwan (a square with a triangle on top of it like a house) and Chung, meaning middle (shaped like an open book). I was pleased with myself because I'd found the right bus, but like all the other passengers I wasn't so pleased with the driver who, for reasons known only to himself, refused to open the luggage bays under the bus. Everybody was sitting there with their possessions and livestock on their laps. We started off, and something dawned on me: I knew what the Chinese words looked like, but had no idea what the place looked like. As you can imagine, nobody understood English, and unless there was a sign outside the town anywhere we went through could have been it. After a couple of hours, as we drew into a more built-up neighbourhood, I drew my house and book on a piece of paper, showed it to the Chinese woman with the pig on her lap next to me, and she nodded. I arrived at the hotel and was immediately whisked by the guys from Pearl to a very upmarket karaoke bar. I say karaoke bar, but this place was the same as the German clubs I'd played in during the sixties – simply a place for people looking for very short-term romance.

I was issued with my very own bottle of Johnny Walker Black Label as I arrived, and was joined by a giggling bunch of Oriental babes. These women hung on my every word, without having even the vaguest idea what the hell I was talking about. No problem . . . by the time I'd witnessed the ritual of all the Japanese guys from Pearl singing 'Rock Around the Clock' as if their lives depended on it, I was at least a third of the way through my bottle of 'pimple and blotch' – and I couldn't understand me either. Now I like the distilled product of the grain as a chaser with a beer, and preferably spelt whiskey, but drinking just that all night is not for me. So by the time they marked the level of the 'water of life' in my very own bottle and put it safely away, in the unlikely event that I go there again, I'd had more than enough.

Unfortunately this wasn't my last trip to a karaoke bar. I went to another at the end of a Kinks tour in Tokyo, with quite different results. I'll try to remember to tell you about it in the pertinent chapter. There's no point asking Jim about it. It's not so much he's obliterated it from his memory; it was never in there.

OK, if you're that desperate I'll tell you now.

Touring Japan is not like touring any other country in the world, because the gigs start (and finish) so early there's no chance to eat before. Since the promoter is contracted to feed you he, or one of his representatives, will invariably take you out after the show. Eating in Japan is a time-consuming and food-sharing business. A meal can easily take a couple of hours, during which time you're squatting on your haunches. The only thing that made it bearable was the copious amount of lukewarm sake which was delivered with reassuring regularity to the low table we were sitting awkwardly next to. Now it's this rice wine combined with karaoke that caused the trouble.

To set the scene, it was just about the last day of a tour, and the record company (Sony) along with the promoter took us out to a very large Oriental restaurant. I knew we were in trouble when we all trooped in because there was a very large, highly sophisticated karaoke machine set up on a stage at the far end. We had the road crew, the shadow road crew of exceedingly able Japanese guys, lighting designers, drum techs, guitar techs, sound guys, security guys and so on all sitting around a very long gaijin-height refectory table. The promoter was anxious for us to sample a very special cold sake which came in a huge bottle: you only needed to sniff it to realise it was absolutely chock-full of intoxication. I was sitting with Stubz on one side and Jim on the other, and Stubz and I had a polite sip of the sake and poured the rest into a conveniently placed bonsai tree. Mild-mannered Jim Rodford, though, had quickly developed a taste for the stuff, and was really going for it.

Eventually the fun began when the Sony people got up to sing. Now karaoke is almost a religion. They take it seriously in the Orient, and these record company people put their heart and soul into it. They were good. Eventually, as inevitably happens at these events, it was everybody else's turn to sing, and Ian Gibbons and I decided to get started early. We did a rendition of something with him sitting on my lap like a ventriloquist's dummy. We'd done our duty – and now Jim felt it was his turn. He staggered towards the little stage and tonight, Matthew, he was going to be Frank Sinatra. He selected one of Old Blue Eyes' songs and went for it. When Jim had finished, to tumultuous applause, Dave got up, and took another microphone ready for his turn – but Jim was ready for an encore. He wrested the microphone from Dave, and now had one in each hand. Understandably Dave was put out and tried to snatch his mic. back, but Jim was anxious to give the people what they wanted. A struggle ensued in which Dave grabbed the mic. back and Jim brought him to the ground in a rugby tackle to retrieve it. (The song he was planning to sing next was 'My Way', which as far as Jim was concerned needed a microphone in each hand for a proper performance.) But Dave was still anxious to sing, and obviously needed to be subdued first. Jim accomplished this by trying to strangle him – all in full view of the great and good of the inscrutable Japanese music industry. Big Tel was for some reason slow in coming forward, so in the end Martin, the drum tech, managed to unlock Jim's hands from Dave's neck and remove his thumbs from his windpipe. Jim seized the moment to get on with the entertainment portion of the evening, and sang his favourite Sinatra number – or as Jim interpreted it, 'My Fucking Way'. Having finished the song, he completely trashed the karaoke equipment in a triumphal, Who-like way and like Elvis got ready to leave the building. I stole a look at the audience. Our road crew were struggling to keep straight faces, while the Sony guys and the promoter were wearing huge beams. They thought they'd stumbled into a real rock band, and we Kinks did this sort of thing every night! Common sense took over then, and Gibbo and I decided discretion was the better part of valour – that we should get Jim away from the restaurant before Dave got his breath back: pun intended!

We grabbed one of those cabs with the automatic doors that you can't impatiently pull open quickly without breaking, even if you're completely out of it like little Jimmy. We staggered through the hotel with his arms draped around our shoulders, and eventually got him into his room, dumped him on his bed and put a 'do not disturb' sign on his door. That was that.

We had a gig the next day and needed to get an early bullet train, so were all down for breakfast just before Jim. When he walked in everybody rose to their feet and applauded his performance. Fortunately Jim had absolutely no recollection of the event. Sadly Dave was not gifted with this amnesia, and remembered absolutely everything: he had the thumb marks on his windpipe to prove it. Things between him and his diminutive bass-playing assailant were sticky for quite a while afterwards.

Because you can't throw a television into the audience without breaking it I expected there to have been a huge bill for the damage to the Karaoke tower. It turned out the ever industrious 'shadow road crew' had worked through the night to piece it back together with super-glue and soldering irons and (for all I know) empty yoghourt pots. Evidently it was *almost* as good as new.

Telling you that story means I've moved out of sequence. Thanks a lot!

In 1978 I was booked to play drums on an album with a very surprising artist. It was surprising because he was (and still is for that matter) the best known drummer of all time. Ringo Starr was being produced by Russ Ballard, who had written all the songs, and because Ritchie (to his friends) was a tax exile we were going to record it in Denmark at a studio called Sweet Silence. It was a very interesting bunch of musos who flew out to Copenhagen on SAS one morning: me, John Verity, Dave Wintour and Chas Hodges were going out ahead of Russell B. (whose dad, Leslie, had very recently passed away) to meet Ringo and his manager there. Chas and I lived pretty close to each other, so we travelled together to Heathrow, me with my stick bag and a trusty Samsonite suitcase, which had survived many US tours, Chas with a Tesco's plastic bag containing a demo of the new Chas & Dave album and either a pair of underpants or a pair of socks, not both. As he said, we were only going away for a week or so. We found the others and joined the check-in queue, and I recognised the guy behind the desk from school. It wasn't easy because he'd changed a lot, and was now gay and camping it up behind the counter. As soon as he saw me he straightened up to deal with us. Unfortunately whatever else Chas Hodges had in his Tesco's bag, he didn't have a passport, which presented a real problem. Anyhow, he must have produced some form of identification because the next thing we knew we were on the plane heading towards Scandinavia.

Arriving at Kastrup airport we were surprised to find nobody waiting for us, so Chas steered us all at the bar to wait. Obviously musicians couldn't sit at a bar without drinking, and Chas asked the barman what strong beer he had. His response was Carlsberg Elephant. Those of us who have worked in Denmark a lot know that Elephant is probably the strongest beer known to man – outside Belgium. But Charlie Hodges didn't have that knowledge. Even though it only comes in regular continental-sized 275ml bottles he ordered us a pint each, and having disposed of my pint I realised I was drunk. There was still no sign of anyone to pick us up, so Chas did the necessary and ordered us another pint. This one went down slightly more slowly than the first and we were all having trouble talking intelligibly, but since we still hadn't been picked up it was obvious someone needed to talk to John Stanley, Russell's manager back in London, to see what was happening. I managed to dial the number with difficulty, and somehow talked to John, who informed me the reason no one was picking us up was because we were a day early. In the furore caused by Chas's lack of passport and my old school pal trying to prove he wasn't gay, they'd failed to notice the tickets weren't for the right day.

So we took a cab to the Grand Hotel, and on our way in caught sight of Noddy Holder from Slade dragging a heavy crate of beer across the Axminster carpet to the lift and up to his room. I'll draw a discreet veil over the rest of the proceedings that night, but we continued as we'd started. One of our number went to sleep leaving instructions that he should only be woken up when the drugs arrived.

The next day we went to the studios to meet Ringo, soon to be known to us as Ritchie.

Chas came into his own once the sessions were over for the day. He'd play piano and Ringo would play drums and sing songs like 'Red Sails in the Sunset' and other tunes we knew and loved from the Beatles' Hamburg repertoire. (Paul McCartney once told me they never had an ending and kept repeating 'Oh carry my loved one, home safely to me' until they'd had enough, whereupon they'd stop abruptly.)

I remember John V. was nursing a hangover after an evening out with Ritchie and fell asleep in a cupboard the next morning at the beginning of the sessions. He woke up hours later when it was dark outside, the studio was closed and we'd all returned to the hotel.

For one reason or another Ringo's record didn't come out in the UK, but one of the songs, 'On the Rebound', was eventually recorded by Russell and became a hit in America. It was also covered by Uriah Heep.

The next time I saw Ringo was when he turned up late one afternoon at Drumstore to buy a set for his young son Zak. I sold the world's richest drummer a brand spanking new Yamaha kit at a cut-throat price, and as he pulled a wad of notes from his back pocket like an old-fashioned used car dealer, he had the cheek to ask where his professional discount was. I was happy to tell him it was already included!

Sometime during 1977 Derek Griffiths, my old pal who'd played guitar in Unit 4+2 for a while and the bluesy solo on Argent's song 'Christmas for the Free' when Russell was just beginning to be overtaken by depression, wandered into Drumstore. Because I'd pinched the lovely Ricki from him I was always a little bit unsure of him, but he never seemed to bear a grudge and we repaired to the Ship for a chat. The Ship was the pub next door and always full of musicians like Phil Lynott, so the obvious place to chat about a musical project Derek had in mind. He wanted to start a ten-piece rhythm and blues band: was I interested? Jim Rodford was going to play bass, along with Mike Cotton's horn section (recently with The Kinks), with John 'Boat' Beecham on trombone, Nicky Payne on sax, Noel Norris on trumpet and a keyboard player so far unselected but eventually Eddie Spence. Root Jackson, a great Grenadian singer from the sixties, was going to be taking charge of vocals. I jumped at the chance because years earlier I'd turned down the opportunity of joining Mike's original band – I wasn't going to let it slip this time! Of necessity it was going to be a fun project, because while you can easily divide ten into any fee you can't reasonably expect the quotient to be a very big number.

So we decided to get a rehearsal room and see what happened. We wanted it to be a bit different from the usual 'I woke up this morning' type of blues thing, and the horns worked up great versions of highly unusual songs like 'Purple Haze', which were stunningly effective. As usual, the *raison d'être* for GB Blues Company was, as for most of my 'project' bands, have fun, make great music and if at all possible don't lose any money! The first two reasons were easily accomplished, while the third certainly wasn't.

The idea was we'd get to play at jazz and blues festivals around Europe, and sometimes we did, but because of other musical commitments we mostly played around London, or occasionally ventured a couple of hundred miles up the M6 to Manchester.

We all supplemented Blues Company with other gigs: Jim was in The Kinks, Nicky Payne was in an early version of Culture Club with Boy George, 'Boat' and Mike did pick-up gigs with jazz bands, as did Noel. I was with Phoenix, Charlie, Ian Matthews and Don McLean (depending what year it was, since we ran from 1977 to 1985). Derek played in The Tornadoes. Jim being in The Kinks caused a few problems, but Guinness (John Gordon) filled in admirably so long as I was there to make eye contact with him. Providing Jim or I was part of the rhythm section it was always possible to keep the whole thing together. Things weren't quite so good when I was working on long tours with Ian Matthews and Don McLean, and Jim was also away. And when I joined Jim in The Kinks the writing was on the wall for the Blues Company. We'd be in the studio doing demos with Ray, knowing we had a gig to get to within an hour, and hoping he wouldn't want to do another take. This wasn't good for our collective blood pressures or our churning stomachs. It was our fault because we tended not to inform Ray exactly what was going on, lest we be in breach of the increased retainer I'd negotiated for us all when I joined in 1984. But I'm sure Ray knew what we were up to. Blues Company was great while it lasted.

I was very nearly in a band with a Canadian prima ballerina named Lynn Seymour. She had decided she'd done enough classical ballet, so the only proper way forward was to have a rock band. It wasn't so much new wave as punk, and I'm sure if we'd ever got to playing any gigs she would have turned up with ripped tights and T-shirts with pithy slogans on them. Unfortunately we never got past the rehearsal stage in her house in Parsons Green, and it's probably just as well for all concerned that her alternative career ended right there. Years after the event, a punk band with a prima ballerina now approaching seventy years old dancing in it seems so preposterous that I wonder if I'm a victim of false memory syndrome or memory influencing drugs. Jim wasn't destined to be in that band, so I certainly can't ask him – but Dave Wintour should know. As I wrote I thought of Vivienne Westwood, so maybe it's not that preposterous after all.

As it happens, I had played on some punk records so I knew exactly how to go about it. It wasn't that I was protesting against anything in my mid-thirties, but the punk movement coincided with the opening of Drumstore, which was situated in Wardour Street just around the corner from both the Marquee and Trident recording studios. Frequently record producers rushed from the studios into the shop in a panic, asking if any of us were available to take over on a punk recording session where the drummer refused to play the song again. If he'd played it once and the producer wasn't together enough to get the performance on to tape, never mind the bollocks – he was off down the pub! Punk drummers could easily play hard and fast, but weren't interested in the principle of doing just one more take for insurance purposes. They were picking up the same sort of big advances from the record companies as mainstream bands, but God knows what they did with them. Punk groups spent as little as possible on making an album, and we certainly never made any money out of their drummers in the shop. These guys were more interested in their Mohican hairstyles than their instruments, and wanted second-hand drums, cymbals, drumheads and even drum sticks.

They were very entertaining and full of attitude when they came into the shop, though. A guy called Decca, who had the 'talent' to out-prank Keith Moon, was my favourite. One band who never made it big (maybe they were too good?) rejoiced in the imaginative name of the Four Skins (geddit?), although that doesn't come close to my favourite, which was Touching Cloth. One of the nicest of these so-called punks left a polite message on the shop's answering machine which went as follows: 'Hello, Gerry, hope you're well. It's Chris here. You know, Rat. Rat Scabies . . .'

I was playing in GB Blues Company when I got a call to do a tour with a chap called Ian Matthews. To be strictly accurate, his manager came backstage at a gig at the Venue, which had sprung out of an old theatre in Victoria. Sandy Roberton asked me if I was interested, and I was intrigued since the last I'd heard of Ian he was something of a folk singer, and I only really knew him from Matthews Southern Comfort, who had had a number One hit with a cover of Crosby, Stills, Nash and Young's 'Woodstock'. The gig was a tour of France supporting a Canadian band called Saga, and playing with an American guitarist called Bob Metzger, an English bass player called Dave Wintour, and an equally English guitarist named Mark Griffiths, who had been with Ian in Matthews Southern Comfort.

The first time I met Ian, Bob and Mark was at a large rehearsal complex with studios on several floors in Tooley Street, just over the Thames at London Bridge. We shook hands and began to play through Ian's songs as soon as we were set up, and had been banging on for an hour or two when the deafeningly loud fire alarm began to sound all over the building. This would have been the late seventies, when punk was beginning to invade the mainstream, so we gathered outside on the pavement with various other bands, mostly wearing ripped jeans or bondage trousers, T-shirts held together with safety pins and printed with slogans like 'never mind the bollocks' and the ubiquitous Mohican haircuts. We watched with boyish interest as the engine arrived and the firemen ran out their hoses. They were rolling them back up as we were waiting for the all clear, when another group of punks, the Monochrome Set, wandered out of the building and stepped over the hoses on their way to the pub. They'd been rehearsing so loudly they hadn't heard the alarm, and continued obliviously while the fire raged in the basement!

There's another rehearsal studio story that leaves a bad taste in my mouth a quarter of a century later. We'd been rehearsing with Ian in Ritz Studios in Putney, and having been bashing away for several hours we decided to repair to a local hostelry for some refreshment. I ordered a salad sandwich and a pint, and immediately bit into something slightly more slimy than I was expecting. It was indeed a slug, and I felt suitably sick and outraged about the inclusion of something I hadn't ordered. To make matters worse they changed the name of the pub to the Slug and Lettuce! On that occasion we were rehearsing for the French tour, on which a great time was soon to be had by all – unless you count the Scottish tour manager who had to deal with our misdemeanours and subsequently discipline us. The chemistry between us four (who I recently discovered with some pride were called The Insults) was fantastic, and musically what we achieved was exceptional, but so was the mayhem. I was a thirty-something married man with a mortgage, wife and two kids (with another on the way), and found myself behaving like a teenage hooligan on his first tour – and I loved it. I'm almost ashamed to say that we wrecked rooms, but since we were made to pay through the nose for everything by the tour manager I refuse to be too concerned.

Al Gallico, who was Argent's music publisher, once told me that he took care of Johnny Cash's music during his days of acute substance abuse. Johnny would be incapable of sleep, and would turn his hotel rooms into neat bundles of debris tied around with string. His tour manager would check out of the hotel and literally pay for the hire of the room and replacement of its contents every day.

There's no doubt it was mayhem with us, but it was never vicious or really life-threatening, always light-hearted and absolutely creative. (For your information, the going rate for recharging a fire extinguisher a quarter of a century ago was £250. This alone ensured we didn't let off too many of them!)

Ian was quite a laid-back guy, who was completely different to the rest of us. Mind you, he did have Judith, his American girlfriend, with him – so he had responsibilities! That said, he played hard musically, and I was most surprised at the first rehearsal to discover we weren't playing anything that resembled folk music. It was aggressive 'garage' rock.

Ian had moved to Seattle and had been well and truly caught up in the beginnings of the Nirvana grunge scene. He'd become involved with a guy called Jules Shear and the Polar Bears, who wrote a lot of great songs including 'I Survived the Seventies'.

Ian (aka Iain) had sold lots of records in France, and had not long since had a hit single there with a John Martyn song called 'Man in the Station', which was why we were going there. I was never sure whether Ian liked me. Believe it or not, he felt I was 'too much into advertising' because I wore Zildjian T-shirts with slogans on them. He was certainly frightened of what the rest of us became when we were together. He was also inexplicably frightened of my effervescent wife.

Saga were a revelation to me. I'd never heard of them, even though every US tour I'd ever done had included a stint in Canada – and they were really big in Europe. We criss-crossed the continent in the usual haphazard way, hitting as many large cities as we could in the time allotted by the record company's budget. Unusually we had security. This was composed of three French Hell's Angels who Metzger immediately christened Animal, Vegetable and Mineral. I'm sure these guys were really dangerous if you crossed them, but they loved Bobbie, and even though they wore all the right gear (denim jackets with 'colours' on the back, Levis and biker boots) they managed to look menacing yet chic at the same time. Their T-shirts were always sparkling, their boots shiny and their hair clean. They'd left their Harleys behind, and were driving around in a hired Peugeot that only Metz dared go in.

Saga had brought a complete North American road crew with them who seemed to be thrilled to be touring Europe for the first time. They treated it like a regular American tour, which turned out to be a huge mistake. I can't remember where the first gig was, but having finished our set we were amazed to hear Saga's intro music before they launched into their act. It was 'Jump' by Van Halen, which had recently been a huge hit for Alex and the boys across Europe. I'd never heard of any group coming on stage to somebody else's music, other than Argent with Ravel's 'Bolero', but strangely the audience didn't seem to care. Saga came on to a great welcome. They had a pretty big on-stage production going on, with ego-ramps, stairs and various other trappings of stardom. Steve Negus the drummer (who made no bones about telling us on a day off in Switzerland that he was off to Stuttgart to buy a Porsche) had a regular drumset *and* a Simmons on stage. Cool or what?

Every morning we all had a copy of the *Hooterville Times* pushed under our doors, which their tour manager, who obviously couldn't sleep, had produced overnight. Underneath the Mast Head was the slogan: 'An army marches on its stomach, a road-crew marches on its nose.' This might just give a clue to the reason for the guy's inability to sleep.

The sort of things we Insults got into trouble for with our tour manager were basic room adulteration. Fusing the electricity on one floor by removing a light bulb, putting a penny in and replacing the whole thing was one of the favourites. Normally this was done when you left the room for the last time, and mostly as a result of (arguably) having been given a hard time by the management, or bad service. One time, though, we were enjoying a day off before a gig in Dijon when two of our number fused the whole floor when they took control of their room for the first time, because they were curious to see the results of this prank. I went in to see Griff shaving by candlelight in the bathroom and Metz lying on the bed with an inoperable television, soaking wet carpet and a broken French window onto their balcony. Water bombs were responsible for the flood and the broken window. That was another innocent diversion, which worked well providing you had an easily accessible balcony and the plastic bags filled with water from the bath were kept small and easily portable. However, if as happened to Metz and Griff, you decided to push the envelope by introducing a binliner into the equation it was a recipe for disaster. Two slightly inebriated guys can't carry a garbage bag full of water: it absolutely has to end up on the floor before it's thrown out of the window. The reason the TV wasn't working was because a beer had been poured into the top, so they could watch the picture slowly disappear into a small dot. I'm told it would eventually come back, but not immediately. I never believed this, but turned a blind eye to it. Of course there were other liquids you could use that were closer to hand. I'll leave that to your fertile imagination: we certainly never went there!

There were other things you could do to keep yourself insane while on tour. Plugging a vacuum cleaner into a wall socket and switching it on before sending it off in a lift was a good one, but not as good as the wheeze we carried out with an unwisely abandoned and fully laden tea trolley and an empty lift shaft. That's simply too embarrassing to publish. I was interviewing Chad Smith from the Red Hot Chili Peppers one day, and the discussion somehow gravitated to hotel pranks. Thinking I'd found a kindred spirit, I was chastened when he asked me if I'd do that sort of thing at home.

Griff always spoke fondly of some water bomb mayhem on a Cliff Richard tour, where a Volkswagen Beetle ended up with a dented roof. Unfounded rumour has it that Sir Cliff became interested in this extra-curricular activity, and Griff told me at one time they were seriously contemplating having special plastic bags made up printed with 'Cliff Richard Tour' or 'You've been soaked by Cliff, have a nice day'.

We had to be rotated every night, because we got into too much trouble in any combination. Even if we were staying for more than one night we needed to be separated the next day. Ian made the mistake of allowing the rest of the band to do an interview with an important music magazine in Switzerland (or was it France?) without him. We decided to rearrange the room before the interviewer arrived, and turned everything that normally stood on legs upside down; everything else we simply upended and leaned against the walls. The journalist arrived to find us sitting on the floor in the middle of the space we'd cleared. He looked around for somewhere to sit, and realised the only place was the floor. He really didn't know what to make of the situation, but put his questions to us in a highly professional manner. We were anything other than professional with our answers. Recently Bruce Hazen reminded me of the incident, and how we cited Paul Bocuse and Rene Descartes as being our biggest musical influences.

We had a Scottish road crew who joined in the fun. On a day off these guys could drink everything from a mini-bar and, by the judicious use of various liquids at their immediate disposal, make it look like nothing had happened. They could open a bottle of champagne, drink the contents, fill it up, shave the cork enough to get it back in and even replace the foil and the muzzle. They had a tool kit full of all the necessary tools to make this happen.

Griff also had an on-the-road tool kit to help him wile away the long hours in hotel rooms. It consisted of screwdrivers, pliers, scissors, scalpel, glue and a generous supply of pictures of body parts taken from various soft porn men's magazines. When we arrived at a new hotel he'd do a recce looking for pictures he could work his highly creative magic on. In the main these were pictures of the restaurant and were ideal for what he had in mind. He'd lift them from the walls, or better still unscrew them from the lift, and take them to his room. Then he'd take the pictures apart and find a suitable photo of a body part from his collection to carefully (and literally) cut and paste onto the picture. He'd then put everything back together and replace them exactly where he found them.

In time people would glance at the pictures and do a double-take. Griff had put a breast with a nipple on a plate that someone was eating from, or maybe a penis sticking out of a bowl of fruit, or even someone's ear. Once on a picture of a solitary diner he superimposed a pair of legs wearing stockings and high heels sticking out from under the table. He had infinite patience, and his efforts were real works of art. For all we know these adulterated pictures are still on view in some of the hotels we visited. Of course all this was pre-CCTV, and he'd be caught bang to rights if he carried out his innocent hobby these days.

There was an Ian Matthews Band before me, which comprised Metz, Griff, Jimmy Russell and a great English organ player called Mick Weaver. They had also been guilty of causing mayhem. One of their pranks will take some beating, and ranks with Keith Moon's Cadillac in the swimming pool. While doing a gig in Salt Lake City, for a lark they drove a hired station wagon onto the Great Salt Lake, and skidded around having a great time until they realised they were sinking. Panic set in when they realised they couldn't go backward or forward – only down. They clambered out of the windows and stood on the roof working out what to do. Eventually they realised that they had to jump ship, and they were relieved to discover they could stand on the salt lake – they just couldn't drive on it. Eventually the car sank till only its roof was visible, and they had to think of a plausible excuse for losing a Hertz car in the middle of a salt lake! The estate car had to be abandoned, since only a helicopter could have retrieved it.

Keith Moon was creative with his pranks. My favourite and the most printable one concerns a can of Campbell's vegetable soup smuggled surreptitiously aboard the flight, opened and secreted in his hand luggage. Upon boarding the plane he turned left for first class and took his seat. While no one was looking he emptied the contents of the can into his sick-bag and replaced it in the seat-back in front of him. He then chatted to the people around him, saying he hated flying and was a terrible passenger. Eventually when the great and good had settled into champagne and gin and tonics Moonie somehow made himself look as if he had motion sickness. He started to moan and groan, reached for the sickbag and buried his face in the open end. People around him looked on with genuine concern as he struggled. When he had their undivided attention he lifted the bag to his mouth and drank the contents with relish. First class passengers would faint around him at the sight.

In the halcyon days before electronic room keys Metz never returned keys to reception when he checked out, keeping them just in case he returned. If the room was unoccupied he had free lodgings for the night. If someone was already occupying the room he simply said he'd been given the wrong room key. The worst risk was if he took charge of the room, made it his own and then the hotel allocated it to someone else. But he was prepared to risk it.

In the days of being able to check in at Victoria for a Heathrow flight, Metz fainted on the floor rather than pay excess baggage on the Fender amplifier he'd brought with him. They were going to allow his guitars for free with his suitcase, but when they asked if he had anything else he pointed to the heavy Fender Twin that he was standing in front of. The very British lady at the check-in told him he'd have to pay £100 excess baggage for the amp and he promptly fainted. I had no idea what he was up to, but improvised and picked him up. The concerned airline lady stood up and peered over her desk, and wondered whether she should call a doctor. Eventually he got himself together and told her he was OK but simply didn't have the money. Couldn't she help him? He gave her a sob story about being ripped off in the UK, and she agreed he could take it with him for £20. Bobby put his hand in his pocket and peeled just one £20 note off the top of the large wad of banknotes he had, having just been paid from a Randy Crawford tour. He was just about to pass the money over when he pretended that a new thought had hit him: if he gave her the money he wouldn't be able to get home from Los Angeles airport. He would be stranded. The exasperated lady gave in, and he put his money back in his pocket. It wouldn't have worked at Heathrow, and Metz knew that. Anyway he went home and bought a brand new mint green Saab 900 Turbo with air conditioning and sunroof – with the pocketful of cash he had on him at Victoria. Oh, I forgot to mention he'd ady been paid for the excess baggage transportation of all his gear as a tour se by Ian's manager Sandy Roberton. Sandy frequently told us in times of adversity, or while negotiating for more money, how he just happened to have been the boxing champion of the King's Royal Kenya Rifles. Danger, danger, danger!

We recorded with Ian Matthews as well as touring with him, and put out a couple of pretty good records: *A Spot of Interference* in 1980 and *Shook* in 1984. The first of these was made at a residential studio next to Sir Winston Churchill's modest stately pile in Woodstock near Oxford. The studio was at Chipping Norton, a village that is justifiably celebrated for a traditional ale called Hook Norton. It was traditional to supply the band with a pub-sized barrel of this amber nectar at the beginning of the sessions. This was meant to last until the album was completed, but we needed another after three days. Live-in studios around the world were all the same, deliberately kitted out with lots of diversions (pool, darts, backgammon, videos and so on) to stop the band working, and thereby elongate the time spent there. And there were never any clocks! *Shook* was recorded in part on a farm in Wales grandly named Mountain Studios, which belonged to one of Hawkwind's bass players. He had a rehearsal studio in the middle of the mountains with only sheep and low-flying fighter jets to keep us company. The fighters ruined many a take by strafing us, but nobody seemed to care. We'd taken the ex-Fleetwood Mac mobile up there as a control room and we set up our instruments in various dank barns. In an attempt to recreate the drums of doom we ended up sending the sound of a Simmons electronic snare drum out through a speaker cabinet and bouncing it around the mountains before committing it to tape. Outside the control room it sounded like a pile driver echoing round the peaks, and went on constantly while we played.

The bass player's wife/mistress did all the cooking and was christened Nutcase by Metzger because she was responsible for all the vegetarian cooking. At this time Ian and Griff weren't eating anything that had once had a face, apart from in Griff's case bacon sandwiches. We were put off Nutcase's cooking when we discovered a filthy towel covered in flies in the kitchen. Of course as musicians we should have known better: it's a terrible mistake to go into any kitchen that produces good food – but in our defence we were looking for something of an alcoholic nature to drink late one night.

We returned to London to do the overdubs to *Shook* at my old schoolfriend Nic Kinsey's Livingston Studios in that funky converted church. We spent many a happy hour waiting for our turn to overdub our parts sitting along with Nic in the Duke of Edinburgh, conveniently situated a 100 yard stumble from the studio. We also found time to indulge ourselves at the most unassuming but indisputably the best vegetarian Indian restaurant in London, also situated a short walk away down Wood Green High Street behind Turnpike Lane tube station. According to Ian's website, *Shook* represented the low point of his career, which surprises me. There was some great stuff on it, including a great version of The Yardbird's 'Over, Under, Sideways, Down', where I got to play a ride rhythm on a Chinese cymbal for the first (and probably last) time in my life. The Yardbirds' drummer Jim McCarty happened to be in Livingston Studios when we put it down, and was amazed at what we'd done to it. This didn't necessarily mean he liked it, though.

I can't remember how I got the gig with Don McLean, possibly via good old Bob Metzger, but I know I deliberated for some time about doing it and finally gave in – mainly because it was to be with an orchestra and I'd have to be using my decidedly rusty reading skills. So I agreed to the challenge, did a bit of homework and at the first rehearsal with these guys from the London Symphony Orchestra in autumn 1980 wondered exactly what I'd got myself into. Fortunately Bill Justis, who in the fifties had had a hit record with 'Raunchy', had written the parts and given me a great deal of leeway – so in the main the manuscripts weren't the proverbial 'flyshit' but were simply a 'road map' to tell me where to start and stop, rather than dictating *how* to start and stop. The reason for having an orchestra was because Don had just had a huge worldwide hit with Roy Orbison's song 'Crying', and we had a very interesting bunch of serious and not so serious musicians on the road. The leader of the orchestra was as usual a violinist, but the conductor was Ian Green, a keyboard player with what the 'proper' musicians called an erratic sense of timing. This meant the orchestra watched me instead, which would have been a huge responsibility had I only known. We had a violin section led by Robin Williams, a bunch of violas and cellos, a flautist doubling as sax player, a piano player called Jimmy Horrowitz who also co-owned Riva, the record company that Rod Stewart was signed to, Dave Wintour on electric bass and Fred Snell on something called a Z bass (like a double bass without a body), Les Morgan playing percussion and the indefatigable and completely unsinkable Bob Metzger on guitar.

The first gig was a comprehensive soundcheck for everybody, with microphones being attached to all the orchestral instruments. This was the first and last time the orchestra soundchecked because, believe it or not, it wasn't in their contract. So we rockers arrived at the gig and soundchecked at around 4pm while the 'proper' musicians headed for the pub. They returned in time to go on stage at precisely 8.50!

Musically the tour was a lot of fun and very enjoyable from that standpoint. We played a lot of songs in the act and the only one I wasn't happy with was 'Dreidl'. Nothing against the song, but it was very long and in a fast 2/4 so the bars on the music went by at breakneck speed. There were some stops in it, so you really needed to know exactly where you were. Because the song was so long it went over several pages, and since a drummer is playing all the time with all his limbs it ain't easy to turn the pages. I solved the problem by writing the words at the beginning of each verse on the manuscript paper. It's not cool, but neither is not stopping at the right place. I don't know why everybody doesn't do it.

Metz and I got on particularly well with McLean and taught him a couple of things, one of which was a game that for all I know he still plays. It's called 'I'm thinking of a person' and the only answers are supposed to be yes or no. It goes like this:

I'm thinking of a person . . .
Living ?
No
Male?
Yes
Showbusiness?
Yes
Singer?
Yes
Actor?
Yes
American?

Yes

Elvis Presley?

Sometimes we'd cheat by doing Mickey Mouse or Lassie, but the game would keep us going for quite a few miles till we got bored. When we finished the tour and everybody spread to their corners of the globe, every now and again my phone would ring at 3am and the American voice on the end would announce 'I'm thinking of a person'.

I also taught Don how to drink tequila, which I was astonished to find he'd never done before. There's only one way to deal with the liquor of the cactus and that's to have one (at the most two) with salt and lime, experience the best alcoholic rush in the world, then move on to something less dangerous, like beer. Unfortunately Don discovered he liked tequila, and kept on drinking it until it was too late.

I got on with gigs with GB Blues Company and sessions and things, and the next time the transatlantic phone rang it was 1981. That same 'American Pie' voice asked me if I wanted to do a US tour lasting several months. There wasn't going to be an orchestra but Metzger was going to do it, as was Fred Snell (on upright bass). Jimmy Horrowitz was busy with Riva Records so Garth Hudson would play keyboards, accordion and saxophone. I was a great fan of The Band, and that swung it for me: I really was looking forward to playing with him and hearing the stories. Being an enemy alien I asked about a work permit, and was told everything was under control. So I turned up at Don's place on Old Manitou Road somewhere in upstate New York and we began to rehearse a new orchestraless set. Pearl had provided a drumset for the tour (which Mr McLean still has), and we eagerly jumped onto the Silver Eagle bus that was to be our home for the next few months.

For once the tour was set up reasonably logically, and if we needed to retrace our steps for a recently added gig we'd fly there and meet the bus later. If we travelled overnight we always turned up at a hotel the next day so it was civilised, and we had bunks on-board. We had a tour manager called Ira with us, an equipment guy called 'Rabbit', Fred the Dutch bassist (known to me and Metz as 'Nee' which is Dutch for no – a word he used a lot), Garth and the driving duo (one side of which was called Lois), who belonged to the hippy commune that owned the bus. They were great people who had a neat trick: they could change drivers while speeding along the highway. The driver taking over sat on the other's lap, took over the accelerator and steered until the other driver slid out from underneath. We drove thousands of miles, and finally ended up on the West Coast in LA. Obviously we spent an awful lot of time on the bus, and I enjoyed every minute of it. I'd sung backing vocals on 'Hold Your Head Up' and 'God Gave Rock and Roll to You', but Don took my singing to another level. I discovered his favourite song was 'Since I Don't Have You', and he taught me to sing those harmonies with him. He was really into the close-harmony groups of the fifties and Don, Metz and I sang doo-wop songs like Don and Juan's 'What's Your Name?' till we got it right. In the end Don admitted I wasn't that bad – for a drummer! (Don had recorded with the Jordanaires so we even had a bash at their stuff too, as well as those ridiculously close-harmony cowboy tunes of the Sons of the Pioneers.)

I was told I had a work permit, but since it wasn't actually stamped in my passport that was being economical with the truth and professionally dangerous. I could be sent home unless I kept out of the way of the American Federation of Musicians – whose representative uncharacteristically turned up at every gig. But I almost came to grief coming up from the Mexican border around San Diego, where there's a surprise customs and immigration post well within America to catch illegal Mexicans and perhaps the odd British musician. I had a visitor's visa but any customs officer would have been crazy not to have been suspicious of my presence on the tour bus of a multi-million-selling singer. My American accent was the equivalent of Dick Van Dyke's English one and wouldn't have fooled anyone. Somehow I slipped through, but my suspicions were raised when it was decided not to take me to a gig in Vancouver 'just in case something unexpected happened and I couldn't get back into the US!' I never did get to see my permit.

Garth Hudson was the most enigmatic character I've ever met, which after fifty years of rocking and rolling is saying something. During soundchecks he absentmindedly played snatches of Band tunes like 'Rag Mama Rag', 'The Weight' or 'This Wheel's on Fire', and I enthusiastically leapt in to play along with fours on the bass drum, just like Levon Helm! As soon as I joined in he stopped, and said he hadn't meant to play that tune at all. Sometimes we got him to talk about Dylan and the rest of the guys in The Band, and he explained that the only way his parents let him go on the road (first with Ronnie Hawkins and the Hawks, then with Bob Dylan) was because he told them he was teaching the others music. For the record, Garth referred to the greatest poet of our time as 'Shithead'. I assumed it was a term of endearment.

Garth was a narcoleptic, which meant he could fall asleep at any time – and he frequently did. I'd expect something from the keyboards and, hearing nothing, I'd look across to see he was asleep with his head on the keys – during the show. McLean used to wind him up and announce one song and go into another, leaving Garth genially making his way to the microphone with the wrong instrument. It didn't faze him, and he'd just get on with it and play his solo. Don joked that the reason he'd employed Garth was because he'd always wanted to play with the Hudson Brothers! For those of you out there who don't recognise the name, don't feel bad: the Hudson Brothers were a family pop group with their own TV shows, a bit like the Monkees. They had their five minutes of fame around the time the Osmonds were happening during the seventies. Coincidentally Bob Metzger was their guitarist and was based in the UK filming *Bonkers!*, their TV variety show, a year or two before I knew him. Bill, one of the brothers Hudson, married Goldie Hawn and sired Kate Hudson. I'm not sure if not a lot of people know that.

We had a day off somewhere on Route 66 heading west, and Garth dragged his Prophet 5 into his hotel room to programme some stuff on the day off. We didn't see him till the next gig, when we discovered that for the piano intro of 'American Pie' he'd programmed in wind noises. At the end of the tour Garth asked what he thought was a perfectly reasonable question: 'Where's my tour bonus, Don?' McLean replied, 'You can have your bonus when you learn the chords to "American Pie"!'

We found our way to Chicago, and arrived the day before the gig to discover a new Irish band were on at the Riviera that night. They were called U2, and since I vaguely knew their manager Paul McGuinness I wanted to see them. They were really good, but it was so early in their career it seems they didn't have any songs left for an encore. Having secured one, they apologised before launching into their first song again.

In the beginning I couldn't play with poor old Fred – a double bass doesn't work in the same way as a bass guitar as far as the feel is concerned, because the note is more contained. I was worried. At the end of the tour I *could* play with him. and was even more worried!

We did a week in Lake Tahoe at Harrahs, which is primarily a casino, which (like its counterparts in Las Vegas) has rock shows to suck in the punters of a certain age. We followed Diana Ross into the main room, and the surrounding bars had great acts like the Nitty Gritty Dirt Band playing for a week. (The first time we were in Vegas in 1970 we were amazed to discover the Beach Boys were working there.) Metzger and I drove across the desert to Tahoe in the aforementioned Saab 900, and Ricki flew out to join me, Metz and his English girlfriend Ann-Marie for a week. This was followed by our first trip together to Big Sur, on our way to LA. At the time the Henrit family was a four-piece, comprising me, Ricki, and Lucy and James, who would have been seven and four at the time. Just as soon as we'd had time to be reintroduced to each other Joseph would be along, and since he arrived in March 1982 it's safe to assume he was conceived on US soil. I don't think Mr McLean was too sure about the girls arriving, because needless to say it changed the demographic of all the boys together.

Don was really into cowboys, and had written songs about them: 'Yippee kai ai oh, yippee kai ai ay, one man's work is another man's play, Oh Lord how I worked my dreams away . . .' So very early one morning the Silver Eagle bus drew up outside the Tom Mix museum in Dewey, Oklahoma. Dewey was a real Wild West town with tumbleweed blowing down the main street, which was built wide enough for a wagon, or a stage coach pulled by a team of horses, to do a U-turn. The early morning sunlight was blinding as they opened the museum up especially for Don McLean and friends. It was an impressive place, mainly because Tom Mix, the guy in the white hat who appeared to throw his bullets at the bad guys, was a proper cowboy. He'd found his way to Hollywood, and became a huge hit because he wasn't pretending to be something. He could shoot, ride, rope and herd cattle and did his own stunts. I knew all about him, and how he was driving to Hollywood in his 1937 Cord Phaeton when a flash flood took away the road. He plunged down a ravine, whereupon his Haliburton briefcase shot forward from the ledge at the back, hit him on the head and killed him outright. Among all the fascinating debris of a cowboy's life: pistols, rifles, holsters, saddles, chaps, boots, lariats, ten gallon hats (which couldn't even hold a single gallon) and gold shaving kit was an aluminium Haliburton briefcase with a head-sized dent in the corner.

We watched a couple of Tom Mix films before we staggered out into the daylight in the direction of a shop which sold western boots – not because they were cool or trendy, but because that's what people in that part of Oklahoma wore. I didn't buy any because if you can't play drums in Chinese policemen's boots you certainly can't play in cowboy boots either. I believe Don treated me, Fred, Garth and Metzger to western shirts.

In the fullness of time I came back to the reality of the UK, and got on with the job of being a professional musician, writer and drum shop owner.

During Drumstore's third year I was going to New York on Phoenix business, and I asked the guys at the shop if there was anything they wanted me to bring back.

The UK at the time was in the grip of electronic drum fever brought on in part by the drums on Carly Simon's 'Nobody Does it Better' in the James Bond film *The Spy Who Loved Me*, as well as some ridiculous 'diddley-doo' sounds on other hit records. I remember one American band that put some really inappropriate electronic drum sounds on their multi-million selling record, and years after the event said they put them on the track as a joke! There were three American drum manufacturers whose products were in demand here, but the one the Brits coveted most was Syndrum. This had been invented by a guy called Joe Pollard, whom I'd toured with when he was playing with the Beach Boys. Glyn Thomas, a busy drummer-cum-percussionist friend of mine, had asked if I could get him a set, so once I'd concluded my record company business I marched down Avenue of the Americas and into Manny's Music on 48th Street and bought half a dozen sets with my American Express card. Needless to say Manny's did me a good deal on the six sets, and I duly received a kosher receipt. Since I was going to have to declare them on the way through UK customs and pay tax and import duty, I also asked for a receipt for a considerably lower sum just in case I felt lucky. I sat on the plane agonising over which one I should use. As good (or maybe bad) luck would have it, the customs guy I went to recognised me, because he lived near my mother. He politely enquired how she was. I was completely sucked in, and having showed him the Syndrums pulled out the dodgy receipt. My customs official friend examined it closely, and looked me up and down before walking off to talk to someone behind that two way mirror you're not supposed to notice. Eventually he returned, and invited me to join him in a little room behind the mirror. Things were hotting up. He asked me ever more searching questions before reading me my rights and advising what would happen should I be trying to smuggle anything or avoid proper payment of duty. He then asked me for my wallet, which he emptied out to discover the Amex receipt. As he got the rubber gloves out of his drawer I realised the game was up and I was caught bang to rights. It was a fair cop, guvnor – but society was to blame. Several hours later they released me, having fined me and confiscated the drums. They were no longer my property, they were the Queen's, but I could buy them back from HM's warehouse in Isleworth in a day or two. Eventually we did this, and sold them instantly in Drumstore – although at a somewhat reduced profit.

After a while I learned the truth. While I'd been away HM's Customs and Excise had put on a seminar where a guy called Glyn Thomas, who had ordered a set of drums from me, had public-spiritedly advised them that unscrupulous people would probably be trying to smuggle Syndrums into the country. He even told them what the true price was at Manny's! To add insult to injury, Glyn used the Syndrums I'd managed to retrieve from the Queen's warehouse on Amii Stewart's 'Knock on Wood'.

Before this we'd been making our own electronic drums in conjunction with Dave Crombie, a boffin who worked for Argent's Keyboards, and with whom I eventually wrote a book about electronic drums. Our version was called Humdrum, a name that I cooked up in Tupperware (pun intended), which we bought from my sister Patricia who was a Tupperware representative. She drove all her friends mad with her 'parties' and everybody who knew her had cupboards full of the stuff. Ours looked great (like Adamski's flying saucers), although we never wanted to rule the world with Humdrum – just to stem the flow of orders until we got a reliable supply from America.

When Drumstore went bust I was hugely disappointed, because up until then in my professional life I'd been pretty much calling the shots, and if I changed direction it was because I had made the decision to do it. But here was a situation I couldn't control. We'd been trading for four years or so and weren't making enough money to stay where we were in the West End. We'd had our chance to sell out in the very first year of trading when a Japanese drum company had offered half a million pounds for the business. We declined, on the not too implausible grounds that we'd get twice as much for it the next year. Wrong! To be frank, 1981 was not a great year for the music trade. No one was spending real money on instruments. To add to our woes our landlord, the Duke of Westminster, was putting up the rent and Westminster Council was increasing the rates, so it was tough to make money. Add to that the fact that we took a gamble by trading in instruments in an area away from the mainstream music streets like Charing Cross Road, Shaftesbury Avenue and Denmark Street, where traditionally only sex shops and service industries were making any money. I'm sure you'll see our dilemma. Believe it or not, it's over a quarter of a century since we closed Drumstore and I still can't bring myself to walk past the shop. I unhappily walk for an extra half mile to avoid it. (Mind you, I don't suppose that's any different to holding my breath when the tube doors open at Arsenal station and not breathing again until they close. Arsenal moved from Highbury to the Emirates in 2006 and I still don't breathe when I get to Gillespie Road.)

We struggled on for another year, and then had to call it a day because of problems with the Zildjian room. This was a brave venture, in which we devoted a whole room to one make of cymbals, with a stripped-down, tom-less drumset in the centre. We spent a small fortune on fitting the area out with signage, carpets, lighting and racking, and every different size, shape and weight of Zildjian cymbal we could lay our hands on was hanging on the wall waiting to be tried under supervision by our guys (Steve Gadd, Mike Dolbear, Steve Rodford, Mark Brzezicki and various other resting drummers) – all wearing white gloves. It worked wonderfully well, and drummers benefited greatly, but because of the astronomical cost of a whole roomful of hundreds of cymbals they had to be provided on sale and return, as I'd agreed with my pal Bob Zildjian. Along with his brother Armand, he was indubitably the manufacturer of the best cymbals in the world. After a time, though, Rose-Morris, Zildjian's UK distributors, decided they didn't like us or the deal and sent an invoice for all the goods. This coincided with a terminal dispute between the Zildjian brothers, which left us friendless and completely unprotected against Rose Morris' demands. That was that. To cut the story short, they took their gear back and we had a large Zildjian cymbal room – without any cymbals!

We used to get quite a few foreign people coming into Drumstore, looking to buy equipment in bulk to take back to their own countries to sell. Frequently they wanted other instruments besides drums, and we contacted our suppliers to buy amplifiers, guitars, horns and various other bits and pieces, which as a drum shop we didn't normally sell. Often this worked OK, with transactions to middle European countries taking place without too much hassle (although they were never problem-free) because they had to pay up front. But selling to African chiefs was another thing entirely. They paid with letters of credit from their banks, but not before they had been back to the shop three or four times to negotiate a better deal because we were 'ripping them off'. A transaction that contributed to our demise was from Nigeria and the bank, call it the Nigerian People's Bank for argument's sake, refused to honour their own letters of credit. Since the gear was on its way to Nigeria we lost something like £30,000, a lot of money for a shop. After protracted negotiations with the bank we were told they weren't allowed to send the funds out of the country, and the only thing we could do was donate the money to the Red Cross. If the money ever got to the Red Cross I'd be interested to know what they bought with it.

As I said, I don't walk past that part of Wardour Street any more, but I do still wander around Soho from time to time. To be honest it doesn't hold the same vicarious thrill it used to all those years ago, but I'm amazed by what it's become. Of course it's got its seedy parts but 'pink power' appears to have transformed the place beyond recognition. Who'd have thought?

We moved out of Drumstore, suppliers took their goods back and that should have been the end of the story – but there were to be a couple of twists. A high-profile business doesn't go into liquidation unnoticed, and Drumstore was no exception. We'd closed the doors but HM's Customs and Excise felt they should investigate the circumstances of our demise. There's an official department called the official receiver, which at its discretion investigates limited liability companies that can no longer continue trading. The managing director was summoned to give evidence to the Receiver at Atlantic House on Holborn viaduct, but Norman Sheffield claimed he was too busy and anyway he'd always been non-executive, so, since Gerry Evans was very ill with Crohn's disease they not-so-politely requested the presence of the guy whose name was above the door. I had spent the six months up to our demise in America with Don McLean, so I knew I was going to be useless explaining exactly what the circumstances were that led up to it, but they insisted.

I turned up at the appointed time to meet a rather severe lady of indeterminate age who unsuccessfully grilled me for a couple of hours, before warning me that ignorance was no defence. She arranged to interview me again in a couple of weeks after she had returned from a holiday in New York. Seizing the moment to ingratiate myself, I switched on the charm and asked if she'd been before. She hadn't and, softening slightly, asked if I could recommend any interesting places to go. Having spent a lot of time in the Big Apple I reeled off the obvious attractions: the Statue of Liberty, museums, Carnegie Hall, Rockefeller Plaza, 42nd Street. She asked about restaurants, and I listed a few like The Stage, ending with my wife's favourite, the iconic Russian Tea Rooms on West 57th – once immortalised in paint by Beryl Cook. When we reconvened I asked politely how she'd enjoyed her holiday. She told me she'd found it exhilarating, and I was relieved enough to ask how she'd liked the Tea Rooms. She looked at me coldly, before scathingly informing me it was far too expensive for her! An even lengthier and highly uncomfortable interview followed.

The other Drumstore twist was that the family Henrit were all enthusiastic members of Vicars Moor LTC (our local tennis club) and our boys spent so much time playing there that we seriously thought it would be a good idea to buy one of the houses that bordered its courts. We started negotiations to buy one only to discover that we couldn't sell our own house. Norman Sheffield, one of the four partners in Henrit's Drumstore, had somehow managed to place a lien on it through Lloyds Bank over money he was allegedly owed, but had never bothered to ask for. We couldn't sell our house with this lien on it, so we were advised to take action against Lloyds and Norman. We were to be the plaintiffs; they were to be the defendants. I called in at Shepherd-Harris, a highly recommended firm of local solicitors, told them the whole sad story and eventually, after various claims and counter-claims and the usual issuing of writs, I had to unwillingly drag my feet to the High Court of Justice in The Strand. Unfortunately, a couple of unsettling things happened at the eleventh hour. First, my solicitor from Enfield informed me he was unable to represent me but was sending A.N. Other in to bat: not to worry, he was fully briefed on the case. Then Norman Sheffield called at midnight to try to get me to settle out of court. Since my legal argument wasn't with him but with Lloyds Bank that was a red herring, and I declined. I left home early for my day in court and, as normally happens in these times of stress, decided to go via my local church to cure my nerves. Itt worked until I was standing on the steps of the High Court and saw all these guys in wigs and gowns waiting to go in and act on our case as posted: 'R.J. and A.E. Henrit v Lloyds Bank in the Chancery Bench.' The enormity of the situation wasn't lost on me: if the case went against us I'd be paying all these guys, and ownership of the house would be immaterial – they'd have had to let us sell it to finance my day in court. We all filed in and stood until the judge appeared, sat down and brought his court to order. Only then did he look at the papers, for the very first time. As I recall, I was warned that as the plaintiff I wouldn't be able to say anything, but it appeared I wasn't the only one. Lloyds Bank's QC tried to say something and was advised to be quiet in no uncertain terms by His Honour, who appeared to be concentrating hard.

I held my breath while the judge went through the case papers. Halfway through, he looked up and addressed a question to the open court. 'Why is a family bank like Lloyds persecuting poor Mr and Mrs Henrit?' I began to breathe again as he aggressively cross-questioned the bank's brief, and eventually concluded that what they'd done was unfair practice. He found for the plaintiffs: me and the lovely Ricki. 'Case dismissed!'

As is the nature of these things, people stood discussing the verdict on the steps of the High Court, and one of the more eloquent solicitors put his face close to mine and said it wasn't over yet – and that he would see me in court. I told him this wasn't Hollywood, and since they'd just lost the case it was unlikely any of us would meet again.

Around this time Adam Faith asked me to come to a theatre in the West End where he was playing himself in *Budgie*. He had secured a commission from a newspaper to write 'Faith in the City', a weekly page on investments. I'd never been too sure about his prowess with money, but that wasn't anything to do with me: my role was to teach him how to use a laptop while he got ready for the show that night. I'd just finished a book on Simmons drums for Music Sales, and had written it using a Radio Shack Model 100, which was an early form of laptop with a rather small screen. It did the job, but compared with modern PCs and Macs couldn't possibly be described as user-friendly. It needed knowledge of computer principles to get the best out of it, and I doubt Tel ever cracked it. But he wrote his column for quite some time, until something went wrong and he got into trouble because of the advice he gave. As I recall, Michael Winner had taken some of this advice and regretted it vociferously.

He famously said: 'Adam Faith is to finance what Frank Bruno is to the English language.' In my experience Bruno was more *au fait* with the English language than our Tel would ever be with computers!

Rod Argent and John Grimaldi

Argent at the ICA

More TLR

Argent on Brighton beach

Tuesday 13th July, 1971

Argent looking jaded

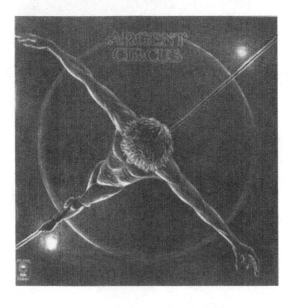

John Grimaldi's Argent cover

Argent 2: my favourite pic

A most uncomfortable way to hold a gong-beater

Argent outside New York's Summit Hotel

Argent at the EMI canteen

CBS

Columbia Broadcasting System, Inc.
51 West 52 Street
New York, New York 10019
(212) 765-4321

Clive J. Davis, President
CBS/Records Group

Dear Mel:

I'm sorry we didn't see each other when you
were in New York. I do want you to know
that we will be completely behind Argent in
their tour of the United States. You will
be hearing from the appropriate people in
our company to that effect. Our plan and
objective is to break the group wide open
once and for all. I hope the tour dates
will be effectively booked to do just that
as naturally the aura surrounding the group
is important.

Warm regards,

Clive

Mr. Mel Collins
Active Management
22/23 Dean Street
London W.1, England

April 27, 1972/ob

Letter from Clive Davis

Fred in his office

Ricki's dad,
John Hedderick

John and Harry

JV supporting Argent at home in St Albans

Argent reunited

Russell
Glyn
Ballard,
USA

The sweaty drum solo

Chapter Seven: THEY REALLY GOT ME

In mid-1984 I was playing on a wet Sunday evening in North London at the Torrington with GB Blues Company. Jim Rodford, who had left Phoenix a few years earlier and joined The Kinks, was in the band that night, and once we got started I looked out into the audience and thought I saw Ray Davies. There was a lot of playing to be done in that band, so I paid no attention and got on with it. It turned out it really was Ray, we chatted over a beer afterwards and that was that. Some time later I got a phone call asking if I'd like to record with The Kinks. I'd been auditioned at the Torrington, and evidently passed the test.

I was no stranger to Konk Studios, having made two albums there a year or two before with Dave Davies: *Glamour* first, then *Chosen People*, so I knew my way around the place. In June 1984 I found myself working on an album that was eventually to be called *Word of Mouth* and enjoyed myself immensely. Even though I say it as shouldn't, I acquitted myself pretty well. The album was for Arista Records, which was run by Clive Davis: he had guided my career and positively guaranteed us success with Argent when he was with CBS in the early seventies. It was my introduction to the new generation of Kinks songs, and they were pretty far removed from the charming, quirky and invariably poignant (intentionally ingenuous?) songs they'd been successful with in the sixties and seventies. 'Do It Again' was a throbbing rock song that was right up my street, and we opened the show with it for most of my career in the band. 'Standing in the middle of nowhere, wondering how to begin, lost between tomorrow and yesterday, between now and then . . .' I also had a soft spot for Dave's 'Living on a Thin Line', which had a great groove and featured a pretty imaginative Latin-inspired fill from me. At the time I wondered about the real message of songs like 'Word Of Mouth', 'Sold Me Out', 'Guilty' and 'Going Solo', and who they were aimed at. Eventually I made up my mind that they were subliminal messages being sent from Ray to Dave, and vice versa.

I say I'd passed the test, but as far as I knew I wasn't actually in the band: I was only what the Americans call 'guesting' on the record. Then I was offered a tour with someone else, and phoned Ray to see if they still needed me for recording because I had a tour to do. Ray's response was, 'You can't tour with anyone else. You're in The Kinks now!' That was that.

In a few weeks I'd be on my way to the States for a proper tour with proper money, but first I needed to learn the live repertoire. I knew all the obvious Kinks songs, but since I hadn't really seen them since Nobby's birthday in Cincinnati twelve years earlier, when we'd been unceremoniously removed from the stage, I hadn't heard too much. It was twenty years since their first record, so obviously I had a great deal of catching up to do.

Before I went to America, though, there was a video to be made for 'Do It Again', and I found my way to Brighton Pier with all the others to film it. Julien Temple was directing it with Ray, and I was dressed as a clown with those great big boots, which made it impossible to play the drums. Fortunately this didn't matter, because Ray played drums and I played guitar! This was a couple of weeks after the IRA had blown up the Conservative conference at the Grand Hotel there, in a failed attempt to assassinate Margaret Thatcher. The bomb killed my local MP Anthony Berry, who had once canvassed me on my doorstep when we lived in Winchmore Hill. Standing on the end of the pier and looking back at the promenade, the devastation was still very much in evidence.

My life as a musician has necessitated a great deal of flying, so it's hardly surprising I've had my share of aerial adventures. My very first engagement with The Kinks involved a Boeing 747 belonging to Pan Am. Jim Rodford and I were on our way to *Saturday Night Live* in New York. (Ray, Dave and Ian Gibbons had gone the day before, and we were travelling with the road crew.) We were upstairs enjoying the complimentary liquid amenities and getting our steak cooked by the side of our seat while the road crew were downstairs doing exactly the same, but without a personal seat-side chef. Then the captain came on the intercom to tell us there was a problem with number two engine and he was dealing with it. Jim and I had at least another couple of whisky sours by the time he came on to say in a slightly higher voice that there was a real problem with engine number two and he was going to have to switch it off. We didn't think anything of this, because after all a 747 has four engines. Eventually it appeared the problem was bigger than the pilot thought, and he came back on to say that for safety's sake we'd land in Gander. Eventually they closed the bar and we began our descent. I was excited because I'd read a lot about Gander in the aeroplane annuals I got every Christmas as a child: it had been a jumping-off post for the transatlantic Stratocruisers on their way to and from Britain in the fifties. I looked out of the window and was surprised to see snow on the runway even though it was September, and remarked on this to Jim. We landed on this 'snow' and taxied well away from the terminal building while fire engines circled us warily. Eventually we were given the all clear, and we finally disembarked, stepping out onto the foam they lay down for aircraft that were on fire and making an emergency landing! It turned out that the road crew down below had watched number two engine burst into flames. It was extinguished, whereupon it burst into flames again. We'd been oblivious to the danger and the excitement.

It's not good in any city when 350 or more people are delayed and need to be housed, fed and watered overnight, but it's a great deal worse when they descend on a small Newfoundland town whose *raison d'être* disappeared with the advent of jet travel. Gander was blessed with only a couple of hotels, and once passengers are on the ground their airside status disappears. First-class passengers like me and Jim queued for rooms to share and sandwiches to eat with everyone else. The little town very quickly ran out of food and alcohol. But we survived, and continued the next day to New York, where I think I remember we stayed in the Waldorf Astoria. There I had the surreal experience of sitting at the bar with Ginger Rogers on one side and Holly Johnson from Frankie goes to Hollywood on the other! After *Saturday Night Live* I had my very first argument with Dave. Our own soundman sat in on the gig, and for want of something else to say when asked about the sound he said the hi-hat had been too loud. I was taken aback, and then walked into a propeller from Dave – who used every adjective he could think of to express his perfectly balanced view. I was ready to go home the next day, but Ray took me off and got me drunk and on the Sunday I flew to Germany for my very first official Kinks gig in Frankfurt. In those days Pan Am planes all had names, and we took the same Queen of the Seas that had deposited us in Gander: it had a new engine and scorch marks on the wing. I didn't tell Ray and Dave, because surprisingly they weren't good flyers, even though like members of all successful bands they'd been on literally hundreds and hundreds of planes and no doubt accrued millions of air miles.

Having always been friendly with Mick Avory, I was really concerned about taking his place, but it was put to me that Ray wanted to investigate electronic and computerised drums and Mick had no knowledge of these things at all – and no desire to explore them. That said I was half prepared for the road crew to hate me because easy-going Mick had been so well liked. Fortunately this didn't happen at all, and after the first rehearsal in SIR Studios in New York I overheard Ray talking about me to Bob Suzinski, one of the American security guys. I was reassured to hear Big Bob say that I was 'all business'.

We'd had a couple of days rehearsal at Konk Studios in Crouch End before the first gigs, and on the first day I scribbled down the odd note about song shapes, beginnings and endings. On the second day, though, some of the songs ended differently. Naturally I questioned this, and was told that this was quite normal. At that moment the penny dropped, and I realised I wasn't in an ordinary band: the only way through was to watch Ray like a hawk. From a technical point of view, like most drummers I preferred to play with my head in the direction of the hi-hat. Unfortunately Ray was over on the right side of the stage so that wouldn't work. I had to change the habit of a lifetime to keep my eyes on him. It's an ill wind, and being forced to face stage right might have helped realign my back.

We all had a set list gaffer-taped to the floor next to us, and if we were really lucky the first song would be as it said. After that it was anybody's guess. None of us minded this: all we could do was go with the flow, and there was never a train-wreck. Ray would start a song, Jim and I would catch each other's eye, I'd play a suitably obvious short drum fill and we'd be in. We might not know what the song was, but we'd be ready for it. Sometimes I hadn't ever played it before: after all, The Kinks had been going for twenty years before I joined. There were even times when Ray would seize the moment and make up a song on the spot. We played in Cincinnatti at a festival by the river, the Ohio River Regatta, where Ray spontaneously wrote a song on stage called 'Regatta my Arse'. The huge audience loved it.

When I joined in 1984 computerised lighting systems were in their infancy, and we were using a state of the art Showco sound system out of Texas. Showco were involved with Veri-Lights, which was an ultra-sophisticated lighting system that Genesis once had an interest in. Each single light could rotate through 360 degrees horizontally or vertically, and change colour and intensity: it was absolutely cutting edge. But each different song's lighting plot needed to be chained to the one in front, so it could be stepped through. It all relied on one song following another without deviation. Unfortunately for the lighting director that wasn't the way Ray worked. Because he changed direction all the time we sometimes found we'd have full rock and roll lights for a ballad like 'Celluloid Heroes', and subdued and intimate lighting for 'All Day and All of the Night'! The sound guys had a problem too, since they never knew which vocal mics needed to be in use and which needed to be muted. It certainly kept you on your toes, because you really didn't know what was coming next. In other bands I'd had a bottle of beer before I went on, but with The Kinks there was no way I could drink that much: I needed to be on the ball from the moment the intro tape finished. I had to make do with a couple of swigs of a bottle of Heineken, which was the beer we had on the dressing room rider. The old Kinks had a deserved reputation for being drunk on stage, but in my day we never were. In all the time I was with the band we always managed to start and finish anything Ray launched into! I'm not saying the old Kinks invented binge drinking, but they certainly liked to be 'loose' on the stage, and in the studio and on the plane, and just about everywhere really. Things had changed by the time I joined, although Dave carried on the tradition. To give him his due he could happily drink more than anybody I've ever met – even more than dear old Chas Hodges who could drink eight Carlsberg Elephants without noticing.

Speaking of intro tapes (which we weren't), Ray and I had a Spinal Tap moment at a gig in New Jersey. We had our allotted sides to go on from, and although technically I could have gone on from either side because the drums were centre stage the vibes on stage right were invariably better, so I went on with Ray and Gibbo. We couldn't find a grown-up so set off under the stage without a security guy or a torch, and promptly got lost. We could hear the intro music above us and knew from the 'Really Got Me' guitar intro embedded in it that we were in trouble. With milliseconds to spare we found the stairs, and made it onto the stage by the skin of our teeth.

The on-stage monitoring was always set up on stage left, where Dave was – and if it wasn't it would invariably be moved there. He liked to tinker with sound as the show went on, and had instruments brought up and down in his and everybody else's monitor mix. There was a memorable moment early in my Kinks career when he took the drums out of my monitors completely. Fortunately I'd survived the 1960s, when I didn't have monitors anyway (or even microphones), so it wasn't the end of the world.

It would be an understatement to say Dave didn't like toms much: he hated them and trumpets in equal measures. He certainly related strongly to Mark Knopfler's lyrics to 'Sultans of Swing': 'They don't give a damn about any trumpet playing band, it ain't what they call rock 'n' roll!' Since I had at least five toms in my set up, I was on a hiding to nothing. If I made the mistake of doing a perfectly valid fill around the toms, I could expect to be told about it in no uncertain terms. It wouldn't be couched as nicely as Donald Auty's 'Now, boys' speech to the Roulettes, and he would certainly mention 'see you next Tuesday' in the conversation. (This was a word he enthusiastically used at a time when it wasn't at all fashionable.) Dave never actually told me how to finish any Kinks song, but having looked daggers at me at the end of every song during my first real gig at the Festhalle in Frankfurt he immediately took me aside to explain. He wasn't diplomatic in his explanation, and our heads were uncomfortably close together too long for my liking. It didn't take me long to get the picture. Because of this embargo on toms I wasn't able to 'build a shed' properly at the end of any of the songs, which was a shame because I pride myself on being able to thrash exuberantly and effectively on the final chord. I had to make do with rolling on the cymbals with a bit of bass drum underneath, which I felt was lightweight and didn't add anything to the drama. As Evie Taylor said in about 1962, 'If they can't tell it's the end how the fuck will they know when to clap?'

I had a friend called Frank Ippolito who owned the best drum shop in New York City when I first went there. He was a real Anglophile, and even though he was my father's generation I had an excellent rapport with him. (Drummers, or maybe crazy drum shop owners, have a lot in common.) Anyway, Frank had played with what was called the Army Air Force Band based in the UK during the war, which was really the Glenn Miller Orchestra, and once when we were taking tea in Professional Percussion on the corner of 8th Avenue and 49th Street he told me how Glenn Miller kept the band on their toes so they didn't get stale. He changed the intros and outros to tunes like 'String of Pearls' and 'In the Mood' almost every night. Like a fool I told Ray about this, and I believe made a rod for my own back.

Ray was really good at instilling something called creative tension into us, which I believe is a theatrical device for putting artists on their mettle. How it worked was like this: just before we went on he'd say 'I think we'll do "20th Century Man" tonight"', which would make me, Stubz and Midget sit up and take notice. That particular song had no arrangement, and we'd have to do a lot of concentrating to perform it without a train wreck. So we were on tenterhooks expecting this song, and if we relaxed and presumed it wasn't coming it would and if we were tense and ready it wouldn't. There was one night when we opened with it instead of 'Do It Again', and didn't know it was coming till Ray started the intro riff.

We also didn't know how Ray was seeing the shape of a song on any given night. His great strength was reading the audience and giving them what they wanted. The last album before I joined was actually called *Give the People What They Want*. We had to be aware where any song was going, because if he wanted to do three verses instead of two, or two choruses together, we had to react. I used to think some of these commands came through the ether, because they were never spoken. Another thing Ray liked to do was stop the band with a hand signal at the end of a chorus or middle section, to get the audience 'at it' – going for a call and response thing with them. I was never sure whether I was meant to stop with the others or if I was meant to keep going, so I got to a situation where if I was meant to continue playing I could pick up on the very next offbeat.

One of the greatest drumming thrills ever (make that *the* greatest) was when Ray stopped the band halfway through 'Lola' and I continued playing. The lights were turned on to the audience and I watched thousands of people clapping and moving to the simple rhythm I was playing: 1 and 3 on the bass drum (sometimes with a sixteenth in front of the 3) and 2 and 4 on the snare. I could make the audience move a little or a lot simply by slightly adjusting the position I put my beats in: this was real power. Ray contributed to the intensity by shouting 'Dayo', which the multitudes shouted back, and then 'Lola', which again they responded enthusiastically to. I imagined this was the power that the great dictators had over their subjects as they harangued them at those monstrous rallies around the time of the Second World War. I once stood on Hitler's podium at Zeppelin Platz in Nuremberg, and imagined the same power I got from 'Lola'.

It's interesting to note that being in The Kinks didn't provide a particularly diverse range of experiences: tours, gigs and recordings were so well set up that it was all pretty much the same each year: only the songs would change. I'm not knocking anybody here, but we often did the same old gigs where we were successful every time. I don't believe this was any different to other bands at the high end. Much like the hotels, limos and gigs that drove some bands what Adam Faith referred to as stir crazy. But it was certainly never the 'same shit, different day': how could it be with Ray and Dave?

The latter Kinks years were invariably feast and famine, inasmuch as we were going full tilt at doing something or we weren't. Nevertheless we certainly earned the retainer we received every week from the management. We found ourselves in the studios putting down demos or over at Ray's place in Effingham (which was hell for me to get to since it meant negotiating at least 50 per cent of the busiest part of the M25) working on lots and lots of new tunes. These demos were invariably routined then recorded on home ground in Konk Studios, which was an easy journey for me – four stops on the overground from Winchmore Hill station to Hornsey. Frequently we arrived at these sessions and kicked our heels till RD arrived, so we routined the songs in Konk in one of the rooms adjacent to the big studio and eventually moved into it to record. Konk One was (and still is for that matter) a fully equipped professional studio, initially with one then two twenty-four track analogue recording machines but eventually with one (sometimes two) synchronisable Sony digital tape machines, giving a total capability of up to a hundred tracks to record on. Making demos in this fashion was overkill in the extreme, but it never stopped us!

The conundrum has always been that if professional musicians are recorded in a professional studio with professional equipment by professional engineers, what is the difference between a demo and a master? The answer is very little, not when you played a piece to the best of your ability to get the job done and not let yourself down. There was never a thought that if you made a mistake (played a bum note or wandered off out of time) this would be acceptable because it was 'only' a demo. We always gave the track 100 per cent. So when it came time to make the master it was difficult to change the mindset you'd had previously. In short you could always do something differently, but not necessarily better. Frequently for the master Ray wanted to hang on to a section from the demo, so we'd edit each track severely. Sometimes this worked. In reality there was always a reason why a verse or a chorus sounded good – because of where it came from; so putting a good verse from take one with a good chorus from take two wasn't necessarily a licence to print money. But it didn't stop us (make that one of us) from trying. To be fair, it sometimes worked but mostly it was a pain in the arse. To make this happen with a pair of analogue tape recorders was very time consuming, but to do it with digital recorders

You all know my track record . . .' I don't believe it was quite what Pat's family were expecting. Ray had already been married to Alessa, as well as being heavily involved with Chrissie Hynde with whom he had had a child. I remember seeing her standing across the road from Konk once as we came out of a Dave Davies session there.

The Kinks never had a big road crew. We had enough guys on the payroll to get the job done, and that was pretty much it. Probably the only luxury was a wardrobe person, but since Ray liked to change his clothes a lot during the set he or she was in fairness pretty essential. Malcolm was the first wardrobe guy, who also did luggage, and he was replaced by the slightly more attractive figures of Julie and someone whose name I really can't remember. Jim will be able to help, though! There was a limo driver in New York who drove us around the city a lot, whose name I've carefully erased from my mind just in case I'm ever invited to appear before a grand jury. He wasn't always available, because every now and then he went to south-east Asia to settle old scores for the government, no doubt with extreme prejudice. I'm told SAS guys never leave the regiment, so our security guys became unavailable too when things kicked off around the world. We used these guys instead of the gung-ho cowboys who were out there looking after most bands at the time. They were trained to see trouble and manoeuvre us or the potential trouble-maker out of the way before it happened. Everybody else's cowboys didn't: they waited until the bother occurred, then they waded in to sort it out. I guess they needed to justify their positions – and I suspect they actually enjoyed the violence. We were forced to use non-SAS guys a couple of times when we couldn't find our usual minders. Each time their absence was followed within a month or so by a 'spontaneous' invasion of a Balkan or an Arab country. Of course all this is conjecture on my part, and certainly not an intentional contravention of the Official Secrets Act. Those chaps were quietly tough and unassuming, and very reassuring to have around – particularily on the other side of the Atlantic, where over-enthusiastic Americans invariably felt they were entitled to a piece of you. They were also very interesting guys to have a quiet drink with, because even though they didn't boast they had such great bloodcurdling stories. And like all soldiers they had instant and brutal solutions for all the world's ills, which unfortunately (unlike our New York limo driver) their political masters were loathe to let them use. I earned their respect, believe it or not, because of the way I shaved. Like all the men in my family I've always had a tough beard, and over the years I've learned that the only thing that works is a completely dry shave with an unsophisticated razor. These tough guys from Hereford were aghast when they saw me, and said no-one in their circles would be brave enough to do it. I felt I was ten feet tall. They told me one story about how a very young 'Rupert' had joined the regiment and had started throwing his weight around. Showing off, he invited one of them to attack him unarmed, and the soldier did as requested – whereupon the Rupert produced a knife and asked what he would do now. The exasperated SAS chap lost his rag and, grabbing the knife by its vicious serrated blade, ripped it from his hand and knocked him out with the haft. He then went straight to hospital to have major surgery on the severed tendons of his hand. I preferred to show my bravery by shaving without soap and water!

Though most of these security guys came and went, big Terry Draper was around for most of my time with The Kinks. I'm not sure if Big Tel or Ken Jones invented the hiding room, but like just about all of the crew he used it from time to

139

time when he didn't want to be captured by the management or Ardy or Mr Russell, known to the crew as the Dangerous Brothers. The funny thing about this story is that at every gig the rooms were labelled catering, wardrobe, production and so on. Eventually there was a room away from the mainstream officially labelled Hiding Room!

The Kinks had had several managers before I got there, including Robert Wace, Grenville Collins and Larry Page, but by 1984 Ken Jones appeared to be taking care of day-to-day events in the UK while Elliott Abbott was guiding the band in the USA. Towards the end Kenny Laguna, who had been in Tommy James and the Shondells and recorded 'Mony, Mony', took over the reins, and the US touring began to speed up a little.

Like most drummers I've had a lot of problems with my hands from playing, and of course the more frequent the gigs were the worse it became. I play with what they call a traditional left-hand grip, which means I hold the stick like a marching drummer would, with the business end going between fingers two and three and the fat end resting on top of the pad between my thumb and first finger. This pad was frequently abraded from the stick bashing on it, and most of my fingers and thumbs had blisters on them. This made playing difficult. Now I know there are those who say I must have bad technique to get blisters, but I'm not buying that. Being out in front of thousands of over-enthusiastic people and propelling the band under intense lights, which meant you were soaked with sweat that ran down your arms during the first number, has very little to do with technique and finesse. Frequently the pad between thumb and first finger on my left hand (which was responsible for what the Americans call the backbeat) was skinless and bloody. I used to say you could see the bone there, but I might be exaggerating just a tad. That said, over time a corn has grown up there. When it was examined by Bill Graham's doctor in San Francisco, he offered the opinion that it might be carcinogenic. Cancer of the hand? It's not the most well-known form. Through all the sixties and seventies I put up with the pain and only put a plaster on it when it was necessary – usually two days into a tour. But when I joined The Kinks in the eighties I saw the light. Why not put Elastoplast on the places I knew would blister *before* it happened? I found some great stretchy fabric sticky tape in New York made by Johnson & Johnson and I've used it ever since. I had a couple of false starts with The Kinks using Nuskin, which I discovered in New York. Depending which one you bought, you painted or sprayed it on to create a film over the wound, which was good. But the pain of applying it to raw flesh was unbelievably bad.

When I was a teenager older drummers told me that the way to toughen your hands up was to wee on them. I honestly never did this but I'm pretty sure it's an old wives' tale, up there with sending apprentices out to get a can of elbow-grease!

All my life I've been fascinated by the magic of steam radio, and embraced it even more when I discovered I wasn't growing old quite as gracefully as I'd hoped. There was (maybe still is) a desire in me to be a presenter, so when out of the blue I was asked to make a programme for the BBC I jumped at the chance. It was to be called *The Drum*, so no prizes for guessing what it was about. To tell you the truth I'm struggling to remember all the details, and especially how I was pressed into it. I can tell you where it was recorded – in one of the warren of studios in Maida Vale; who was in it – Jack Parnell and Dave Simmons; where the music came from – the world-famous BBC Gramophone Library; who the actors were – members of the BBC Repertory Company; and who helped me with the music – the BBC Radiophonic Workshop. (No prizes if you're British for knowing they were responsible for the evocative *Doctor Who* music.) The reason there were all these BBC departments involved was because they didn't impact on the minuscule budget: they were already being paid by the Corporation.

This was a couple of decades before Google, so I spent a lot of time in the BBC library at Broadcasting House researching the subject. It was worth it because I discovered a few great stories about military drumming, which with the help of the actors we were able to turn into little dramatised plays. At a time when armies used drums to signal orders on the battlefield, a very young British drummer boy was captured at Waterloo, the battle not the station. His captors wanted to shoot him as a spy, but when Napoleon wandered over to see what was going on he said that if the lad was really a drummer he would be able to play the command for retreat. The boy faces up to 'Old Boney' and angrily informs him there is no such command in the British Army. Napoleon orders his release.

For some unknown reason the French march more swiftly than us Brits, and they have frequently chided us on the subject – what you might call 'se foutre de la gueule' or, for people with French as a second language, prener le piss. However, we're able to retaliate that although this may very well be the truth we've marched slowly all over France and they have never managed to march quickly anywhere in Great Britain – without our permission.

The programme ended with a great rendition of 'Drake's Drum' by Sir Henry Newbolt:

Take my drum to England, hang et by the shore,
Strike et when your powder's runnin' low;
If the Dons sight Devon, I'll quit the port o' Heaven,
An' drum them up the Channel as we drummed them long ago.

I hadn't been in The Kinks for more than a year when I got a call from the elder daughter of the Barkers, who had lived next door to us in Waltham Cross at number 17 when Cliff's people had lived on the other side at number 21. They'd moved south of the river to Eltham years before, and even though Christmas cards were sent every year while our parents were alive that had now stopped, and I had no idea what the girls, Joan and Maureen, were up to. Joan explained exactly what she was doing. She was in films, knew all about Drumstore and asked whether I was still in the music business. I explained what I was up to and she told me about this film Julien Temple was beginning called *Absolute Beginners*. She told me who was in it: Bowie, Patsy Kensit and Ray Davies. (I already knew Ray was going to be involved because we'd recorded some music for it: a song called 'Quiet Life'.) Eventually she told me why she'd called. She was the art director for the film, and looking to find someone who would be able to source the necessary instruments for a major musical set in London in the fifties. I had no idea what an art director did: I actually thought it was something to do with painting the scenery. Once Joan filled me in I figured by networking my crazy musician friends with vintage instrument collections to get the job done. The set was already being built at Pinewood so I went along to take a look. It looked fabulous and depicted the West End exactly as it had been when I'd gone up there with my folks to buy my first drum kit a quarter of a century earlier. The only things missing were the 'ladies of negotiable affection' leaning provocatively on the lamp-posts.

The Kinks were off the road between tours and recording, so I was able to throw myself into this. I enlisted the aid of Mark Griffiths because he had by far the biggest selection of vintage guitars, while I had more than enough suitable drumsets for the various locations. This stuff, known to my wife as 'my crap', was spread between my overflowing garage in Winchmore Hill and the storage bay at Konk Studios in Hornsey. *Absolute Beginners* was set at a period before American instruments were available here, so we needed to find British, German, Italian and French stuff. Mark Griffiths came up with the right guitars, Egmont, Grimshaw, Rogers, Antoria and even a couple of highly collectable plastic Macaferris made by Selmer – recently found by a publicist pal, Max Kay, in the back of a French warehouse. I came up with a Trixon Speedfire, an ancient Premier and a few bits and pieces like snare drums, cymbals and so on to dress the window of the music shop in the film. Since it was the heyday of the dance band we also needed trumpets, saxophones, accordions, and even jews harps, harmonicas and kazoos.

Unfortunately for me and the British film industry *Absolute Beginners* wasn't a success, and didn't pave the way to fame and fortune for me in the film business as Joan had promised. But I did go to a film premier for the first time in a while and got to see my name on the silver screen in the credits.

Nevertheless there was another film for me to dress. Hard on the heels of *Absolute Beginners* came another film about music – although not a musical as such. The plot of *John & Yoko – a Love Story* was contained in the title, so it certainly didn't need a trailer. It was set against a background of famous gigs and the different musicians Lennon had worked with. It needed to be dressed as accurately as possible (unlike *Back to the Future* and *The Buddy Holly Story*, which I was shocked to see had a couple of glaring inaccuracies in the guitars used). Anyway, this film was being made for HBO by a company owned by Johnny Carson of *Tonight Show* fame. and had Mark McGann starring as John Lennon. I had a lot of the drumsets necessary in my vintage collection, and once again Mark Griffiths had just about all the guitars. So I shipped various Ludwig sets and the odd Slingerland (for Alan White in the Plastic Ono Band) to Wembley Conference Centre, where they did a lot of the filming. Griff, meanwhile, loaded himself up with Fender, Gibson, Rickenbacker, Hofner and Gretsch guitars, and various amplifiers including Vox. Interestingly all The Beatles' bass drums needed to have logos on the front, so I got a half dozen or so made up on modern Remo heads. I have no idea where they are now, but experts claim that far more Beatles logoed heads have been sold at auction than there actually were. My Catholic upbringing wouldn't allow me to keep one back for myself as a hedge against inflation!

Ray Minhinnett had been in Phoenix's second emergence from the fire after Jim had left for The Kinks in about 1977. This was the time we had two guitarists, in John V and Ray, and no bass players. At the time it didn't matter because JV played bass on the records, but fortunately (aside from a showcase for an agent) the studio was as far as we got. If we'd ever had any live gigs we'd have been in trouble! When the whole thing metamorphosed into Charlie (also known jokingly as Char-Phix by Trident), it didn't include Ray but did include JV and me along with Terry Thomas, Steve Gadd, John Anderson and Terry Slesser (who had the unique distinction of turning down AC/DC). So Ray and I sort of lost contact musically, until sometime after *Absolute Beginners* he called me to talk about a film he'd just finished called *Curves, Contours and Bodyhorns*. To the uninitiated this meant nothing, but to anyone who knew about Fender Stratocaster guitars it meant a great deal. The documentary bravely concentrated on a single instrument and the many guitarists who had played it since its inception in California in the very early fifties. Everybody whom he could get a clearance for was in the film, from Buddy Holly, Hank Marvin, George Harrison, Jeff Beck and Yngwie Malmsteen, all the way through to Eric Clapton. This had worked well, and the film had received critical acclaim: it had been up for several awards and the book of the film had been published. On the grounds that nothing succeeds like success, Ray's suggestion was that we made another film concentrating on drums, drummers and drumming. *Crash, Bang, Wallop* was the title I came up with for what we wanted to be what the Americans call, succinctly and embarrassingly, an infotainment. It was specifically designed to appeal first to people who knew nothing of drums and second to people who did. Everybody who was anybody was due to be in it, from Moonie to Buddy Rich, Gene Krupa to Ringo. Charlie Watts was to be in the opening scene. Initially we were looking at a film for broadcast followed by what was then called a long-form video but would now be a DVD, with a book alongside, which I was eventually to complete: *The A to Z of Drums*. Within a month we had a dynamite treatment, which we planned to be voiced by Ringo and were ready to present to interested parties.

There was an evocative cover, which my daughter Lucy had painted when she was a toddler at nursery school. I'd always felt it looked like a modern art painting of a drummer, so we used it.

Picture if you will an aborigine sitting under a Joshua tree in the desert outside Five Palms. He's playing a primitive 'hambone' rhythm on a small ethnic drum with a large thigh bone. After establishing the rhythm he stands up and throws the bone in the air, and the camera pans back and follows its trajectory. It spirals up in an arc and eventually comes down into the concrete canyons of New York City, whereupon a hand reaches up to grab it, and it turns into a drum stick that crashes down on to a cymbal. The camera zooms back and we discover Charlie Watts at the Times Square end of Broadway sitting at his drumset. He launches into 'boof, daff, boof-boof daff, boof-boof, daff, dada-dada-dada-dada . . .' For those of you who don't read drum, that's Charlie's intro for 'Honky Tonk Woman'. The screen behind him (where they show the count down to each new year) bursts into life, and the film begins.

It seems the golden rule is that you never use your own money to make a film, which was just as well because we didn't have any to spare. We set off to Hollywood to drum up (sorry) the necessary million quid or so. I was nervous about exposing ourselves like this in the movie capital of the world, but since at the time I had forty-odd years invested in the project and all the necessary contacts I reasoned it wouldn't be that dangerous – especially since we had the protection of the disclaimer at the back of the treatment. More of this later. We based ourselves at the Sunset Marquis and were very well received in California, but pretty soon realised we were barking up the wrong tree. We were trawling for money among the musical instrument industry, where traditionally the million pounds we needed represented the profit on three million pounds' worth of sales. Even the very biggest drum and cymbal companies we approached, like Remo, Sabian and Zildjian, who were excited by the project and could have benefited from the exposure, were scared off by these dollar signs with too many zeros after them. Still, we made the best of our time in Hollywood until one night we found our way to The Rainbow to see Stevie Winwood. The upstairs section there isn't exactly massive, and we discovered our table was next to Tony Curtis's. He came in a little late, and promptly leaned over and shook hands warmly with me, Ray and Bob Young – none of whom he knew from brickdust!

Eventually, to get the ball rolling and give any potential broadcaster something to get excited about, we decided to break the rules and invest our own money. We started filming at a musical instrument show in Wembley Conference Centre with my skiing pal Mike Edwards, who was a freelance cameraman. We got some great footage there, including some of Cozy Powell and some equally amazing stuff from Peter Green, who talked exclusively about Tony Meehan and Jet Harris from The Shadows, citing them as huge influences on his career. The next thing we planned was to make a start on the intro, and hearing that the very next year was to be a Stones year, when Charlie Watts would only be available for their concerts, we began to panic. We started our negotiation with his pa/manager, but this wasn't easy because Charlie, like all the Stones, is very well protected and nothing is done in haste. We had meetings with his people and eventually it was agreed that Charlie could do it, but only on one particular day just before Christmas: we would need to pick him up, take him home, provide special food and drink and cater for his every whim. Readily agreeing, we sent over a shooting schedule so Charlie would know exactly what we wanted him to do. We booked a studio and I contacted Bill Harrison, who was Charlie's drum-tech, about getting an evocative drumset for the shoot. We decided on his Cadillac green Gretsch set from the fifties with gold fittings. When we arrived we set up the studio, complete with Charlie's drums on a riser in front of a blue screen. The special food, coffee and milk arrived just before 'Old Stone Face', who wandered in and shook hands before looking in bemusement at the drumset. 'What's that doing here?' he asked. Ray and I looked at each other, and said, 'It's for the film, Charlie!'

'I don't do drum solos,' he growled.

We told him we didn't want a drum solo, just what was in the script, and we'd talk to him on camera while he sat on the riser in front of it.

'What script?'

I explained what we wanted him to do and play: the intro to 'Honky Tonk Woman'. 'How's that go?' Charlie asked – so I hummed it to him!

To begin with, he had to sit at the drums in front of the blue screen, hit the cymbal and throw the stick into the air. The idea was we would reverse the shot and the stick would look like it was coming into Charlie's hand; then we'd superimpose the whole thing on a moving shot of Times Square. Charlie got started and soon warmed to the task, but having thrown the stick in the air left the drums to catch it. We explained the situation and he nodded, but once the cameras were rolling he did it again. After quite a few false starts we managed to get the shot we wanted, and we launched into the interview with him. Charlie sat on the riser with his fantastic drums alongside him, and we talked drums and drumming for a couple of hours.

144

The next time our paths crossed was years later at the presentation of a lifetime achievement award to Ginger Baker, when he embraced me warmly. Charlie was presenting the award and I was introducing a film I'd put together about Ginger with the Zildjian Cymbal Company, who were presenting the award. I'd also written the programme notes with Geoff Nicholls. I'd like to say Ginger behaved himself, but that would be a gross exaggeration. He took exception to the programme notes, which didn't list his favourite drummer (Phil Seaman), although the film certainly did. He managed to antagonise everybody backstage as well as the cymbal company people who'd crossed the Atlantic specifically for the event. Russell reminded me how he completely blanked us when we were the only people crammed into a four-person lift in a hotel in New York during the early seventies.

In hindsight we should have gone immediately for an alcohol or tobacco company to sponsor *Crash, Bang, Wallop*, and not worried about the moral issues involved. But as usual I had my principles, and because of them we're still looking.

We actually had several treatments for musical films and long-form videos, all with the very important disclaimer page at the back. In our enthusiastic, naïve way we felt we only needed one to take-off and the others would have followed. *Ebony, Ivory and Rock* was about Cristofori's far-reaching invention of the piano, and we hoped to get Elton John to voice that one. *Voices* was about the power of the human voice, and what makes it commercial or not. Why did Mick Jagger's completely untrained voice appeal to the masses when, pre-Italia 90, Pavarotti's didn't? *Rock and Roll Cities* was to be a guided tour of the world's capitals by the stars who lived there, who knew where all the action had been and where it could be found now (the Beach Boys in LA, Debbie Harry in New York, John Lydon in London, Morrisey in Manchester, Johnny Halliday in Paris, Willie Nelson in Texas, Dan Ackroyd in Chicago, Dolly Parton in Nashville; that sort of thing).

Another, slightly more unusual, treatment was for something I called *Rocking Good*. One of my contacts in the record industry had told me in passing how Jack Good, the Godfather of musical television, whom he knew well, was now a monk living in Santa Fe and existed by painting naïve religious scenes. If he needed more funds than a picture of the Sacred Heart could get him he unashamedly asked his high-profile pals in the music business for a handout. He told them that without him to propagate popular music on TV, it might never have taken off. Jack was right, of course. I thought this was an interesting story which I felt would make a great film, and immediately started work on a treatment for the documentary. It was a deceptively simple format: interviews with Brother Jack with great establishing shots in the desert interspersed with footage from *Six-Five Special*, *Oh Boy!*, *Boy Meets Girl*, *Hullabaloo* and *Shindig*, and interviews with the artists (Cliff Richard, Adam Faith, Marty Wilde, the Vernons Girls) now. Ray presented this to several broadcasters, who duly deliberated before passing on it. Not long afterwards the whole thing came out with somebody else behind it. So much for a confidentiality clause! Ray was uncharacteristically sanguine but I was uncharacteristically livid. I'd sweated blood over it and was really proud of my work. And my pal had told me about it in passing and nobody else. Curiouser and curiouser, as Alice says in Wonderland as she begins to grow taller (or is it smaller?).

It was the end of a long North American tour for The Kinks. We'd finished somewhere in mid-America (possibly Cincinnatti) and sat expectantly on a plane bound for New York's Kennedy airport. The idea was to make a connection there and arrive in the UK early enough for a pint down the pub followed by roast Sunday dinner. As we sat there a storm of biblical proportions began, so we couldn't take off. Eventually the rain abated, but when we prepared for lift-off there was something else wrong: the plane's brakes were seized on. Eventually they found another plane for us and we headed for La Guardia. Unfortunately the London plane was going from Kennedy, so by the time we got there Pan Am was halfway across the Atlantic. The airline said they'd put us up for the night and send us on Concorde the next day. Unfortunately the lunatics had taken over the asylum and we decided to take a plane to Zurich, with a quick connection to London. This, I was assured, would get us there in time for a pint down the pub. Unfortunately once we got underway we discovered the plane was heading for Frankfurt not Zurich, and we'd be having a five hour wait once we arrived there for a plane to London. We finally got to Heathrow, and there was the Concorde we could have taken cleaned and refuelled on the runway, ready for its next Atlantic crossing.

We never did get to the pub.

Aside from my brief visit to the police station in Santa Maria, apart from three driving offences and a few parking tickets I've never been in trouble with the law. But several guys (and one girl) around me have.

The girl in question was Annie, the first dancer to partner Pat Crosbie when Ray brought a new dimension to both the live and recorded Kinks performances. She was young and I don't believe paid too much attention to the consequences of having a good time. She was arrested by security leaving Milan airport on the way to a gig in Zurich at the start of a European tour. A police dog named Bingo made the bust, having discovered some recreational drugs in the pocket of her Levis. We continued while she helped the Italian police with their enquiries, and she caught us up quite some time later.

She wasn't the only one to be arrested during my Kinks years: Dave Powell, a guitar tech, and Bobbie Zinzer, who ran security, also absented themselves from the entourage for a time at the president's pleasure during US tours. Dave's was a more serious offence than Bobbie's, although with the same result – incarceration. Before I became a Kink DP had lived in the US with a young lady, and after an altercation with her had set fire to their house in a fit of testosterone. Needless to say he'd been arrested and bailed to appear before a judge to answer serious charges of arson. He hadn't liked the idea of that so had elected to go back to England instead. As I said I knew nothing of this, and had passed safely through US immigration with him several times on the East and West coasts. However, while crossing from Canada into America at Toronto airport, he was apprehended in front of me and immediately whisked into custody. He was eventually dragged off to the infamous Rikers Island, the world's biggest penal colony, in New York City. (I've always been wary of the big book they look into at immigration on the way into America, wondering whether something innocent I'd done had inadvertently put my name into its frightening pages.) DP came back several weeks later a changed and chastened man!

Bobbie Zinzer was also changed by his time 'under canvas' – although his misdemeanour wasn't quite as grave. We'd just arrived in Los Angeles to begin an American tour and as usual had started off with a drink (make that three) with the US guys in the road crew who, since they didn't do Europe with us, we hadn't seen for a while. Bobbie Z. was a sort of doctor since he'd been a trained medic in the military who had failed his medical exams; but he was still a very useful person to have around. (The Kinks never had a huge crew like Genesis, but everyone was experienced and well rounded so they could cover for each other if something untoward happened – like getting sent to jail.) Anyhow he'd obviously missed the lecture during his medical training that warned you about the effect a great deal of alcohol could have on your driving abilities in the vicinity of Sunset Strip on a busy Friday night. Bobbie left the Sunset Marquis Hotel going in the direction of fun and games, and contrived to drive into several cars parked innocently down a side street leading to the well-known Rainbow bar and grill, infamous for big hair, tight pants and spandex, up the road from the Whiskey-a-Go-Go on Sunset (the scene of the first Argent gig in LA almost twenty years earlier). As usual we stayed up drinking at the hotel until we couldn't stay awake any longer – to beat the jet lag and force ourselves into West Coast time – so we knew nothing of this until Ken Jones, our tour manager, told us the whole sad story at breakfast the next day. Jonesy told us Bobbie was likely to be helping the police with their enquiries for quite some time. He was a big guy, but he too returned to the band a changed man.

If the US police weren't to be trifled with, the rent-a-cops we had at gigs could be even worse. Neither of these law enforcement agencies had any of the special rules for celebrities that seem to prevail here in the UK these days. Don't get me started on Kate Moss, Amy Winehouse and Pete Doherty! Security guys at gigs were sometimes off-duty cops, but whoever they were they were armed. We supported Black Sabbath at a huge gig in Lexington, Kentucky, during their scary 'Out, demons out' days, and after our show were playing football with a tin can in a parking area behind the auditorium when this rent-a-cop came up to us and ordered us to stop. We said something along the lines of: 'Hey, man, we're the band,' and carried on. But we stopped immediately he got his gun out.

These guys were interesting because they were local guys who were paid by us. During the settlement after the gig their wages appeared as a debit from monies earned. This settlement thing was something that happened after every big gig, but I only ever witnessed it once. As I recall we were 'between records' and doing an East Coast tour of very large clubs: we had just played somewhere in New Jersey. For some reason I was sitting around in the dressing room on my own when Dave Bowen rushed in and asked where everyone was. I said I had no idea. He replied that he desperately needed one of the security guys, but in their absence asked me to do him a favour and come along to the settlement for moral support. I had nothing better to do so I did. A couple of too-young brothers, whose names unsurprisingly ended in a vowel, owned the club, and when we went into their ostentatious office one of them had his feet up on the desk and a large pile of white powder on a piece of glass in front of him. He explained his brother was getting a blow-job next door and if we were interested we could be next. In the meantime what about a toot. We politely said no thank you to both offerings, and he said he'd had a thought: as he had so much of this valuable white powder, why didn't we take it instead of the money? Of course there was absolutely no danger of it happening, but I had to laugh at the thought of us going back to the guys and showing them what we'd got instead of cash. It would have been like the magic beans in Jack and the Beanstalk.

Speaking of blow-jobs, we were in New York when the movie *Deep Throat* came out. The music for the film was published by a chap called Al Gallico, who also published the Zombies and Argent – and he arranged free passes for us to see it. As it happens there wasn't enough plot for me, but it certainly made Linda Lovelace and those two guys from the Washington Post famous!

I hadn't long been in The Kinks when I got a call from a very unlikely person, a chap with the same surname as a Scottish city who just turned out to be a Queen's Counsel who did a great deal of work for Paul McCartney. I'm not sure if this is sub judice so under advice (from my learned wife) I'm going to leave out the names to protect the guilty. I turned up in his chambers in Holborn to discover my QC friend wanted me to act as an expert witness for a well-known insurance company who were the defendants in a case that involved an equally well-known drummer whom I knew pretty well from all the various watering holes and TV studios we visited together in the sixties. We'd also done gigs together in America in the previous decade.

He'd been in a car driving home along a motorway with his girlfriend when another car had crossed the central reservation and crashed into them head on, injuring them both. As I recall my drummer friend was less seriously injured than his partner, but because he needed to recuperate the accident scuppered (for the moment) his plans for a new band, with which he was guaranteed to dominate the world. The gist of the case was that because of the time lost to his injuries my drummer friend (call him Deep Throat) would be unable to make the record, unable to make the sell-out tour and unable to make the millions you immediately get for this kind of success!!! (I don't normally subscribe to more than one exclamation mark, but since they didn't even have a record deal in this case I feel I must.) To add insult to injury, the plaintiff claimed that as soon as the first album was a success they'd rush to the studio and make the next, which would be even more successful, and consequently they'd do more tours with more bums on seats and make even more money – for as long as the band could stand each other. So the prosecution was demanding obscene millions in lost revenue, and the whole case revolved around whether the tracks to be presented to prospective record companies would give rise to those riches. My role was to listen to the tracks and say whether, in my professional opinion, they had the potential to secure a recording contract. I took all the tracks home and was shocked (make that amused) by what I heard. I was expecting sparkling new material, and was confronted by a bunch of ragged demos of my favourite old R&B tunes put down hastily in a cheap and cheerful demo studio, or possibly (in several cases) someone's bedroom with a drum machine.

I have no real objection to unworthy people making undeserved money, it happens all the time in show business, but I do object to the prosecution's layman's formulaic view of how you make it in showbiz – because I know it doesn't work. It flies in the face of all reason, and the more you apply a formula to it the worse it becomes. By and large it's the 'luckiest' people who happen to be the ones who work hardest at it. Even in these days of *X-Factor* and people making fortunes in no time at all I know someone, somewhere has to put in the hard work to make it happen – be it record company, management or more likely their stylist. And don't get me started about Oasis bass player 'Bonehead', who allegedly left the band because he had enough money!

There's a story, which deserves to be a modern parable, about a musician who wins millions on the lottery. Upon being asked what he plans to do with the money he replies, 'I'm going to keep on being a professional musician till it's all gone!'

Anyhow, I reported my findings back to the QC and thought that might be it. For some reason I felt it might be settled out of court to everybody's satisfaction, so wasn't unduly concerned about confronting Deep Throat in a courtroom. The wheels of justice grind slow and the legal eagles took their time, but eventually I was asked if I would appear in the High Court as an expert witness for a fee. I wasn't too happy with this until the QC explained that if Deep Throat won the case then motoring insurance policies for musicians (which were already prohibitive) would increase, as would public liability insurance premiums for gigs. So I agreed to appear, but at the eleventh hour the case was settled out of court – presumably to Deep Throat's satisfaction, because even though he knew I'd been involved for the defence the next time we met he was nice as pie. (By the way, Deep Throat is a pretty good name for a band.)

Ian Gibbons, Jim Rodford and myself were what the Musicians' Union would call non-contracted members of The Kinks. This meant we'd frequently find ourselves on TV or radio programmes which we should have been paid for (maybe even had been paid for) but the money never filtered through. The various record, TV and radio companies didn't understand the concept that freelancers – who by definition weren't participating in any profit-sharing scheme or share of record royalties – needed to be paid. We did many programmes without being remunerated, and none of our protestations to the various record companies made any difference. They offered The Kinks to a TV company free and gratis for a plug on their show, which could of course result in a hit record.

One of these situations very nearly got me into trouble with the good fellas whose names end in a vowel. Very early in my tenure in the band we did a live broadcast from Chicago, which was standard practice if the gig was sold out – because it didn't affect the bums on seats. Everything went well and the stereo broadcast aired without problems. That was that until a bootleg CD appeared, and was snapped up by voracious Kinks fans everywhere. It was the Chicago show from the Riviera Nightclub: the producer had recorded it directly in stereo from the radio, put his name to it and turned it into a record. Nobody at the office seemed that fussed, and the guy was untraceable since the label on the CD box simply had an Illinois PO box number on it. Fast forward to the nineties, and a Kinks live programme on Radio 2. There was no advance information on the broadcast, and having listened with interest to the hour-long programme I was surprised to discover it was that Riviera Live show from several years earlier repackaged as the King Biscuit Hour. I bypassed the Musicians' Union and called the BBC to inform them where to send the cheque, because I had a new address. They responded with 'What money?' I explained the non-contracted members thing, and they told me that since they'd acquired it 'free to air' there wasn't going to be any money. My next conversation was with the MU, who said they could do nothing, so I got back to the BBC who helpfully furnished me with the contact details for the chaps in New York who'd supplied my services for nothing! I took a deep breath and phoned a chap whose name ended in an A, E, I, O or U. He listened to my story with interest, before politely asking me how much I wanted to go away.

Segué to another story along the same lines. Late one night I was channel-hopping and heard some music playing over the credits of a Channel 4 programme. It sounded pretty good, and unusually it played for several minutes, which didn't normally happen because if you used under thirty seconds you didn't have to pay the musicians. As I idly listened a familiar Latin American drum fill came along. The penny dropped, and I realised it was me playing on a Kinks track written and sung by Dave Davies called 'Living on a Thin Line'. The programme was *The Sopranos*. (This not recognising yourself playing on record is right up there with being attracted to someone across a crowded room, and realising she's your wife – embarrassing and satisfying at the same time!)

I decided to bang my head against the brick wall yet again, and contacted the MU, with the usual plea to send the money to my new address, not the office. They asked me what the programme was. There was a sharp intake of breath when I told them, followed by a pregnant pause. I'd better say no more . . .

Sports and music go hand in hand, since at the top level they take place in the same venues. At least three guys in the various groups I've been in had trials for professional football teams: Russ Ballard, who was on Tottenham Hotspur's books, as were John Rogers and Buster Meikle. Ian Matthews was also signed to be a footballer by Hull City. In Russ's case the injury to his eye put paid to the idea of sporting fame and fortune. In Buster's case I guess he found tennis instead, then women, then music. Brian Parker also found tennis, and actually died on the tennis court. I'd seen him not long before while taking part in a charity bike ride from London to Cambridge, which just goes to show that being fit is no guarantee of longevity. Funnily enough, Brian's funeral was the first time I heard Eva Cassidy's beautiful version of 'Over the Rainbow' in a church, and because of those connotations every time I hear it it brings tears to my eyes.

My father-in-law was working for a bicycle maker in the Midlands. He got me an unmissable deal on a sample model, and I returned to riding about twenty years ago – mainly in an attempt to get even fitter and thereby prolong my life. (I'm just a little concerned that this might jsut give me a few minutes more at the 'last knockings', when I'm gasping for breath and happy to let go.) Mind you, cycling can be life-threatening: I've had a few near misses. Once I was riding along a designated cycle path when I was very nearly wiped out by a huge Dutch lorry.

The Kamikaze Downhill Cycling Club is a sort of cycling gang formed of like-minded hedonistic pals from various dubious walks of life like the tennis club, 41 Club, skiing and the golf club. We do one or two 'proper' rides a year, where we put in 40 or 50 miles a day before over-eating and over-drinking. We started out very ambitiously with a tough sea to sea ride across the Pennines from Whitehaven to Sunderland,. and followed that up with what we hoped in vain would be less arduous runs, including the Ring of Kerry, Ilfracombe to Plymouth across the Devonshire moors and eventuellement le Canal du Midi in France. There is talk about having a bash at the big one – Land's End to John O' Groats. As we know, talk is cheap . . .

I don't believe I knew any wrestlers back in the sixties, a period I can remember vividly by the way – it's yesterday I have problems with! But at that time it was very popular, and one particular grappler owned the 2-Is coffee bar in London's Soho, which gave a start to rock 'n' rollers like Cliff Richard and Adam Faith. Paul Lincoln was the proprietor; he was professionally known as Doctor Death. He wore a mask, like they did in Mexico, and since you never knew who you were watching he could arguably fight in several places on the same night. Mod Rogan shared a flat with (as opposed to lived with, which is an altogether different thing) a wrestler called Bob Anthony, who co-owned The Cromwellian with the aforementioned Paul Lincoln. Bob Anthony may or may not have turned out as 'The Death'.

I was making the second Phoenix album in LA in 1975 at a time when soccer in North America was just about as popular as it was going to get, until twenty years later when American women took it over and turned it into a world class sport. Anyway John Verity, Ray Minhinnett and I decided we should support our national game, and drove somebody else's rent-a-wreck to the Rosebowl in Pasadena to watch the predominantly non-American footballers representing LA Aztecs playing another bunch of non-American footballers representing Tampa Bay. For the first (and last time) in my life I sat with a load of Arsenal supporters, and was astonished to find Sir Stanley Matthews (one of the heroes of my youth along with Jackie Milburn, Stan Mortensen, Tom Finney, Len Shackleton and Ted Ditchburn) kicking off. The match continued and Sir Stanley, the 'wizard of the dribble' as he was billed in the football annuals I got every Christmas, left the field without any security and walked through the crowd on his way to the car park. We couldn't let the opportunity pass, so by the time he got abreast of us we were standing in the gangway. He was genuinely pleased and probably relieved to see us, having been completely ignored by the crowd. We chatted to the greatest English footballer of all time for a while. He had been doing some youth coaching in California, perhaps to supplement the meagre income he'd received as a professional footballer. This was in 1975 when he was aged sixty but still not exactly retired. It wasn't until he hung up his heavy, dubbined boots for the last time that even ordinary footballers, supported by oligarchs using other people's money, received tens of thousands a week for their efforts.

Rodney Marsh was on the pitch for the Rowdies that day, not too long after his iconoclastic speech where he broadcast that 'Football in England is played on grey days in grey stadiums in front of grey people.' In those pre-oligarch days he was absolutely right.

In Argent we made a film (long before video and MTV) for America of us playing soccer at Spurs' old training ground in Cheshunt. Thanks to some Oscar-deserving editing the finished result seemed to show that we knew what we were doing. The camera never lies? Of course like all young baby boomer Brits I played football and cricket at junior school, although I never played in goal as I did when The Kinks played a team made up of dozens of record company people and DJs from the Chicago area during a summer US tour around the middle of the eighties. It was a rolling five a side game, which means you could substitute whenever you wanted, something that the 'Chicago all stars' with their packed bench took great advantage of. We would have too, had there been more than the four of us in the band (without Stubz, who had the good sense to be elsewhere) and Terry, a very useful merchandising guy. As I said, I was playing in goal, and since I had one of the new-fangled digital watches I was made official time-keeper. Ray and Dave were accomplished footballers, having played in the sixties with the Show Biz XI, made up of guys like Harry Fowler and Kenny Lynch (aka Alcock and Brown for reasons that were obvious at the time) and Jess Conrad. But because of the opposition's unlimited fresh legs we struggled to hold our own against a bunch of experienced ice-hockey, baseball and basket-ball players. But they reckoned without a certain amount of guile on my part. Obviously we couldn't afford to lose our national game against this bunch, so when we managed to draw level with them I blew the whistle for the end of the match. Possibly there was a minute or so to go, but without the glasses I'd only just begun to wear I may have mis-read my Seiko watch. An innocent mistake.

Another semi-sporting activity I was involved in with Argent was the shooting of the *In Deep* album cover, which was done by a company called Hipgnosis, the wonderful Storm and Poe, who did all the best album artwork of the early seventies. We hired Crystal Palace's Olympic-sized swimming pool at great expense, because it had several large portholes in the side. We dived in and swam 25 metres under the water towards Storm (or Poe), who sat there taking photos in the dry. Now everyone of a certain age brought up in the dark days before digital cameras knows there are thirty-six shots on a roll of Kodak or Fuji 35mm film. As a consequence, Jim and I, the strongest swimmers, swam under water for 36 x 25 metres, a total of 950 submerged metres for each film. After each frame we ran halfway round the pool and did it all again. Rod and Russell weren't great swimmers, so all they had to do was tread water and submerge while little Jimmy and I were going for the rock-world's unofficial underwater swimming record. This was the time of Russell's nervous breakdown, and having spotted he was struggling I went in to fish him out. Don Broughton, who was married to our publisher's assistant and eventually became our first expert soundman, took over; and it's him on the cover holding Russell's dark glasses.

It's debatable whether ten-pin bowling is a real sport, but when we first arrived in LA we were invited to a bowling tournament held at an alley off Sunset amusingly called The Hollywood Bowl. This was long before the days of the A-lister goody bag, but we were all issued with a vibrator when we arrived, inscribed 'Good Vibes from the Canned Heat Invitational Bowling Tournament'. As I recall, Aynsley Dunbar carried his around with him for years. The next time we saw Canned Heat their drummer's Aston Martin DB4 had broken down in the white zone (for immediate loading and unloading) at LAX airport. He got us to bump-start it. Fred was ready to get underneath and sort it out then and there, but fortunately we had no time.

Aynsley flitted in and out of my Argent years when he joined another couple of ex- Turtles, and ex-Frank Zappa's Mothers of Invention, who were known as the Phlorescent Leech and Eddie. They toured America with us just before Russell left the band. I knew Turtles songs like 'Happy Together' and 'She'd Rather Be With Me', which had that great drum fill out of the chorus, but had never intentionally met them. I say intentionally because Howard Kaylan and Mark Volman had both been with the Mothers of Invention at one time – but possibly not when we'd toured with the band in 1970. It wasn't until 1972 when I finally met them in their new guise. It's safe to say they'd had eventful careers – so much so that they couldn't call themselves The Turtles, or even use their own names. Eventually they became plain Flo and Eddie.

Eventually I discovered Flo and Eddie came from the same mischievous mould as Keith Moon: they were very funny guys and great to tour with. At their sound-check at the first gig at which they supported us they unexpectedly launched into an Adam Faith and the Roulettes tune 'It's Alright', which had been our only hit in

America and subsequently used in Robin Williams's film *Good Morning Vietnam*. Unfortunately it didn't find its way on to the film's soundtrack album, so we never got paid.

Sporting charities for musicians were not quite so popular in those days, although we've always done our fair share of charity gigs for organisations like the Stars Organisation for Spastics and Buckets and Spades. Strangely I don't recall ever doing anything of that nature with The Kinks; maybe we were never asked.

While playing with Adam Faith and the Roulettes I took part in a charity cricket match in Margate against the Mayor's XI. I opened the batting against the worshipful mayor's dodgy bowling, and was out first ball to a ridiculous daisy-cutter that I could easily have stopped by lying my bat horizontally in front of the wicket. Instead I tried to hit it out of the ground. Anyhow the umpire deemed it a no-ball, and I was saved. I went on to hit a respectable score of thirty-odd runs, but the poor old mayor didn't live long and prosper. Within very few days of the show opening he had joined the 'choir invisible', and we were singing 'To be a pilgrim' at his funeral.

Over the years I've played summer gigs in a few ski resorts with The Kinks, in the Northern states like Illinois, New York, Wisconsin and Colorado. Invariably we played in the open air, and the stage was set up right at the bottom where several slopes merged together – a surreal experience. I enjoyed these gigs because I took up the gentle art of skiing just after I joined The Kinks, although for obvious reasons didn't tell anybody. As the old joke about wanting to be a drummer when you grow up goes – don't be silly, you can't do both – I decided to embrace multi-tasking and investigate my more macho side. The lovely Ricki was a skier and had long wanted to take me with her, but I'd always resisted vigorously. However, when a group of friends from Winchmore Hill decided they wanted me to go with them I felt it churlish to refuse. As it happened the first holiday I was booked on in 1985, to Crans Montana, had to be cancelled because The Kinks were unexpectedly in the studio. I passed my place on to our friend Joy Ayton, who served as first reserve during all my Kinks years.

The reason why I resisted for so long was that like all pro drummers I thought if something happened while racing down a mountain I'd never work again. To get used to skiing I went to the dry slope at Hemel Hempstead, and felt it was exceedingly dangerous, especially if you got your fingers caught in the plastic bristles you slide down. Fortunately I didn't have those problems on real slippery snow. My only problem was standing upright and getting to the bottom! But I persevered, and by the time we left Chatel in the French Alps I could keep up with the big boys and girls. Mind you, I had no style, just grim determination. I was hooked, so much so that I idly wondered how I could combine skiing with making a living. There was no way I was going to take the traditional chalet maid route at the age of forty, so it was but a fleeting thought. As I say, I hadn't told anybody what I was up to, and apart from my panda eyes (where the goggles had kept out the sun) nobody in the band would have known.

The next year we went to Les Deux Alpes. Again I felt discretion to be the better part of valour, and I didn't broadcast what I was doing. It wasn't out of the question that a surprise recording session or rehearsal might be called and I'd miss out again. Anyhow, in those days before mobile phones I managed to remain incommunicado for a week and nobody would have known a thing, had it not been for some idiot on a snowboard taking me out from behind and bending my left thumb back – a condition known to physios as rugby player's thumb. I went to the Cabinet Medicale at the resort and they gave me a special aluminium splint so I could still ski. When I got back to the UK a consultation with Jo Durie's physio told me what exercises to do. But before she could see me I had a big problem: the day after I got back I had a session at Konk. I'd exercised my thumb like crazy for hours but I still couldn't hold the stick properly in that hand. I didn't want to draw attention to my predicament and have to answer awkward questions about how it happened, so I developed a method of playing that sounded OK but looked ridiculous. The right hand did all the work playing the hi-hat for three beats, but returned to the snare drum for the fourth beat – the all-important off-beat. The overall effect was very like what Charlie Watts does, but I didn't like the fact that there was a missing beat on the hi-hat. To compensate I brought my otherwise useless left-hand up to play it. It was very unconventional, but so effective that I've used that pattern with two good hands for many years – when I want to sound a bit different. This wasn't too much of a problem because I was surrounded by several of those sound-absorbing double screens with glass on the top and carpet on the bottom, so my face was visible but nobody could see what my hands were up to. It worked perfectly for playing time, but when it came to playing a fill it was a different matter. I could probably have got away without any fills, but that ain't me, so I had a single hand to play something without nuances yet scintillating and evocative. Single beats from tom to snare and back again sounded surprisingly good. Fortunately I only had to do a few takes of that particular track before I was able to escape. Unfortunately I don't recall what the track was, so I can't draw your attention to how clever I was. It's a fact of life that often the first tracks made by a band embarking on an album don't make it onto the album, simply because the ones that come later, when the momentum has begun, are always deemed to be better. The Kinks were no different, but since we always put down twice as many tracks as found their way on to any particular album it may find itself one day on a bumper compendium of previously unreleased tracks.

I continued to go skiing for the next twenty-odd years with the same hedonistic bunch of miscreants, and as I got better at it the dangers of a recurrence of rugby player's thumb receded. Now I have a bus pass I have a concession on the price of my ski-pass too, which is a very welcome addition.

In the mid-nineties my youngest son Jos played mixed-doubles tennis with a girl called Susie Coates, who ran her own successful PR company in London. We saw a lot of her. She was dynamic and committed, with several lucrative contracts with various publishing-type companies. One day a water company she'd already acted for decided it wanted to move itself further up-market with a new 'sporty' product. Now for me and a lot of other people water is water, even if it's been passed through alpine volcanoes. But this particular Ale of Adam came from deeper in the Wiltshire hills than any regular water, so it had lots more healthy bits in it. The idea was to call it a three (possibly four) digit number to show how far down they had to drill to get it. I was intrigued when Coatsie told me about the project and inexplicably asked me to help. I'd been having a love/hate affair with drinking water all my life, so I thought why not?

We drove down to somewhere in the West Country to meet the water people and make our pitch. They were serious, and wanted us to provide them with an equally serious advertising campaign and a sporty shape for the bottle. We gave it a lot of thought and came up with a plan. This was a time when a young athlete named Du'aine Ladejo was beginning to cut a swathe through international 400 metre runners and, given a legal prevailing wind, could have been on the podium for the upcoming Atlanta Olympic Games. He'd won the silver medal at the Commonwealth Games in 1994 and was joint British recordholder for a while in the 4 x 400 relay – and he fitted the demographic perfectly: young, gifted and black. I negotiated with his people and things looked promising, but eventually the trail went cold. I don't know what happened. Did they run out of water? Was the generous deal insufficient? Did he have a sudden loss of form?

Anyway the project didn't happen. The web tells me he's now in the British two -man bobsleigh team, and every now and then turns up on television taking part in celebrity sporting events.

I'd always been thrilled to go to Germany: it was like stepping into the pages of a John le Carré novel. I'd say the country appealed to my baser instincts, and venturing into the East felt positively dangerous. Before the Wall came down we were playing in Berlin and I decided to take a trip into the DDR. This was easier said than done because they wouldn't just let you in: you had to have a minimum of 30 Ostmarks with you, and to prop up their economy you had to spend there; and they had to want you too. So Big Tel, Stubzie and I crossed the border over the infamous bridge at Checkpoint Charlie. We showed our passports and money to an armed soldier sitting behind a desk in a long corridor, with just enough room to get by walking sideways. He held me there while he looked into the same sort of large book full of miscreants that they have at American immigration. I held my breath.

All my life the first thing I did on taking possession of a foreign hotel room was look in the telephone directory to see if there were any other people called Henrit listed. There never were: the closest I'd got was in Sydney, Australia, in 1962 where I discovered a Henritze. Because of this I'd always romantically suspected that my ancestors had fled from persecution in Eastern Europe, and dropped the ze off the end of their name once they'd arrived in Britain – so any secret policemen pursuing them wouldn't recognise them. Was I in the book? Had my family done something illegal before fleeing? Was I a wanted man? Did I own a vast country estate somewhere behind Churchill's Iron Curtain? The soldier stamped my passport and waved me through, so I presumed the answer to all these questions was a resounding nein.

We wandered into a spinetinglingly different world, where nothing was the same as in the West. The streets were somehow different: cars, buses, shops, advertising; even the buildings. Only the large paved squares created by the bombing that had ended the Second World War were new. This wasn't completely surprising since we'd seen all the spy films, but it was really like stepping from colour TV into black and white. We wandered around like tourists for an hour or two, imagining we were being followed by the Stasi, and with our Ostmarks intact we sat down at a café to work out what to do with them. With a cup of coffee costing just a couple of marks, and an unappetising sandwich only bringing it up to 5 marks, it's not easy to spend 30 Ostmarks when there's nothing to buy other than vodka, binoculars, cameras, harmonicas, trumpets and accordions. So rather than being arrested for smuggling worthless currency into the West we ended up tipping the waitress 25 marks each! She must have thought all her birthdays had come at once.

We retraced our steps through Checkpoint Charlie to the Café Adler, and breathed a sigh of relief once they'd consulted the big book again and we were allowed to cross from the Motherland back to the Fatherland.

When the Wall unexpectedly came down in the first year of the nineties, politicians in West Germany realised there were votes to be gathered in the East, so set off to capture, for the first time, the hearts and minds of their suddenly avaricious countrymen in the old DDR. This would help their parties' coffers, since every vote cast in Germany accrues money. Oskar de la Fontaine was the figurehead of the SPD who decided to travel to the 'Neu Deutschland' looking for new friends and, to ensure people came to the hustings, decided it would be a good idea to take some rock bands with him. In November 1990 he took The Kinks, the Gypsy Kings, Donovan and various German bands on his 'Stimmen für Oskar' tour. To us it was just another series of big gigs, with the usual German faces outside the halls looking for autographs holding every album we'd ever made during our various careers – many of which we were seeing for the very first time. For Oskar, though, it was an opportunity to put his story across during the show. Unfortunately for him not enough people in the East bought into his philosophy and ideals to make him Chancellor. He was SPD: the S stood for Socialism and they'd had as much as they could take of that dankeschön Now they were free they wanted what the rest of the world had: capitalism. Oskar would have done better if he'd changed the name of his party to Kapitalisten Partie Deutschland.

As we travelled around Germany on that tour we saw broken down Western European cars littering the roads. The Trabants of the East went on for ever, while the more sophisticated (not to mention sexy) status-symbol vehicles that they'd been bussed into the West to buy (thousands of opportunist dealers had gathered together on football pitches) were on their last legs. And with sophisticated engine management systems they could only be resuscitated with difficulty.

Mind you, the less opulent side of the border had its own things to sell too. Rather than return to Russia, the soldiers in East Germany happily sold everything they had to finance their desertion. We weren't too thrilled when an armed soldier in full uniform leapt out in front of us on our way down that corridor-like road to Berlin where the old tank is parked with its gun pointed menacingly towards the West. Fortunately we were being driven by Germans who knew the score, and they backed up quickly to go round him. It turned out he simply wanted a lift, and this was the best way to get one. He and his comrades would sell you Kalashnikovs, landmines, pistols and grenades for very few dollars. Even the places these guys lived in were under threat. Before long we saw army camps proudly flying Volkswagen, Mercedes and Opel flags – as what seemed to me to be the Americanisation of the 'other' Germany got under way.

Cars play a very important part in a jobbing drummer's lot. Some work well for the carting around of drums; others don't. Alec Issigonis's Mini, which burst onto the scene in 1959, wasn't fit for purpose – so I had two (one of which went like shit off a shovel). Next came a Renault 4, which had a hatchback so was better, then a Renault 5, which was also ideal, then a Beetle, which was useless and which my Lucy very nearly managed to fall out of by opening the door as I did a U-turn in the middle of Green Lanes. Then we bought a Citroën GS, which wouldn't have been too bad but it had difficulty starting. Since its suspension pumped itself up when you turned the engine on, in repose it looked like a dead tortoise. It was eventually swapped for another Beetle! A Ford Capri with a hatchback replaced that, and that in turn was replaced by a Citroën 2CV – when a nice lady wrote off the Ford, whenn it was innocently parked. Next came a black Saab 900, then a white one, then a Saab 9000, and a Saab 9-3 in 2001: that was meant to last for ever, but for ever was sooner than expected. In early 2009 it gave up the ghost, whereupon against Ricki's wishes we (I) bought an identical one. The moment the warranty ran out it needed a new turbo.

I've agonised about this bit, and wasn't going to include anything about the use of illegal stimulants. But I feel nobody would believe me if I said I'd never indulged, and since writing *Banging On* is meant to be cathartic I might as well get it off my chest. Mind you, I don't want this to be used as a weapon against me by anyone, especially my kids. I don't condone drugs at all, and truly subscribe to the fact that it's God's way of telling you you've got too much money. But, like Robbie Williams, I've spent time in the company of people with whom I have nothing else in common other than that insidious Class A drug. I've never smoked anything at all, so had no desire for that particular nasty mode of getting high – but the 'Colombian Marching Powder', with its more exciting paraphernalia, was slightly more interesting – and certainly not quite so smelly. I was first introduced to cocaine (there, I've said the word) in New York in the seventies in a posh hotel, and can remember that feeling of euphoria even now. I felt super-confident, and at that precise moment could have accomplished anything. Of course it's the classic confidence trick, which indirectly ruined the lives of a lot of my contemporaries, like Jimi Hendrix and Jon Bonham, along with a lot of jazz guys I was too young to know, like Charlie Parker. The first time you take any drug, even an aspirin, it works better than the second time. After that you're simply unsuccessfully trying to recreate the high of the first time. I don't want to be judgemental, but I watched at close quarters intelligent guys who (like Eric Clapton, Ginger Baker and countless others) discovered that cocaine on its own wasn't doing anything for them any more, so they mixed it with a little of what The Stranglers called 'golden brown'. Once you got used to this the next step was to do away with the cocaine, which was more expensive anyway, and just take the heroin. That was it – they were hooked.

Perhaps it'll be entertaining to mention that when cocaine first became fashionable it was ingested in a completely different and decidedly less elegant way – via the most sensitive but, unless you're in Ibiza or St Tropez, discreetly covered part of the anatomy. And when one very famous and to my mind exceedingly attractive big-haired seventies female singer's septum disintegrated from too much nose-action, she had to resort to this method. She would leave the stage and crouch on her hands and knees inside her backstage 'dressing-tent', so her assistant could blow the stimulating powder in the right direction with a straw. You couldn't make it up. This gave rise to much banter amongst musicians parodying Pete and Dud's famous 'what's the worst job you ever had?' skit!

So from time to time I indulged, but I really hated myself and didn't like what I became when I was doing it.

The other thing to mention is that you never know what you're getting. I once sat in a hotel room while someone 'stepped on' a great many grams, thereby making them twice as valuable. It's the closest thing to turning lead into gold I've ever seen. And when someone offers you a 'toot' there's no way you can know whether it's going to kill you. I was friendly with Robbie McIntosh from Dundee's Average White Band, who took something he thought was innocuous and turned out to be anything but. Poor Robbie died in a star-studded environment, with the highly glamorous female side of a mega-famous sixties singing duo walking him around and feeding him coffee to try to save his life.

Just say no.

Winnebago complete with suspect spare wheel

Argent Mk 2 live

Argent after live Encore album at The Nightingale, Wood Green

Argent Flyer

Phoenix 2

Phoenix glam rock

le Funky Château

My Bowie-sighting room at Château d'Herrouville

Winnebago: 10,000 miles doesn't seem so far

Phoenix in LA recording Full View

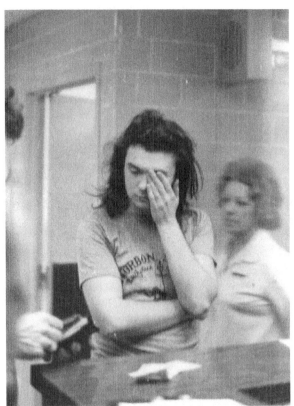

*Andy after the
Bakersfield affair*

Dave Courtney at the Château

Clean Charlie

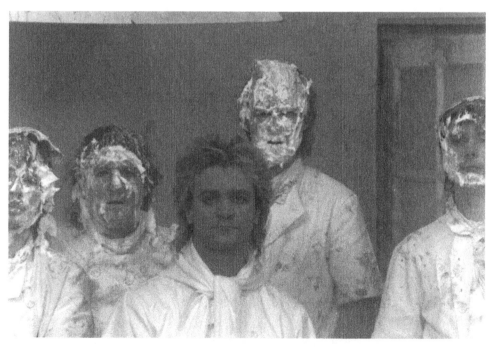

Dirty Charlie: it's inevitable

Jos with first set

The Juniors

Dirty Angels with Jos

Argent 40 years after

Grown up kids

James at 30

Chapter Eight: AFTER THE DANGEROUS BROTHERS

An innocent remark from me to Ray after a gig called Norwegian Wood in Oslo on 15 June 1996, when Van Morrison supported us (with his back to the audience), set-off a profound chain of events as far as The Kinks were concerned. Deke Arlon (who was just about the only embryonic English pop singer we didn't back with The Daybreakers) had taken over as manager, and appeared to be doing a good job inasmuch as he ensured we were paid proper money for gigs, even though the weekly retainer that I'd negotiated as a new boy when I joined in 1984 was long gone. We were reasonably busy and no earth-shattering arguments were taking place between the siblings. Anyway, over a cup of tea I suggested to Ray that he was the Noël Coward of our generation, and that songs like 'Waterloo Sunset' had pretty much the same resonance on society as 'Mad Dogs and Englishmen'. Ray smiled benignly, and the die was cast. The next thing we knew Ray was putting all his energy into a one-man-show called Storyteller, and writing an autobiography called X-Ray. The one man show by definition had no room for a drummer.

I had unintentionally shot us all in the foot with my chance remark, because it gave Ray the opportunity to get cracking on a solo career. Obviously if the rest of us played with Dave we'd be The Kinks, and Ray might threaten to sue – and vice versa. So we all needed to find something to do to pay the mortgage while waiting for something to happen with The Kinks. I guess we're still waiting. Strangely, in the same way that I wasn't told I had joined The Kinks in 1984 I still haven't been told a quarter of a century later that I've left the band. Maybe I haven't!

It was something of a rite of passage for any musician of my generation to play with 'Screaming' Lord Sutch. My turn came when I was in the house band with Jim Rodford at a restaurant known as Blues West 14 in London's Holland Park. It was owned by a vivacious lady called Ramona who felt that if she could provide a place for musicians and singers working in musicals in town to eat a late supper and sit in with the band if they fancied it she might create a nice little earner. For a while she was right, because it was just a few stops on the tube from the West End. The gig was frequently packed, and lots of famous people like Mike Berry and Hank Marvin were coerced there to drag people in. The house band was fronted by a possibly American keyboard player, Johnny Casanova (probably not his real name), whose mother happened to be Scottish. Johnny fancied himself as a Jerry Lee Lewis impersonator, so we played many of 'the Killer's' great songs, albeit invariably too fast, too loud and too long. The house band kicked things off before guys in the audience were allowed to get up. Fortunately we weren't forced into accompanying too many twelve- bar blues tunes in the key of E with turgid and unimaginative guitar solos, but we did have to put up with a certain number.

The aforementioned David Edward Sutch turned up one night and was in his element: he specialised in frenzied versions of old rock tunes like 'Johnny B. Goode', as did Johnny Casanova. I liked what Dave Sutch stood for, and the way he stuck his fingers up to the establishment with his Monster Raving Loony Party. However, not to speak ill of the dead, playing with him wasn't the zenith of my career.

In the end people stopped coming to Blues West, possibly because the West End guys wanted to show off their talents with more sophisticated and complicated jazzy stuff, which they expected the band to play without music. In the end I wanted to stop because I was getting in at 3am every Wednesday, and since I was involved with Arbiter at the time I needed to be back in Hendon not too long after 8am. (And for my money the place never completely recovered from its sewers inconsiderately blocking up towards the end of our time there!)

Around this time I was approached by my bass-playing pal Mark Griffiths, who said Hank Marvin was looking for a drummer for a tour. Was I interested? I liked the idea of standing in my old pal Tony Meehan's shoes so said yes, and after having had a blow with Mr Marvin at Blues West 14 with Jim Rodford and Johnny Casanova I was hired. We really rocked that night, and Hank played brilliantly on a borrowed Fender Strat without a whammy bar. He must have liked me, and said he was amazed at how much like Tony I played. (Since it was probably getting on for forty years since he'd played with him I was surprised he remembered!) All the recordings were sent to me, and I duly wrote out my parts and turned up for rehearsals at Nomis studios ready to rock.

There were two weeks of solid rehearsals booked at Nomis, and I was amazed to discover I was expected to play all the songs in their entirety immediately – as if I'd already been in the band like the rest of them. Coming from a completely professional but ostensibly ramshackle situation like The Kinks, where I coped perfectly well even though I never knew what was coming next, or how many choruses, verses and middle eights Ray was going to put in the song, I was shocked. I was also angry to discover that, aside from Mark G, nobody was interested in working these things out with me. Hank came into the rehearsals several days earlier than expected, and I was told by the management he wanted everything right immediately. My response was that if they wanted it right on the first day why was I booked for two weeks' rehearsals? Not surprisingly, the Musicians' Union agreed with me. It was a shame, because I didn't do the gig and was really looking forward to playing with Hank. I had a lot of rock 'n' roll 'chops' to bring to the party. Years after the event it occurs to me that one of the guys in the band (who wouldn't swing if you hung him) possibly had a different agenda, and wanted one of his drummer pals in from the start.

When the legal dust subsided and my wounds were sufficiently licked, I got a call from an Anglophile friend called Wayne Blanchard who worked for the Sabian Cymbal Company in Canada. I'd had dealings with him over the years when I was writing for various drum magazines. His company was hosting a bunch of British drum dealers in Meductic, New Brunswick, and since their UK distributor was going to be there too could I give some pertinent background on him. Ivor Arbiter was the distributor in question, and I'd known him since the fifties when he sold me my first proper drumset – and I often saw him at Drum City in London's West End. I'd also reviewed many of the products he distributed – from Rogers, Autotune, Sabian, Paiste and Hayman. Wayne was delighted with my contribution, as was Ivor who, after the event, enquired where all the inside information had come from. When Wayne called me to say how well his speech had been received he suggested that Ivor might be interested in someone writing his life story, so it wouldn't be lost. I was on the look-out for something to get my teeth into, so I called Ivor and set out my writer's stall. He called me to a meeting at his North London offices, where after the usual hard negotiation he agreed to pay me £5,000 in stages. I became his official biographer in October 1996, and set about getting his highly colourful life story down on paper. (I say I was Ivor's biographer, but it would be more accurate to describe me as his auto-biographer: he told me what to write!) I turned up at the Arbiter offices in Hendon a couple of times a week, and Ivor made mostly hilarious, sometimes explosive, frequently shocking revelations to me and my recently acquired mini-cassette Dictaphone.

Ivor was a big man, a larger-than-life character who had grown up in London's East End where his father Joe was first a dentist and then a professional musician playing with Harry Roy's band, one of the most popular dance bands of the war era. Unusually for a young Limey, he'd been evacuated to the east coast of America at the beginning of the war and lodged, safely out of harm's way, with relatives there. He spent his formative years in the States, went to school in New York and mixed with some very interesting people. These included a gangster called Louis Buckhalter, 'Lepke', who was head of Murder, Inc. and had married into the Arbiter family. Lepke was to be electrocuted in Sing Sing for ordering the executions of at least 100 people including 'Dutch' Schultz, but Ivor was on his way home long before this happened. (My new mate Tony Curtis played Lepke in the Hollywood film of the same name.)

Upon his return to the UK, on a luxury liner turned troopship and after a decent interval, Ivor took up the calling of saxophone repairer doing jobs for the likes of Dizzy Gillespie before joining his father in Paramount, the Shaftesbury Avenue music shop. At this time guitars were just becoming part of the music scene. Ivor sourced them in Holland and imported them in a van driven by his jazz-playing friends who'd been working there. To ensure that would-be Tommy Steeles looked at their best wearing these guitars, he installed a full-length mirror in the shop so that rock 'n' rollers could get the full effect. The fact that many of these guys couldn't play a note was irrelevant: neither could the guitars.

When Ivor opened Drum City a few doors east at 114 Shaftesbury Avenue in 1962 I was an enthusiastic customer: the vibe was great and lots of my chums (like

Gerry Evans, Dave Golding, Johnny Richardson and Dave Mattacks) were working there. It was loosely modelled on a drum shop in LA partly owned by Remo Belli, and where the Weatherking plastic head, which changed the world of drumming, was invented. Ivor's shop was unique on this side of the Atlantic in that it only sold drums: until then drummers were pretty much consigned to the scruffy, damp, badly lit nether regions of general music stores known evocatively as the Drummers' Dive', or Drum Cellar. Before the Beat Boom, which brought guitars to the fore, the ground floors of these musical emporia invariably had a prevalence of saxes, trumpets, trombones, violins, accordions, banjos, harmonicas, jews harps and of course the inevitable kazoos.

Ivor freely admitted that all his life he'd been fortunate in being in the right place at the right time, but to give him his due he'd been responsible for importing and even inventing many instruments which have shaped the lives of me and a great many other wannabe rock stars. He'd imported Fender guitars and Ludwig drums to name but a couple, and these makes became world famous mostly because of him. Certainly when Ringo Starr came into Drum City with his manager Brian Epstein looking for a drum kit at a time when the Beatles were just beginning to make waves, by accident he was turned on to Ludwig. Ringo fancied a Trixon set, and tried to order one in the grey and black oyster-striped finish he saw in a collection of plastic drum coverings on the counter. Upon being told those finishes were for Ludwig, not Trixon, he did what few other drummers would do: he went ahead and ordered the Ludwig set because he liked the colour! Evidently 'Eppi' tried to drive a hard bargain to get a deal on the drums, claiming The Beatles would be so famous it would be well worth Drum City's investment. Ivor was no slouch at bargaining either, and having deliberated for a while he came up with a deal whereby Ringo's old and decidedly beaten-up Premier kit (which was about to disappear to Australia and become for ever the Holy Grail of celebrity-owned sets) would have to be taken in part exchange. According to the Ludwig website, having successfully pulled- off the coup of the century with the Ringo deal, he telephoned Bill Ludwig and negotiated his own deal, whereby the Ludwig company gave him a full credit on the set he'd supplied to The Beatles. As I said, Ivor Arbiter knew how to negotiate, but Ludwig and Drum City and arguably Ringo were the winners. Within days of The Beatles famously appearing on the Ed Sullivan TV show the Ludwig factory in Chicago was working round the clock to keep up with worldwide demand, and Ivor was struggling to take delivery of enough sets for the home market.

The Fab Four's old Premier bass drum had a clumsy-looking logo on a strip of cloth across it, which I always thought read 'The Silver Beetles' with a double 'e' and a couple of the antennae you see on cartoon drawings of insects on the capital 'B'. This was evidently the name they went under in Hamburg. (I'm prepared to admit I might be wrong on this, because all the pictures of Ringo I've seen of late that show this set have the regular 'ea' spelling.)

You might not know this. A one-armed signwriter named Eddie Stokes worked across the road on Shaftesbury Avenue, and he wandered into Drum City in his lunch hour to see if any drummers needed bass heads sign-written. Upon being told that a new group called The Beatles was looking for one he immediately drew four different logos on a cigarette packet, and the Beatles (or possibly Mr Epstein) picked out the one they liked, with the raised 'B' and dropped 'T'. Eddie Stokes received his usual fee of five quid for creating what was to become arguably the third most famous logo on the planet! For years this design was attributed to Ivor Arbiter, but my pal Gerry Evans (who was there at the time) assured me in all honesty it was Eddie. For my money the one he did for The Beatles wasn't even his best effort. My favourite was the one he did for the Undertakers, which had a top hat and a pair of horn-rimmed glasses sitting on top of the capital 'U'.

But as usual I'm digressing.

Ivor and I put our heads together on the book project a couple of times a week, and at the end of one session in the confessional box he spilled the beans about his new drum venture and asked my opinion. It was another single-screw tuning system, and in the light of the fact that he'd already had a 'close but no cigar' brush with the concept a decade before, with his 'Auto-Tune' drums, I was sceptical. We'd struggled to sell Arbiter Auto-Tunes in my Drumstore, so I counselled him to make sure that it worked this time (since the original one didn't), and make it look as much like a regular drumset as possible. Ivor never liked being told that his babies were ugly, so bridled at my criticism of the original concept – until I mentioned how he'd had to adapt the system by fitting small 'fine tuners' tapped into the counter-hoops. This made it work, but ruined the idea of a drum tuned with a single screw.

Bob Zildjian, who was at the time co-owner of his family's cymbal company, always said that Jimmy Reno, an eccentric Mancunian inventor and shop-owner who was said to drive around with a priceless Stradivarius in the boot of his Rolls-Royce, beat Ivor to the punch with a single-screw tuning system .which he introduced halfway through the fifties. Ivor Arbiter didn't get on with him. While I think of it, Reno's shells were made from war-surplus plywood he bought for a bargain-price from the MOD. It had been stock-piled to make Mosquitos and other wooden-framed planes during the war. Actually Reno wasn't the first either, because Leedy and Ludwig's equally unsuccessful 'knob-tension' drums were introduced at the beginning of the fifties. They and Reno had to deal with awkward and unpredictable animal skin heads, so didn't really have a chance.

If you're not a drum technophile I suggest you skip the next few paragraphs . . . Auto-Tune's Achilles heel was actually that, since it worked on the principle of a glass-topped pickle jar with the counterhoop taking the place of the lid screwing down and thereby tensioning the head inside, because it was effectively running down a thread there was always a leading edge that would be tighter than the following edge. Therefore the pitch dropped slightly as you tapped around the head anticlockwise: hence the need for fine tensioners. But unfortunately, since they made contact with the brittle glue channel of the head and dug in, it could be caught in the twisting motion and rotated against the fibreglass bearing-edge. This sometimes cut through the plastic and thereby destroyed the head.

I knew Ivor's son Johnny had even made visits to shops to change rollers on the drums so the mechanism worked properly. I think we agreed to differ, but I know Ivor looked at me in a different light from then on. I never found out whether this was a good light or a bad one. At the end of one of our sessions he asked me lots of technical questions about shell materials, thicknesses, construction and finishes, as well as the relative virtues of pressed steel or cast counterhoops and various other drum fixtures and fittings. I was slightly reticent at first, since that would be consultancy and I was simply playing the role of a biographer, but in the end I threw caution to the winds and told him what I thought.

There was one memorable moment when at the end of a confession session Ivor presented a very old-fashioned extra deep counter-hoop for my approval. I had no reason to lie, so told him in my not so humble opinion it was ugly, old-fashioned and the drum world wouldn't go for it. I caught sight of my old mate Dave Caulfield standing behind 'Mr A', and as I delivered my condemnation I saw him put his hands together in supplication and raise his eyes to heaven. He'd been trying to tell Ivor this for some time, but he wouldn't listen. I also suggested while I was on the subject that there was no need to reinvent the wheel with accessories at the very end of the twentieth century, and saw no point in him investing money in designing his own bass drum and hi-hat pedals, since they were already out there. He listened to me on both these topics, although as you'll see this wasn't exactly a regular occurrence. Ivor Arbiter had had a lifetime of practice at keeping a dog and barking himself.

Eventually he showed me the prototype. To set the scene: while sailing in the English channel on his motor yacht (the *Jolly Rotter*) close to the Goodwin Sands, Ivor had suffered an oil pressure failure in one of his engines. Having gone down to see if he could fix what he thought was a turbo leak, he discovered that the pipe wasn't held on with a jubilee clip but with a completely different animal – a vee-clamp. He was unable to move this sideways, and when he eventually got it off and held it in his hand a metaphorical light-bulb went off over his head. He realised that here was another way to tune drums from a single position. It was a much purer solution to drum tuning than Auto-tune, since it didn't rely on the complicated moving parts of a rack and pinion. The vee-clamp was a very sophisticated piece of equipment often used in jet engines: precision made from steel, it was C-shaped in plan, with a nut and bolt bringing the open ends closer. It was sectioned like a 'V' with a very slightly flattened bottom, and this encompassed two equal and opposite angled flanges formed into the ends of the pipes and drew them together until they touched. This was accomplished by decreasing the circumference. I assume it worked really well, otherwise we would have heard reports of a great many aircraft losing engine pressure and falling from the sky.

So Ivor produced a prototype drum fitted with two flanges, one on the hoop facing down and the other fixed to the drum below the bearing edge and facing up. The head sat on the bearing edge in the normal way, the counterhoop went on top of it and the vee-clamp fitted around both flanges. Once the screw on the clamp was tightened it drew the two open ends closer together, while squashing the film of the head down against the bearing edge and thereby tuning it. Because of the metal to metal contact of the vee-clamp on the flanges there was a certain amount of friction, which Ivor overcame by hitting the outside of the clamp with a hefty chunk of wood. The whole thing worked, but Ivor freaked out the Boston Symphony Orchestra's principal percussionist turned drum-stick maker Vic Firth when he saw the way he adjusted the prototype so the tensioning was equal all over the head. Vic still talks about it to this day!

As I said, Dave Caulfield was masterminding the project but he was a guitarist not a drummer, and knew he was out of his depth. That said, Nigel Robinson, the guy at the Arbiter factory working on the engineering side of the project and turning Ivor's ideas into reality, wasn't a drummer either. A potentially dangerous situation, you might think. Dave suggested to Ivor that since I was a drummer and already involved to a point, why not rationalise the situation and bring me in for real. The die was cast, and Ivor called me in, taking me for tea and toast in his mate's café round the corner on the Edgware Road and offering me a position within the organisation.

'What would I do?' I asked. 'I'm the drummer in The Kinks.'

His response was that I should simply help out the non-drumming guys when I could, and when it was nearly ready to be launched bring in some pals to see it and get some feedback. I said I'd give it some thought. Eventually I gave in and threw my lot in with Mr A. Once we had a product I went down my address book and invited all the guys I knew to see the drums. They were impressed, and I have to say I was already hooked on the tuning system, even though it was still very much a prototype with a few loose ends. I felt that its ease of tuning would save fortunes in the recording studio. Please allow me to tell you what persuaded me.

Like every other studio drummer, in those halcyon days before sampled drum sounds took over, I would be booked to make an album. On the designated day I would turn up at the studio with a drum tech (or two) and a pantechnicon full of a great many different sized snare drums, bass drums, toms, cymbals and heads. The producer would have set aside a day or three to get a drum sound before the band came in. So by a lengthy and arduous process of elimination we picked out which drums and cymbals made the best sound – all this without having any idea how they'd sound with the band: it was invariably only by accident that it was compatible with the other instruments. But in the days when record companies had more money than sense and producers were getting $40,000 as an advance against royalties, that's the way the game was played. Of course state-of-the-art studio time was never cheap even if you'd negotiated a deal for a month's worth of 'lock-out'. (This meant the studio and its staff were at your disposal for a whole month, day and night, and nobody else could get in.) So since it could easily take two days to work out which drums and heads to use, you could end up paying £2,000 to £3,000 to get a drum sound. Eventually I learned the salutary lesson that the more you took into the studio the longer it took to eliminate the ones the producer didn't like – at that particular moment.

I've heard of well-known drummers taking fifty snare drums into a session, and can't for the life of me see why. Any producer worth his salt is going to want to hear them all before he makes his decision, and just setting up that number of drums is hugely time consuming – never mind tuning them and changing heads. In the end I just took a handful of snares into the studio and saved the one I knew would work best (a cheap and cheerful Ludwig Acrolite I'd bought in an American pawnshop) till last. If I tried it first it never got the gig. And this drum sound thing wasn't like playing with a band. I called it coitus interruptus. I never found any fulfilment at all in the nonsense of getting a drum sound. Now where was I? To get to the point, Ivor's invention would do away with all this experimentation and save eons of studio time, and therefore lots of money.

I sat down and gave a deal of thought to this. I worked out the number of times where I'd gone into the studio for a couple of days and contributed, willingly or otherwise, to this initial expenditure. I stopped at thirty-nine albums and multiplied by 3,000. This gave a grand total of £105,000, the asking price for a very nice cottage overlooking the sea at somewhere like Weymouth, possibly with a small yacht and a

Land-Rover thrown in! I think you can see where this is going. Surely drummers and producers would want to save that money if they could?

So, even though I was still self-employed, I started the very first proper job I'd ever had towards the end of 1997.

Since the vee-clamp tuning system was considerably more expensive to produce than a regular version, we were forced to look outside the UK to get the job done, and we started negotiations with various Taiwanese companies about sourcing the necessary componentry. Shells weren't deemed to be too much of a problem – they just needed to be made from the right materials, in the right thicknesses and in the right colours. This proved to be a great deal easier said than done. Where the rest of the world had access to various indigenous woods like birch, beech and oak, the Taiwanese didn't. They had basswood and mahogany, which grew abundantly in the Orient. Maple, which because of its tonal qualities had become the material of preference for shells, needed to be imported from North America. Obviously it was priced at a premium. Initially the shells were made from nine plies of 100 per cent maple – at least the samples were. However, when we finally took delivery of the 'production' shells we weren't so sure. Many of them had been filled and repaired where the bearing edge would be, and when inspected by the very knowledgeable Mark Pressling, who set up all the Fender and Guild guitars, they were pronounced maple mix. What this meant was that the outside and inside plies were maple while the inners were basswood: a completely different animal at a considerably different price. The Taiwanese swore the shells were what we expected, and I remember standing face to face with the inscrutable guy who made them saying they certainly weren't. After much argument Charlie Tye, who should have been aware because he wore glasses with the thickest lenses I'd ever seen, admitted that they weren't completely maple after all. And he'd never meant us to think they were! And shell material was the least of our problems: colour matching was our nightmare. Don't get me started.

One day Ivor called me in to his big office, which adjoined the board room with its huge posh table which bore the scars of all the dismantling, assembling and 'cutting and shutting' of the prototype AT drums that took place on it. He wanted to talk about what the initial shell order should look like. He knew what diameters he wanted, but he and I disagreed on how deep they should be. Extra-deep drums called 'power toms' were already an outdated concept, as they didn't respond as well as shallow drums and didn't sit comfortably on top of regular bass drums either. But the chairman wanted them so we had them. Otherwise we knew what the different sets were going to be: fusion, rock, jazz and so on in four, five or six pieces. I'd done a lot of research, so when Ivor asked me what colours were the most in demand I was able to tell him black and natural maple were pretty much the only ones wanted in new sets. The on-the-road sales reps, who were in on the meeting, agreed with me. OK, he said, we'll have fifteen red, fifteen blue, fifteen green, fifteen black and fifteen natural maple! I take no satisfaction in the knowledge that we struggled to get rid of the coloured drums, especially the green (which Ivor eventually deemed to be an unlucky colour).

As I said, I was always consulted but not always listened to. One thing I managed to put my stamp on was the name of the set, which became Arbiter AT, short for Arbiter Advanced Tuning, which I felt summed up the product admirably.

166

Eventually the lacquered shells arrived for our first production run, and we oohhed and aahhed' about them until, having machined the shells to accept the lower ring (which for the time being was carried out in the UK) and put the drums together in sets, we discovered a problem. There were subtle differences in colour shade within the drums in each set. To be fair, all the same-coloured 10 inch toms matched one another, as did the bass drums and all the various other sizes. They would, as they were sprayed at the same time. This was to prove unacceptable to the public who (surprise, surprise) wanted a completely matching set and wouldn't be placated by being told it was one of a kind! The problem was even more acute with the natural finished drums, where not enough care had been taken at the factory to match the important grain of the outer ply of maple when the shells were constructed. Some were really grainy and interesting while others were bland and just – well, wood really. We were able to juggle a bit with these, but even their shades didn't always match and once we'd mixed and matched as best we could we always ended up with at least a couple of dodgy-looking sets.

At the time all the big drum companies were looking at ways of isolating their drums from mounting systems, and I felt we should too. The others had to adapt their drums, but since we were new guys this didn't impact on us – we simply built the mounts into the design. So by welding small brackets to the lower rings we fashioned a fixing point for our rails system, which retained a mounting boss for tom holders, bass drum spurs and, for the first time ever, snare throw-off and butt end. All without touching the shell and (arguably) muting its resonance.

Time went by, and with less and less Kinks activity and more and more Raymond Douglas Davies activity, I was available to spend more time on the AT project. By default, since I was the only one who knew the product (and the only drummer), I found myself the AT product specialist – and in LA at what they call the NAMM show. This was in 1998. By then Dave Caulfield had progressed to pastures new, and Ivor had taken on a general manager to oversee the day-to-day running of the project. Tony Ferris was a big part of the Thames Motor Yacht Club of which Ivor Arbiter was the commodore, and a thoroughly nice chap. He knew a great deal about the stress of selling supertankers: the problem was he didn't know anything about drums other than what we paid for them. We were team-handed on our first expedition to the Los Angeles Conference Centre, a great looking place in the middle of a pretty dangerous area. Still no matter, we were staying on Sunset Strip in my old stamping ground; the Hyatt House, which was the only hotel I ever stayed in with a cinema-style marquee above the entrance announcing 'The Hyatt House proudly welcomes The Kinks and Argent.' It had somehow managed to shrug off its image of being the perfect place for musicians of my generation to behave badly in. (The Who had taken hotel wrecking to its logical conclusion there, and Led Zeppelin had ridden motorbikes along the corridors. Although I don't believe anybody was ever banned from the Hyatt, Argent were banned from two hotels: the Holiday Inn in Westwood, because mild-mannered Fred Wilkinson had done a bit of damage there once, and the Four Seasons in Toronto because of the Dayvilles ice cream incident. I told you about earlier.)

No expense was spared for this first Namm show. Ivor wasn't flying transatlantic too much by this time because of his tinnitus, but he turned up nevertheless for the worldwide launch of AT. So did his wife, the hugely supportive

Adrienne. Otherwise Tony Ferris was there helping man our stand, which was rather large for a new company. Still, it showed we meant business. It was a huge success from the marketing point of view, although that particular word was not part of Ivor's vocabulary. It was known to us as the 'M' word , and Ivor was only interested in the 'S' word: sales. Anyway, the great and good of the music world turned up, and we received our fair share of plaudits.

There had recently been an influx of Russians into Los Angeles, and they had taken over a huge area around SIR rehearsal studios on Sunset and La Brea to create Little Moscow. They also drove all the dodgy-looking taxis parked haphazardly outside the Hyatt House. Not only that, in common with cabbies with English as a second language in big cities all over America, they had very little idea how to get anywhere – so a request to one of these guys to take us to the Convention Centre elicited a meeting between all the Russian cabbies and much discussion about the route. Eventually one of them would produce his secret weapon, a dog-eared map of Los Angeles, and we'd be on our way.

Deep Purple had reformed for a series of gigs across the road from the Hyatt at The House of Blues, and one day I found myself riding shotgun alongside the fierce shaven-headed young driver, who looked to me as if he'd just left Spetsnaz and relocated directly to Los Angeles. He engaged me in conversation, and I was most surprised when he asked whether I'd seen Deep Purple. I said I had, and his next question was how Ritchie Blackmore was – and was he still doing drugs. It turned out that although he might well have been a soldier in the Soviet special forces who could kill in many different ways, he'd moved to the US to make it as a guitarist! He reeled off all his favourite English bands, including Uriah Heep, Gentle Giant and all the English bands of my era. Just in case he mentioned Argent I thought it prudent to change the subject. I said I doubted Ritchie still did drugs, because like his contemporaries he was becoming too old for it. The Russian wanted to become my new best friend and visit me in my room, but I'm ashamed to say I wasn't ready for that.

A few paragraphs ago I asked whether drummers embraced the Arbiter product. Well, the truth is, aside from me and a couple of Nashville studio guys and the Moody Blues, they stayed away in their thousands. Ivor Arbiter always said there were two hundred reasons for not buying something, but only one for doing so. Unfortunately too many drummers had two hundred reasons to buy something else! Too many people listened to AT with their eyes. They were put off by the look, because it didn't have lumps of gleaming chrome-work to break up the expanse of polished wood. They also professed to not liking the isolation systems we'd worked so hard on, to allow the drums to sing properly, and which most drum companies didn't have. But while this lack of interest was potentially going to become extremely serious, fortunately there was another unexpected throw of the dice – but not for a couple of years.

In the beginning a great deal of money was spent on publicising AT drums with double-page-spreads in all the appropriate music magazines, and having taken great care to explain the advantages of the single-screw tuning concept to editors and critics around the world through erudite and readable press releases and adverts, we received more than our fair share of glowing reviews. (Editorial and advertising people are supposed to work independently of each other but in practice they never do.) I had only recently stopped writing instrument reviews for *Rhythm Magazine* in the UK and the editor (the lovely Louise King) felt, since I knew the product, I'd be the perfect person for the job. So I wrote their first critique of the new product – and needless to say I was enthusiastic about it!

Things moved along pretty smoothly in the UK after this, with the Arbiter Sales reps managing to get a reasonable amount of product into the shops with a mixture of the old pals act, promises of special treatment and veiled threats that if they didn't take them they wouldn't get the best deals on the other products Arbiter handled: Sabian, Remo and Fender. As you can imagine, Ivor used his connections with the mighty Fender to get distribution overseas, and we had quite a few of their main distributors handling the drums. These guys were not as successful as Ivor would have liked, mainly because the drums were expensive and not what drummers wanted. Frequently I was sent to shows around the world to support these guys and demo the drums. One of these springs to mind as an indication of how the world is shrinking. I went to a show in Italy to help a company called Casale Bauer, Arbiter's distributors, and having said my goodbyes I left the seaside resort of Rimini at noon on a spring Sunday to return to London. A taxi took me to the station, whereupon I journeyed up to Bologna on a train that had originated in Bari at the foot of Italy and was filled with passengers with livestock in cages and their belongings stuffed into pillowcases on their laps. At the station in Bologna I took a bus to the airport and had the usual wait for a delayed plane to Heathrow. Having landed safely in London I went downstairs to the tube, which took me to Finsbury Park, where I boarded an overground train home to Winchmore Hill – where Ricki had a meal waiting. After this early supper I loaded my car with drums, and seven hours after I left Rimini I was setting them up for a Phoenix gig with John Verity and Jim Rodford in a Hertfordshire town!

The next show we went to with AT was the biggest of them all at that time: the Frankfurt Music Messe. Here again we had a large, expensive and business-like stand showing absolutely everything we produced in every size and colour. It was here that Ivor pulled rank on me and insisted I took a drumset out of the show and delivered it personally to a hotel – something that was far, far easier said than done. Security was extremely tight, and just getting the equipment into the show at the beginning was difficult. Taking it out halfway through was nigh-on impossible, and to make it worse taxis weren't allowed anywhere other than at the very front of the building, which was miles away. Fortunately my old friend Axel Mikaelovich, editor of a German drum magazine called *Stix*, spotted me sweating and swearing with the boxes I was struggling to get out of the Messe complex. He took pity on me and being German was able to intercede volubly with the authorities on my behalf. The reason for removing the set from the show was that every year Fender, the mighty American guitar company, of which Ivor just happened to be a director, held a soirée where they gave their awards away, slapped each other on the back and generally had a very good time. A jazz trio was invariably playing softly in the background. Ivor thought this would be perfect exposure for his brand-new AT set. The problem was that the German jazz trio's drummer wasn't happy: he was endorsed by a rival drum company and wanted to play his own set. Needless to say, Ivor came out on top in that argument. After delivering the drums to the Intercontinental Hotel in the centre of Frankfurt, lugging them up escalators and setting them up I assumed the job was over. Not so. Having arrived at the gig, the drummer decided he wanted to dampen the bass drum, so he took it apart. At this particular stage of AT's development this wasn't a good idea because it was exceedingly tricky. Well, he certainly couldn't do it, and under the eyes of a few hundred Fender distributors, who Ivor wanted to carry the sets in their respective countries, neither could I. My only chance was to take it off the bandstand dismantle the bloody thing and reassemble it in one piece. The problem was with the lower tuning ring, which had sprung out of its slot in the shell. I knew how to fix it, but it took time and a certain amount of brute strength. I struggled for a while under Ivor's malevolent and unhelpful gaze, and eventually managed to replace it in the nick of time. This was just one of the Advanced Tuning System's Achilles heels that eventually needed to be fixed. The inventor of the product wasn't at all pleased with the guy who was struggling to fix it. In these highly pressured and red-faced situations he tended to get my name wrong and call me John (after Hiseman)!

To be frank there were a few problems that only me, Nigel Robinson and Nick Hudson (Dave Caulfield's replacement) were aware of. We didn't want to be shot as messengers, so we worked on these ourselves without telling the old man. The biggest problem was that once attached to the flanges the vee-clamp, the heart of the tuning system, tended to lose its circularity where the two open ends were held together by the single tension screw. This meant that around the screw there was more tension than anywhere else around the circumference, thereby resulting in a slightly higher pitch. In an instrument boasting equal tuning this was not ideal.

We had another drumset in the roster by this time called Vibrasonic, which we were showing at Frankfurt for the first time. It used the same cripplingly expensive tuning system, but its basswood shells and bolted-on fittings meant it retailed for slightly less than the AT maple-shelled drums. Vibrasonic was actually the name for the special polyurethane interior paint on the inside of the old Hayman shells, which was an acrylic you could buy in any hardware shop at that time. (It was also the name of a Fender amplifier, which Ivor had borrowed when he launched Hayman at the end of the sixties.) The other thing that made Vibrasonic cheaper is that the shells weren't lacquered on the outside: they were wrapped in solid-coloured plastic, which meant no matching problems. And we had a secret weapon, which was a covering that looked exactly like natural maple with a very distinctive grain – so every drum matched.

The drumhead company Remo had been using a photographic process to make jazzy patterns to cover their Kidz drums, and I asked if they could produce a natural maple finish. They didn't think there would be any problem, and simply asked for a good quality photo of a natural maple shell to be sent to California. Nick Sharples was the in-house photographer and digital layout person at the time, and he and I went down the road to Ivor's Hendon Football Club to take the photos. We chose an interesting piece of grain on a bass drum, and Nick took several different shots with slightly different exposure times. Once they were processed the transparencies were sent off to Remo. The next thing we knew was that a very large roll of realistic wood-look plastic film arrived. The Vibrasonics looked great, and aside from the join, which without nutboxes was difficult to hide, they looked just like the real thing. Unless, that is, as we discovered a little later, you put them in a shop window and let the sun get to them. The photographic pattern was bleached away and you had a nice white drum! Ask yourself, was this a marketable concept?

Lots of AT maple drums were covered a little later on once retro drum finishes (glitters and sparkles) from the fifties and sixties were back in demand. This gave us the opportunity to use up some of the lacquered shells that didn't really match. (It's amusing to read on websites a decade or so after the event how guys have discovered different colours under the plastic wraps and wonder what the significance is!)

A chap called Mel Gaynor was between endorsements, and came to see me about the possibility of throwing his lot in with us. He was playing in Simple Minds, and had a lot going for him as far as the drum world was concerned. Ivor liked his image, so he was chosen to be the face of AT drums. A budget was drawn up for a clinic tour of the UK and France, and to kick it off Ivor ordered cripplingly expensive, stand-alone, life-sized cut-out photographs of Mel mounted on cardboard to go into key shops around Europe.

Mel was around 6 foot tall, and so was his cut-out, which meant it was impossible to send it safely to shops without the carriers breaking him in half. I remember I drove to the important accessible shops with Mel's facsimile sitting awkwardly in the back of my car. For the rest of the shops he was wrapped carefully in cardboard by a nice chap, Sang, who had been the warehouse manager for many years.

The metal-shelled AT snare drum was made differently from the wooden drums because its thin shell couldn't be grooved to take the lower ring. The solution was to throw a 'Z'-shaped circular flange and make it fit snugly over the raw edges of the shell. It worked very well. One day I was messing around in the workshop and managed to separate this complete top section. I realised I had the world's shallowest drum in my hand. Rewind to 1981 . . .

On our very last day in Drumstore a mobile crane-driver called Len Bailey wandered in with a bunch of shallow drums under his arm and asked for help in marketing them. I pointed to the remnants of a dream all around me and suggested I wasn't really in a position to help anyone; but when he contacted me again later I lent a hand. He was reasonably successful with his Melanie Fantoms – with guys like Trilok Gurtu still using them to great effect. I used these shallow drums years later when space was at a premium (if I was travelling a long way with Jim Rodford and car-sharing). They worked reasonably well, but this section I'd pulled off a 14 inch AT snare drum worked even better.

I was fired up, and the guys at the Arbiter factory were instructed to cut down a regular wooden set to produce single-headed drums with the shallowest shells possible. Lo and behold . . . even though they appeared to transgress all the laws of drum building, they worked, and sounded pretty damn good. Nigel Robinson at the factory put a set together and I showed them to the old man. Mr A. was very impressed, although disappointed he hadn't been consulted and part of the development. Within a very short time we had a unique product on the market: a drumset that sounded like a drumset, played like a drumset and fitted into one bag had been my dream (and that of many other drummers) since I had first carried a drumset and here it was, a reality. We needed a name, and having batted it around I suggested Flats. Ivor preferred Flat Hats until I told him Zildjian already had a pair of hi-hat cymbals with that name – so Flats it was.

At first the drum world was sceptical, but once they realised it sounded pretty good sales began to happen. The first sets had wooden shells fastidiously (make that laboriously) worked by hand from full-sized left-over basswood shells down at the Arbiter manufacturing facility near Bournemouth. They also had the metal vee-clamps, counter-hoops and mounting brackets – in short all the expensive attributes of the AT. So they didn't come out that much cheaper than the regular sets, even though they had no real shell and aside from the snare drum only one head. This would have been more of a problem had the drum world not liked what they'd seen – and heard. When Flats were unveiled there was a certain amount of disbelief among the cognoscenti as to whether they sounded like drums. I evolved a ploy where I sent these guys out of sight round the corner – at the show we were exhibiting at – and played regular drums and Flats and asked them to differentiate. They had great difficulty in doing this, and grudgingly admitted how good Flats were. I immediately stopped playing my favourite little Pearl kit which I'd had since 1970 for my casual gigs, and transferred my affections to Flats. The main benefits were that they were contained in two bags, which fitted unobtrusively into the boot of my car, and they could stay there till the next gig.

We were into the new millennium before the first phase of the next Flats innovation was unleashed – plastic shells. While the guys at the factory were struggling to build Flats from wood, discussions were going on as to whether the shells could be built from anything else. The idea was to form them from ABS and spring-fit the expensive metal lower ring in. I asked why the angled lower ring couldn't be built into it, and the die was cast – pun intended. The sets came out with this refinement, and various other differences, in time for the Music Show in Birmingham. This coincided with the death of John Hedderick, my father-in-law, who over the years had been able to translate even my most ridiculous drum ideas into reality from a mechanical standpoint. This was another idea that Ivor hadn't been involved in, since the shells were made by Alchemy (a company owned by Nigel Robinson and his family), not by Arbiter Manufacturing. For the first time in my experience Ivor allowed control of something to slip away from him.

When Flats Lite were released with vee-clamps made from plastic, the original drums with metal clamps were elevated to pro status. Mind you, this time the old pals act didn't work as far as reviews were concerned. Andy Doershuck, editor of *Drum!* magazine in the US, hated them and refused to review Flats Lite, even though I was writing a vintage article bi-monthly for them.

I had another trick up my sleeve: regular wooden-shelled drums with specially rebated Flats Lite pushed onto their open ends to create 'real' drums, thus doing away with the need to laboriously cut a bearing edge. We made some prototypes but they never found their way into production. It's a shame, because that idea could have changed the way drums were constructed. However, all Flats shells had the rebate formed into their inside – just in case.

I learned from Dave Caulfield that Ivor was never big on the written word. This was a pity, because looking back over the thousands of words I wrote for brochures, press releases, adverts and the like, it appears (not to beat about the bush) that I did a very good job. As I said, I even wrote the first review of the new drums for *Rhythm Magazine!* In the end I learned, like all the other Arbiter guys, not to show Ivor anything contentious. The only adverse effect was that he began to question what I was up to.

I was given a room away from the main offices, behind the warehouse building at the far end of the workshop, where guitars were set up, amplifiers repaired and karaoke machines resuscitated. I was comfortable here on my own, and in time (even though it was dangerously close to the railway) I turned it into a place to which I could invite prospective endorsers, pals from the press and visiting dignitaries from drum companies. We had pictures on the walls, filing cabinets, prototype drums, samples and so on. Eventually a chap called Nick Hudson came on the payroll, poached from Tecconex, who initially made the vee-clamps for Arbiter. Guess what, he wasn't a drummer either – he played bass. He took up his position in what had once been a large cupboard next to me. Later I was moved back into the main building and into an office with the percussion guys, whose job was to deal exclusively with telephone enquiries from the drum trade. Here we were known strictly among ourselves as the coffee club, with a whip round for chocolate biscuits every Monday .We were in our element speaking about drums, drummers and drum concepts all day long while the phones weren't ringing. We respected each other and, aside from having a lot of fun, we did the business. It was a great team. At the time I was only responsible for AT products but Jerome Marcus, Darran Bramley and Martin Potts dealt with Remo, Sabian, LP, Gibraltar and Toca.

Arbiter had a computer system for orders, which told all the different departments what had been sold, what had been put on back order because it wasn't in stock, what could be expedited from the warehouse and what could be invoiced. Even though it wasn't part of my job description (what job description?) I learned how to do this, and was therefore able to help dealers with orders for the staple drum items, like heads, cymbals, sticks and the like.

We even had 'drum circles' to bond the various departments together, but as you can imagine only us percussion guys really got into this. I watched the various telesales and office guys leaving promptly at 5.30 every evening, and privately thought that they could never have made it in showbiz. In time various initiatives were brought into play, including seminars which entailed role playing. Having once been an all-round entertainer, I was rather good at this – but others couldn't get into it at all. The purpose of these seminars was to expose the weak links in the teams and fix them, but frankly once these people were exposed nothing much happened. One of them (an attractive woman) went on to sell a great many Flats drumsets without the essential profit margin to a chain of toy shops. Don't get me started.

Speaking of toy shops, we once put on a presentation at a faux-chateau in Warwickshire where we introduced Flats drums and Fender guitars and amplifiers to the assembled staff. They were about to be selling them at Christmas in the toyshop chain's many stores. I was working alongside Damon Chivers, a guitar sales guy, and Howard Rogers, a bass player and singer who was in charge of logistics and shared the new office we'd been put into next to Ivor's (probably so he could keep an eye on us). We put together a power trio, and played for the delegates. How it worked was that teams from the various stores around the UK traipsed around a myriad of different rooms full of baby clothes, nappies, dolls, kids' bikes, sports equipment and so on – lots of stuff they'd never seen before. Their last task was to wander into our room filled with instruments. As they entered we began to play Robbie Williams's 'Let Me Entertain You', brilliantly lit and wreathed in dry ice. It was a complete surprise for them, and a huge relief after all the boring stuff they'd had to digest. Each group spontaneously began to dance, and they all overstayed their allotted time because they couldn't get enough of us. We couldn't miss! So they started selling our gear. As is the nature of these things they took on a lot of seasonal staff, and the only way there was a musician in any of their vast warehouses was by accident. They couldn't answer questions, so their punters found their way to me.

Now the good thing for the consumer as far as that particular chain with the backwards letter 'R' was concerned was that they guaranteed you could send your purchase back within thirty days if you didn't like it – giving only a vague reason why. Some things written on returns authorisation dockets accompanying the returned goods were risible at best and ridiculous at worst. 'Couldn't play it' on a drumset was one; 'Couldn't set it up' another; and on a guitar I saw the classic 'Broken string'. All these items couldn't go back into the food-chain and had to be sold as A2 stock, with the low profit margin eroded even more. The fact that they were sold into 'consumer' shops like the world-famous toyshop, where they worked on a smaller margin than the specialists, annoyed the regular dealers so much that they lost interest in selling the product.

I think the parents who bought our drums on a whim for their budding Keith Moons had no idea how to put them together, even though we supplied a detailed sheet of instructions. Once, when talking the tenth lady that day through the set up, I apologised for the fact that she obviously hadn't received a manual. Upon being told that she'd got one, I snapped a little and asked if she knew what the letters RFM stood for. Naturally she didn't, so I informed her it was a mnemonic where the first letter stood for Read, the last stood for Manual and the F in the middle was for whatever word she could think of that made sense in the context! Worse still, punters had seriously underestimated the aggravation and the noise produced by drums in untutored hands (far worse than the violin and clarinet we put up with in the Henrit household when Lucy searched for a second instrument to play). So, as far as the shop in question was concerned, they could legitimately have written 'too loud' on a returns authorisation and got away with it.

This ridiculous returns nonsense was bad for any manufacturer. In exchange for selling truckloads of goods, he had to cheerfully put up with it whether he liked it or not. Ivor certainly didn't.

Arbiter had a Christmas party every year for the staff, and to tell you the truth I really didn't enjoy it as much as I should have done. However, Candy Kendrick, loosely described – just by me – as my assistant, and I did our duty, and found our way to the banqueting suite at Hendon Football Club. Every time we sat through the congratulatory speeches which eulogised the Fender department, and never mentioned our AT drum department at all. That is, until one memorable December evening in 2002 when Nigel and the guys from the factory made the mistake of turning up for the first time. Seizing the moment to take a pot-shot at the chairman, the sales manager congratulated us on good sales figures in America, and followed up with applauding the way we'd managed to get all those goods back safe and sound when the distributor had rejected them. Ivor and Mrs A. looked angry, but Dave warmed to his theme. He welcomed the guys from the Bournemouth factory with these memorable lines from an ancient joke: 'Ah yes, Bournemouth . . . it's like a clitoris. You know where it is but you don't want to go down there.' Dave lasted a couple of months longer in the company than I expected him to.

It was 1999, and the Winchmore Hill ski mob were going skiing as usual. I was to catch them up in Austria a couple of days after the holiday began. To be honest I should have cancelled the trip, because I had to get from Los Angeles (where I was at the NAMM show) to a small skiing resort called Kaprun, which was at least three hours outside Salzburg. Intrepid to the last, I left LAX on Sunday evening in my spring clothes and flew to Amsterdam in the worst wide-bodied jet I've been on since we used to fly to America via Prestwick. It had overhead screens and, since I'd forgotten to order the vegetarian option, seriously dodgy mystery-meat food. It takes just as long to get from LA to Amsterdam as it does to get to London, and twelve hours after take-off I landed in the Netherlands. After a short layover of three hours I was on my way, with a dozen other people, in a packed plane to Salzburg. Arriving at the airport, which gave us *The Sound of Music* within two minutes, I was almost the only passenger in the terminal. I chatted with a girl who also needed to get up to the mountains, and we discovered that we knew how to accomplish *most* of the journey: tram from airport to hauptbahnhof, train to the mountains, then . . . we had to work it out for ourselves. The problem was that the tram stand was empty. My new travelling companion and I stood waiting, but nothing turned up. Suddenly there was a flurry of activity: a plane landed and three coaches turned up out of the mist. Suddenly the airport was full of French schoolchildren chattering excitedly. Seizing the moment, I ran towards them and spotted some older children – who turned out to be teachers. In my best French accent, learned while accompanying Richard Anthony many years before, I asked if they were going to the mountains. On being told they were I offered them a deal: if they would give us a lift I'd speak English 'avec les enfants pour toute la journée'. They cogitated for a brief moment and, realising they had plenty of room and my presence would give them a rest from les enfants terribles and more opportunity to flirt with each other, they agreed. We set off, and everything went really well until a couple of hours later when the driver told me he was turning off – and I needed to get off!

I was wearing a snazzy linen suit, which was the height of comfort in Southern California, where it never rains, but pretty useless in Austria, where it frequently snows. As a matter of fact it was snowing as I stood, with my Converse hi-tops covered in snow, by the side of the road with my suitbag over my shoulder and wondering what to do. It put me in mind of one of the first of Ray's songs I recorded with The Kinks: 'Standing in the middle of nowhere, wondering how to begin, lost between tomorrow and yesterday, between now and then . . .' Now, gentle reader, lest you think I'm stupid enough to contemplate skiing in those togs, perhaps I should let you know that the lovely Ricki had taken all my skiing clothes and winter woollies with her from the UK. I was freezing, and there was absolutely no-one around to rescue me. But as I always knew, there is a God, and he sent me salvation in the form of a seriously dodgy grey van which I summoned up the strength to flag down. It turned out to be a taxi van but you'd have been disappointed to be picked up by it if you were wearing your best suit, unless of course you were about to freeze to death in it. I jumped inside, and told the driver where I was hoping to get to. Then I realised I'd need to pay him. I didn't think for one moment he'd be interested in the Amex card I'd been planning to use for the train journey, so I opened my wallet and showed him English money, Austrian shillings, French francs and American dollars. Would he take me to Kaprun for all this accumulated wealth? He bit warily into some of the coins, and eventually agreed to deal. I must say I was expecting to be ripped off, and that's probably what you're thinking too: Joe der taxi would simply drive round the corner and drop me at the chalet. As it happened, I was still miles away from civilisation, but at least I was warm. The driver couldn't accept I didn't speak German, and spoke to me for a long time. All I could do was nod or answer with the phrases I knew, like 'die plattenspieller ist kaput, Wo ist die buhne, haben sie eine zimmer frei', or Jim R's favourite, 'Omelette surprise bitte!'

Much, much later we pulled into Kaprun. By then I'd put on every freebie drum T-shirt and sweatshirt I had in my bag, which was just as well because the driver couldn't take me up to the chalet: the road was too steep and narrow. So I slogged up from the main road and arrived just in time for tea. I wandered into the bar where all the guys were having the first of many pre-prandial drinks. They all greeted me as if I'd just come up from the village, which was a bit galling since I'd been ricocheting around the world for at least eighteen hours!

James with master mariner's beard

Lucy and James

Kresse at thirty

Lucy at the piano

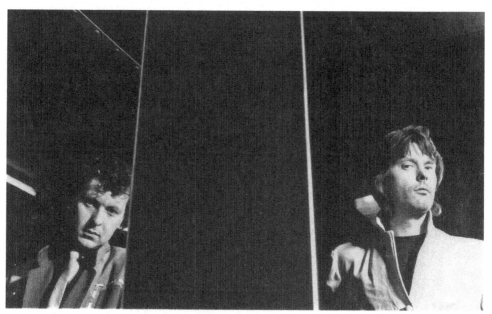

The somewhat embarrassed Juniors

Probably enough said

My very own Drumstore

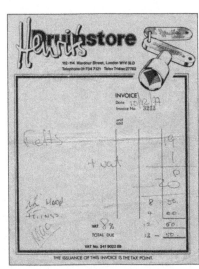

Big deal: Henrit's Drumstore

Drumstore sticker

With Metz and Griff

Don McClean at home

Big Sur road trip 1981

Ann Marie, Don McClean and Ricki

McClean era cowboy shirt

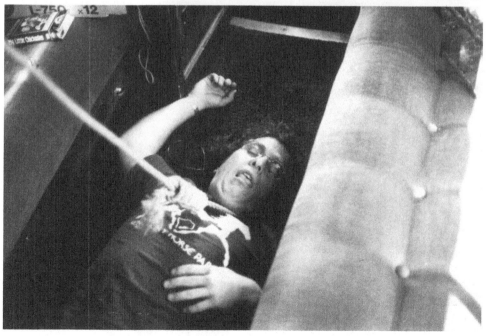

Don McClean at the end of his tether

*Silver Eagle
drivers*

The Insults

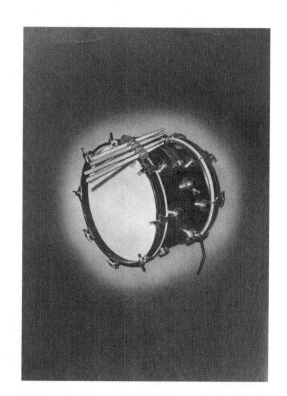

*Gerry Evans's spring on
my bass drum*

GB Blues Company at the Dominion

Ricki at Napenthe on Big Sur

Three Insults

Chapter Nine: BAD NEWS

This is a part of the *Banging On* story I never dreamed I'd be writing. To blow my own trumpet, having been involved with Arbiter and their undeservedly ill-fated AT project almost from the beginning in the late nineties, and having the vision to make Flats drums happen, in 2005 I moved on to the next project: Traps. In tandem with Nigel Robinson, an engineer who until then had run Arbiter's manufacturing arm in Bournemouth, I knew the portable drum project could be elevated to another level, and from the feedback I'd been receiving from around the world, I knew exactly what to do. What we had with Flats was a great start, but I knew there was a lot more that could be done.

While with Arbiter, even though my responsibility was to the drum lines they manufactured, from time to time the phone on my desk rang with enquiries from retailers around the UK about products they distributed, like Remo, Sabian, LP and Toca. Rather than make my excuses and pass these on to the other sales guys, I did my best to save time and do my best to help the customers (most of whom I knew anyway). This went on for some time and, because I knew lots about heads, cymbals, sticks and so on, retailers would often ask for me, and we'd chat about whatever we had in common (drums, drumming, football, mutual friends) before getting down to their enquiries. In the end I was deemed to be part of the team. But not long after Ivor had left the company Andrew Landesberg, the managing director, called me into his office to tell me they'd decided they couldn't afford me. To be frank, from the very beginning I didn't think I was getting paid enough at Arbiter but, ever the optimist, I imagined things might change eventually.

Ivor and I met up at Copthall Sports Ccentre in Barnet, where he was planning to move Hendon Football Club, having acrimoniously tried to sell off their old grounds to developers, amid outrage within the local community. I bought him lunch in the café, and we discussed what was going to happen with 'our' Arbiter drums. By this time there was no interest in the regular drums, which were consequently out of production, but Flats Lite were still being snapped up in the UK and around the world, in Japan, America and Germany. We debated the issue, and since I had nothing to lose I told Ivor he couldn't afford me, and even elaborated on the subject by saying that to my mind I'd never been paid properly. He promised to give it a lot of thought, and that was that.

As it happened I knew I was destined to defect to the new company anyway, but Ivor Arbiter really made up my mind when he phoned me to say that he'd decided he could offer me a couple of hours' work a week marketing and working with Flats. I don't think he could believe it when I said no to such a great opportunity.

Over a glass of Scotch at close of play one Friday evening Ivor had admitted to me that I'd saved the Arbiter drum project by coming up with Flats. Unfortunately like my contract and job description he didn't put it in writing!

So I got on with plans for the new project. We needed to come up with a name for the new portable kit and I thought of Traps. (It had good connotations for those knowledgeable people who knew that it was a diminutive for 'contraptions', which came into use when the first drum kits were introduced at the turn of the last century. Initially there had been a bass drummer and a snare drummer in a theatre or cinema orchestra, but with the advent of Ludwig and Ludwig's foot pedal for the bass drum they could save a player's wage. To accompany the pianist in silent films they began to add cowbells, woodblocks, coconuts for horses hooves, train whistles, pistol shots, glockenspiels, orchestral bells, thunder sheets and gongs to the drummer's armoury. These were collectively called contraptions. Traps was as catchy as any other name for a product being launched in the fifth year of the twenty-first century. (There was actually an initial suggestion from Nigel Robinson that the drums might be called Henrit, which, in my self-effacing way, I didn't think was a great idea. In the light of what eventually happened it's lucky for them I vetoed it. That said, it wouldn't have done me any harm at all!)

From conversations with colleagues, teachers and retailers we knew that the drum world was clamouring for an electronic drumset at a reasonable price, and the idea was to get to that eventually. For the moment, though, we needed to proceed with a superior portable *acoustic* version. To be frank, there had been portable drums before Flats, but they were mostly built to be easily transported. None of them had really been built to sound great, and in this they didn't disappoint. The metal Flatjacks from the sixties simply went clang, Len Bailey's Fantoms from the late seventies weren't a kit, just toms, although a little more ballsy than most; Gary Gauger's Purecussion from the eighties (without shells) went blat and Remo's Legero from the nineties, with resin-impregnated, wood-fibre shells, never really took-off – even though they didn't sound too bad.

So the Traps project began slowly but surely, and within just a few short months we had great-sounding acoustic drumsets which I began to use enthusiastically for all my gigs. These drums were very much prototypes, but it's a testament to the product that I was still using the very first set I had three years later. It's certainly been put through its paces, and I've given it a good workout two or three times a week. Traps were so superior to the competition that things went very well from the word go, and we, make that I, managed to get us into all the shops that I'd been selling drums into while I'd been at Arbiter, as well as picking up quite a few new customers along the way. With a bit of tinkering the parent company (Alchemy) managed to produce A400, the world's finest portable drumset, out of a large barn and an office above a launderette in Christchurch, Dorset. Lots of the parts were made from industrial-grade ABS, which was squirted out of moulds in factories in the home counties. All the other necessary bits and pieces were imported from Taiwan. Carriers turned up late every afternoon at Christchurch to take the single boxes, each filled with a complete acoustic drumset including cymbals, to far-flung corners of the world. OK, initially we settled for far-flung corners of the UK, but in time we picked up distributors for Traps around Europe and then in a decent slice of the rest of the world.

Nobody was getting rich, but I kept plugging away at the marketing, and visited foreign trade shows on the evidently exclusive understanding between Nigel Robinson and me that there were some spare shares returned by his stepbrother that would be coming my way in lieu of remuneration. I continued funding my own expenses for day-to-day stuff like phone, petrol, insurance and so on, until one day on a trip down to Bournemouth I brought up the subject of the shares. Nigel's reaction was genial, and he said he'd bring the subject up with the other guys. A little later I heard from Nigel's stepfather, Chris Fletcher, who told me there were no shares available, nor were there ever going to be. That was that. I ruefully asked myself what on earth the point was of continuing with Traps.

I hung on because after my outburst I began to be paid a retainer, and what used to be known as a piece of the action. It wasn't a fortune by any means, but it meant I didn't have to do live gigs simply to finance being part of the Traps organisation.

When we began the company (which Nigel said he wouldn't do without me) it was very much a family business, with Nigel's stepbrother Nick a shareholder as well. Being an IT specialist, his responsibility was initially to set up the website and produce various other necessary bits and pieces like brochures and price lists. He and I also got together briefly to work on some aspects of R&D of the electronic project, which was taking place near him at a factory in Luton – about 30 miles away from me in Enfield. Being the only drummer in the organisation, I was heavily involved in recording drum sounds in the studio with Jay Stapley, before sending them to an enthusiastic boffin called John Catchpole who was working on the electronics of the 'brain'. He was a nice guy and a fledgling guitarist, but he knew little of acoustic drums and even less of their electronic counterparts. He learned quickly. Twenty years earlier I'd been involved in sampling drum sounds for Simmons's all singing, all dancing SDX, so I knew what I was doing. Having recorded the sounds of just about all the many acoustic drumsets that were cluttering up my outbuildings, we set to work sampling them into the brain of the microprocessor attached to our newly designated E400 drums. (E stood for electronic with Traps, while A stood for acoustic.)

I crave your indulgence if you know how this process works, but for those of you who don't I'll explain. A strike on each of the various elements of the set is recorded at various (say five) different dynamic strengths from soft to hard, and then those sounds are digitised before being encapsulated into a memory chip that is eventually inserted into the microprocessor in the brain. So every time you hit an electronic pad (or drum) it calls for the digitally sampled sound associated with it and, depending on the force you hit it with, will activate the correct one of the five samples.

Our Traps were rather different to the other drums on the market. They used same-sized rubber pads to initiate the process, while Traps had soundless woven heads attached to our regular-sized drums, which enabled them to be played like a proper set. It was a bold step forward, and it worked so well that we immediately ate into the sales of everybody else's electronic drum products. Obviously they didn't like it, and one of them took steps to stop us in the New World. Roland have a patent on the use of the silent mesh head in electronic drums in America, and this was brought to our attention just a week before a prestigious summer music show in Austin, Texas. (They actually asked quite nicely how we were getting around their US Patent 6271458.) Of course we knew of this, and hoped we'd bypassed it; but, realising we were rumbled and that the way we thought we were getting around it (with two heads on the batter side) wouldn't hold water in an American court of law, we were forced into changing tack. For the time being we fitted electronic pick-ups to our regular drums, but while this worked to a degree and triggered our brain surprisingly well, you could still hear the acoustic noise of the drum. This wasn't ideal, since the reason parents around the world were investing in electronic drums for their offspring was because they were almost completely silent: you couldn't hear them except through headphones – unless of course they were amplified. (In America it seemed parents who wanted peace would happily pay twice the price for an electronic set for precisely this reason.)

So while we were doing OK in territories where the Roland patent couldn't be applied, we couldn't sell into what is potentially the biggest market in the world. We simply had to find a way around it in America – and I had a great idea. This is where the story gets complicated.

Since I'd first become involved with Simmons and begun writing reviews about electronic drums for magazines and books in the mid-seventies I'd had a bee in my bonnet about a pad with a sensor inside. It would sit on top of an acoustic drum, attached to an electronic brain. This would serve two purposes. First, it rendered the acoustic drum pretty close to soundless, while allowing the aforementioned samples to sound in the headphones – perfect for silent practice. It also allowed the player to add lots of electronic sounds to his regular set. I discussed my idea with the Alchemy guys, who liked it of course. Work began on the pads, which were to use the same piezo transducers that triggered our mesh-headed E-sets, embedded into a sandwich of rubber that was eventually stiffened with metal. The results were initially positive, and even though we knew the pads needed a little more tweaking I took them to America for another music show. People from around the world were exceedingly enthusiastic, and wondered why nobody had thought of it before.

A nice chap called Joe Cappello was distributing Traps in the US and was pleased to see the new product (now using my name E-pad), because he could legitimately sell electronic drums using our original brain without being asked to 'cease and desist' by Roland.

The original 408 brain, as built by John Catchpole and his guys under the flight-path at Luton Airport, with a great deal of drumming input from me in their smoke-filled workshop, was intentionally an entry-level, plug-and-play unit that, had it been working with immutable rubber pads, would have done the job admirably. Unlike all the competition's sets you only needed to press one button to step through all the different 'kits'. But unfortunately Traps didn't use rubber pads like everybody else, so if the flexible heads weren't tuned correctly the response left something to be desired. Unfortunately we couldn't guarantee people would get the set-up right, and the other problem we had was that people wanted more from their set than the price warranted. The fact that it was child's play to operate, could be turned into an acoustic set in minutes by changing the heads and was just about the cheapest on the market wasn't enough. (I frequently asked people who complained that our £400 unit didn't do what a £5,000 Roland did if they could point me in the direction of a Rolls-Royce for the price of a Ford!)

The feedback I was getting was that while the drums themselves were fine, the Traps 408 brain wasn't as sophisticated as the Roland or the Yamaha. We certainly knew that and, worse still, knew it was expensive to produce in the UK. Even though that was crucially important, there was no way to make it cheaper. So the company decided to look round for another cheaper off-the-peg brain, and eventually at the end of 2006 found one in China. It worked like the most affordable Yamaha and seemed to fit the bill. Poor old John Catchpole was summarily kicked into touch!

The Achilles heel of Traps wasn't just the brain; the top-of-the-head triggering system frequently got in the way of the sticks. We explored the possibility of reversing our trigger and its mount, thereby putting it under the head and moving it out of the line of fire. This worked to a degree, but it was still positioned towards the side. It was glaringly obvious that to work really well it needed to be mounted in the centre. Unfortunately Roland had been granted another patent on that too! Both these patents could be challenged in a court of law as being unfairly restrictive to trade, but at what cost? The Roland Corporation was the market leader, and extremely rich from various other highly popular electronic music products they were responsible for. We weren't. And if we'd managed to go to court to refute their patents we could be absolutely certain that the other electronic drum companies would be waiting in the wings geared up to take advantage of the level playing-field that we'd created. (One or two of the US electronic drum manufacturers were already paying thousands of dollars a year to Roland for the licence to use mesh drum heads within their own systems.)

We desperately needed E-pad for America.

One day just before the end of 2007 Nigel Robinson let slip that Joe Cappello had asked for protection on E-pad, and negotiations were proceeding for a patent. I innocently asked whose names would be on the patent, and was told Joe's and Nigel's! I was flabbergasted, and when I asked why RJ Henrit, as the inventor, wasn't participating in the patent, was told that since I hadn't paid to develop the idea I had no rights. Nigel Robinson and the other guys at Alchemy had their own ideas about what constituted intellectual property!

As time went by the major customers I'd brought in were gradually taken over by others in the company, since they didn't need to be educated or nurtured any more and simply sent in their orders by email. I was left with the poisoned chalice of bringing in new retailers. Because of my early efforts all the big guys in the UK were happily selling both acoustic and electronic Traps, so the growth area was a difficult one – what the Americans call mom and pop shops. These people traditionally prefer to order a set once a punter shows an interest. They don't carry stock just in case they get stuck with it.

Not long after this I went away for the usual week of snow fun in Austria, and on my return on the Sunday found this email in my inbox, sympathetically entitled 'Bad News':

Dear Bob

It is with great regret that I am mailing to tell you we will have to let you go.

This is due to financial reasons due to the lack of extra sales growth. This means that is it unsustainable for us to carry on with you selling in your area.

We will settle the December invoice within the next few days. January pay and any commission will be paid within this month.

We deeply regret having to do this but I am sure you understand that with the rest of us taking very little money on a monthly basis Alchemy will either have to cut its costs or close.

Kind Regards

Nigel

I sat there stunned for a moment or two, and didn't mention it to anybody at home for several hours. The bottom line was they couldn't afford me, and this was something I'd known for a very long time. Some might ask the question that my son did – was a company that was trading without paying anybody properly actually a good idea?

John V. phoned me later that day to check that I'd survived skiing in the Austrian Alps and talk about some prospective gigs, and I told him what had happened. We'd been having problems with the concealed lights in our kitchen at home, and for a very long time he'd been threatening to come over and sort them out. He said he'd be round the very next day to fix them! Sure enough, on the Monday morning he turned up bright and early on the doorstep, with his collection of pliers and electrical screwdrivers.

My relationship with JV over the last thirty-five years or so, besides making great music together, consisted of me giving him the benefit of my advice on various subjects, but mostly on marriage – something which, since he was now on his sixth, he had considerable experience of ignoring. Marriage was something he was either particularly bad or very good at, depending on your viewpoint! But this time he came round to give me timely advice for what I suspect was the first time ever. John's view was that I could fight them and maybe I would win – but so what? It might take years, use up all my energy and become something of a money-pit, which I still might not get anything significant from. He also pointed out that it would use up a lot of the time which, aged nearly sixty-four, I was fast running out of. He felt it would be more beneficial to simply turn my back on Traps, write it off and get on with something more positive, like writing this book and making music. I took his advice, and didn't even give myself the satisfaction of telling Nigel what I thought of him.

I'm guessing, since I haven't been in contact with him since, he probably has a pretty good idea.

Despite being a self-confessed absentee father, I've managed to achieve what a great many fathers haven't – witnessed all three of my children's births.

Lucy was our first born, and I knew that when she was due I was going to be in attendance: Argent had just returned from a US tour and had nothing planned for a while. With the certainty of first-time prospective parents, Ricki and I were convinced she was going to be a boy and therefore had no female names in mind. Lewis was the name we were going to give him. Ricki had some problems, so they took her in a couple of days early in preparation for a caesarean. We set off in the morning in our battered Renault 4 for the maternity ward at Chase Farm Hospital. They admitted her, and nothing happened for a couple of days. Our friend (and hairdresser) Teddy Sparrow turned up with a bottle of champagne to celebrate the birth, and since nothing was happening they decided to drink it in advance. This meant several things: the expectant mother got drunk and went into labour, but they couldn't give her the caesarean or an epidural. We were introduced to the midwife who would be looking after the two Henrits in their hours of need, who promptly left me in charge of dispensing thirst-quenching water, mopping fevered brows, proffering reassurance, sympathy and possibly advice on when to push. I was surprised they didn't ask me to boil any water like they do in Hollywood films! However, since I was to be responsible for the important task of administering gas and air to the patient, they showed me where the tank was. I had to work out for myself how the air turned on and where the mask went. As far as I could ascertain nothing happened for quite a while, except perhaps some gentle moaning from the mother-to-be. I was sitting there as the night drew-in, being reassuring and writing notes on the story of Lewis's birth (which I was planning to turn into an article for one of the many women's magazines available in 1973), when I'm sure I heard the sound of rushing water. Ricki told me her waters had broken, and I sat bemused, weighing up the importance of this information, before Ricki shrieked, 'The waters have broken. TELL THE MIDWIFE!'

I rushed out, found the midwife and breathlessly said, 'The waters! The waters!' The midwife was unruffled, and replied that she'd already put water in the room. Eventually I made her understand what had happened, and I reluctantly allowed her to take over.

Ricki made relatively short work of giving birth, possibly because I administered gas and air so expertly. Eventually this adorable maroon-coloured infant with masses of dark hair found her way into the world and into Ricki's arms. I grinned inanely as the jolly midwife took the bundle of baby away to clean up. She shouted over her shoulder as she cleared airways, mopped delicate things, wiped and patted, to warn us we were the proud parents of a bouncing baby girl! It was a wonderful moment, to realise we were responsible for this beautiful life. She asked what names we had for her, and we said we thought Lucy was nice and feminine. And so our first-born was named Lucy Ann Joan Henrit. I was delirious until the enormity of it all came flooding in: one day boys would be pursuing her.

The next time Ricki and I turned up at Chase Farm's maternity unit (we'd been to A&E with Lucy several times during the previous three years) was on the first night of February 1977. Another little Henrit was on the way. We were more prepared this time, and when the contractions began we waited until the end of the late-night film we were watching before setting off from our flat in Village Road, Enfield (directly opposite where Ross McWhirter, the founder of the *Guinness Book of Records*, was brutally murdered in November 1975 by the Provisional IRA). By this time we'd moved up to a Volkswagen Beetle. We also had names ready for either eventuality. Again I took charge of gas and air, and this time the labour was more protracted: James Robert Henrit was born at roughly 3pm on the 2nd. There were no problems with the birth, but we did have a slight problem with the accommodation the family was returning to. Ricki and James left the hospital to go immediately to a brand-new house in a cul-de-sac in Winchmore Hill – but it wasn't quite finished. To make things worse, I was off to Europe with Phoenix, supporting Aerosmith. Poor Ricki. She was left with Lucy, on the way to being a boisterous four-year-old, a new-born baby and no carpets, heating or useable kitchen. It sounds dreadful as I read this, and I apologise wholeheartedly. There's no excuse, except to say that in those days the only way forward for a successful musician was to be constantly on the road. (In 1966 I met the captain of a US aircraft carrier, which was on an official visit to Majorca, and for some obscure reason we sat together in a restaurant. I asked him how he liked being in charge of a dangerous warship in times of peace. He replied, 'If you're a fireman you need to go to a fire from time to time.' So it is with musicians. I rest my case.

We had two children, so as far as the statistics of the seventies were concerned we had 0.4 to go to come into line with the average. So we decided to go for it again. Ricki fell pregnant shortly after meeting me in California after a long Don McLean tour, and with this baby we knew what we were getting – Joseph Charles Henrit. Ricki had been offered this information as a by-product of a routine amino-synthesis test, and since we already had one of each sex we were happy to know so we could buy babygros in the right colour. By this time I was driving a snazzy 2 litre Ford Capri hatchback in metallic silver, which we loaded up to drive once more to Chase Farm. Jos was born late at night, but not without fuss. For a long time Ricki and I were sitting quietly in her room, where she was attached to a monitoring system, waiting for his appearance. All of a sudden medical people burst into the room shouting that the baby was in distress – and why hadn't we called. It turned out that the umbilical cord was wrapped round his neck, and the next few minutes were dramatic and critical. Eventually they sorted him out, and he was born a fine healthy baby boy – immediately nicknamed Lumpy by his father.

Sibling rivalry was about to begin. James turned up to see Joseph for the first time, and tried to pronounce his name. The best he could manage was Jos, and the name stuck. (Mind you, he actually thought his brother should have been called Charlie Prince Henrit!)

All the young Henrits had tennis lessons, to prepare them for the genteel side of society in the leafy suburbs of North London, and from where I was sitting watching them it didn't look *that* difficult. So when Vicars Moor, our local tennis club, decided to change the rules to allow adult beginners in, I was there like a shot (make that a smash). As with most physical things in my life (including skiing) I arrived on the plateau reasonably quickly after investing money in tuition. I'm never going to win the club championships (I'll leave that to Jos and Ricki), but it gives me the opportunity to sit and drink a slightly subsidised beer with friends at least once a week – whether I need one or not.

Every now and then we'll play a Henrit 'fixed four', where Jos partners me against James and Ricki. Jos normally only takes an interest when we're 4–0 down, whereupon he goes into overdrive and we take the set 6–4. Needless to say this bugs the hell out of James, who would rather die than get beaten by his brother at anything.

Jos really is the prodigal son, and unfortunately for him has inherited his father's laissez-faire attitude, even though he's not a 'pro' musician - *yet*. (He's actually a really good drummer in a band called The Dirty Angels, but outside of music he epitomises the phrase 'you can lead a horse to water but you can't make him drink'.) Tennis for England, cricket for Middlesex and a natural talent for golf that disappears after nine holes. It's a good job we love him – unconditionally. He's the only kid in our circle who felt the need to become engaged, instead of plunging into living in sin like his parents. The lovely and fragrant Ricki and I had to examine our consciences as to what we'd done wrong with his upbringing.

James, though, is a completely different kettle of fish. For a start he's organised. Preparation is everything to him, and because of that he's succeeded at everything he's tried. He often found himself outside the headmaster's office at his junior school, not for being naughty but more for being bored with waiting for the rest of the class to catch up. He's always had a very low boredom threshold, especially at church. Our church at Enfield had a large room to the side of the altar with a glass wall, so all the little Catholics could see what was going on. For many little children this was enough: they could happily sit there colouring in their religious books and paying attention to the altar at pertinent moments like the consecration or the communion. James wanted more, and was prepared to search the church to find it. .

Aged five or six, Jos would be standing with his mother or me watching James playing football, tennis or cricket, jumping up and down and itching to get out there with his big brother. Eventually, after he'd agitated enough, the coach would invite him to get on the court, pitch or field for the final five minutes, where he normally acquitted himself admirably. When he joined Winchmore Hill Cricket Club I dropped him off for the first time to practise at the ground. I stayed for a while to see him settled in, and went for a beer in the pavilion with the other dads. One pint later I came back to find him batting for the first time, and whacking the ball all over the place. But something was wrong. As a sportsman, Jos has the advantage of being left-handed like his sister Lucy, but he was facing the bowler with his left leg forward and his bat on the right side. One of the coaches was standing next to me, and told me he was very impressed by my youngest son. I asked why they had him batting right-handed. He said Jos marched to the crease and put his bat on the right like everybody else. Upon being told he was a leftie, the coach changed him – and he then really came into his own.

At seven years old Jos wasn't big enough to play proper tennis like his brother, so we enrolled him in a short-tennis course. A few weeks later he came back with this huge cup: he was Middlesex short-tennis champion.

Jos has a low boredom threshold as well. He doesn't do patience – which for a sportsman is not necessarily an advantage. Like Kevin Pietersen, before he became England captain, if he's batting he wants to attack from the word go. No forward defensive shots for Jos: if he could get his feet to the pitch of the ball he was going to hit it hard. When he first moved to QE Boy's School he was selected to play for the second XI, and I went along to watch. Jos's team won the toss and elected to bat, and I took a seat waiting for him to come in at number five. It was early afternoon, and I sat next to the only other spectator. He turned out to be Rod Argent's production partner, a drummer called Pete Van Hook, whose son opened the bowling for the Mill Hill team. We chatted about an island he was buying (honestly), until Jos came in and set about his son's bowling. Eventually Jos bashed one back at him no more than six inches above the ground, and somehow Pete's son got his fingers to it. It remains the best catch I've ever seen!

James was a completely different animal on the cricket field. He would patiently build an innings. I went to see him playing a house match at Haileybury and was asked to umpire. The other umpire was a teacher, who advised me not to give anybody out LBW, and everything went swimmingly until one of James's team was hit on the pad right in front of the middle stump. Everybody looked at me with expectation, and I found my right index finger rising all by itself. Like a true gentleman the batsman obediently walked, and James wouldn't talk to me all the way home.

Mind you, James wasn't quite so patient at tennis. That desire to win I mentioned earlier often took over: at best he'd throw the racquet; at worst he'd smash it to pieces. He also came out with words on the court that he hadn't heard from me – maybe it was his mother! In the end I couldn't watch James or Jos playing singles because my stomach churned too much. Doubles or team sports were never a problem, but when it was one on one I didn't cope too well. This stomach ache also beset me with Lucy in her piano competitions.

Like her mother, Lucy was a seriously accomplished pianist, who whizzed through the piano grades to eight with her teacher Mrs Foster, and frequently took part in recitals with her. Lucy was incredibly artistic, and a born performer, but I worried about her performance to such a degree that I had to leave the room. I guess I was concerned that if anything went wrong I wouldn't be able to do anything about it. Of course it never did.

Lucy was very bright, and earned a place at the local school for high-achievers, but having deliberated for a long time for some reason we decided to send her to Haberdashers a very good school in Elstree. Her forte was sculpting, and she turned out some great pieces: dancers, hitch-hikers, even her grandfather sitting in his armchair. Unfortunately she wasn't allowed to take her talent further because she preferred to get her hands straight on to the clay without what the school felt was the essential step: working sketches.

In the end Lucy wasn't as sporty as she could have been, although she swims like a fish and runs with a lot of stamina if we shame her into it.

Both my boys played Fives – James at Highgate School and Jos at Queen Elizabeth's Boys' in Barnet. (I hope I've got the apostrophes in the right places. but it's been a while since I wrote them a cheque!) Fives is a version of handball played on a three-sided court with protuberances called buttresses: if you hit them the small, hard rubber ball heads off in a completely different direction, frequently making it unplayable by the opposition. Jos' ambidexterity gave him an advantage, since his playing was solid on either wing. Anyway they were both England School champions at different times, albeit representing different schools.

I'm boasting, but it's my book. Jos played cricket, tennis and fives for Middlesex as well as representing England in tennis; James played tennis, water polo and hockey for Middlesex along with hockey for Leeds University. He was to my knowledge the first Henrit to go to university and used his time well reading Modern Languages. I remember driving him the couple of hundred miles north to Leeds for the first time. He seemed pretty reticent and unusually uncommunicative, so we left him slumped in the back of the car keeping himself to himself. We arrived at his hall of residence, and as we carried his belongings upstairs he bumped into 'Dirty' Helen (a term of endearment) and another girl he knew from Channing School, around the corner from his alma mater in Highgate. Immediately he brightened up immensely, and Ricki and I might just as well not have been there. He was gone, and apart from high days and holidays we didn't see much of him for several years, what with a year in France followed by a year in Spain studying, before eventually a life-changing move to Hong Kong, working himself to a standstill for a company that specialised in mergers and acquisitions. This was where he met the delightful Kresse not long before he came home to become a master mariner.

Lucy didn't get away with just being an artist, dancer and musician. She was also subjected to tennis and swimming – a sport she is still very strong at, probably because she has the right build. She's dogged in her approach to strenuous activities, but prefers to do them indoors away from the wind and rain. I'd like to describe her in the nicest possible way as something of a diva but wouldn't dare. Unfortunately she's cultivated the view that since her mother managed to find love and happiness with a musician there's no reason why she can't. Unfortunately I'd like to say I'm the exception that proves the rule, and apart from Jim Rodford and Rod Argent most of my musician acquaintances haven't managed to remain married for as long as Ricki and I have. (John Verity, whom I love dearly, is on his sixth and final marriage and (depending on how long it takes to get this into the bookshops) hasn't even arrived at his bus pass yet!)

Anyhow, after running a couple of restaurants for a while upon leaving school, for most of her working life Lucy's been in the music business and would appear to be really good at it. She's diversified, to say the least, having been Harvey Goldsmith's PA before moving sideways to become PA to the indefatigable/ inimitable/incomparable Osbourne family, a vocation that demanded far more time to be devoted to it than 24/7.

Towards the end of the seventies JV and I were at the NAMM show, in the days when it was held at McCormack Place in Chicago. John was there to launch the Phoenix amplifier he had invented and I was there reporting on drum trends for *International Musician*. We were looking through a free newspaper and discovered there was a blues jam out at East Chicago, and we made up our minds to go. We called a cab and the driver looked at us very strangely when we told him our destination. We drove around the lake for quite some time through darker and darker streets before pulling up in front of an unlit building, without even the ubiquitous neon light over the double doors. This was it: we steeled ourselves and walked in. The place was dimly lit, as those clubs invariably are, and it went frighteningly quiet as the door closed behind us.

We were the only white guys in there, and we looked at each other quizzically to see whether we should brave it out or back out quietly and go back to the hotel. The main problem with that plan was that if we retreated we'd find ourselves back on the pavement and have to walk to who knows where to find a taxi. So we decided to brazen it out. All the guys looked like old-time Blues heroes: gold rings, gold watches and gold teeth. They looked the part, but in the end they couldn't play as good as they looked. (The women were styled like the men. It's none of my business, but they may have been otherwise employed out on the street once the club closed.) Apart from the music side we were seriously out of our depth, but decided to brazen it out. We walked over to the guy in charge, who entered our names in a book: different columns for drummers, guitarists, bass players, singers. We didn't play together at first so didn't really have a chance to do our thing, but when we did eventually coincide the place went rather quiet at first and finally the audience became vociferously appreciative. Of course we didn't play exactly like the greatest Chicago blues guys, but then neither did they. And as it happened we were a lot closer to the real thing than they were, having been listening to the guys who played Chicago blues best for years. I certainly knew more about Freddie Below (who played on Chuck Berry's 'Schooldays'), Earl Palmer (who played on everything I loved from the late fifties) and Johnny Otis (who introduced me to Hambone rhythm) than any of the other drummers there.

Eventually we decided we'd shown off enough, and it was time to get back to the hotel. As we left the club we discovered the same young cab driver was waiting outside, because he was worried we might get into trouble. On the way back downtown he surprised us by asking what was going on with Argent.

Around this time I received a call from a guy whom I'd never expected to work with in a million years. I'd seen Richie Havens on the Woodstock film, opening the whole festival, and from that appearance considered him to be a folk singer, so I was surprised when he told me he was looking for a drummer for a handful of dates. I agreed to do it and got myself to the old Embassy club in Bond Street for a rehearsal before the gig. He seemed to have reinvented himself in the decades since Nazgur's farm in Woodstock and instead of being a folk figure with a single tooth and the battered guitar tuned to D (giving him major chords with his thumb barring across the frets) he now wore Armani suits and looked like Marvin Gaye!

Of course we did all the tunes like 'Here Comes the Sun', 'Motherless Child' and others, but he had some funky stuff too that just happened to be on the record he was plugging.

He had a new record company based in Newcastle, so we slogged northwards across all the roundabouts on the A1(M) to do what I think was a showcase there. We were all in the same minibus, pulling the gear in a trailer. I can't remember the other guys in the band. They were so intent on getting laid back that I found myself passively joining in with them, which made me wobbly, gave me short-term memory loss and is not my thing! Unlike President Clinton (at whose inauguration Richie played, coincidentally) I had to inhale – it would have been impossible to hold my breath all the way from London to Newcastle.

My generation of drummer invariably traded one set in when they progressed to a slightly better one. This was as much to do with not having the space to store two drumsets in a semi-detached house as needing the pittance you got for selling your original set to finance the next. Having boarded over the floor and transformed the loft in the Winchmore Hill house, I had the room to store drums, and I began my quest for world domination! I had a plan that as far as I know is unique. I contrived to buy a version of everything I ever owned. Owning a drum shop helped no end, because guys traded in their old stuff, which wasn't worth too much, and I snaffled it. Eventually, as Don McLean had described me (and he should talk), I became an excessive and ended up with more sets in my loft than I had room for. So I stacked them one on top of the other. There were twenty-four collectable sets at one time, lots of cymbals, footpedals and more snare drums than you could shake a stick it (pun intended). There were fifty, to be precise – spanning the twentieth century. To be honest I was concerned that all my 'crap' (my wife's affectionate word) might well bring the roof down, but Tim Harper, a surveyor friend who just happened to be a drummer, said that providing the weight wasn't in the middle it should be all right.

It really was an Aladdin's cave, because besides drums it was full of magazines, books, computers, stage clothes and two ancient air pistols confiscated from my sons, which we couldn't find when we moved. (As is the manner of these things, once we moved to the new house surrounded by woods and fields our rubbish came under attack from squirrels and we needed the pistols just to frighten them away. Honest!)

I used to trawl through the pawn shops of America's major cities, which always seemed to be situated in the slightly less salubrious parts of town. My nose invariably took me in the right direction: on a good day I would find something good and on a better day I'd find something outstanding. If I hadn't been touring with The Kinks it would have been a problem, but as it was I consolidated the stuff with the rest of the onstage gear, and the next time I saw it would be when it arrived at Konk Studios in North London, where the gear was stored.

I never wanted to pay real money for any of my stuff, so I wouldn't dream of buying from a vintage drum shop or a collector. I enjoyed the thrill of the chase and wanted to find the stuff myself, not buy it at a premium from someone who got there before me. Inevitably I ended up with far more than I could chew, and one day I woke up feeling that I was being selfish, and imagined myself like Blofeld in the James Bond films with vaults of stolen treasures that nobody could see. Of course mine weren't exactly stolen, although I did like to buy them as cheaply as possible.

Ricki's friend Wendy split from her musician husband Lem Lubin (of Unit 4+ 2, Rocket Records and my stag party fame) and decided it was a good idea to see the world, this at a time when only youngsters did that sort of thing. So she reinvented herself and got on her way. For a start she took ten years off her age, which was only dangerous if you were doing scuba diving. Of course the first thing she decided to do was a little scuba in Israel. And while she was too far under the water for her age, she suddenly got an attack of whatever old people who dive too deep get (the bends?), and needed to be rescued by the allegedly attractive diving instructor.

Wendy fetched up in several far-flung places, and we got the odd late night call from her, telling us how she was getting along. By far the strangest of these came one Sunday afternoon when she was in New York. She informed us that someone very upmarket living on Park Avenue with a double-barrelled name would be phoning me the very next day, and all I needed to do was be economical with the truth, say what a great nanny Wendy had been for our kids, and how I trusted her implicitly. Sure enough, on Monday the phone rang and I was quizzed about how strict she had been and was she of good character. Wendy got the job, and began to travel all over the world again – but getting paid for it this time.

Eventually she found herself wandering along the beach in Ghana, not far from Accra at a place called Kokrobite, when she saw a large patch of mud for sale adjoining a wonderful expanse of white-sanded beach. She bought it for £1,000, put up her first mud hut and stood by to receive backpackers. As her finances grew, with more and more kids struggling to find themselves on their gap years, she put up more huts, and by the time we were ready to make the trip to Africa it was a fully fledged backpackers' hostel with dozens of huts, a communal longhouse, a restaurant and a bar – called Big Milly's Backyard. Toilets were primitive by our standards and needed to be flushed with a bucket, but since we all eventually got the runs, primitive was a great deal better than nothing.

Ethnic drummers visited Big Milly's every day and played what I presumed were Ghanaian tunes accompanying various shapes and sizes of thumb pianos. They asked me to sit in one night and I emphatically said no: I don't play hand drums. Course you do, they said, just play one song with us. They showed me the rhythm and I got started. Twenty minutes later my hands were giving me excruciating pain, but I gritted my teeth, thought of England and concentrated on the rhythm. A funny thing happened, because on concentrating on the melody I figured I was on the wrong beat and moved my rhythm along a little bit from what we Westerners would probably call the downbeat to the offbeat. Everybody turned and looked at me with surprise.

Drumming is very much a part of the culture in Ghana. We went along the beach to see a performance, at a once luxurious German hotel, of the Royal Drummers of Ghana. These were guys who went all round the world giving concerts, and they were absolutely stunning players and dancers. You couldn't allow yourself to home in on what one guy was doing because if you did it would appear to be wrong against all the others. But if you listened to the big picture you could see how all rhythm is divisible, and sooner or later everything that was being played, however diverse, coincided with what the others were doing. I was absolutely entranced. When the show was over I was dawdling along this dusty red African road with the jungle on one side and the Atlantic on the other, taking photos, when this guy on a gleaming Hercules-type bicycle caught me up. He was the bell player who, like the claves player in Latin-American music, gave the key to the rhythm. I'd met him the day before at Wendy's, and as you'd expect we chatted about drums. I asked how the Royal Drummers learned the complex rhythms I'd just heard. Were they reading music? He told me they were taught by rote, and if they got the drum part wrong they were whacked hard over the knuckles with a drumstick! We spoke animatedly for a few miles as the sun sank into the ocean. As we walked along in the dust I realised just how comprehensive and transcending the language of drumming really is.

We Kinks played at West Point, which is America's most prestigious military academy. It was pretty close to where Don McLean lived in upstate New York. I called him and he came to see us. It was an interesting gig, playing to officer cadets who, since they had to be on their best behaviour, were not exactly the perfect audience for rock 'n' roll. There was a certain frisson before we went on between the Dangerous Brothers, which transferred itself onto the stage. Now I know people don't just go to Kinks gigs to see a fight, but I also know they like the idea that if they're lucky there might just be one. Anyhow, McLean happened to pick a gig where there was a fight on stage, and it was in full view of the faculty of West Point. Perhaps all the testosterone put out by those warriors was contagious. I'm sure punters thought these shenanigans were part of the act but they weren't: something that had happened during the day might trigger it, or perhaps it really was just sibling rivalry. I'd say Mr Ardy and Mr Russell meant it when they hit each other but there appeared to be an unwritten rule – never in the face.

Anyhow, all the officer cadets in the audience loved it, but Don decided discretion was the better part of valour and that perhaps it wasn't a great time to visit the dressing room. He was absolutely right. The after-show dressing room was always a dangerous environment, with lots of colourful and sloppy Indian food in evidence that could easily be thrown around. Walls were often decorated with orange-coloured masala sauce or yellow turmeric sauce.

I wasn't particularly interested when these things went off on stage and invariably discovered an urgent problem with my bass drum pedal immediately after the fisticuffs started.

I actually haven't seen Mr McLean since that day. I'm off his Christmas card list – having asked him for money. Every time he has a new record out they use a flattering piece of film of himself with a youngish Henrit in the background, with thick hair and a black and cream western shirt with embroidery on the shoulders. This clip was part of the show we recorded for an album at the Dominion in Tottenham Court Road. There was payment for the album, but there wasn't any buy-out for a video. The story at the time was that there was no video, but a long-form video does actually exist, and there's never been any payment to us poor professional musos for it. Even our all-powerful Musicians Union has been unable to get the money.

If you're interested in seeing this video that doesn't exist check out YouTube!

Every year at the NAMM music exhibition I used to talk to Billy Zildjian who makes Sabian cymbals and is McLean's next-door neighbour in Hertford, Connecticut. He tells me Don sends his best. For the last quarter of a century my response has always been, 'Thanks, but did he send anything else?' Maybe I'm being a little harsh here and shouldn't be. On his website Don describes me as being: 'one of the best drummers he had ever heard,' and on a personal level he thought I was open to every kind of music and a hell of a lot of fun to be with. I guess I should settle for that!

A drummer's lot in the rehearsal studio is very much to keep quiet while the other guys are learning the chords, play when they need you to and make suggestions only when you know what you've suggested won't be ridiculed. So you generally sit there quietly looking at your drums, wondering why components do what they do, and in extreme cases having a bash at reinventing the wheel. Most drummers have an idea for an invention that will first change drummers' lives then, because of the increase in fortune from royalties, change their own. I admit to having been caught up in this too, but though I say it

191

myself I've been responsible for some cool stuff. I invented a drum key that had a thread inside the square which fits onto the tension screw. This meant it could screw onto the top of a cymbal stand so you always had a drum key to hand. Zildjian took the project on and put it out, and when the split between the two brothers came in 1980 the patent passed to Bob Zildjian's new company, named for his three children and called Sabian. So there are (better make that were) Zildjian and Sabian threaded drum keys. The *pièce de résistance* as far as my inventions are concerned was a Roto-tom pedal for Remo. I bought a Roto-tom when they came out in 1969 or '70 and used it at the beginning of Argent – it was something else to hit during my drum solo. I liked the simplicity of turning the drum to change the pitch, but examining the thing one day in rehearsal I felt it could be more useful if it was adapted to a foot pedal, leaving both hands free to produce a glissando. I worried at it with my father and brother-in-law and produced plans for a pedal with a hole in the middle of the centre bolt, allowing a push rod to go through it and change the pitch. I attached this push rod via a cantilever to a hi-hat pedal and it did the job. Remo liked the idea and developed it way beyond my affordable version. Theirs was affordable providing you had the money and the need, and lots of them were used for film soundtracks. I had always wanted a Chevrolet Corvette, and having turned up at the old Remo factory in North Raymer to pick up the money my idea was to go out in LA, buy a Sting-Ray and ship it home. In the end I chickened out, brought the money home and frittered it away on my kids' education! But my Roto-Tom footpedal is still regarded as a very elegant solution and has become something of a collector's item. (I also adapted a Roto-tom to a snare drum but couldn't get anybody interested in the concept. In the meantime a chap called Randy May came up with the same idea and sold it to Pearl.) Something I did suggest to Pearl was a stick bag that came with a knee pad made from the same material, which tied to the knee for less painful practice. (Most drummers of my acquantaince warmed up on their thigh, and I still have a very dangerous-looking mark above my right knee from years of playing there.) Pearl thanked me profusely for the idea and gave me my very own sample, which was not quite the financial result I was expecting!

In the sixties I developed cymbals with various different shaped and sized holes in them to make them speak differently. Unfortunately I was forty years ahead of my time, because those designs happened in the 'noughties'. I also worked on square, hexagonal and unevenly shaped cymbals, which at the time cymbal companies laughed at. I'd always used a Chinese cymbal for punctuation (or even riding on, as with Ian Matthews) when only that sound would do, but didn't like the way it needed to be mounted upside down, making it awkward if spectacular to play. It also denied access to the bell sound. So I came up with one with an inverted bell, so it could sit on the cymbal stand properly but still allow access to the different flanges *and* the bell. Paiste liked the concept and put it out in the seventies under the name Novo. I'm still waiting for the royalties and my own cymbal.

I was working in an anechoic chamber testing drums for *International Musician* in the mid-seventies when a light bulb went on in my head. If I took cymbals into the controlled conditions of the chamber, played them and sampled the results I could come up with a series of numbers unique to that instrument relative to its fundamental, highest pitch, lowest pitch and various other parameters. These would be printed on the cymbal whether it was a Ride, a Crash or a pair of hi-hats, and when you wanted an exact replacement you'd simply match up the numbers as closely as possible. Even before I owned a drum shop I knew this was a great starting point for standardising something that was (and still is) a completely arbitary thing. Again I couldn't get arrested with this concept.

I used to put these ideas into letters, which I posted to myself and didn't open. One day I got Barclays Bank to put a date stamp on a design – something that ultimately saved me from disaster with my Remo pedal.

My most useful invention by far is along the lines of a piece of string, which you'll only get to see when it's launched – which will be when I can work out how to make money out of it!

I've been employed as a consultant on several projects over the years. Nick Kinsey's Inpulse One drum machine for AHB was the first and the second was for the Simmons Drum Company, who asked me to sample some drums before I wrote *The Complete Simmons Drum Book* for Music Sales.

Like most musicians I've been happy to do gigs for charity, although as my late drummer pal Bobby Graham said there came a time when they were the only gigs he could get! That said, over the years I've done stuff for the Stars Organisation for Spastics, Buckets and Spades, Breakthrough Breast Cancer and even charities in Africa and India. I guess the most prestigious festival we did along these lines was at the London Palladium, in front of royalty. I'm not sure who was there but it wasn't the Queen; it was probably the Queen Mother. This was close to being Mod's first gig, and I could tell he was nervous as we waited under the stage with our gear sitting on a rising lift waiting to go up. The amps were plugged into the mains so were live, and the stage manager, dressed in black tie and tails, warned us not to attempt to plug in until we were safely on stage behind the curtains. Unfortunately Mod was anxious to see that his amp worked, and plugged it in with the volume turned up. As the amp barked back the stage manager rounded on him and hissed, 'D'you mind? This isn't a gig, it's the London Palladium!'

Sporting charities for musicians were not quite so popular in the sixties, although Ray and Dave played for the Showbiz XI football team. Strangely I don't recall ever doing anything of that nature in my time with The Kinks. Maybe we were never asked.

My dentist in Winchmore Hill was involved with a very worthy charity called the Teenage Cancer Trust, and one day while I was lying on my back trying to hold an intelligent conversation with his fingers in my mouth he asked me if I'd like to help with something he and his wife were involved with. Since he had the dreaded drill in his hand I thought it was prudent to nod enthusiastically. I was willingly inveigled into a charitable organisation, at that time called the Adolescent Cancer Trust, which existed to provide wards for young cancer sufferers in hospital who were too old to flourish in baby wards and too young for the geriatric ones. It was also blindingly obvious that teenagers get on better when they're with others who are in the same predicament. They lose their hair together, cry together, feel sick together, listen to music together, talk about the opposite sex and console and support one another. It's a very worthy and positive cause, and I was an enthusiastic supporter during the time I was involved with Pepsi and Shirley, Nigel Benn the boxer, Nigel Kennedy the violinist and Bob Holness. We were all together at a fundraiser with Sarah Ferguson, who was the patron of the charity and looked absolutely stunning. Anyhow, I was standing with Bob Holness, who was once a Radio Luxembourg DJ (but was never the sax player on 'Baker Street'; this is an urban myth) and the presenter of *Blockbusters*, in which contestants had to tell him the letter they wanted to answer questions on. Invariably they would say the letter and 'please, Bob'. We stood together at the event, chatting with various supporters. He asked if he could get me anything, and I nonchalantly replied (wait for it), 'Tea please, Bob!' He looked over the top of his glasses at me and laughed. The guys behind the charity like Dr Adrian Whiteson are highly experienced, and realise that well-wishers only have a certain time to effectively rape and pillage their friends within the organisation; in time everybody moves on and others come in. Now under its new name the charity is alive and well in the safe hands of Roger Daltry (responsible for the annual Albert Hall concerts) and those thoroughly nice chaps McFly.

Even though Northern Ireland was in turmoil during the Troubles, we still went there to do gigs. The first time I went was in 1962 after a tour of ballrooms in Eire, when things were reasonably peaceful. I bought an American Ludwig snare drum in Dublin, which I have to admit I smuggled across the border into Northern Ireland before sending home via the Royal Mail. I didn't do this to defraud HM Customs and Excise, and I hope the statute of limitations will save me after almost half a century. The reason I did it was because at that time American instruments weren't allowed to be sold in or imported into the UK, and I wanted one badly. I'd also bought a cheap and cheerful watch in Dublin, which the customs officer at Newry couldn't miss gleaming on my wrist, and I happily allowed it to be confiscated: this took his attention away so he didn't discover the valuable snare drum in a box under the seat! It was at the border crossing at Newry, not too far from where those poor guys from the Miami Showband would be cruelly murdered by UVF machine guns firing dum-dum bullets thirteen years later.

I was drawn to the romanticism of the struggles in Ireland in a *Boy's Own* adventure way, and had read a lot about Michael Collins and the flying columns. For a short while I believe I actually sympathised with their struggle.

Each time we went to Ireland we were stunned by how long it took to get from towns that by mainland UK standards weren't far apart. (Even in the twenty-first century it could easily take four hours to drive 100 miles over there.) Clodagh Rogers's dad Louis was our agent there, and as we drove from one dancehall-sized barn to another he'd assure us that it was 'just down the road'. It never was, and the roads there are so narrow that it only needed a tractor in front of us to put half an hour on the journey.

The sixties were the heyday of countless Irish showbands like The Royals, Nevada or the Miami Showband with Dickie Rock, known to us as 'Sticky'. The dancehalls were absolutely packed with over-enthusiastic dancers, many of whom were looking for love. The Roulettes once played at a dancehall called The Hangar, which was literally that and situated like most of its kind in the middle of absolutely nowhere. Afterwards we left the stage and sat outside, exhausted, to cool down and get our breath back. Looking back we saw steam pouring out of the top of the building from people inside, perspiring, glowing and maybe even sweating!

We kept going back to the Emerald Isle and were in Cork on Friday 22 November 1963. I was wandering around the city when I learned by looking at the one black and white television in an electrical store window that JFK had been assassinated.

I was there in the seventies towards the end of the struggles, playing at Queens University with GB Blues Company at a time when the Europa Hotel had sandbags in front of its revolving doors and the streets were patrolled by cautious squads of British troops, along with battleship grey heavily armoured Land Rovers, with skirts to the ground to protect them from bombs being rolled underneath. It seemed more frightening then it had ever been.

Once it was all over I was with Big Tel and Dave Davies driving from a hotel up near Stormont to the gig at Ulster Hall. Dave decided he wanted some cigarettes, and we stopped outside what seemed an innocuous pub on the way in. For some reason I followed Tel inside and the noisy pub immediately went deathly quiet. Big Tel had been in 'the Regiment' in a previous life, and it seemed everybody in the pub could tell. It was a decidedly sticky moment, which illustrates that feelings still run high in the North.

There were several TV programmes in Ireland that we flew over to take part in – some of which like *The Kelly Show* in Belfast you got paid for and others, like Gay Byrne's show in Dublin, you didn't – no matter how hard you tried. Don't get me started! We appeared on one directed by Michael Lindsey-Hogg (allegedly Orson Welles's illegitimate son), who not only directed *Let It Be* for the Beatles and *Jumping Jack Flash* for the Stones but also *Brideshead Revisited*. For some reason, in summer season style we weren't playing instruments but stood behind four huge polystyrene blocks spelling Adam. At a predetermined moment we had to appear from behind these blocks, clicking our fingers on the offbeat and kicking our feet alternatively on the downbeat. Or was it the other way round? You know, just like the Jets in *West Side Story*. Anyway, this time I wasn't responsible for Russell going too soon: he did it all on his own. When he realised he turned to us before retreating backwards with the same cool *West Side* movements whereupon Thorpey, Mod and I went forward. We knew Michael pretty well by this time from *Ready Steady Go* and I'm pretty sure he kept Russell's blooper in. A true *Spinal Tap* moment!

Needless to say, I have a great many more stories about the sixties, seventies, eighties and nineties, but I normally recount them better with a glass in my hand. Cheers . . .

Every picture tells a story

Convenient bass pedal problem

The Kinks with Mark Haley

With Ray D and Mark

Video shoot: me on guitar, ray on drums

Live Kinks

Konk

Konk sign

With Ray and Dave

Ivor Novello awards

Henrit coast to coast ride in Consett

With Flats pro

Screaming Lord Sutch's banknote

What became of Hentrit's Drumstore

Lucy Bad Finger by Jack Osbourne

James takes up the drums

Teenage Cancer charity lunch at London Zoo

Chapter Ten: SO FAR, SO FAR

Russell called me early on the morning of Saturday 8 March 2003 to say Adam Faith had died. We were shocked, of course, anxious to know what had happened and when the funeral was. In the event I was telephoned by Alan Field, a guy I didn't know, who was Tel's agent, who told me when the funeral was and how Jackie (Tel's long suffering wife) wanted me, Russell, Thorpey and Mod to carry the coffin. We were all touched and agreed immediately. Believe it or not, I was the only one who'd carried a coffin before, so I was slightly nervous, but the others weren't. Ignorance is bliss! When you're a pallbearer you're always concerned you won't be able to do it and you'll drop the coffin! I was even more concerned when I heard Jackie and her daughter Katya had ordered a wicker coffin. They're very trendy and eco-friendly but very unstable things to carry, because they twist and bend like an unwieldy laundry basket.

So Mod, Russell, Chris Andrews and I left my place and headed for Tunbridge Wells for the funeral. Without a tour manager, and a year or two before sat nav, we got slightly lost, but managed to find a pub to have a couple of swift halves in to calm our nerves. Thorpey met us outside the chapel and we bumped into people whom it seemed to me we hadn't seen for a lifetime: publicists, record company guys and Leo Sayer. The hearse arrived with Tel in his basket, and we prepared to take him his last few yards. (The last time we'd carried him was in the sixties at Bobby Jones's ice-rink in Ayr, where he'd slipped and banged his head so badly that the noise echoed around the deserted rink. We thought he'd killed himself and we'd collectively joined the ranks of the unemployed. We carried him off to the dressing room till he came to his senses.)

We picked the long wicker basket up, and were surprised at how heavy it was. There was a reason for this. Jackie and Kat had put a lot of stuff in there with him for his journey: a big box of Maltesers, his favourite clothes and even the clogs he wore when he was playing Budgie. Fortunately they'd taken his mobile phone out at the last minute otherwise, since he was being cremated, the funeral really would have gone off with a bang! Michael Parkinson gave a wonderfully humorous speech about

Terry and, turning to us, remarked how unusual it was to find a sixties band where all the members were still alive! We were truly grateful.

As we left for the reception with the great and good of the entertainment industry, we bumped into Sandie Shaw. She had flown in from abroad and her plane had been delayed. I understand this might not have been such a bad thing, because funerals affect her so much that she has a propensity to throw herself onto the coffin and wail. She seemed to have a problem remembering us, and we put this down to jetlag. Things warmed-up once we got to the wake at a local hotel. In my experience musicians' funerals are unusual in that they seem to be happy affairs and invariably billed as celebrations of life. Tel's was no exception. We reminisced, laughed and joked, and probably told a lot of unintentional half-truths, (much like Keith Moon). A very pleasant couple of hours were spent wending our way down memory lane for the last time as far as Adam was concerned, all without knowing anything of Tel's famous last words about Channel Five. Afterwards all but one of us wended our weary way home.

My pal Nobby Dalton, who had been in The Bluejacks with me and eventually played bass with The Kinks, had lost a son to leukaemia in the late sixties and ever since had put on a charity gig every year to raise money for the Leukaemia Foundation in Broxbourne Civic Hall. Just about every local muso had been involved over the years, including Chas and Dave, Mike Berry, various Kinks offshoots and now, not too long before his death, Adam. We arranged to rehearse at Hoddesdon Conservative Club, where Mod was the manager, and having not been together for thirty-odd years reminisced for a long time and drank pots and pots of tea. We sat around holding our instruments, but Tel seemed reluctant to get on with it. In the end I said something along the lines of, 'I think we should get started because I've got a gig tonight.' So we went into the intro of 'What Do You Want'. The usual four bars with the pizzicato strings went by, and Tel didn't come in. Then eight bars passed, twelve bars, and still no vocal. Eventually we stopped and started again, but he still didn't come in. We asked what was wrong, and he admitted he'd forgotten how to sing it.

Fortunately I did a pretty good impersonation, which involved singing from the back of my throat and not moving my lips, although I'd never done it in front of Tel. As I sang it he twigged, and switched into his old Adam Faith voice.

The gig went well and most of the audience got very excited. My youngest son Jos, who was about seven at the time and had been dragged kicking and screaming to see his dad that night, turned to his mother and asked, 'Who's that old grey-haired guy up there on stage with Dad?' The dangerous pop idol my wife had come to London to marry was being described by my youngest son as a greying old man. Yes! Yes!

In the very late sixties Adam had a new programme coming out, and to publicise it was a 'surprise' victim on *This Is Your Life* with Eamonn Andrews. I realise this is a jaundiced view, but for my money they invariably seemed to have someone in the big red book who had something to plug. By this time Russell and I were in Argent, while Thorpey and Mod were out of the business as far as doing it for a living was concerned. So when we 'pros' went on to tell our various anecdotes about Tel we had long hair down our backs (with green streaks in my case), while the others who weren't in the business were close to having short back and sides haircuts. Good old Eamonn picked up on this and asked, 'Guess which guys are still in the business?' We all went to the green room afterwards and I seem to remember Eammon was far more interested in talking to Diane, one of my very attractive female friends, than talking to us. We were no competition at all!

Speaking of being attractive, there was a time when I was reasonably so as far as the opposite sex was concerned, but now I have my over-sixties travel pass I'm not so much unattractive as invisible. There was even a time when I suspect I was attractive to the same sex, although unlike some of my more versatile friends I was never compromised. I remember making my excuses and leaving after a big TV show in Paris where I was evidently in grave danger. Tommy Moeller and I went out for a meal with the white-haired director of the programme and his sound man pal. I think we both knew that the well-known guy with the long white hair, famous for his 'Super' Saturday night programme, batted for the other side, and suspected his pal did too, but I certainly thought we were going for a bite to eat. There was no suggestion initially about anybody changing my life and making me a star! Well, the whole thing hotted-up and the two pals started moving in. As I always do in complicated situations, I deduced the best way to deal with it was to drink. Unfortunately before long I was pissed – don't worry, gentle reader, I wasn't that pissed! Once they started to get to the point, which was unsurprisingly not long after we'd been to the top of the Eiffel Tower, I made my excuses and left, as they used to say in the more salacious Sunday papers I used to deliver! I somehow got back to the room I was sharing with Russell, who was fast asleep, whereupon I accomplished my first (and so far my last) projectile vomit. This was long before the phrase was invented. RGB woke up to me trying to mop several square yards of marble floor with a rug, which I then had to wash out in the bath. It put me off same-sex liaisons for life.

Having once played a leading part in the movement, I don't do 'rock scruffy' very well any more. Sartorially I suppose I'm too old to really carry it off these days. When you're of a certain age, scruffy dress equates more with down and out – certainly in the eyes of my loved ones. I'm fortunate in that my hair is still dark, although with a little blond at the sides, and there are no real holes in it. My beard, though, is another kettle of fish. I've never taken to shaving, and now I get away without it when I can, although the colour of my stubble is not at all attractive – no wonder Sting decided to dye his. I try not to look in my mirror too closely these days, and since shaving properly needs me to put on my new varifocal glasses, whereupon my once God-like features come into even-closer focus, I don't recognise the face looking back at me. It looks much more like my father's. He, of course, had no need to keep up the appearance of a rock god.

Now to be fair, like all the men of his generation my old man used Brylcreem all his life, and died with hair so black it looked like it had been boot-polished; and he only had a half-crown-sized bald spot on the back of his head. I'll happily settle for that – although not the Brylcreem.

It was my sixtieth birthday on 2 May 2004, and we were going to celebrate the acquisition of my bus pass properly. We'd put up a marquee for the band and our friend Tony Anderson had miraculously created a new patio from left-over York stone slabs the afternoon before the event. Working like a dervish, he'd lifted whole patches of grass so he could excavate underneath them and level a whole area. It was brilliant, and still looks great. James had come back from Hong Kong for the event, and was running the barbecue and about to make a very touching speech. Jos was helping him in his own inimitable way, getting drinks for himself and generally dancing around his brother. Lucy was busying herself being the 'hostess with the mostest', and the lovely Ricki was wondering what life would be like with a sexagenarian. We were parking in the field next door to the house and I was standing at the farm gate when Rick Desmond arrived with his wife Janet in his ragtop Ferrari. I pointed to a parking place and said how overwhelmed I was by the present, gesturing towards the car with the prancing horse badge. I mentioned I wasn't worth it and that one of the boys would drive him home. I could see indecision in his eyes, and wonder how close I'd got to scoring the red Ferrari. Anyway, we laughed and he gave me this fabulous framed cover of *OK!* magazine featuring me in all my musical guises. As it said on the cover – priceless!

Johnny Vee, Rod, Russell, Derik and Mod played, with Rick sitting in on drums, and as I often say a jolly good time was had by all. At about 9.30pm almost everybody had gone home. Ricky and I were just thinking about having a proper drink when we discovered that someone had redecorated the downstairs loo with coleslaw, tomatoes and the inevitable carrots. We'd just set about clearing up this colourful mess when the phone rang. It was a still inebriated Verity to tell me that he loved me. I suspected this might have been his way of apologising about the mess in the downstairs bog, but it was worse than that. After a pregnant pause I intuitively guessed what was coming next. After a short courtship of twenty-six years (with two or three wives and one husband in between), John and Carole were going to get married. Would I be best man? I was drunk enough to point out that this wasn't actually my first shot at being best man for Mr Verity, but I assured him it was definitely my last!

In late spring one year we Kinks were touring around prestigious American universities. This was something many bands did, because it resulted in important plays of your latest record on college radio stations, and maybe would catapult it onto mainstream stations, which would make or break it. At this time of year well-heeled students were treading water before heading home till the next semester, so were ready for some harmless fun. During one particular gig at Rutgers, a prestigious Ivy League university on the East Coast, we were playing in a giant gym, and as usual got changed into our stage clothes in the same locker rooms where the athletes changed. These places reeked of fitness, Ben Gay liniment and musky jockstraps. On the way to the stage I passed one of those weighing machines with the huge round faces and weighted balance levers we used to see in Woolworths when we were kids. For no reason at all I stood on it, to discover I weighed my usual 147lbs. Two hours later, after various encores, I stood on it again and weighed 137lbs. No prizes for working out that I'd lost 10 lbs, but it was all water – and I put it back on in a very short time by taking on-board a beer or two. We always played for a couple of hours, and at the end I'd be pleasantly exhausted, with my head between my knees on the side of the stage and soaked in sweat down to my socks and underpants. Because of this aerobic activity I always suspected that drumming kept me fit and that I was giving my heart a good workout – until I had an 'episode'. As a self-employed musician I've always been obliged to enjoy good health – and aside from the scarlet fever (or was it measles) when I joined Adam Faith, I'd pretty much sailed through my adult life unscathed . . .

It was sometime in May 2007 and I'd come back on a rush-hour train from a drummers' get-together which the Zildjian Cymbal Company had put on in a rehearsal studios in Putney. I'd been pushed up against a great many other people, yet still determined to read my *Evening Standard* with my arms crushed against my manly chest. When I got off the train my arm muscles felt really sore, and I put it down to cramp. As I arrived home the phone was ringing, and an old pal, Dave Caulfield, was calling me to book me with his band for a weekend of gigs in Ireland at the Kinsale Blues Festival. Around the time he got round to telling me there wouldn't be much money in it, I felt this strange pain across both shoulders. I put the phone down and sat for a while wondering what was going on, whereupon it moved downwards and became a band of discomfort around my chest. I wouldn't have described it as painful, but I thought that if it was still there in the morning I'd go to the doctor. This, I now know, would have been my first mistake. Doctors can't do much in this instance except call an ambulance. Ricki was at the theatre and needed to be picked up from the station. When I drove there I suddenly felt really cold, but in my manly way said nothing. We went to bed, and I promised myself that if this 'heartburn' was still there in the morning . . .

Waking up for my usual bathroom visit at 1am I realised the pain was still there, and at 5am it woke me up. It was now the traditional very tight band around the chest. I woke Ricki and spilled the beans. We threw on some clothes, got in the car and drove to the hospital. Mistake number two. (If anything untoward happens in your own car you're screwed, whereas if you're in an ambulance there are lots of frightening things they can do to save your life.) I was lucky, and arrived at the hospital. They started doing things immediately to help the pain. By 9am I'd had every test known to man and was feeling better. I was reading a chapter of Bob Dylan's *Chronicles* when an impossibly young doctor came to talk to me. He said, 'You've obviously had a problem with your heart; the blood tests show that. We need to do another blood test twelve hours after the worst pain.'

'No problem, Doc. I'll get myself back here for 5pm.'

'It doesn't work that way. We need to keep you here.'

The next thing I knew I was lying on the bed I'd been sitting on, being wheeled to a cardiac ward. Aged sixty-three I was being admitted to hospital for the first time in my life. I wasn't happy.

They looked after my every whim, including lunch, which was a vegetable burger that, if I hadn't put the salt on it I was forbidden at home, wouldn't have tasted of anything. Lots of people came to gather around the bed, many of whom were sympathetic doctors. Others were my family, summoned from the corners of Britain by Lucy – just in case. In the event, given the option of going home or staying for the weekend (now let me think!), we all left the hospital together that night and that, apart from a huge bag of take-away drugs picked up the next day, could well have been that. I went out for a ride on my bike the next day to see what would happen, and fortunately nothing did.

On the Wednesday I reported for a stress test on a walking machine, where they increase the gradient to see what you're capable of. I'd walked 25 miles the weekend before with my family along the Dorset coast, so this was a doddle. Twenty minutes later, after the technician and I had discussed a mutual drummer acquaintance who taught in his studio at the bottom of her garden, she told me sternly to go home and put my feet up for the night because I'd worked so hard. 'I'd like to,' I said, 'but I'm playing tennis, and since it's a fixed four if I don't turn up I may not get asked again.' She looked at me resignedly, and told me there was no point wasting her breath.

I arranged for a consultation with the registrar, who told me that as 'the episode' was a thing of the past I could do what I wanted now. I was due to go on a German tour with Russell Ballard, so asked if it would be OK to play the drums. Only if you could play them before was his predictable answer. 'There goes another rib' was my almost immediate response.

I went off with Russ and enjoyed myself immensely. The other guys in the band were seriously miffed about missing the sixties, and couldn't get enough of the stories we invariably tell when we're together. And even though it was very hot and sweaty I survived, and didn't need to use the life-saving, under-the-tongue aerosol I hope I still have in the bag-full of drummer's stuff I invariably take to gigs. (Besides sticks, a towel, Converse trainers, shirts, drum keys, pliers and the like; this has always contained a microphone and guitar lead for Mod Rogan, who invariably needs one. My wallet always has plectrums in it for Russell for the same reason!)

I arrived home, and things continued as if nothing had happened until I received a letter from the hospital requesting a visit. I turned up thinking it would be short and sweet – just a quick check to see how I was. Nothing could have been further from the truth.

Mr Schaeffer, a German surgeon, told me sternly that my recovery rate from the exercise they'd monitored just after 'the event' wasn't good enough, and they needed to do an angiogram to check the arteries for blockages. I was surprised, and asked how long it was likely to be before they needed me. I was off to Texas the next Thursday to a music show. He let that pass without too much comment, and asked if he'd know any of the bands I'd been in. 'You'd certainly know The Kinks and probably Argent,' I replied. He was from Hamburg, and asked if I'd played in any of those clubs along the Reeperbahn. I said I had, and many others like them, and having assured him I'd never smoked was most surprised when he asked me how long I'd been breathing in other people's smoke. I told him probably sixty-five years, and he said that was the reason for 'the episode'. He asked me to grab a cup of coffee and made some calls. Twenty minutes later he came back to tell me a place was reserved for the very next day at the London Chest Clinic, and that I was going to be admitted to my local hospital before an ambulance took me first thing the next morning to the clinic for an angiogram. Having been admitted to hospital for the second time in my life, I sat outside the ward in the July sun writing this very book. Fortunately, when I returned much later, I had a sign on the end of the bed that said 'nil by mouth', so I wasn't allowed to eat any of the food the other patients were subjected to.

The next morning I rode in an ambulance for the first time without a siren. I was admitted to the London Clinic in Bethnal Green at about seven o'clock, and they began to get me ready for the procedure. This involved them inserting a tube into an artery. As it journeys up to the heart it squirts out ink every few seconds. It's linked to an X-ray machine. (Blood doesn't show up on an X-ray but this dye does: they can immediately see if there are any blockages, and immediately clear them by inflating a balloon at that point. Normally they go in from the groin but once in a while they gain entry from the wrist, because it's a slightly shorter journey.)

As a drummer I wasn't too happy when, after having shaved my pubes, they also shaved my right wrist. Eventually I was wheeled into the operating theatre and introduced to a bunch of cheerful young people in whose hands my life rested. As bad luck would have it, they decided to access my heart through my wrist and prepared to cut into it. As good luck would have it, the door burst open at that precise moment and a doctor from my hospital, sent to keep an eye on me, burst into the room. When he saw them about to cut my wrist he asked what they thought they were doing. 'Getting the patient ready for the procedure,' was their response.

'You can't go through his wrist,' he said. 'The guy's a drummer!' I was saved, because judging by the amount of cutting and shutting that subsequently went on in my groin, they might have put paid to my drumming career.

Eventually they got the probe all the way round to my heart and found nothing. I suggested they inserted a couple of stents while they were in there just in case, but they declined because those small honeycombed cobalt tubes cost a couple of grand each. So while they retrieved their equipment I chatted and asked what would happen next. They said that since they hadn't found any problems there was nothing more for them to be interested in. I seized the moment, and asked if I could carry on normally. Three days later I was on the plane to Austin via Chicago to the Summer Namm show, wearing anti-DVT socks from Boots the Chemist, with a collagen sponge plug in my groin, and having taken an aspirin before we took off from Heathrow.

Eventually Herr Doktor Schaeffer got to the bottom of my problem, and decided I had a larger-than-usual heart, known in the trade as an 'athlete's heart.' He assured me mine was as good as anybody else's but needed to be warmed up before strenuous exercise. (Since my house is situated between two inclines I don't really have the option to build up slowly when I leave home on my bike.)

On the subject of health, I was enjoying a deep sleep one Friday not long after my sixtieth birthday in 2004 when the phone rang. It was three in the morning, and it turned out to be Dave Davies. Typically he got straight to the point. He was beginning a German tour the next day, and his American drummer had been on his way through immigration at LAX when it came to light that his passport had expired. As my wife knows to her cost, these people at Los Angeles airport are completely intransigent, and he wasn't going to get even as far as the departure lounge: he was grounded! I'd like to have heard a recording of the conversation he had with Dave to make him aware of the situation. Could I make it to the airport first thing and do a week or two in Germany? As it happened I had loads on in the immediate future, so I had to tell Dave I couldn't make it, but suggested some guys who might be able to help, including Jim Rodford's son Steve. I apologised for not being available, and the next thing I knew was that poor Dave had suffered a hypertension-induced stroke while at the BBC. I don't know too much about it, other than the fact that it took out one side of his body. Of course this made it difficult to play the guitar. I felt guilty, and thought I hadn't helped matters by not being able to do his gigs. Anyway, I spoke to Ray on the subject of Dave's health some time later, and he confided that his brother was having difficulty playing and singing at the same time. (I deliberately didn't catch Ray's eyes, and have resisted the temptation to put an exclamation mark after that sentence.) Anyhow, this was around the time of Ray being shot in the leg, and I'm told that when they were both recuperating Dave moved in with Ray, at his house behind The Flask in Highgate, for mutual support. Some malicious wag told me they were now known as the Sunshine Boys.

I've always considered myself to be naturally fit without the necessity of going to the gym every day or hiring a personal trainer. However, I'm well aware of the fact that once my endorphins begin to flow there's no stopping them. I recall in my days of going to aerobic classes and exercising to 'Beat It' (with a teacher who annoyingly heard music in counts of ten rather than the eight that most songs are written in) that once or twice a week was never enough. That said, having always run with my sons and in the early days let them win, the first time I realised I wasn't going to be able to catch them was hugely chastening. The worst thing was they could tell by my face I hadn't let them win. Bummer!

Early one morning towards the end of 2008 I turned on the news to discover that we drummers were as fit as Premiership footballers. A couple of universities in the UK had got together to work with Clem Burke, Blondie's drummer, to see how much energy he used up when he was playing the drums, and their results showed he used as much at a gig as a top-flight professional footballer. Now I'm reasonably fit, I play tennis once a week, ride my bike at the weekend when I can, walk if I have to and ski at least once a year. But there's no way I'm as fit as someone whose day-to-day job is keeping fit. How the hell could I be? I resolved to investigate, and emailed my mate Clem Burke to talk it through and to publish my findings on the website that takes the majority of my ramblings. We set up an interview for the following week, when Blondie were going to be playing in Docklands, and the story rumbled around the media all day. A researcher from the BBC's News 24 phoned me in the afternoon, saying they wanted to take the story further and would I come along to the studio to comment. I thought it was BBC Radio until they told me the car was taking me to the TV Centre in Wood Lane. I'd need to wash my hair. I was whisked into the studio by a researcher, and Robert Hall and Joanna Gosling interviewed me 'live'.

I'd never been in a modern news studio before, and it was a revelation. There were a desk and a long settee behind it, with room for the guests, the presenters and four static pedestal cameras (like they used when I first went on TV), and that was it. I told them I was very flattered to be told I was as fit as David Beckham, but it was ridiculous. My fitness allowed me to drum live for several hours without passing out, and his fitness allowed him to run up and down a football pitch for ninety minutes (on a good day) without falling over from fatigue. David couldn't do what I do and I certainly couldn't do what he does – as much as I'd like to! I pointed out what to me is blindingly obvious: there's no such thing as crossover fitness. Marathon runners aren't fit to swim long distances or ride the Tour de France. Curiously they asked me whether I felt Led Zeppelin would do a world tour again. I said that if they did they certainly couldn't get up to the tricks they used to. To get through it they'd need to husband their resources: nap in the afternoon, warm-up properly, get to bed early, avoid the excesses. Unfortunately, in my experience energetic heavy rock can't be played properly for a really long tour by old farts from the sixties like us, even if we want to. A month would be an elegant sufficiency.

A week later I met up with Clem and the lovely Debbie Harry and talked about the fitness project that he'd been involved with for several years and still had a long way to go. He persuaded me to sign up for it, but having had a heart attack (there I've said it) I may well turn out to be the exception that proves the rule.

My wife, the lovely and fragrant Ricki, has a degree in maths that she got in her spare time when she was bringing up me and the children. She began her teaching career with degrees to enable her to be a music and PE teacher, until a couple of decades later she was told the only way her future could be guaranteed was by retraining as a maths teacher. It puts things into perspective, I suppose.

After bringing up our offspring Ricki went back to teach in her old school in Winchmore Hill. But because of its intake it had become an Inner London school, even though it was actually in what they used to call the leafy suburbs. She enjoyed teaching there, although in the twenty-first century there were an awful lot of kids who weren't interested in learning and were prepared to make things as difficult as possible for anybody who wanted to get an education, or show them how to. (I always felt she should ask her classes how many grams there were in an ounce. Anybody who knew the answer had obviously already found a career – dealing drugs or preparing to.)

Eventually Ricki retired from that school and moved to an agricultural college just down the road from our new home, where students had to learn maths to complete their diplomas, otherwise they'd be kicked out. She wondered why she hadn't done it twenty years earlier.

We Kinks were playing at an outdoor gig in northern Wisconsin called Jurassic Jam which took place outside Appleton (where Harry Houdini once lived), and while I was relaxing in my room before the gig and zapping around the channels I discovered that Conway Twitty had died. I mentioned this to Ray in the mobile home we were changing into our stage clothes in, and he expressed his sorrow. We hit the stage to a huge crowd and went through the act. Somewhere towards the end Ray turned towards us, played a major chord and, having showed it to everyone, turned back to the audience and sang:

> *People see us everywhere,*
> *They think you really care,*
> *But myself I can't deceive,*
> *I know it's only make believe . . .*

We all came in playing the triplets on 'lieve', and it was an electrifying moment. Somehow the audience seemed to know the original singer of the song had died, and held their breath as we played the whole song, eventually bathed in the light of literally thousands of lighters held aloft. It was without a doubt the very first time we'd played this song together, although Ray seemed to know all the words. I doubt if any of us had played the song since the early sixties, but we made a great job of it.

Conway Twitty would have been delighted.

To entertain ourselves we often played old songs in soundchecks and also adapted various Kinks songs into reggae versions, slow blues versions or even shuffle versions. We once played 'You Really Got Me' as a shuffle, and it worked amazingly well. I think Ray may well have played that version in his one man show. The soundcheck always began with the drums: bass drum first, then snare, then toms, hi-hat, overheads and so on. By the time Jim joined me on stage I'd be playing whatever rhythm was in my head and the bass would join in while they sorted out his sound. By the time Gibbo joined in on keyboards Ray would walk to the front of the stage with his bag, reach inside and surreptitiously switch his tape machine on. This rhythm might well resurface as a brand new song for the next album.

Every time I'd been skiing I'd wondered what the ground underneath would be like to ride down on a mountain bike. Ricki and I decided to go for a biking holiday in Bavaria with our friends Joy and Phillip Ayton to see if we could put it to the test. Joy had once taught with Ricki, and these old friends had accompanied us on several adventuresome holidays over the years, both with and without our children. We soon had the answer to the question. Having taken the cable-car up alongside the ski-jump at Garmisch-Partenkirchen with our bikes onboard, we discovered you can't ride down a regular piste. Any ski slope that looks really smooth when covered with snow turns out to be completely unrideable, with potholes and boulders and tree roots in the way. After a very few yards we discovered the only way down was on the green paths that novice skiers tend to use, which traverse from side to side. They're built on shale: when coated in snow it's easy on skis, but not on a bike.

   The slope was actually called the Wank (although in Germany the letter w is pronounced as v), and we felt we should do our best to go down it so we could boast about it to anyone with a smutty mind at the tennis club.

   The holiday was really about following the Romantischer Road, which extends through Bavaria from Wurzburg to Fussen via Augsburg, Friedberg and Landsberg. We even managed to fit in a visit to Oberammergau, although we were a few years early for the next passion play, which was due in 2010.

On Labor Day weekend in 1995 we Kinks flew to Cleveland for the inaugural concert of the Rock and Roll Hall of Fame. The gig lasted almost eight hours, went out as a simulcast on HBO to tens of millions of people around the world and included just about everybody I'd ever admired in music: Chuck Berry, Bob Dylan, Al Green, Jerry Lee Lewis, Aretha Franklin, Johnny Cash, The Pretenders, John Fogerty, Lou Reed, Iggy Pop, George Clinton, John Mellencamp, Bruce Springsteen, Booker T. and the MGs, Eric Burdon and Martha Reeves. Unfortunately Elvis had left the building eighteen years earlier. Seeing him there would have been the icing on the cake.

   For some political reason getting to the gig wasn't without problems, and I remember we were sitting in Air Canada's first-class lounge on the Friday evening with boarding passes waiting to take off when for some reason plans changed. (I never understood why.) The next thing I knew we were booked into one of those airport hotels out at Heathrow. On the Saturday morning we took Concorde to New

York, then a somewhat larger, although slightly less supersonic, plane to Cleveland for the show.

I was surprised that the Hall of Fame itself had ever happened, because years earlier I'd been asked by the curator to help to secure British artefacts for it, and when I'd asked what sort of budget they had to bid for famous instruments and machinery, like the Studer four-track tape recorders the Beatles had chained together at Abbey Road, was told there was no budget. All the record company money had been spent on the building! But they managed to get the whole thing together somehow and made a fabulous job of it. The halls were packed with memorabilia, all of which they told me they'd got for free.

Though I say it as shouldn't, I'm not without my romantic side. I always kiss the lovely and fragrant Ricki goodnight wherever I am. But I'll reinforce the point with an anecdote. Towards the end of the eighties Ricki came to visit me in LA halfway through a Kinks tour. This was before the days of visa waivers, so you had to have a B.1 stamped in your passport – which meant you could come and go until it was rescinded: it didn't run out even if your passport did. All you needed to remember was to bring your old 'clipped' passport with the visa in along with the new one. Unfortunately Ricki forgot hers. So after a horrific flight where the plane had dropped thousands of feet in seconds and even the stewardesses were screaming, she arrived at immigration with the other Kinks' WAGS without the necessary second passport.

This would appear to be the worst thing you can do in LAX, and they held her for several hours before preparing to put her on a plane home. Eventually she managed to persuade them to phone Washington and to check she'd been issued with a visa. In the end they let her in with a stern warning about flouting the immigration laws. Meanwhile, of course, illegal Mexicans were streaming across the Rio Grande and terrorists were arriving to learn the rudiments of flying while immigration dealt with this dangerous schoolteacher from leafy Winchmore Hill. (What this meant to Ricki and I was we wouldn't be able to go to Tijuana, which may of course have turned out to be just as well. We were going with Metzger and Ann-Marie, so we could have got ourselves into tequila trouble.) While this was going on The Kinks were finishing that leg of the tour in Vancouver. It's a tidy step down the Pacific coast to LA, so I didn't contact my wife until I was in the lobby of the hotel we were staying at in Westwood. I pretended to be delayed in Canada while I phoned the room, and a couple of minutes later I was knocking on the door with a red rose between my teeth! Not bad, eh?

As I said, I got to the ripe old age of sixty-three without ever having been in a hospital, and Ricki got to be sixty-four without being admitted – other than the three times necessary to give birth to our children. Then, bang, it all went wrong! It's a well-known cliché written by Henry Wadsworth Longfellow and sung by The Inkspots that 'into each life some rain must fall'. My deluge, make that ours, came in the form of Ricki's breast cancer.

Shortly after my sister died from the same smoking-related disease that carried my parents off, after a routine mammogram Ricki received a follow-up letter that said they'd like to see her again. The bombshell fell when they told us some white spots had shown up on the mammogram and she needed a biopsy to determine what they were, which they did then and there. We were shocked, but slightly more reassured when they told us that it might be nothing, and even if there was something nasty there a lumpectomy might well deal with the problem. (Notice the reassuring use of the word might!)

A couple of weeks later we were back in a place I knew well, the old Boosey and Hawkes drum factory in Deanswood Road, Edgware, which was now the breast clinic department of Edgware General Hospital. The news was good and bad. Ricki needed a lumpectomy because they'd found two lumps, which was bad, but there were only two small ones, which was good. Not long afterwards I dropped her off at the Royal Free in Hampstead for her wire-guided lumpectomy in the safe hands of a nice South African surgeon called Tim Davidson. The prognosis was good after the operation, and they were *almost* 100 per cent certain they'd been able to remove all the nasty bits.

Ricki stayed in for five days and came out with two breasts, albeit one of them ever so slightly dented. This wasn't of any real concern: no doubt they'd be able to sort it out sooner or later. Unfortunately they were working on her again much sooner than expected, because while the surgeon was inside he took away various other bits and pieces from around the infected area for biopsy. There was more carcinogenic infection, and the lumps were considerably larger than first diagnosed: my lovely Ricki needed another operation asap. Christmas and New Year came and went, and in January 2006 Mr Davidson had another go at cutting out the cells. Five days later Ricki was out, and we were waiting apprehensively for the results of the second post-surgical biopsy. Poor Ricki's left breast was even more dented now. I think at this stage she was resigned to the idea of losing the whole breast if they discovered more cancer, so she wasn't as devastated as I was when we were told that because there were so many small infected sites the only way to be sure that the problem would go away was by removal. In February 2006, within six months of her last mammogram, Ricki had a breast removed.

I didn't cry until I accidentally saw the result of the amputation just after the dressings were taken off, when Ricki was putting a T-shirt over her head in our bedroom. I rushed to the bathroom and sat glumly on the lid of the loo with tears running down my face. Of course I realised this wasn't about me, and however bad I felt Ricki felt worse; I was crying for her. Some time later she asked if I'd like to see the result of the surgery, and it wasn't quite as bad as it could have been: having seen it earlier I was over the initial shock. Ricki could have had a reconstruction then and there, had she allowed them to take the necessary flesh and muscle from her back and under her arm, but as a very, very sporty woman she decided she didn't want to run the risk of being unbalanced, so she could still play tennis (she's been the Vicar's Moor LTC Ladies' singles, doubles and mixed champion several times), swim, sail, run, ride her bike and play golf.

Ricki's now had the reconstruction from her abdomen; this is called DIEP flap. She'd been growing her stomach with this in mind, so she'd end up with enough spare flesh for a couple of big 'threepenny bits', and with that finished she's pretty much back to her svelte pre-offspring shape. (As I'm writing this

I'm wondering whether that sentence will survive her red teacher's pen when she demands to proofread this! You lot won't know if it doesn't!)

So, I'd like to hear you ask, what are you up to now? Like most other musicians I respond to the telephone for gigs, and find myself having fun playing with a lot of people whom I might not otherwise have expected to be playing with.

There's also John Verity's band with Mark Griffiths, Jim Rodford or Bob Skeet on bass, which is a joy to play with and far too much fun. We're pushing the envelope as much as we can every time we play, and mostly it works. We decided to make a 'live' album. JV put it on his website that we'd be recording at Cardington Village Hall in 2007, and anybody who wanted to be part of it should be there at 6.30pm with their own beer! The place was full, and as a tribute to the ill-fated R101 airship which was built in, housed in and launched from Cardington, the CD was entitled *101*. It was such a successful way to get people to come and see us that we felt perhaps we should use that method for all our gigs.

Talking of live records, towards the end of my time in The Kinks it was decided we would make a record in front of the fans, rather like 'Faith Alive' with Adam, but thirty years later.

The internet tells me it was 5 March 1994 (which is close enough for me) when we gathered at Konk to record an almost 'unplugged' record called *To the Bone*, which remains my favourite conglomeration of Kinks tracks. The idea behind it was for us to make do with the least equipment we could and see what happened. As it happened, using minimal equipment we sounded more like the original Kinks than we normally did in the studios. That said, we certainly weren't trying to sound like the old band when we made records in the eighties and nineties. The proceedings were filmed for posterity, although I haven't seen them. But I enjoyed making that album because it was so uncomplicated.

I've done several live albums in studio conditions, and it really worked. *Faith Alive* was one we recorded with Adam at EMI's Studio 2 in 1965 in front of a live audience. The difference with JV's album was that we went straight to computer and the whole thing cost just £40, which was the hire of the hall!

From time to time I play with a bunch of guys called the Cruising Mooses, whose bass player, Jimmy 'Classic', was in Unit 4+2 after Russell and I pushed off to join Argent. The Mooses are a fun band too, and frequently start a song without telling me what it is. Their guitarist Martin Matthews has rowed me into another band he's in, called Van the Band. It's not a tribute band, but there are no prizes for guessing that they only play Van Morrison songs. Anyone who thinks it's an easy gig would be seriously misinformed. Van appears to write songs a lot like Ray, with half bars here and there, middle nines or tens instead of middle eights, and lots of unexpected odd bar sections that you simply can't busk successfully.

When I replaced Mick in The Kinks he started playing in a band with Mod Rogan, who'd been in the Roulettes with me, and Russell's brother Roy, called The Organizers. I substituted for Mick in the band if he was busy doing Kast Off Kinks or Class of '64 stuff, and when Roy died unexpectedly, while in hospital being examined after chest pains, they called it a day. But Mod kept going, albeit sporadically, playing weddings and birthdays (no funerals so far) with whoever was available: Jim Rodford, Mark Griffiths, Derek Timms, Russell B., Geoff Nicholls, Rick Desmond and yours truly.

I was at Arbiter when I received a panic call from Andy Scott who was still rushing around Europe with his version of Sweet. I'm pretty sure the excessive Brian Connolly (who JV and I had recorded with and very nearly been a band with) was dead by this time. They had a tour of Lithuania, Latvia or somewhere equally Russian coming up, and Bruce Bisland, their drummer, had fallen off his mountain bike and broken one of the limbs he needed to play drums successfully. Could I help them? As it happened I could, until Andy told me there was a catch: the work permits had already been issued and couldn't be changed. Therefore I'd have to carry Bruce's passport. Now not only was I taller than him, older than him and arguably more handsome, I had long darkish hair with just a hint of silver at the sides, while his was short, blond and spiky. I deliberated for almost a couple of seconds about the consequences of turning up in a Communist-bloc country carrying somebody else's passport – before deciding against it. I wasn't interested in being forced to play drums in a gulag in the Arctic Circle if I was caught.

The versatile Mick Avory called me towards the end of 2007, asking if I could do his gig with The Hitmen with my old mate Eric Haydock (who used to be in the Hollies), Martin Lyon and Ted Tomlin from the Love Affair. I agreed too quickly, and the next thing I knew I had two CDs of Hollies, Kinks and Love Affair songs to learn. So I got down to it, and by the time we got to rehearse with the guys at the local studios I didn't realise were there I was more than ready. I could play all the fills Bobby Elliott, Bobby Graham and Clem Cattini had recorded – and in the right places! I did just one sold-out gig in a theatre in Burgess Hill, and I was amazed at how excited the audience were. As a sign of the times we and the ageing audience had a comfort break halfway through. Over a cup of tea I told Eric Haydock a joke Jim Rodford had told Mod, about a balloon family. He didn't seem to be paying too much attention, but once we were back on stage after a couple of songs he wandered unexpectedly to the front and went into a hilarious Bernard Manning-style stand-up comedy routine. 'There was this family of balloons . . .' The joke ends with the immortal words, 'You've let me down, you've let your mother down and worst of all you've let yourself down!' He made the gag his own, and told it better than anyone I've ever heard.

Mick called me a while later to see how I'd got on, and I told him I really enjoyed it. He said he thought it would be good fun too. I'm pretty sure I'd depped for him on a gig he'd never played before.

There's one band I'd like to have been playing with which, inexplicably, I'm not. At the most creative time of my life all my energies were invested in Argent, so not to be included in the offshoot Zombies revival when I'd played on their last records was really rather disappointing. Somewhere around the turn of the century there were very positive moves to get Argent back together with Russell B., although we were all determined it wasn't going to be a 'bank raid', i.e. just for the money. Not just to tour, but to actually have a crack at doing it properly, by recording then touring. Believe it or not, Rod and Russell had never written songs together, so we figured that if they got into it seriously with the usual input from me and Jim, there was every chance they'd come up with something special.

Brand new records are not something bands usually do when getting back together after a hiatus. Many never record again, other than the odd live album to sell at gigs, or new recordings of the hit songs to bypass the original record company that has rights to the original performances. Some have been known to transfer the songs from the mastertapes if they've got them (or the actual vinyl records if they haven't) with the addition of something that wasn't on the original, like backing vocals, keyboards or even tambourine, to disguise it. We weren't aiming to do this and anyhow, there was no reason why the sum of Argent's parts wouldn't be better than ever. Unfortunately this didn't happen at the time, and the best laid plans were eventually superseded by the excellent Zombies thing with Colin Blunstone. Not until July 2010, that is when almost out of the blue, Argent played a festival in a North London park followed by a UK Tour in 2011 and another in 2012, which may well preclude a full-blown revival. It's a crying shame Argent never managed to begin the project, even though we're told there's certainly a market for it. Maybe one day . .

During our 'holiday of a lifetime' in 2008 we went to see Ray's one-man show at a folk festival in Calgary. I'd been surprised to bump into him at Nobby Dalton's sixty-fifth birthday where, even though he'd said he was coming, I'm not sure anyone was holding their breath. We man-hugged and discussed what we were up to. I said I was getting ready to go to Canada, and Ray said he was going there too. It transpired we were both in Calgary on 14 July, Ricki's birthday. He suggested we meet up at the gig, and that was that. I went back to the marquee in Nobby's garden to play in one of the bands I'd been in fifty years earlier, and by the time I finished Ray had left the building!

I called Konk and spoke to Linda McBride, who gave me all the contact numbers to set the thing up. Several weeks later, after our long weekend on the houseboat on the Shuswap Lake, Howard and Jacki Stainsby (our pals with us on the trip) and two of the three in-laws to be (God willing) turned up at the Jack Singer Hall for Ray's two-man show with Bill Shanley.

We'd been up to see the whales and the icebergs in Glacier Bay, and then drove a Winnebago down to see Ray. While I think of it, I picked up a birthday card that I didn't have the courage to send him when he became an OAP. It said: 'The years have been kind to you, it's the weekends which have done the damage.'

Ray came on stage to huge applause, and I looked round the audience to see many of the happy faces I'd been used to seeing from the stage during my Kinks tenure. After the first couple of songs Ray explained that there wasn't a drummer in the band, although he understood there was one in the audience! We all sang-a-long-a Ray, and as usual he set up all the songs with a brief dialogue before launching into them. Before singing 'Days' he mentioned how the band (us) used to refer to the song as 'Thank you for the raise'. I was very surprised Ray knew anything about this, because we all thought it was a well-kept secret. 'Thank you for the raise, that didn't come in one lump sum, in time to save me!' There were a couple of new songs I didn't recognise. One was 'Morphine Song', which he'd written while he was in the hospital fighting for his life after getting shot in the leg in New Orleans in 2006. He set it up beautifully: 'I was shot in New Orleans. It's not like Hollywood – it fucking hurts!' (While I was researching Ray's shooting I came across a very unkind quote entitled 'You really shot me.')

Afterwards we were backstage and Ricki, who'd been celebrating her birthday for quite some time, invited Ray to drop his pants. Ray was shocked, until she said she only wanted to see his wound. Fortunately Ray declined, and we enjoyed a couple of beers in the dressing room. He told me about *Come Dancing*, the musical he was working on that was opening soon at the old Theatre Royal in Stratford

Fast forward to September 2008 when we old Kinks (Mick, Nobby, Jim, Ian, Shirley, Debbie, Nick Newall, Nicky Paine) and of course the ubiquitous Olga were all gathered at the press showing. The plot of the musical is pretty much the lyrics of the song with embellishments of the dance hall days period, when people looked to ballroom dancing to magically transport them away from the drudgery of post-war Britain. At these massive dance-halls, mostly owned by Mecca, the hoi polloi waited expectantly all week to go dancing on a Saturday night. Love, hate and all the emotions in between were lived out in these places, where big-bands played strict tempo music to propel the desperate dancers in the traditional, well-defined movements of the quick-step (slow, slow, quick, quick, slow), waltz (1, 2, 3, 2, 2, 3) or foxtrot; and the much more modern and exotic tango, rumba or cha-cha-cha. Woe betide any Teddy boy in drainpipes, draped jacket, string tie and crepe-soled shoes who decided to break the rules and attempt to dance the creep or the jive in a fifties dance hall. He'd be vigorously encouraged to leave the floor by a large, make that fat, bouncer wearing the same sort of big-shouldered coloured jacket with black-rolled lapels that was available from Cecil Gee in Shaftesbury Avenue for something like 5 guineas, which the fifteen guys in the band were wearing.

Rock 'n' roll was in its infancy in the UK in 1955, and wrongly epitomised – in my opinion – by Bill Haley's seminal record 'Rock Around the Clock'. (Little Richard's 'Tutti Frutti' and Chuck Berry's 'Schooldays' should both share that distinction.) That said, Haley's song was the antithesis of what was going on in the world of strict tempo and the BBC's Light Programme. It was exactly what we soon-to-be-named baby boomers were looking for – our own thing, not something our parents (and our parents' parents) had grown up with.

All this was thoughtfully and accurately captured by Ray in his show, which was set in a dance-hall with musicians on their own stage, a bar stage right and tables for the cast stage left. Centre stage was a revolving dance floor with mood-changing mirror-ball suspended above. It had all the required elements, including the novelty of black musicians who were beginning to make their way to Britain, Borstal boys carrying flick-knives, skiffle groups with tea-chest basses and guitars they couldn't really play, determined sisters looking to better themselves by moving to one of the healthy new garden cities, or even as far as Australia. There were skeletons in the cupboard too, with siblings sired out of wedlock by family 'uncles', who then contracted one of the life- threatening juvenile diseases prevalent in those days; and there were also inter-racial love and manslaughter. The story was narrated by Ray, seated at the bar of the Palais in what I'd describe as his Pagliacci persona and he kept the audience enthralled until the very end when, typically, they didn't all live happily ever after. There was a real Kleenex moment at the end when the cast individually confessed what had happened to them in the fullness of time. The pathos of this scene was soon dissipated by the entire cast (and eventually some of the audience) dancing vigorously to Ray's song 'Come Dancing'.

The critics were kind, and for once agreed with everything I thought about the show. Ray sent me an email thanking me for coming. In my reply I mentioned that I'd chanced on a blog where a guy said he didn't get the plot. Of course we all understood it perfectly because it was our generation, and we knew the lyrics intimately: there was only a problem if you hadn't been in The Kinks or had been born too late. I suggested Ray could justifiably tell me to make love elsewhere but it might be a good idea to educate the generations after ours by giving them the lyrics, or better still the sheet music, before the show started.

In June 2009 it was forty-seven years since I began with the Roulettes and forty-six years since Russell joined. Thorpey, Mod, Russell and I got together for lunch at an Italian restaurant in Ware and a jolly good time was had – although being responsible drinkers, we only had a couple of small glasses of Pinot Grigio each. There are no plans to record for the moment, we're all too busy with our gardens for that, but here's to the next half century!

The years after my sixtieth went by in a flash, and before I knew it I was sixty-five years old! To be honest, even though I was away with the Kamikaze downhill cycling club riding along the Canal du Midi to the Mediterranean, I didn't cope too well. Even though I could still rock and roll, ride my bike, play tennis and ski I wasn't happy about attaining the age of retirement. Of course I'm not going to retire, but from where I was standing on 2 May 2009 the finishing line appeared a lot closer than it had ever been.

Since this is my first autobiography I have no idea how I'm supposed to finish it. Technically I suppose it should end when I shuffle-off this mortal coil, but if you're reading it the chances are I was still breathing when I delivered it to Bank House Books. If that's the case then the lovely Ricki and I will be doing our best to continue our latest hobby – seeing the world. I always thought that by joining a band I'd see the world at someone else's expense, until the record company sent the bill!

In 2011 (despite all the odds) we'll have been married for forty years and plan to go to India to celebrate our achievement. The idea is to visit Kerala in the lush south-west of the sub-continent for a 'ruby'. (For the uninitiated a fortieth anniversary is a ruby wedding and Ruby Murray, a singer on the wireless when I was endeavouring to grow up, is rhyming slang for curry.) I once suggested to my lovely wife that we renewed our vows, and was somewhat taken aback by her response which was along the lines of 'If you didn't hear me the first f***ing time . . .'

I've taken to making public speaking engagements to various baby boomers organisations on the subject of sex and drugs and rock 'n' roll, although I always seem to run out of time before I get round to the sex and drugs. Through the auspices of Chris Wright, the owner of a very busy drum shop in Reading, I'm doing more of this public speaking lark to drummers – preaching to the converted you might say. This is with my pal Clem Cattini, whom I get on really well with even though he's a Gooner! We certainly talk volubly about rock 'n' roll, but I'm not sure whether either of us can accurately remember enough about the sex and drugs side to really expound on the subject!

It's no secret that Jim Rodford, Ian Gibbons and I were brought into The Kinks for a reason – not just because they needed a bass player, keyboard player or drummer. They needed intuitive and schooled players who were on the same wavelength as Ray and could instinctively follow him wherever he went, often without being given any direction at all. In my case I could do it because I'd never been a musical snob, and if somebody wanted me to play a certain kind of music – be it hillbilly, country and western, ceilidh, reggae, disco, rock, funk, jazz or any other genre – I'd put the work in to get it right. To illustrate the point, I was once doing a clinic for Arbiter in the Guitar Center in LA, and one of the hot-shot drum salesmen, who was over-endowed with technique, felt the need to show me what he had. I listened politely, and once he'd finished in an absent-minded way I started playing a rhythm I've always used for mid-fifties rock 'n' roll, where some of the instruments are playing a shuffle and the rest are playing straight eighth notes. My right hand plays the shuffle, my left plays the straight eights and accents the offbeat and the bass drum plays a typical New Orleans marching figure. The guy pretended to ignore me for a while, but I could see his hands and feet moving as he tried to work it out. Eventually he came over and grudgingly admitted, 'Hey, man, I can't play that.' My response was, 'I'm not surprised – it took me fifty years to work it out!'

Anyhow, as far as my status within The Kinks is concerned (even though I sometimes wonder if I was ever there.) I seem to be getting very good press among the fans on the internet, and many of the tunes I worked exceedingly hard on, like 'Scattered', 'Missing Persons', 'Now and Then', 'How Do I Get Close', 'Did Ya', 'Do it Again', 'Living on a Thin Line', 'Video Shop', 'Still Searching', 'Over the Edge', 'Welcome to Sleazy Town', 'Only a Dream', 'Lost and Found', 'Don't', 'The Road' and 'Looney Balloon', are making their way onto lists of favourite Kinks songs as 'modern classics', which is extremely reassuring.

Thanks are due to Russell Ballard's band, Steve and the two Chrisses, who made me aware that in their opinion there was a market for these ramblings. They'd better be right!

I'd just got back from a tour of Europe with Russell when I got a phone call from Linda at Konk Studios – Ray wanted to speak to me. He asked what I was up to and I said I'd just come back from tour. Ray said, 'I wanted to know if you'd been playing for real recently'. I gave him my 'use it or lose it', 'putting myself through hoops' speech, and he told me he was doing some gigs and suggested we got together. Was the merry-go-round about to start up again? Well no, not so far but time is on my side, I can wait.

Three men die in a plane crash and are waiting to enter heaven.
St Peter: 'What did you do on Earth?'
Man #1: I was a doctor.
St Peter: Go right through those pearly gates.
St Peter: And what did you do on Earth?
Man #2: I was a school teacher.
St Peter: Go right through those pearly gates.
St Peter: And what did you do on Earth?
Man #3: I was a musician.
St Peter: Go round the side, up the freight elevator, through the kitchen . . .

Outside International Musician offices in Covent Garden

Photo on back of Complete Simmons Drum Book

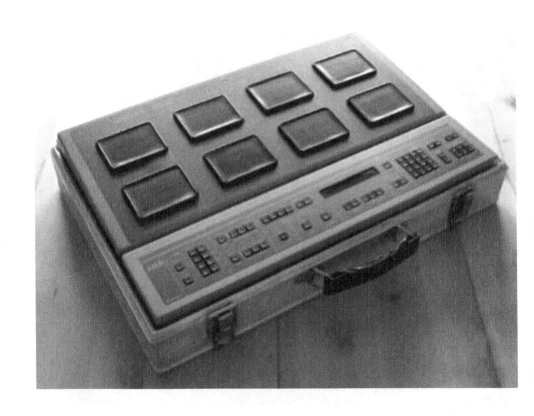

Impulse One drum machine

Rototom pedal prototype

Ricki, Lucy and my afghan coat

Deutchland mit Russell

Le Peloton

Nana Ricki

You looking at me?

With JV and Griff

Let there be drums: with Brian Bennett, Johnny Marta, Nigel Shipway,
Rick Lee, Mark Brzezicki

With Ricki in our woods

Phoenix from the ashes again at Cambridge Rock Festival

with Raymondo

We Got A Friend with Sue Marchant and Ben Taylor

Duly signed Sir Cliff 50th Anniversary Tour ticket

The Ballard Band

Harry Polson Henrit: my old man

Argent reunited

Russ Ballard Band

Lulu and Jos

Grandbob

Russell in action

With Elvis Dalton

Jos after London Marathon

Lucy pregnant

Caution,
granddaughter inside

Roulettes plus 50

Fifty years with Zildjian

Acknowledgements

Dave Randle at Bank House Books for liking my musings – at least enough to send me a contract.

Russ Ballard, Johnny Mod Rogan, Peter Thorp, Jim Rodford, Rod Argent, John V and Mark Griffiths for putting me right on certain facts – some of which I chose to ignore. (See the Keith Moon reference about the truth and a good story.)

My parents for believing in me enough to let me do what I wanted – within reason. And mostly to the lovely Ricki for supporting and putting up with me throughout the whole adventure – so far.

Good News!

While I was editing Banging On! for the very last time a stork arrived on our doorstep at 2.13 pm on Wednesday August 8th with Elesa, Vanderluce, Marcella Henrit in its bill. We are now extremely proud grandparents henceforth to be known as Nana and Grandbob.

Index

Haley, Bill, 7, 212
Hall, Robert, 204
Hallelujah I love her so, 20
Halley's comet, 84
Halliburton brief-case, 125
Hallyday, Johnny, 145
Hambone rhythm, 143, 188
Hamburg, 23, 25, 30, 34, 114, 162, 205
Hamburger, 15, 70
Hamilton, 28
Hammersmith Odeon, 99
Hammond organ, 77, 81, 82, 85
Hammond, Ray, 103
Handlebar moustache, 59
Hannay, Richard, 3, 229
Happy Valley Stadium, 31
Hark, 54
Harley Street, 74, 75
Harper, Tim, 189
Harrahs, 125
Harris, Bert, 24, 34
Harris, Bob, 51, 87
Harris, Jet, 19, 144
Harris, Richard, 56
Harris, Thurston, 11
Harrison, George, 43, 82, 143
Harrison, Rex, 56
Harrods, 107
Harry, Debbie, 145, 205
Hartlepool, 31
Harvey, Alex, 56, 82
Harvey, Les, 82
Hasek, Jaroslav, 28
Hatchetts, 61, 62
Havens, Richie, 188
Hawkwind, 102
Hawn, Goldie, 124
Hayden, Carole, 18
Haydock, Eric, 210
Hayman, 65, 161, 170
HBO, 142
He fought the law, 53
Heart, 109
Heathrow, 113, 120, 146, 169, 203, 207
Hedderick, Ann, 61
Hedderick, John, 172
Helm, Levon, 124
Help me to help myself, 60

Hemingway, Ernest, 28
Henderson, Pete, 91
Hendon Football Club, 170
Hendrix, Jimi, 43, 80, 86, 157
Hendrix, Marcel, 46
Henrit, Charlie Prince, 184
Henrit, Harry Polson, 1
Henrit, James Robert, 184
Henrit, Joseph Charles, 184
Henrit, Lucy Ann Joan, 183
Henrit, Patricia Marie, 2, 126
Henrit, Ricki, 61, 62, 73, 74, 80, 89, 90, 91, 114, 125, 129, 153, 157, 167, 184, 185, 187, 189, 200, 201, 205, 206, 207, 208, 211, 213, 215
Henrit's Drumstore, 86, 104, 105, 107, 128
Henry Barras stadium, 12
Henry VIII, 87
Henry, Stuart, 51
Hepatitis, 95, 101
    Edgewater Inn, 95
Her Majesty's Forces, 30
Herbert, James, 69
Hercules bicycle, 190
Here comes the sun, 188
Herr Doktor Schaeffer, 203
Herr Pieter Neumann, 81
Hesse, Hermann, 95
Hessey's, 34
Hetchin's, 10
Heute, Daddy, 70
Hideously skinny and horrendously loud!, 32
Highgate School, 186, 187, 204
Highway to Hell, 109
Hi-heel sneakers, 80
Hiseman, Jon, 170
Hitchcock, Alfred, 6
Hitler, 2, 30, 79, 136
HM's Customs and Excise, 126, 128, 194
HM's Warehouse, 126
HMV, 55
Hoddesdon Conservative

Club, 198
Hodges, Chas, 13, 31, 68, 113, 132
Hoffmann, Dezo, 103
Holborn viaduct, 128
Hold your head up mark II, 75
Hold your head up, 2, 36, 49, 75, 80, 83, 87, 89, 91, 95, 98, 103, 123
Holden, William, 31
Holder, Noddy, 114
Holiday of a Lifetime, 211
Holland Park, 159
Holly, Buddy, 11, 17, 25, 53, 68, 142, 143
Hollywood, 69, 86, 105, 109, 125, 129, 143, 144, 152, 161, 183
Holness, Bob, 193
Holy Family Convent, 13
Holy Grail, 162
Home on the range, 53
Honey trap, 42
Honeybus, 56
Hong Kong, 28, 187, 200
Honk, 21
Honky Chateau, 91
Hook Norton, 121
Hooker, John Lee, 80
Hooray Henrys, 37
Hora Staccato, 22
Horkins, Tony, 104
Horn, Jim, 100
Horrowitz, Jimmy, 122, 123
Hot pies have come!, 24
Hotlegs, 100
Houdini, Harry, 205
How do I get close, 214
Howard and Jacki Stainsby, 211
Howard Johnsons, 77
Howey Casey and The Seniors, 30
Hudson, Bill, 124
Hudson, Garth, 123, 124
Hudson, Kate, 124
Hudson, Nick, 170, 173
Hughes, Graham, 91
Hugo, Victor, 28
Hully gully slip and slide, 23
Humdrum, 126

227

CPSIA information can be obtained at www.ICGtesting.com
Printed in the USA
BVOW08s0906160814

363139BV00003B/3/P